100
120
P9-DNT-848
Urga
MONGOLIA
KOREA
JAPAN
Tokyo
Seoul
Peking
Hwang
H I N A
Shanghai
Yangtze
B E T
Lhasa
FORMOSA
Brahmaputra
PAKISTAN
Hongkong
Mandalay
Hanoi
BURMA
LAOS
VIETNAM
LUZON
Manila
PHILIPPINE
ISLANDS
South
China
Sea
Bay of
Bengal
Rangoon
THAILAND
Mekong
Bangkok
CAMBODIA
MINDANAO
ANDAMAN ISLANDS
Saigon
NICOBAR
ISLANDS
SARAWAK
MALAYA
CELEBES
BORNEO
SUMATRA
Singapore
INDONESIA
BALI
Jakarta
JAVA
a n
J. TREMBLAY
40
20
0
100
120

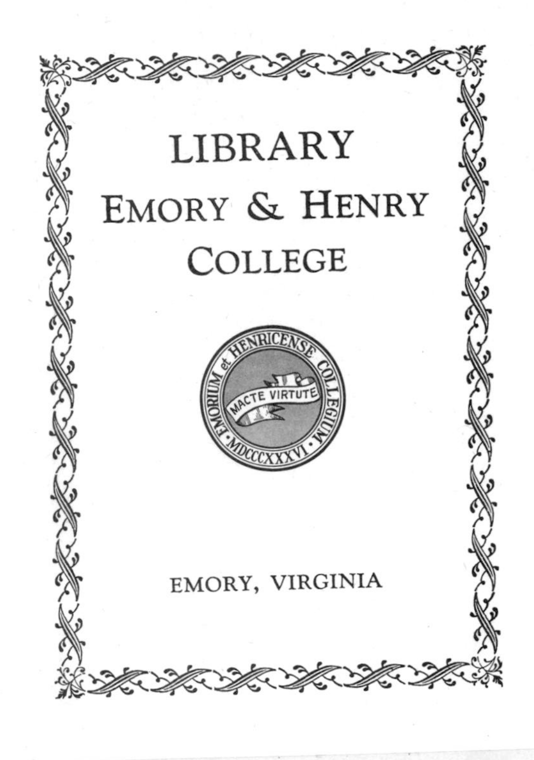

AMBASSADOR'S REPORT

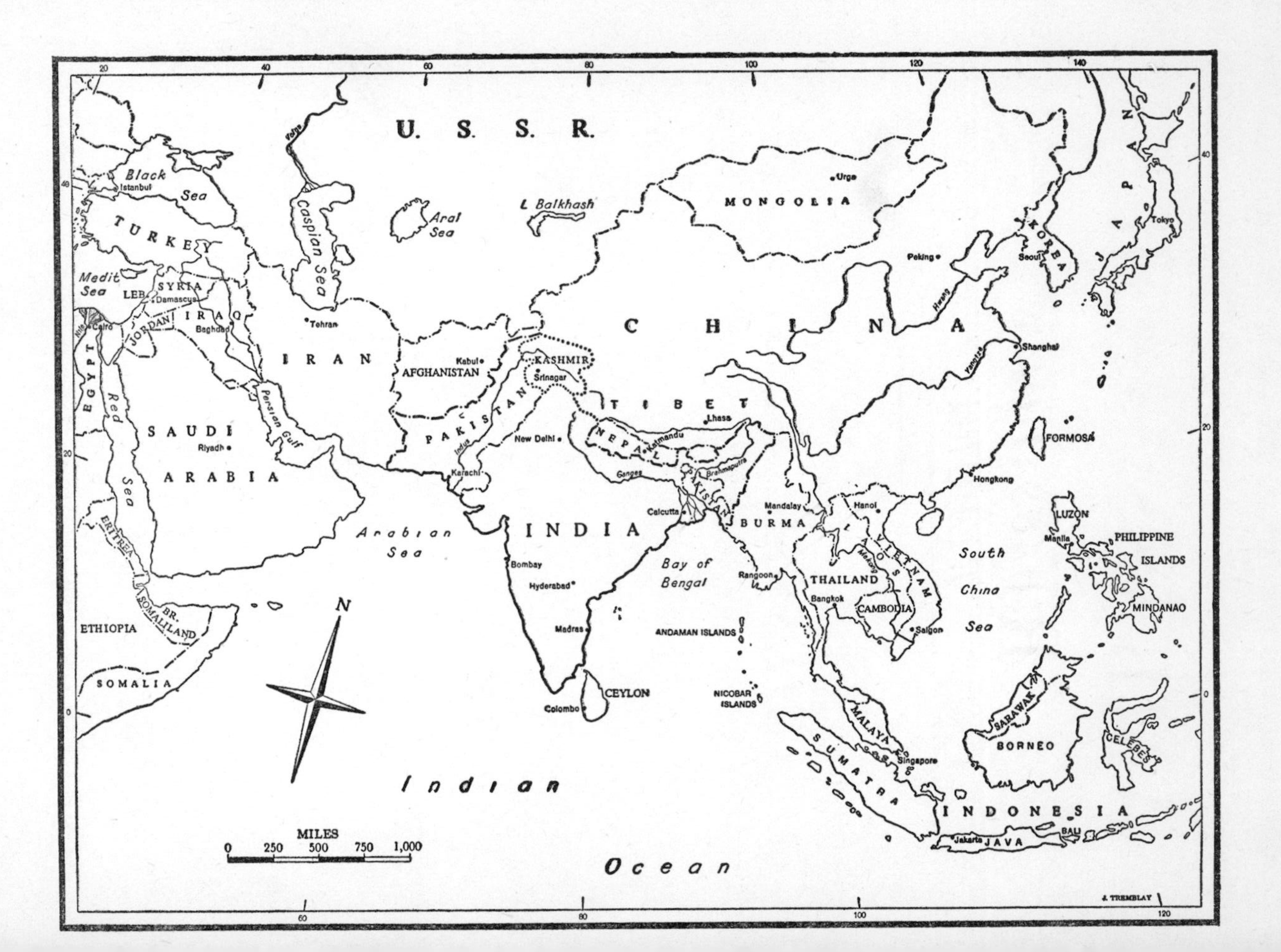
U. S. S. R.
MONGOLIA
Urga
L. Balkhash
Aral Sea
Caspian Sea
Volga
Black Sea
Istanbul
TURKEY
Medit Sea
LEB
SYRIA
Damascus
JORDAN
IRAQ
Baghdad
Cairo
Nile
EGYPT
Tehran
IRAN
Kabul
AFGHANISTAN
KASHMIR
Srinagar
PAKISTAN
Indus
Karachi
Persian Gulf
Red Sea
SAUDI ARABIA
Riyadh
ERITREA
BR. SOMALILAND
ETHIOPIA
SOMALIA
Arabian Sea
CHINA
Peking
Hwang
Yangtze
Shanghai
KOREA
Seoul
JAPAN
Tokyo
FORMOSA
Hongkong
TIBET
Lhasa
NEPAL
Katmandu
New Delhi
Ganges
Brahmaputra
Calcutta
INDIA
Bombay
Hyderabad
Madras
Bay of Bengal
CEYLON
Colombo
ANDAMAN ISLANDS
NICOBAR ISLANDS
Mandalay
BURMA
Rangoon
THAILAND
Bangkok
LAOS
Mekong
Hanoi
VIETNAM
CAMBODIA
Saigon
South China Sea
LUZON
Manila
PHILIPPINE ISLANDS
MINDANAO
MALAYA
Singapore
SUMATRA
SARAWAK
BORNEO
CELEBES
INDONESIA
Jakarta
JAVA
BALI
Indian Ocean
N
MILES
0 250 500 750 1,000
J. TREMBLAY

AMBASSADOR'S REPORT

by

CHESTER BOWLES

HARPER & BROTHERS, NEW YORK

AMBASSADOR'S REPORT

Printed in the United States of America

B-D

Library of Congress catalog card number: 53-11840

To Steb
Who Contributed The Most

CONTENTS

A section of illustrations will be found following page 180

Why This Book Was Written

HOW EASY it would have been to write this book after only three months in Asia! The discoveries were then so fresh and exciting. The problems seemed so much more straightforward and uncomplicated, and the issues so clear-cut.

Now, back in America after eighteen months as Ambassador to India and Nepal the impression that is strongest is how manifold and complex those issues and problems really are. There are certainly no single or easy answers to the future of Asia, and I feel a deep sense of humility at the thought of putting my views on paper.

Yet I believe that the history of our time will hereafter be written largely in Asia. If that is so, and if America is to participate constructively in the unfolding of that history, anyone who has had the opportunity I have had to observe Asia at close hand in the capital of the world's largest democracy has an obligation to offer his report to the American people.

The experiences I have reported here took place not only in India, but in Nepal, a small neighboring kingdom on the border of Communist Tibet; also in many hours spent with visitors from all over Asia and the Middle East; and in three months of travel in all of the countries of South and East Asia, and from Lebanon to Japan. These travels convinced me that what I had learned more intimately about the 360 million people and the 500,000 villages of India applies to a surprising degree to the billion or more other people who live in this vast area.

Sharing my experiences were my wife "Steb" (a nickname derived from her maiden name, Dorothy Stebbins), our three younger children, Cynthia, then fifteen, Sally, thirteen, and Sam, twelve, and a fluffy yellow kitten, Tichat, whose name somehow evolved from *un petit chat*.

For all of us, India became a second home. We grew to love and admire this great nation, newly free, and struggling against heavy odds to build a lasting democracy from the oldest of civilizations. We made many dear friends, not only among the government officials but among the ordinary people of India. Cynthia even decided to stay for a few months after we left, preferring to spend the hot spring and the monsoon summer among friends she will never forget and where history is happening.

This book offers no glib analysis, nor does it propose a precise program for America that will guide us through the maze of conflicting pressures, hopes and prejudices which confuse our present relations with the people of the East.

Rather I have attempted to describe the underlying forces which today influence Asian action and thinking, and to suggest a few essential principles on which I believe any constructive American policy must be based.

Among other things I have sought to bring out that the free nations of the Middle East, South Asia and the Far East are determined to travel their own road, and that the most we can do is to help them meet some of the problems they will have to overcome. In some instances our help may be crucial, but the most critical decisions will probably be made not in Washington but in such Asian capitals as Cairo, Karachi, New Delhi, Rangoon, Djakarta, Manila and Tokyo.

Our ability, in any event, to influence the future of the vast region that stretches from Casablanca to Tokyo, in which more than half of the human race lives, will depend on our ability to listen objectively and with humility and to try to understand.

It is in an effort to contribute to such understanding that I have written this book.

My personal debt to the many people who, wittingly or not, have assisted in its preparation, is very great—my friends and former associates in the Foreign Service and other government agencies in Washington, New Delhi and other posts; the Point Four technicians and consultants with whom I worked so closely; the many Indians and other Asians for whom we developed so much affection and respect.

My particular thanks go to Harris Wofford, Claire Wofford, Abram Chayes and the members of my family, who so generously contributed their suggestions; and to Kay Hart, Jeanne Spallone, Ingebord Bowie, Ruth Merrill and Mae Sullivan, who tirelessly typed and retyped the manuscript. The ideas, analyses and judgments as well as the errors and mistakes in this book are, of course, my sole responsibility, although the problems which I discuss belong to all of us.

AMBASSADOR'S REPORT

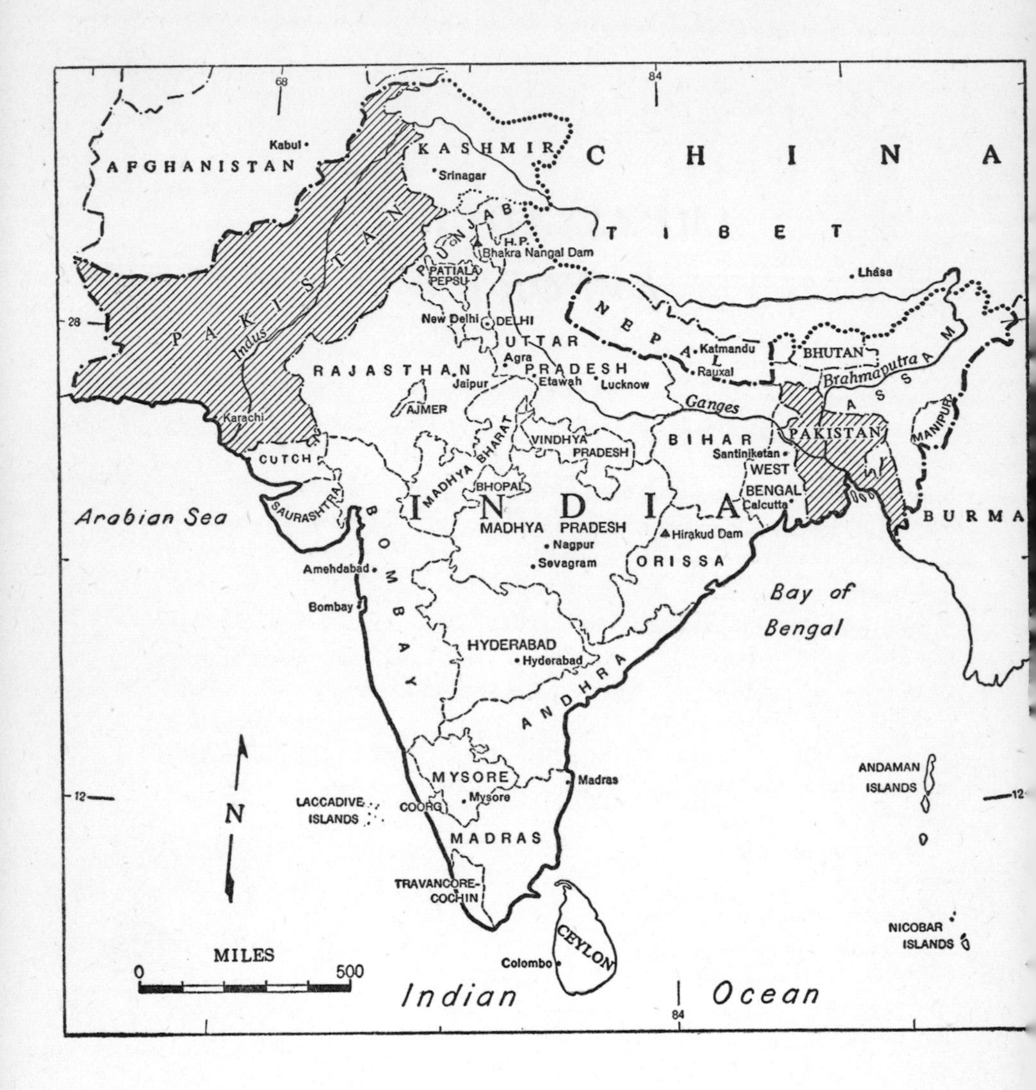

AFGHANISTAN
Kabul
KASHMIR
Srinagar
CHINA
TIBET
Lhasa
PAKISTAN
Indus
PUNJAB
H.P.
Bhakra Nangal Dam
PATIALA
PEPSU
New Delhi
DELHI
UTTAR
PRADESH
Agra
Etawah
Lucknow
NEPAL
Katmandu
Rauxal
BHUTAN
Brahmaputra
ASSAM
RAJASTHAN
Jaipur
AJMER
Karachi
CUTCH
SAURASHTRA
Ganges
BIHAR
PAKISTAN
MANIPUR
Santiniketan
WEST
BENGAL
Calcutta
VINDHYA
PRADESH
MADHYA BHARAT
BHOPAL
INDIA
MADHYA PRADESH
Hirakud Dam
BURMA
Arabian Sea
Nagpur
Sevagram
ORISSA
Amehdabad
Bombay
BOMBAY
Bay of
Bengal
HYDERABAD
Hyderabad
ANDHRA
ANDAMAN
ISLANDS
MYSORE
Madras
Mysore
LACCADIVE
ISLANDS
COORG
N
MADRAS
TRAVANCORE-
COCHIN
NICOBAR
ISLANDS
CEYLON
MILES
0
500
Colombo
Indian
Ocean
68
84
28
12

1. INTRODUCTION TO DIPLOMACY

I. Between Two Worlds

OUR PLANE was high over the Arabian Sea. It was one o'clock in the morning and after a long and tedious flight we were still one hour out from Bombay.

I am afraid we made a rather sorry sight. Sally and Sam were sound asleep, and Cynthia was looking mournfully at the forlorn little yellow kitten in her lap, whose spirits had sunk lower and lower as each new country had been left behind us.

We had brought Tichat along to provide a kind of familiar link for the children between Connecticut and India, but now she only reminded us all that we were a long way from home.

Steb was still quietly reading Gandhi's autobiography. She had spent three months in India right after graduating from college, and we had kept her busy piecing together her memories of places, people and customs.

We had all wanted to come, but suddenly India seemed overpowering, and I felt uncertain about my qualifications for the enormous task that lay just ahead. It was no comfort that in a way I had asked for the job.

"Why in the world would you want to go to India?" President Truman had asked me. "Why not some country in Europe?" After my recently completed term as Governor of Connecticut several challenging government posts in Washington had been suggested, but I had found them surprisingly easy to turn down. When the President asked me to tell him what I would like to do, I told him of my long interest in Asia and particularly in India, which I said would be one assignment I could not refuse.

In answer to his questions I explained to him my deep conviction that India was the key to Asia, and that both India's own course and America's policies toward India were still in a state of flux. If a solid relationship could be built between the two countries, India might find it easier to succeed in establishing a stable and effective democracy in South Asia, and America might unite on an Asian policy behind which our people could stand with assurance.

With China now Communist, Asia and the whole underdeveloped world would be looking to India to see if another way were possible. The Kremlin, too, would be looking to India; for long ago Lenin had said, "The road to Paris lies through Peking and Calcutta." Although the Marshall Plan and related policies for European reconstruction and defense had blocked the direct path to Paris, at least for the present, even a firmly democratic Western Europe might eventually be undermined if all of Asia with its billion or more people should go the way of Communist China.

The debacle in China, which aroused such partisan argument and confusion, had virtually paralyzed American policy making in Asia. It seemed to me that India was a place to start afresh. Indeed if Paul Hoffman was right that India was now where China stood in 1945, then there was no time to lose. The hope that I expressed to the President was that India and America over the years could learn to work together in such a way that a new democratic tide might be set in motion in Asia.

It did not seem likely to me that anything would come from this casual conversation, for the United States had as Ambassador to India one of its ablest career diplomats, Loy Henderson. Unknown to me, however, the State Department had for some time been anxious to send Henderson to Iran.

So the Bowles family was soon faced with a decision. Were we really prepared to leave our home on the Connecticut River for the heat, confusion and frustrations of a Foreign Service post halfway around the world? Steb, who had always shared my interest in foreign affairs and Asia in particular, had immediately said, "Yes." Cynthia, who had been looking forward to her last two years in high school at Essex, had said hesitantly, "I guess so." Sally, who always had a special yearning for faraway places, had approved the idea with obvious enthusiasm. And Sam, after a few careful questions about schools and sports, had also agreed.

Most of my time during the next weeks was spent in Washington. Until my month of briefing by the State Department, I had not realized how badly the relations between the two countries had deteriorated.

Although the loan of two million tons of surplus wheat to relieve India's terrible food shortage had finally been approved by Congress in May, India's "independent" foreign policy had come under heavy fire during the months of delay. In the end the efforts of a few Congressmen to tack on crippling amendments requiring India to meet some of our Cold War demands were defeated, but the day-to-day debates, with many irritable speeches, had been thoroughly reported in the Indian press. Many Indians had become convinced that we wanted to take political advantage of their suffering.

There had also been some differences over the Japanese peace treaty. India felt that she and several other newly independent Asian nations had not been adequately consulted about an issue in which all of Asia had an important stake. Rather than oppose us directly at the treaty conference in San Francisco, thereby benefiting the Soviet delegation, she had refused to attend, expressing her opposition to parts of the treaty in a critical letter to the United States. A bad taste had been left all around.

Beyond this, to many Americans Nehru was a troubling enigma. Mr. Truman told me how puzzled he had been by the Indian Prime Minister during his trip to America. Some officials in Washington actually wondered whether he was a Communist sympathizer. Nehru said that we had no understanding of the "mind and heart of Asia."

Actually, we had not tried very seriously to understand the new Asia. Most of the postwar emergencies, with the exception of China, had been in Europe, with which we were familiar and to which we assigned our ablest diplomats. No American Secretary of State had ever visited India or the rest of South Asia. Yet India more than any other nation was looked to as spokesman by the 700 million South Asians who had become free since 1945. When South Korea, a distant Asian peninsula, was suddenly invaded we reacted with courage and boldness. Could we not help bring strength and confidence to an even more critical area while there was still time to forestall violence and subversion?

My doubts about my own abilities were profound. I had a lot to learn which no books and no briefing could ever teach.

What about the Prime Minister? Would it be really possible to establish a satisfactory relationship? What about India and her tens of millions of hungry impoverished people? Could any ambassador really understand their hopes and fears? Could I cut through the walls of language and cultural differences?

How about Asia itself with its billion or more people which stretched so many thousands of miles beyond India to Japan? Could I hope to achieve any real understanding of what so many Americans still referred to as the "inscrutable East"?

Could I convey to the Indian people some of the inherent good will of the American people? Diplomacy did not usually involve this but it seemed to me desperately important.

What about my new associates in the Foreign Service? When I first walked into the State Department I hardly knew what to expect. Although I did not share a current misconception that our diplomatic officers all wore striped pants and interrupted their work at frequent intervals for a cup of tea, I am sure that, like most Americans, I had subconsciously absorbed some of the propaganda so continuously leveled at the Foreign Service over the past few years. To my relief, the people in the State Department whom I saw turned out to be a hard-working group of high caliber, struggling conscientiously with huge problems and explosive situations.

But I still wondered what the Foreign Service officers in India would be like. Would they be as competent and co-operative as their colleagues in Washington?

My first ambition as a high school and college student had been to work for the State Department. I had been tremendously excited by Woodrow Wilson. His campaign for the League of Nations led to many family arguments with my father, a staunch high-tariff Republican of the old New England school. But a job in the State Department was not easy to find, and when my father's business ran into difficulties, I decided to settle for a business career.

Still, with all the brash overconfidence of a young college graduate I had written to friends that I would stay in business only until I was thirty-five, and then regardless of how far I had advanced I would enter public service. But the years had dragged on and I was thirty-nine before I felt able to cut my business ties, and accept a position with the Office of Price Administration.

In 1945 Secretary of State James Byrnes asked me to leave the OPA and join him in a major reorganization of the Department. Although I was sorely tempted, my commitments had been too great elsewhere.

Later I served as an American delegate to the first Paris conference of UNESCO and as chairman of the National Convention of UNESCO in the United States. I had also worked with Trygve Lie in the United States and in Europe as International Chairman of the UN Appeal for Children. I had taken a particular interest in the Point Four program and long before President Truman's proposal in his 1949 inaugural address I worked with others on the development of this concept.

But these activities had been only on the fringe of foreign policy. Now I would be up against the tough practical day-to-day problems.

My new assignment was also opening a door to another goal which I had thought about for some years. In February, 1942, I wrote my friend Senator Francis T. Maloney of Connecticut:

"Mr. Roosevelt has called this a war 'to establish the Four Freedoms in all parts of the earth.' That great ideal will remain no more than an empty bit of oratory unless it can be developed into a living, breathing, symbol of alliance with the nearly one billion people of the Far East who now consider themselves no more than spectators in the present struggle."

To the Senator and to other friends in government I urged the adoption of a strong anticolonial policy. To transform Asian indifference "into a crusading fight to achieve freedom from all foreign rule," I proposed "a far-reaching workable charter of liberty for all Asian nations."

A decade had passed since those years, and although great changes had taken place, those were still decisive issues.

As our plane cut through the Middle East, over oil-rich Saudi Arabia, with rebellious Tunis and Morocco and an angry Egypt behind us, with Iran to the North, and seething South Asia ahead, I wondered if perhaps the "living, breathing" association I had urged then might not begin between the United States and India.

It was two o'clock in the morning of October 20, 1951, when the lights of Bombay began to twinkle directly ahead. We woke the children, ran a comb through their hair, put the kitten in her basket, and stepped out into the hot, humid Asian night, doing our best to appear fresh, untroubled and delighted to be in India.

2. First Impressions

A NEWSMAN REPORTED that as we stumbled out of the plane we looked less like an ambassador's party than any he had ever met. How other emissaries always seem to emerge from twenty-four hours of flight looking like Anthony Edens I will never know.

But the smiles we had managed to produce for the reporters, photographers and other welcomers gradually faded as we drove from the airport to downtown Bombay. This ride is a disheartening introduction to the new Indian Republic, especially on a dark and sultry night.

The strange new smells, the grim miles through one of the world's worst slums, the sidewalks covered with tens of thousands of sleeping people, some on cots but most of them lying on the hard pavement, the ever-present poverty, misery and squalor, were impressions which we each absorbed silently and apprehensively.

No more reassuring was the fantastic old hotel, named after the Taj Mahal but otherwise coming straight out of the Victorian age. Its enormously high ceilings, the many turbaned servants, its air of elegance and luxury were in shocking contrast to the streets through which we had just passed. As we were led along the great halls to the Viceroy Suite, five large echoing rooms with incredibly large bathrooms, we were all awed, and the childen uniquely subdued.

At the risk of losing face with the servants who assigned us to our respective and distant beds, we soon reassembled in one room, where we slept on beds, sofas and window seats. All of us needed consolation in these strange new surroundings.

Four hours' sleep restored our spirits remarkably and in the morning light everything began to seem possible again. After breakfast Sam took me out for a walk along the broad avenue on the edge of the great harbor, which was alive with ships ranging from dirty freighters to two large modern passenger steamers, and hundreds of sailing vessels with rigs very different from the boats we had sailed for so many years along the New England coast.

We then drove through the same streets back to the airport for the last four-hour hop to Delhi. The poverty was still there, but somehow the sense of a people awake improved the picture. They were on their feet now, talking, shouting, laughing, carrying their wares to market, hurrying to work. The forbidding dreariness of the night had changed to bright-colored saris draped around graceful women, and white garments on the brown-skinned men.

Some men wore only dhotis, skillfully wrapped over their bodies in the manner made famous by Gandhi. Young men were often dressed in long white shirts hanging over white pajamas. Most of the workers wore khaki shorts and undershirts. Some businessmen were in Western clothes. Daylight did not erase the squalor, but it showed the remarkably varied attractiveness of the people, and even disclosed several new housing projects going up in place of the slums.

Loyd Steere, the Embassy's Chargé d'Affairs, and his wife Anna had come to accompany us on the flight to Delhi. Their warm welcome boosted our morale further, and as was always to be the case they were a great help. As we flew northeast in the Embassy's B-17 plane, they pointed out stretches of sparse vegetation on the Rajasthan desert, where only two or three inches of rain fall each year. Then we passed over a more fertile area, and occasionally irrigated sections, whose brilliant greens stood out in hopeful contrast to the otherwise universal gray and brown.

The whole Embassy staff was assembled at the Delhi airport. Although it was a hot Saturday afternoon, they gave us a wonderful reception. We were officially greeted by representatives of both the Indian Government and the Government of Nepal, since I was to be Ambassador to both countries.

The children were delighted with the bearded chauffeur in a bright turban who finally took us in tow. Big, strong, good-humored Jiwan Singh, who had been a sergeant in a Sikh regiment in the First World War and who had driven American representatives in India for nine years, drove us through a maze of bullock carts and dusty suburbs to our new home in India.

We knew that New Delhi had been built next to the ancient walled city of Delhi in 1932, as the seat of British imperial power.

But we were unprepared for the modern, well-planned capital of broad avenues, green trees, and lovely homes and gardens, which in its orderly layout reminded us of Washington, D.C.

Fortunately, we did not have to live where American ambassadors had traditionally resided—a big barn of a palace with endless bedrooms and crystal chandeliers. Knowing of the serious housing shortage in New Delhi, we had asked before leaving Washington to have the great mansion divided into seven apartments for younger members of the staff and to take for ourselves a convenient, attractive smaller house with four normal-sized bedrooms, at 17 Ratendone Road.

Some officers in the State Department had urged that we keep the old palace as a matter of prestige. But this did not seem to us the kind of prestige America should seek.

Perhaps all this was just a rationalization of our horror at the thought of trying to turn a palace into a home. Hence we were rather startled to find lined up by the front door of our new home, twelve servants in full white uniform with six-inch-wide belts of red, white and blue, and huge red, white and blue turbans. In Essex, Connecticut, we had handled a much larger house with one helper.

Cynthia and Sally quickly discovered which baby belonged to the cook and which one to the gardener; who was the wife of the bearer and who was the wife of the sweeper; who were the Muslims, Hindus, Christians, Buddhists and Sikhs. And they in turn did their utmost to make us feel at home.

The next day, a Sunday, we went off to see the old city. We enjoyed wandering through the crowded streets, jammed with window shoppers moving slowly down the long line of open stalls. The hawkers kept up a constant din. Bullock carts, two-wheeled horse carriages called tongas, and hundreds of bicycles made the streets almost impassable for automobiles.

Thousands of Indian families were out in the city parks, enjoying themselves as their American counterparts might on a similar Sunday afternoon. To our surprise several people recognized us from the pictures in the paper that morning and spoke to us cordially.

There were flowers of all kinds and green lawns, but what impressed us most were the birds. Strange bright-colored birds, green parakeets, bright blue rollers, bee eaters, and Indian kingfishers, as well as huge pariah kites that we later discovered would snatch food from our table when we ate under the trees.

The children soon made a discovery. Next door lived the Chinese Communist air, army and navy attachés! Since we did not recognize Communist China and were fighting Chinese troops in Korea, there was no question of a normal neighborly relationship. Cynthia, Sally and Sam, however, were quite unfamiliar with diplomatic requirements, and waved a greeting to the young Chinese children playing outside. At first they were rudely rebuffed but, a week or so later, they reported that they had received some warm, young Chinese smiles as they bicycled by. A day or so later the Chinese children were whisked away and did not again return to the front yard—where the risk of becoming contaminated by capitalist children was so clearly evident.

A few months later we discovered that the Communists really play for keeps. In Delhi, as in all capitals of the world, there were frequent rumors of tapped wires and secret agents. Although I suspected that I might have read too many detective stories, I became sufficiently concerned to request that the State Department send an electronics expert to check all our offices for hidden listening devices.

At the last minute I suggested that our home be included in his check, and it was here that he found a tiny concealed microphone. It was hidden in the library and capable of picking up any conversation within a radius of thirty-five feet. It was tied in with the telephone wire which carried every voice and every sound to a point on the edge of our property where it was tapped. Was it merely a coincidence that the Chinese military attachés lived next door?

We wondered what kind of reception our children would receive from their Indian classmates. In America, both Indians and Americans had advised us that there was no suitable school in New Delhi, and warned that "the *best* Indians and *all* the Westerners" send their children away to Westernized schools in the mountains.

Cynthia was the first to put her foot down on this. "If we are to go to a private school by ourselves, far off from Indian life, we might just as well go to school in the United States!" Sam and

Sally agreed. In Essex, Connecticut, they went to a country public high school, on their bikes, and they wanted to find the nearest equivalent to this in New Delhi, India.

After visiting several day schools Steb reported that four or five seemed quite good, but two of these were rejected because they segregated boys and girls. After a family discussion we settled on the Delhi Public School consisting of thirteen hundred students meeting in some twenty-five tattered tents, with a health clinic in an old temple.

The classes were conducted in English and the textbooks were published in England. Even the principal was still English, although the teachers were all Indian. The students came from families who could afford six dollars a month tuition, which meant mainly government workers and professional people. The only other foreign students were four Indonesians with whom our children became fast friends. Compared with our children's Connecticut school, the Indian school was ahead on mathematics and physical sciences and behind on history and social studies.

At the end of his first day at school I asked Sam how everything went. He had tears in his eyes when he started to talk, and I assumed he must have had a rough time of it. On the contrary he had been emotionally overwhelmed by the warmth of his reception. "I was the only white boy there," he said. "I only hope that if these Indian kids came to my school in America they'd be treated as well. I wonder if they would be?"

The next morning, and every day thereafter, a group of boys and girls arrived on bicycles to accompany our children for the two-mile ride to school. After school they frequently came back to our house to play. Sam's friends were much amused because his white skin showed up so clearly in the darkness and often gave him away in local variations of hide and seek. They gave him the nickname of "Chota bhuti" which in Hindustani means "little ghost."

Actually our children, accustomed to "progressive education," had a hard time with some of their teachers who expected the formality and discipline of an English public school. There was little group discussion or opportunity for student participation. And there was more need for punishment since the strict atmosphere, instead of teaching self-control, only challenged the students to see how much they could get away with.

Ironically, the teacher who permitted the most student initiative was an old lady known as "Ma'am" who followed the Communist line, voted Communist, but who said she was a devout Roman Catholic. In class she scolded and lectured them but none the less encouraged them to talk back.

She seemed to try particularly hard to provoke Sally. One day she snorted that all ambassadors were spies and that America was now as imperialistic as Britain had ever been. When Sally told me that the old lady had said that I was there to ensnare India into a new colonial status, I was annoyed that my daughter should have to listen to such nonsense. But Sally stood up well under the steady barrage, and in the end won Ma'am's respect if not her agreement.

Despite Ma'am's politics, and scoldings, everyone was shocked when she died suddenly of a heart attack, and all the students went to the Catholic Church for her funeral. Sally was touched to learn that one of Ma'am's last requests was that Sally Bowles should conduct her class the next day. I have a feeling that her alleged "communism," like that of many other frustrated Indians, did not go very deep.

Cynthia, who had been the most reluctant to come, soon became our most eager student of India. "The India of India is wonderful," she wrote in her diary. "But," she added earnestly, "there is another India, European or British India, which I have grown to dislike intensely. We have to hunt for Indian things and for India behind her foreign mask. But we have found it and I love it and wish we could live as the Indians do and not as if we were in England."

One of our main worries had been, "How would the children get along?" We soon recognized that they were doing famously. Now it was up to us.

3. America's New Diplomacy

MONDAY MORNING at 8:15 I left for the office two miles from our new home. The drive took us through several broad streets, past rows of modern houses, and across Kingsway with its great India Gate Memorial to the Indian soldiers who died in the First World War.

Although I traveled this route many hundreds of times it always managed to produce fresh impressions. One morning I counted the vehicles which we passed and sent this description of Indian traffic in a letter to our older son and daughter at home. There were 684 bicycles, 41 bullock carts from nearby villages, 36 two-wheel horse-drawn tonga taxis, 28 automobiles, 14 motor trucks, 12 carts pulled by ungainly but dignified camels, and 6 passenger buses.

The Embassy building was simple and all on one floor. It had been converted some years ago from the home of a maharaja but was in no sense ostentatious.

The members of the staff gave me the warmest kind of reception, and went all out in their efforts to be co-operative. With a team that seemed friendly and capable, I quickly began to feel at home.

With three exceptions, the staff were all Foreign Service people or recruited specially for India by the Technical Assistance Administration. These exceptions were: Ed Logue, an able young lawyer from Connecticut, who came with me as my assistant; Jean Joyce, an experienced information specialist; and Bernard Loshbough, a well-known specialist in the development field.

I was not unfamiliar with the setup of an American embassy or of the day-to-day operation of diplomacy, having visited many of our embassies in Europe during previous years, and having known many people in the State Department. Nor was I unfamiliar with the old argument about the respective strength and weakness of "career diplomats" versus people like myself who were appointed directly to a specific post instead of coming up the long Foreign Service ladder.

Our embassies in such European cities as London, Rome and Paris are huge affairs. The ambassador is kept busy from early morning until evening holding staff conferences, sending reports to the Secretary of State, meeting visitors, calling on various ministers of the foreign government, and attending an endless series of social or official functions.

In the old days few career Foreign Service officers could afford the costly living and expensive entertainment that traditionally go with a European post. As a result, ambassadorships in the key capitals of the world were often given to major contributors to the political party in power at the moment. Although some of these individuals were no more than social playboys who left the main burden to their staffs, many of them proved to be excellent and able ambassadors.

In recent years Congress has acted to increase the salaries of the ambassadors at the ten major posts to $25,000 a year, with sizable living allowances and expense accounts in addition, and this has made it possible for career diplomats or other public servants without independent means to occupy any post in the world.

Because of this new approach, some outstanding Foreign Service officers have had a chance to serve their country in the top post which their training merited, and we have had several such refreshing new ambassadors as Mrs. Eugenie Anderson of Red Wing, Minnesota, who won Denmark's heart. Our own salary at the New Delhi post, of $25,000 plus an additional $5,000 for official entertainment, was certainly more than ample.

Unlike the embassies in Europe, however, our embassies in Asia with the exception of Japan are manned by relatively small staffs. For instance, for India, the largest free nation in the world with its nearly 400 million people, I found that we had fewer State Department employees than we had in Greece with her 8 million people. Our staff was only a little more than half that of the embassy in Mexico, less than half of that in Italy, and only one-third of that in France. Pakistan and Indonesia, with more than 80 million people each, had far fewer State Department representatives than did tiny Cuba.

This comparison would be even more startling if the personnel of all the Point Four programs in Asia were compared with the staffs which administer the European aid programs. Our economic aid has amounted to more than $2 billion each to Britain and France, and more than a billion each to Germany and Italy, compared with only a fraction of these amounts spent in the Asian countries, again with the exception of Japan. Nor do the above figures include the military personnel attached to our embassies.

In Asia, of course, there is less travel to America, and our immigration laws, until recently, prohibited the admission of Asian immigrants. But I believe that the explanation for the difference is largely historical. While all parties in America now talk incessantly about the crucial importance of Asia, our long-established habits in dealing with Europe still seem to prevent us from distributing our budget expenditures in a way that will enable us to carry out the responsibilities which we now recognize in theory.

Throughout India there were 148 American employees engaged in political and economic reporting and in administrative and clerical work, the essential basic functions of an embassy. In addition to my chief deputy, Loyd Steere, there were Everett Drumright and Fraser Wilkins, the top political experts, and John Loftus and Clifford Taylor in charge of the economic work. It was a remarkably qualified and hard-working team.

There were also some ten military officers representing our army, navy and air force in liaison work with their counterparts in the Indian military organizations. All of these Americans were stationed in New Delhi or in our three consular offices in Bombay, Calcutta and Madras. In addition there were 69 employees when I left, assigned to the USIS—the United States Information Service.

Fortunately, the American staff was aided by excellent Indian employees, some of whom were experienced economists and political reporters, and others of whom were translators, clerks, chauffeurs and messengers. Without them we would have been lost indeed.

Before my arrival, there had not been many Americans engaged in economic aid programs in India. Point Four activities had been limited to a few American technicians. But in the fall of 1951, just before my departure for India, Congress had provided the far more substantial sum of $54 million to assist the Indian government with its bold program of economic development. An additional $45 million was appropriated in July of 1952 for the following fiscal year.

The operation of this Point Four program involved many phases of the India economy; it was complex and obviously called for the best staff we could assemble. Gradually during my stay we recruited a fine team of 114, headed by Clifford Willson, Bernard Loshbough, and Horace Holmes, and including some able county extension agents from the U.S. Department of Agriculture.

The fact that the Point Four people plus the USIS staff actually outnumbered the regular Embassy employees emphasizes the changed nature of modern diplomacy. An ambassador's job is no longer the relatively simple one of carrying out the policy of his government on a high level in the country to which he is assigned. As I see it his job is also to reach the people and give them some understanding of the objectives and policies of the United States. And it is his job, too, to help work out programs of economic co-operation which would strengthen democracy in the country of his assignment. These were the tasks of the whole Embassy mission.

These first days in Delhi made it clear to me that my efforts must cover three different fields of effort: the traditional all-important diplomacy and reporting represented by the regular Embassy staff; and the new diplomacy, represented by the two new branches, USIS and Point Four.

During my first few days at the office I spent the majority of my time listening, and as usual this was an excellent investment. Among other things I learned that the morale was by no means good. Recently there had been considerable turnover in the staff and, with the exception of a few old-timers, such as Evelyn Hersey, the Social Welfare attaché, Henri Sokolove, the Labor attaché, and Andrew Corry, in the economic section, only a few employees had been in India as long as a year.

The hot season was just drawing to a close and there had been no air-conditioning except in the homes of a handful of senior employees. Because of the intense heat this meant that the office was opened at 7:30 in the morning and closed at 1:30 P.M. for the day. As a result almost everyone had idle time in which to worry and it was not strange that some of the employees had come to look on their assignment to New Delhi as an unpleasant ordeal, a stepping-stone to a more congenial post in Europe or South America.

Among many of the wives and older children there was also a very genuine fear of sickness. Each American Foreign Service post has what is called a "Post Report," describing not only health problems, but also living conditions, climate, protocol customs, general attitudes and other information of interest to newcomers. A glance at the New Delhi, Calcutta, Bombay and Madras Post Reports made it clear that these documents may well have contributed to the general attitude of insecurity and discouragement.

Every page dripped gloom and discouragement. They implied that there was practically no decent food available; that prices were outrageously high; and that almost no goods were available in the stores. They talked ominously of strange new diseases, blistering heat, cobras, sneak thieves and red tape. They emphasized the need of spending considerable time at the "hill station" resorts for relief from the heat, and specified their distance from the main cities.

After reading the report on New Delhi before leaving for India, Steb and I, in spite of our enthusiasm, had come to the conclusion that we were moving into a somewhat uncomfortable situation. As a result, we had shipped endless quantities of canned foods. Fortunately our supplies did not arrive for some weeks and we had a chance to discover that there was plenty of delicious food at prices lower than in the United States. We also discovered that there were clothes of all kinds in New Delhi stores, and what was lacking could be made to order at very reasonable prices.

As far as health was concerned neither Steb nor Cynnie, who spent more time in villages than any of us, had a really sick day in India, although Cynnie contracted a case of trachoma in her eyes. I had dysentery on two occasions, and Sam had a few stomach upsets, probably due to too many Coca-Colas. Sally was the only member of the family who could lay claim to a real two-fisted illness. She was in bed six weeks with jaundice, but, she later discovered, so were four or five of her friends back home in Connecticut.

The Post Report also failed to bring out the fact that for nearly six months of the year the weather in New Delhi is perfect. The spring is extremely hot, with temperatures ranging up to 115 degrees, and the monsoon rains which start in early July are humid and often unpleasant. But it begins to grow cooler in October and by December and January an open fire is needed at night, although the thermometer always climbs above 70 degrees by noon.

For more than half the year there is rarely a cloud in the sky. "The climate—it is heavenly," wrote Steb in her first letter home, describing how we ate breakfast outside on the terrace, and noting that no one thinks to say, "Isn't it a beautiful day?" because all days are beautiful during that half of the year. She sounded like a Californian!

The fourth day I called a meeting of the entire staff. I told them why I had wanted to come to India; why I felt India was so desperately important. I expressed the opinion that they had an assignment which others in the Foreign Service should envy, for it gave them an opportunity for the broadest and most important kind of service in one of the least known and most vital parts of the world. I told them that I understood the very real difficulties they faced, and I assured them I would do everything possible to improve their living conditions and to make their tasks easier. For their part, I insisted on all-out co-operation, loyalty, and hard work.

I went on to say that some Foreign Service officers might be sincerely unable to adjust themselves to India, and in other cases it might be impossible for their wives or children. If such instances actually existed in New Delhi, I promised to try to arrange an immediate transfer to a more congenial post, without detriment to the individual's record. I emphasized that I wanted no martyrs with a grin-and-bear-it complex. There was much to be done, and only an enthusiastic team could hope to do it.

During the following months we were able to make many changes which brought a lift to the morale of the entire staff and their families. We arranged to have the whole office and all bedrooms air-conditioned. When the hot season rolled around in April, I asked the staff to vote whether they would work a full day or go back to the traditional schedule of 7:30 until 1:30. I was enormously pleased when they voted almost unanimously to continue the full working day from 8:15 to 5:30. After closing time, there were always many people working far into the night, even in the hottest weather.

We set up an independent commissary on a co-operative basis where employees and their families could buy food, cigarettes and liquors at prices well below those charged at home.

After some delay, the army agreed to send out Captain John Painter, an excellent young doctor, to support the efforts of our very competent nurse. Within a few months, they had set up a fully equipped clinic which was an immense reassurance to everyone, and particularly to the mothers of young children.

We established free Hindi lessons, not only for husbands on the staff but for their wives, and 110 of our staff members attended the classes. Knowledge of Hindi gave them a new sense of confidence in dealing with Indians. In France, our Foreign Service officers would not think of not learning French, and their wives would take pride in learning it. In India, we are spoiled by the fact that all government officials speak English, but the Indians are as proud as the French, and our effort to learn their national language showed our sincere interest in their culture.

We established a volleyball league with teams made up of Indian and American employees.

We managed to improve the very serious housing situation. In order to avoid any charge of discrimination we set up a committee representing all parts of the Embassy staff, all ages and ranks, to determine who should live where.

Protocol inside the embassy was another problem. According to tradition, the wives of all newcomers were expected to dress up in their Sunday best, complete with long white gloves, and formally call on Steb and the wives of the heads of all the various departments. After a few such sessions, obviously a nervous ordeal for the younger wives, Steb suggested that the system be reversed.

In any New England town, she pointed out, everyone naturally calls on new neighbors to see if they need advice on where to buy things, whom to get to cut the lawn, where to get the washing machine fixed, and a hundred and one other questions. Here we were in a foreign land ten thousand miles away from home and the problems for newcomers were far greater. And so to follow a more American approach, reception committees were set up to greet the new arrivals and to help them in their adjustment to India.

I talked to all the new families who arrived in India and did my best to give them some of my own convictions about the importance of their assignment, and the great rewards which it held for them. Every month we gave a "newcomers" party, where we had square dancing and no one ever dressed up.

Later we set up a two or three weeks' "Introduction to India" course for all new employees, their wives and older children. It included a review of Indian history, culture, languages, an outline of the Indian Five Year Plan, lectures by Indians on the Gandhi movement, visits to hospitals, schools, welfare centers and nearby villages. Although these courses were never as complete as we wished, everyone agreed that they helped immeasurably to make us more effective. One wife told me, "We've been here only six weeks and already I feel that we know India better than we knew our last post after two years."

One evening, three or four months after our arrival, a group of young people were gathered at our home. Someone brought up the matter of the old Post Report. We had already prepared a new Post Report putting New Delhi and India in more reasonable perspective. In it we described the problems newcomers would face, but we also told them of the many good things which they would find in India.

To bring the point even more clearly home, one young Foreign Service wife made a suggestion: "I wonder what an Indian Post Report on America would be like?" she asked. "How would the Indian Government describe the heat in summer, the snow in winter, the high prices and the crowded rush-hour subways?"

During the rest of the evening we entertained ourselves by putting together a list of all the things an Indian might find strange about New York City, from subway rides to baby sitters, snow suits and commuting. The result, which followed the exact style of our own Foreign Service Post Reports, was later reprinted in the *Foreign Service Journal.* It not only created considerable amusement, but helped to put life in Asian "hardship posts," such as New Delhi, in better perspective.

At the end of our first week in India we decided to give a party for the office force and their families. At the last moment we discovered that the invitation had not been extended to the Indian employees. We were surprised to find that it had long been the custom in the American as in the European embassies not to include local employees in most social functions. No one was to blame except the system, which had gone on so long that no one thought to change it.

Hurriedly we invited *all* the staff, and everyone, Indian and American, seemed to have a good time square dancing, singing and eating together. No one had wanted to discriminate, but the old policy had underlined the Asian charge of racial prejudice. Nor could the best efforts be expected of the Indian employees so long as there was the slightest shadow of "second class citizenship." As soon as someone changed the system, everyone approved and felt better.

For Halloween, which came shortly after our arrival, the American women in New Delhi arranged a typical New England county fair carnival. It was magnificently organized and a great success. Some 25,000 rupees were raised for New Delhi charities, which is roughly equivalent to $5,000.

This party was repeated the following fall on even a grander scale, when more than 8,000 Indians came and the charity proceeds totaled 57,000 rupees. Many of them could not get over the absence of servants and the sight of the American wives putting mustard on hot dogs, raffling off everything from dolls to lamp shades, and serving ice cream cones, Coca-Cola, and orange pop to the children. Unhappily there was little in their past experience to prepare them for the sight of "white memsahibs" acting in a normal democratic American manner in an Asian capital.

In early November, after we had been in New Delhi only a few weeks, we received the usual invitation to the annual party given by the Embassy of the Soviet Union. This party celebrates the "October Revolution" when Lenin took power. As in other world capitals, it was a gala and extremely expensive affair. Champagne, vodka and caviar were served in unending quantities to a crowd of at least three thousand.

The point that immediately impressed both Steb and me was that this was not the usual diplomatic gathering. We saw schoolteachers, social workers, minor trade union leaders and other everyday people of New Delhi. Some of them were undoubtedly Communists, but the Soviet Union was reaching out its hand to a much broader group. This was their one big function each year—and there was no doubt of its effectiveness.

As Steb and I were driving home that evening we both agreed that it was silly for our Embassy to give its annual party on the Fourth of July when it is so hot that only a few people can come. We also felt that we had to move far beyond the usual high-level group that normally attends diplomatic functions.

In mid-February invitations went out for a Washington's Birthday party at the Embassy. Seven thousand people were asked and about five thousand actually came. To save money and to respect the custom of a great many Indians to abstain from intoxicating beverages, we set the time at four in the afternoon when it would be easy not to serve expensive alcoholic drinks. At most Indian parties, instead of cocktails, you are offered an amazing array of fruit juices and colored drinks. We tried to follow suit.

The Embassy was decorated with red, white and blue flags and we hired two magnificent Indian army bands. We invited practically every schoolteacher, college professor, welfare worker, trade union leader and businessman in the city of New Delhi, as well as the usual government officers. To each guest in the receiving line we gave the Indian greeting of *namaste* (folding the hands in a praying gesture), or shook hands until our arms ached. When the party ended, everyone was handed a scroll with a red, white and blue ribbon tied neatly around it, dedicated to "George Washington, Father of the American Revolution."

The text presented our struggle as the "first successful revolution against colonialism in the history of the world." It described the decision in 1776 to issue the Declaration of Independence, the terrible privations at Valley Forge, and the final emergence of our free nation.

When the script was completed, there had been a momentary flurry when someone said, "What in the world will the British think of this? Won't they be offended?" A quick call to the British Information Service brought a hearty laugh and good-natured answer. The officer assured us that Britain had long since adjusted herself to the loss of her American colonies.

The second year we gave an equally effective party on Lincoln's Birthday for an even larger number. This time each guest was given a little pamphlet on the life and ideas of Lincoln. The Indians seemed to be particularly interested in the statement that, although many peoples throughout the history had fought to become free, the only time that people of one race had died in great numbers to make people of another race free was in our American Civil War.

But New Delhi is no more India than Washington is the United States. I made it a rule to spend at least 30 per cent of my time away from my desk, traveling into the most remote corners of India, talking with all kinds of people, and learning from them about India and Asia. In eighteen months I crossed India east and west fourteen times and six times north and south. In all I covered some sixty thousand miles, including all the cities and hundreds of towns and villages.

Most members of the staff agreed that they had not done enough traveling and felt as I did that something must be done about it. I urged them to spend more time away from their desks, even if some of their routine work suffered. Once I teased several particularly desk-bound officers by saying that if the diplomatic "cocktail circuit" was abolished and the English-language Indian newspapers ceased publications their reports would be empty of news. Some of our ablest officers in the past had been so trapped by mountains of paper work that they were not able to get nearly as close to India as they should. With a little encouragement and occasional prodding, the previous annual average of less than 5 per cent for embassy travel time quickly increased to better than 20 per cent.

If, over a long period, I introduced some changes in the diplomatic routine, they were changes which it was easy for an outsider, with a new perspective, to make. It is difficult to change a system that you are inside of and of which you have always been a part.

If at a few points the customs of diplomacy have led some of our people into habits which seem stuffy, that is, when they did not act according to the democratic faith and manner they would practice at home, it is only because it is so easy for a Westerner in Asia to slip into the conventions set long ago by the British during their imperial days. Even in free Asia, colonialism's old habits linger and are contaminating.

But with few exceptions the Foreign Service officers in India and throughout Asia whom I came to know were dedicated, devoted Americans, who worked long hours under difficult conditions to represent their country well.

In the last twenty years I think it is fair to say that our Foreign Service has been built into one of the most effective arms of American policy. Although in past years I have tackled various difficult assignments and worked with many fine organizations, I have never experienced a greater sense of mutual dedication and loyalty to a common purpose. I hope the day is not too far distant when they may receive the public and Congressional support which has so long been denied them.

4. Striped Pants and Calling Cards

MY FIRST official act, some ten days after my arrival, was to present my credentials in a formal ceremony to the President of India, Rajendra Prasad. The chief officers of the Embassy were to accompany me. All of us were to be dressed in striped trousers, morning coats and silk hats.

For just such an occasion, I had packed an aged suit which I had not seen since our wedding. But the air freight had not arrived. When I informed our protocol advisers of this, panic set in, and a hurried call for help was sent out to various diplomatic colleagues of my approximate size and shape.

The crisis was finally solved by a miniature Marshall Plan from Italy. The Italian Ambassador loaned me the proper coat, vest, pants and hat. This lend-lease suit probably fitted me better than my own musty outfit which arrived the following day.

The colorful ceremony began in the courtyard of the vast and shining President's House, the former Viceregal Palace, where an honor guard of strikingly tall soldiers in red and white uniforms was drawn up for review. I walked down the ranks to the music of a British waltz and then presented my credentials to the President who stood in ironic contrast to his plush, British-inspired surroundings.

Rajendra Prasad is a simple-living follower of Gandhi, who spent many years in British jails fighting nonviolently for Indian freedom. He wore a white dhoti made of homespun yarn. He has a big walruslike mustache, and his magnificent face always seems to be holding back a smile at the strange twist of history which took him from the British Viceroy's jail into the Viceroy's own palace, with the Viceroy's own bodyguard. He is such a warm and unostentatious person that the great long halls and chambers must have seemed oppressive and unnatural. From time to time members of his huge "joint family" move in with him and help bring the place to life.

My statement to the President was brief. I expressed my earnest conviction that America and India would gradually grow closer together. Both countries were founded on a deep faith in democratic principles. They must not expect agreement on everything, because their people lived far apart, faced with very different conditions. But it was not too much to expect a sympathetic understanding of each other's problems and an abiding respect for each other's integrity.

At the luncheon afterward, attended by many members of the Ministry of External Affairs (the Indian State Department), I was surprised when the President told me that 95 per cent of the servants who surrounded both him and the Prime Minister were Muslims. Like many Americans, I had more or less assumed that since India was predominantly a Hindu country and since Hindu-Muslim bitterness had led to the creation of Pakistan, no Muslim servant would be trusted not to put poison in the soup of the Hindu President. During the coming months, we became accustomed to seeing many such clichés about India, collected in the United States, turned upside down.

The next day I called upon the Prime Minister. I had looked forward to it for many months. In years past I had followed closely Jawaharlal Nehru's courageous part in India's long fight for freedom. I had read his beautiful autobiography, *Toward Freedom,* and his brilliant historical book, *The Discovery of India.* I knew that he had a sensitive mind which had thought more deeply about our present fortunes than most political leaders. Also, I knew that he suspected most Americans of being insensitive, and that he had recently become irritated by what he considered American attempts to badger him into line.

Somehow our first meeting did not come up to my expectations. The Prime Minister was not in an articulate mood and at times it was difficult to keep the conversation going. Even when I started on a new tack, he would answer with a polite sentence or two and lapse into silence, looking out the window. I stayed only about twenty minutes.

Since I was keenly aware that the success of my mission would depend to a large extent on my relationship with Nehru, I was, to say the least, discouraged. But Nehru is known for changeable moods, and I suspected that subconsciously he was a little determined not to have our first session work out as well as our mutual friends had predicted.

A few days later Steb and I were invited to his home for a simple family dinner with him, his devoted daughter Indira and her husband. He had been very close to Indira, his only child, since the death of his wife in the early thirties. As Prime Minister, Nehru lives in the former residence of the chief of the British Indian Army.

Instead of being aloof, he was in high spirits, full of charm, courtesy and friendly smiles, and overflowing with conversation in his inimitable and eloquent English. He joked happily about the pleasant experiences of his sister, Mrs. Pandit, while she was Ambassador to the United States. That night we had mangoes for the first time, and tasted some delicious new fruit from Indonesia, which the Prime Minister showed us how to eat.

After dinner he took me aside and we talked for three hours about India, the Soviet Union, China, the United States, the United Nations, the Cold War and Korea. He did 90 per cent of the talking, and seemed extremely anxious for me to know what he thought and believed. He gave me the impression that although he would, of course, like me to agree with him, the important objective was to make sure I understood his reasons and viewpoint.

I have never forgotten that talk. His deep devotion to Western concepts of democracy was as obvious as his determination to be an Asian, to think and act independently, and above all not to be dominated by his Western training and his Western friends. Over and over again in the coming months I was to hear this viewpoint expressed, although rarely as eloquently, not only in India but in almost every nation from Lebanon to Japan.

A few days later we were again invited to the Prime Minister's house. This time it was for seven o'clock and the children were included. With everyone dressed up in his Sunday best, we sallied forth to what we presumed would be another family dinner. His sister, Mrs. Pandit, whom we had known in the United States, served us fruit juices. The Prime Minister showed the children some statues in his study, and autographed for them a book of letters to his daughter Indira, entitled *Glimpses of History*, which he had written in a British prison when she was a little girl.

Cynthia, Sally and Sam responded easily to his warm friendliness and time passed quickly.

When the clock struck eight and there was still no sign of dinner, it suddenly dawned on Steb and me that we had not been invited for dinner at all. No one had thought to tell us that in India dinner is never announced before eight-thirty or nine, and that seven o'clock simply means tea!

Unfortunately, we had sent the car on an errand to Old Delhi with a request that it not be back until around ten. Steb finally rose to the occasion as a good diplomat's wife and said innocently, "Something seems to have happened to our car. Could we borrow a car from you to take us home?" The children's startled looks ought to have given us away. But in a few minutes we were on our way to 17 Ratendone Road, where we picked up an anticlimactic supper of cold cereal and scrambled eggs. Later, when we got to know them better, we had great fun describing our confusion to the Prime Minister and his sister.

The next official chore for a new Chief of Mission is to call on all fifty or so fellow Ambassadors and Ministers. Since the Russian Ambassador, Novikov, was the senior member of the diplomatic corps, he was first in line.

I found him a large stocky man with huge hands, and a sense of humor. It was the first time that I had ever talked to a Soviet official and I decided that I might as well be frank. I asked him bluntly if there was not some way that the world could be brought a little closer together and the tensions diminished. I described to him our first breath of hope after the war, when Russian and American GI's took a natural liking to each other on the Elbe, and how that hope had gradually faded into suspicion, fear and bitterness.

I told him of my own incredulous reaction to the "Iron Curtain," when I came face to face with it in 1946. Our Ambassador to Russia, Bedell Smith, had invited me and William Benton, who was at that time Assistant Secretary of State, to visit him for a week in Moscow. The Russian Embassy in Paris had readily granted the visas, but our American Embassy plane got no further than Berlin. The local Soviet officials adamantly refused to allow us to take off.

I suggested to Novikov that the arms race could not go on forever without a blow-up, and that against our resources, steel mills and skilled workers they could never win. Nor would America be lulled into indifference.

Novikov replied that if we stopped spending billions on armaments, our economy would collapse.

"If you really believe all that," I continued, "why hasn't the Soviet Union proposed an agreement for the control of atomic energy and the reduction of armies and navies and air forces that we could accept?" I added that our American economy was not going to collapse, that we had learned some fundamental lessons since 1932, and that the Russians must be fully aware of this.

Later, after Stalin's death, when the Soviet Union suddenly shifted its tactical gears, I remembered this conversation. But I am interested to see that there have so far been no practical proposals for disarmament from Moscow, perhaps because their experience in East Germany has convinced them that peace would open up far more problems for them than for us.

Several times during the following months, I saw Novikov at diplomatic functions. Sometimes he smiled distantly and on other occasions he looked grim and uneasy. Even the day-to-day attitudes of Soviet representatives abroad seem to be directed from Moscow. When it suits the zigs and zags of their current strategy, they are all courtesy and friendliness. And then suddenly for several months they will refuse to speak.

During my talks with the other Chiefs of Mission, I tried to learn all that I could of Asia as well as India. I recognized them as trained political observers, many of them of great ability.

Of the Western ambassadors I was deeply impressed with Sir Archibald Nye of the United Kingdom, who has a particularly keen insight into India and Asia. Count Ostrorog, the French Ambassador, is an incisive student of Soviet policy. W. R. Crocker of Australia is a political scientist with particular understanding of Asian attitudes. Joza Vilfan, of Yugoslavia, we found to be very effective in bringing home to the Indians the reality of Soviet imperialism.

Among the Asians, Ambassadors Soedarsono of Indonesia, Qureshi of Pakistan, Ramos of the Philippines, and Kyin of Burma were all men of great ability and experience who were among our good friends. The Soedarsonos, with three children almost exactly the same ages as Cynthia, Sally and Sam, and in the same school, were particularly close.

However, Steb and I tried from the beginning to focus our social affairs on a widening circle of Indian friends, both inside and outside of government, rather than confine ourselves to the diplomatic group. Before our marriage Steb was a professional social worker and has always had an intense interest in public education. Soon she made many particularly good friends among the educational and welfare workers.

But not all of our early impressions were happy ones. From our first conversations after our arrival and the first Indian newspapers that appeared on our breakfast table (excellent English-language papers such as the *Times of India, Hindustan Times, Statesman* and *India Express*), we had realized the extent of misunderstanding about America. The irresponsible statements of some American military men had been fanned by Communist propaganda until a large section of Indian public opinion believed America to be actually seeking war.

Many of our movies, comics and more sensational magazines had convinced a large number of Indians that we were a completely immoral people. Communist reporting of our long tradition of racial discrimination had magnified our past misdeeds and obscured our very substantial progress until many otherwise well-informed non-Communist Indians believed that lynchings in America occur almost daily.

I decided that it would be helpful to hold a press conference. I prepared a three-thousand-word statement and announced that I would attempt to answer any questions about America and American policies. Knowing the intensity of anti-Americanism at that time among part of the Indian press, and being accustomed to more indirect diplomatic ways of doing things, a few of the Embassy staff for whom I had great respect strongly opposed the move, and I approached it with some nervousness.

My statement stressed things about America that we take for granted, but which I discovered were almost totally misunderstood in India. "We believe in freedom of religion," I said. "We believe in the family as the basis of all civilized life. We believe in the right of all peoples to live under a government of their own choosing. And with the most intense feeling, we dislike and deplore the conflict which is now threatening the peace of the world."

I stressed the areas of agreement between India and America, and particularly our mutual desire for peace, disarmament and the rapid economic development of the new free nations of Asia and Africa.

"But," I added, "we Americans believe that disarmament cannot be a one-way street. We believe disarmament must cover all weapons and not simply those in which we are strong and others are weak. We believe that disarmament must include full inspection in all countries to make sure that the conditions are carefully and fully met."

As I later discovered is almost invariably the case in any Asian press conference or forum, the number one question was, "What about America's treatment of the Negro?" This is a situation in which my own feelings run deep, and I answered fully and honestly, frankly describing the problem as I saw it, and reporting with precise examples and statistics the progress which is now being made. I then suggested that, more than any other people, Indians should understand the very real obstacles to rapid progress in America, since they face a somewhat similar problem in dealing with the situation of their own untouchables.

When a persistent Indian reporter asked if America's real hope was not to make India lean toward the Western democracies, I replied: "Certainly. At least we hope you won't lean the other way. But really how you lean is your own business. We only want to see you strong enough and free and independent enough so that you can choose which way you want to lean, and we have no doubt of your answer. What we want in India above all therefore is to see Indian democracy succeed."

The next day all Indian papers printed several columns, covering the press conference in detail. At least a dozen papers printed my three-thousand-word statement in full. Some say that this was the first time a balanced answer to the racial question was ever printed in the Indian press. I felt immensely encouraged, for now it was clear that literate Indian people could be reached with a frank and straightforward talk.

In the following weeks, many stories appeared in the American and Indian press about what was described as a "new kind of diplomacy." We were astonished at the repeated emphasis on my wearing of the Italian Ambassador's dress clothes, the children's enrollment in an Indian school, our preference for bicycles, square dancing and informality, our determination to meet and know Indians in all walks of life, and my willingness to answer questions put to me by Indian newspapermen.

Some of our steps, such as inviting Indian employees to Embassy functions, or Steb's wearing of the Indian sari at evening parties, may have seemed like "symbolic acts," as they were called in some newspapers, but they were not at all so intended by us. We had simply acted as, I believe, most Americans would act who had not assumed it necessary to follow some pompous protocol.

"We want you to know that we are quite disgusted with all this comment on the way we are living and the way Chet is handling things," Steb wrote home in a round-robin family letter a month after our arrival, "because to us it doesn't seem to deserve comment. We are just doing what anybody would do, which is, insofar as possible, to lead a normal life. We have not really done anything at all outlandish, not nearly as outlandish as we sometimes would like to."

The stories grew and grew into exaggerated myths. One account reported that "all India was buzzing" with the story of an evening party which Steb and I were said to have left on our bicycles just as the Soviet Ambassador departed in a great bullet-proof limousine, complete with bodyguards and footmen. Perhaps this could have happened, but actually it never did. It seemed to us that most of the comment missed the essential points. That Indians should be so easily and quickly pleased by our actions simply showed the depths of colonialism's racial wounds.

India and Asia do not expect to find American diplomacy British-bound in stuffy precedents. Prestige in terms of big houses and shiny limousines is out of place in a land of mud huts and awakening villagers.

When Cornwallis surrendered to Washington at Yorktown the band played "The World Turned Upside Down" and that is the music that the people of Asia expect from us today. In many ways this is 1776 in the colonial world. This is Asia's democratic revolution.

Since our purpose in India was to understand the Asian revolution and to find the right role for America, in these first steps we felt that we were only crossing the threshold to our real task. But we were reassured that we were going in the right direction when Radio Moscow found it appropriate to launch a series of violent personal attacks on me in which among other things they called me "the scheming agent of the Wall Street monopolists."

We were even more reassured when Ashadevi Aryanayakam, a beautiful disciple of Gandhi from his mud hut village of Sevagram, told a friend of ours that she felt as much at home staying with us as with anyone in Delhi. We had been a little embarrassed that whenever she stopped with us she had to double up with Sally.

"It is the friendly America, the family America, that India wants to see," Ashadevi said. If this was anything more than a kind compliment, it was only because we, too, were feeling at home.

II. HOMEWORK

5 History Around Every Corner

WHEREVER YOU turn in India history literally stares you in the face. In Delhi you cannot leave your home without seeing a ruined wall, a monument, a mosque, a temple which, on investigation, turns out to be a remnant of some ancient empire, or a relic of an age about which there is only dim knowledge.

On our first day, driving around the ruins of the eight walled cities of Old Delhi, looking at the huge and magnificent Red Fort, built in red sandstone by the seventeenth-century Mogul emperors, we realized how little we knew of the history of the Asian half of the human race.

Ashadevi later drove with Steb through the same streets and by the Fort, telling her tales about the many empires which had once reigned in Delhi, and Steb came home enthralled. When, on a beautiful moonlight night, we went out in the countryside for a picnic supper, and found ourselves sitting in a grassy courtyard in the middle of the ruins of Hauz Khas, a fifteenth-century university, we thought how young America was. This Indian university had flourished long before the first Pilgrims reached our shores.

And yet an Indian friend had remarked, "This school is not old enough to be really famous. Take Nalanda, for example; it began in the fifth century and by the seventh century was known throughout Asia." Later we learned more about this great university in Bihar which was flourishing five hundred years before Europe was to see the beginnings of similar institutions in Paris, Bologna and Oxford. How much we Americans have missed by not knowing Indian history!

In their talks with me, Prime Minister Nehru and President Prasad often said that any foreigner who wishes to understand modern India must first understand India's tremendous past. "To know my country," wrote Tagore, the Nobel-prize-winning poet of Bengal, "one has to travel to that age, when she realized her soul and thus transcended her physical boundaries, when she revealed her being in a radiant magnanimity which illumined the eastern horizon. . . ."

When I was in school we were taught little about Asia as a whole, let alone about India's great ages, and our modern school system still ignores this vast and vital part of the world. Thus when Sam came home from his first day at school in Essex, after our return from India, and announced that next year he was to study World History, I could not resist being skeptical.

"I'll make a bet," I said, "that the world history which you will study begins in Egypt and Mesopotamia, moves on to Greece by way of Crete, takes you through Rome and finally ends with France and England."

"But that's not *world* history," Sam argued. "That leaves out three-fourths of the world." Unhappily I won the bet.

Recently I noted that when students in a large American city were asked to learn the hundred most important dates in the history of the world, only *one* was an Asian event and that was 1857 when Commodore Perry "opened" Japan!

One excuse for our ignorance, which I discovered as soon as I started to delve more deeply into Asian history, is the hard fact that very little about this part of the world has ever been written down. Even after much research and archaeological exploration, great gaps will remain which may never be filled.

During our stay, we did not see Mohenjo-Daro, "place of the dead," near the Indus River, where the evidence of the earliest-known Indian civilization has recently been uncovered and verified by archaeologists.

The ruins reveal a well-developed metropolis which existed about five thousand years ago, almost contemporaneously with the building of the Sphinx and the Pyramids in Egypt. It was a carefully planned city, with broad, straight streets, houses built of burnt bricks two or more stories high, with great public baths and an excellent drainage system, which indicates that plumbing may not be as modern as we think.

Where did these people of Mohenjo-Daro come from, and what happened to them? India, "this lady with a past" as Nehru calls her, is so old that her origins are lost in legend. It is believed that the people of Mohenjo-Daro were of the dark-skinned Dravidian stock whose descendants now live in South India, and that their society was finally overcome by the lighter-skinned Aryans who appeared in India at the dawn of history.

But the common ancestry of most of the European peoples and the Aryans of India is a well-established fact. English, most European languages, and the half-dozen modern languages spoken in northern India are all descended from one original source, the ancient Aryan tongue. The Aryan relationship, for instance, seems clear in the Indian *pita*, *mata*, Sanskirt *pitri*, *matri*, Latin *pater*, *mater*, French *père*, *mère*, German *Vater*, *Mutter*, English *father*, *mother*.

Little is known of the rise and fall of the first Aryan kingdoms on the Indian plains during the next several thousand years after Mohenjo-Daro. Then in 325 B.C. Alexander the Great invaded India.

Every American schoolboy reads of Alexander's march to India, but few ever learn of the marvels which he found there. We study almost nothing about Asoka, the Emperor who, within a century after Alexander, united most of the subcontinent in a reign so remarkable that H. G. Wells, in his *Outline of History*, ranked him as probably the greatest ruler of all time. "More living men cherish his memory today than have ever heard the names of Constantine or Charlemagne," concludes Wells.

About Indian history during the next three hundred years before Christ and the first fourteen centuries after Christ, we Americans study almost nothing, although several great ages occurred for India, such as the Golden Era of the Gupta Kings from 320 to 480 A.D., and the beginning of a series of Muslim invasions which resulted around 1200 in the Pathan kingdom in the North.

India comes into our textbooks again as the fabulous land whose wealth in the fifteenth century drew Western explorers and adventurers like a magnet. We know that India was the aim of the voyage on which Columbus discovered America, and we study how Vasco da Gama finally reached India by sea in 1498. But we find little in our books about the great Mogul Empire which ruled most of India during the sixteenth and seventeenth centuries.

We hear of India again when the British won control over the quarreling rajas and sultans after the Battle of Plassey in 1757, when the Indians first rebelled a century later in the so-called "Mutiny" of 1857, and when Queen Victoria was proclaimed Empress of India at a great durbar in Delhi in 1877. And we know that after a series of campaigns led by Gandhi between the First and Second World Wars the British left India to freedom in 1947.

Obviously my first homework for the Indian assignment was to fill in this sketchy picture of Indian history. I read a number of good books, but the story only came to life for me as I traveled around the country and around Asia, and saw the present impact of that history. This is not the place to try to tell the past of India, and none of my discoveries which are reported here will save anyone else his homework.

What first strikes a Westerner is how much more Western-looking are the Indians than the Chinese, Japanese or Southeast Asians. The ancient historic mixture of the invading Aryans with the Dravidians has given most Indians a skin darker than that of most Americans, but features which are clearly Caucasian.

Though relevant only as a matter of curiosity, it is interesting that in physical appearance as well as language the people of India are closer to us than are most of the peoples on the Asian and African continents.

Out of the relations between these conquering Aryans and the darker inhabitants came caste, which Nehru says "in its origin was based on color." The very Sanskrit word for caste, *varna*, means color. Even today some Indians spend as much time trying to lighten their skins as some Americans spend in an attempt to suntan theirs. While Indians are intensely, and rightly, incensed at color discrimination in the West, they, too, have not freed themselves from the same kind of senseless prejudice.

Many insist that caste is merely a hereditary division of labor, with priestly and intellectual functions reserved for the Brahmans, warfare and statesmanship reserved for the Kshatriyas, trade, industry and agriculture for the Vaisyas, while the Sudras were left with menial and servile work, and the outcastes, or untouchables, assigned to the dirtiest work, such as scavenging and sweeping.

"Our four main castes resemble the members of the human body," a Hindu priest once told me. "They spring from the head, the arms, the thighs and the feet of the Creator."

In any case, the light-skinned Aryans generally took the upper three castes for themselves, and the conquered Dravidians were left largely to the work of the feet. Although South Indian Brahmans are often dark, we never saw a so-called untouchable who was not very dark, nor a very light-skinned Indian who was not among the upper castes. Nehru himself, the color of whose skin resembles a successful Florida suntan, was born a member of the highest caste, a Kashmiri Brahman.

If some Indians take false pride in their Aryan ancestry, all Indians can justly be proud of their Emperor Asoka, who ruled between 273 and 236 B.C. With him Indian history comes, for a moment, into clearer focus. Fortunately, thirty-five of the thousand or more inscriptions which he placed around the country, with some five thousand of his words engraved on rocks or pillars or in caves, still remain.

One of his edicts describes his conversion to nonviolence after defeating the Dravidian kingdom of the Kalingas in the modern state of Orissa in a bloody war in which "one hundred thousand were there slain."

The "conquest of a country previously unconquered," Asoka announced, "is a matter of profound sorrow and regret to His Sacred Majesty." In the full tide of victory, with the rest of South India his for the taking, Asoka renounced further warfare.

Vegetarianism became the law of the royal kitchens. He ordered his governors to think of themselves as "good nurses." He vowed to strive for the happiness of his subjects "in this world and the next."

"At all times and in all places," he said, he would be ready to hear and dispose of "the business of the people." Although there was, of course, an autocratic rule, the Mauryan emperors on coronation took a solemn oath to the people: "May I be deprived of heaven, of life, and of offspring, if I oppress you."

Asoka was the third Mauryan Emperor. The first of this line, his grandfather Chandragupta, was the king who routed the last of the Greeks. In 325 B.C., Alexander had entered northwest India, crossing the Jhelum River and defeating an Indian army of thirty thousand soldiers and two hundred charging elephants. He never reached the plains of Delhi to face the main Indian kingdoms, for his troops refused to go further.

Within two years, at the age of thirty-two, he was dead in

Babylon. In 305 B.C., Seleucus, Alexander's governor of Babylon, again sought to invade India, but Chandragupta, with a reputed strength of 9,000 war elephants and 600,000 infantry, repelled the invasion.

With the chroniclers who accompanied Alexander, and the Greek ambassadors who were later sent to the Mauryan court at Pataliputra, near the site of the present city of Patna in Bihar, the first known direct contact began between Asia and the West.

Often as I traveled over the bad roads of the dusty, poverty-stricken plains of central India I recalled the description of Megasthenes, the fourth century, B.C., Greek ambassador, who went twelve hundred miles across the then fertile heart of India on a "royal road." He pictured it as sixty-four feet wide, lined with trees, and generously supplied with wells, hostels and police stations at regular intervals.

During the next thousand years, the best accounts also come from foreigners, but not so much from Western as from Chinese visitors. The letters of the Chinese, who came in a small but steady stream, tell of India's gradual decline, its division into several kingdoms, particularly that of the Andhras in the South who asserted their complete independence, and its magnificent rise again with the golden age of the Gupta empire in the fourth and fifth centuries A.D.

Fa-Hien, a Chinese monk in search of Buddhist manuscripts, who came across Central Asia between A.D. 399 and 414, reports of the Ganges Valley that "the people are numerous and happy. . . . If they want to go, they go; if they want to stay on, they stay. The king governs without decapitation or [other] corporal punishments. . . ." In the towns he found free hospitals: "Hither come all poor or helpless patients, orphans, widows and cripples. They are well taken care of, a doctor attends them, food and medicine being supplied according to their needs."

The great Emperor Asoka's old palace in Pataliputra left the Chinese visitor so wonder-struck with its huge stone blocks and inlaid carving that he imagined that no human hands could have built it.

Two famous Chinese Buddhist scholars came in the seventh century, Hsüan Tsang and after him, Yi Tsing. They both studied at Nalanda University, and wrote detailed accounts of the life of the ten thousand students and monks who were in residence there. They described the vast libraries in which Yi Tsing copied four hundred manuscripts.

India's store of knowledge was then as great as any in the world. Although our numerals are called Arabic, the Arabs apparently passed on to us the inventions which they learned from Indians, including the zero and nine-figured place value system, which made possible advanced arithmetic and algebra. Indian doctors in the first Christian centuries stressed the study of anatomy, made use of the pulse rate, and experimented with vaccination for smallpox. They took care of their patients' teeth, and had a high standard of surgery.

During this long stretch of history, India was not only a center of advancement to which people came from Asia and Europe, but it was the major expansive force of South Asia. "Greater India" was the title of a chapter in the Indian history text which Sam studied in the Delhi school. Its map shows Indian settlements in Ceylon, Burma, Malaya, Java, Sumatra, Bornco, Bali and Cambodia.

India's chief influence came through its radiation of culture and religious ideas. Even to this day, as we discovered on our later travels, the island of Bali in Indonesia remains dedicated to Hindu culture, and there are many beautiful old Hindu temples in daily use. In a museum in Saigon, capital of Vietnam in French Indo-China, we saw accumulated evidence of India's once dominant role in Southeast Asia.

Asoka, for whom religious tolerance was the rule ("All sects deserve reverence for one reason or another," reads one of his inscriptions), was perhaps the world's greatest royal propagator of a religion. He was such a serious Buddhist that he became a monk, much like two later kings of Christendom, St. Louis of France and St. Ferdinand of Castile, who became members of the Third Order of St. Francis. He had 64,000 Buddhist priests on his personal payrolls. He sent forth missionaries "to the utmost limits of the barbarian countries," to "intermingle among all unbelievers." They were ordered never to convert by the sword, and, no matter how great the provocation, to continue peacefully "in foreign countries, teaching better things." His missions are credited with the founding of Srinagar in Kashmir and Lalita Patan in Nepal.

Hinduism, the older of the two great religions or cultures to which India gave birth, has had no single champion like Asoka; but has an almost infinite line of philosophers, poets, and ascetics, going back from Gandhi in the twentieth century to mythical figures before recorded history.

In early April, 1952, on a ten-day cruise down the Bombay coast, Steb and I caught some intimate glimpses of the way Hinduism has passed itself on from generation to generation of illiterate villagers.

We were off by ourselves on a small sloop for our first vacation. We sailed up coastal rivers and into little back harbors. We passed dozens of old forts, built by pirate chieftains several hundred years ago. We anchored off isolated fishing villages and drank leisurely cups of tea with peasants, fishermen and shopkeepers, most of whom had scarcely heard of America, let alone of an ambassador from such a place.

One night, while anchored behind a little Hindu temple on the banks of a river, we listened to a village celebration which continued almost to dawn. We heard a familiar dance with clashing sticks, and above all the songs from the Hindu holy books, which recount the myths and preach the mores of several thousand years of Hinduism.

Although we could not hear the words, we knew that most of the verses came from the two epic poems, the *Mahabharata*—"Story of the Great Bharata War"—and the *Ramayana*—"Adventures of Rama"—the Indian equivalent of ancient Greece's Iliad and Odyssey.

For fifteen hundred years these books have been recited and copied in their present textual form, but their origins are much earlier. They are as rich in human drama as our Old Testament and probably older. In them, the characters which can be seen as gods on Hindu temples come to life in legends and parables.

We heard these same songs throughout India, in the cities, in village development projects, and in the most remote rural areas. Often when we would find ourselves in a wholly modern setting a flute in the distance would take up a familiar ancient tune; or we would come suddenly upon a Hindu performing one of the religious rites which is prescribed for every change in his life, from prayers at dawn and sunset, to celebrations of spring and fall, of birth, marriage and death.

One section of the *Mahabharata* is the *Bhagavad-Gita*, a philosophical poem which Gandhi took as the highest embodiment of Hinduism. He himself reinterpreted it into a gospel of nonviolent action as a means of defeating evil, although orthodox Hindus believe that this was not its message at all. It is a conversation between a Hindu warrior, Arjuna, and the divine Krishna, on the eve of a terrible civil war.

Standing on the battlefield of Kurukshetra, Arjuna asks if it is right for him to fight his brothers. "I would not kill them, even for the three worlds; why then for this poor earth?" he asks. "It matters not, if I myself am killed."

Krishna shows Arjuna the various ways to God, the path of the intellect or knowledge, the path of action, and the path of faith. He enjoins against "being enamored of inaction" and asks of Arjuna "selfless action": "Thy thoughts concentrated on the Absolute, free from selfishness and without anticipation of reward, with mind devoid of excitement, begin thou to fight."

For Gandhi, "The battle of Kurukshetra is in the heart of man." He often said that he could not "see any difference between the Sermon on the Mount and the *Bhagavad-Gita*." To him the Gita taught men to resist evil by pure and non-violent means. Nehru says that every school of thought in India looks to the Gita and interprets it in its own way.

A visit to a South Indian Hindu temple on a religious festival demonstrated to us the vast, many-sided nature of this, the world's oldest surviving faith. In the architecture were represented all kinds of gods and symbols, taken from the innumerable holy scripts. The ancient temple was a gathering place, with room for the bullock carts of pilgrims, for cooking fires, for stalls of itinerant shopkeepers who supply the needs of faraway visitors.

One American missionary describes it as a combination of our old-fashioned tent revival meeting with a county fair. Since there is no congregational service, each individual may worship when, where and to which god he wishes. "Some of us profess to believe in no god, others in many gods," a Hindu explained to us. "Some believe in one personal god, others in an impersonal universal moral law. Most of us believe in reincarnation."

Much remains of the spontaneous Aryan nature worship which is reflected in the *Rig-Veda*, probably the oldest book humanity possesses. The *Rig-Veda* attributed divinity to every element and force of nature, although it stressed that despite its various names, "Truth is one." At least six distinct schools of Hindu philosophy, with many subsystems, have flourished inside Hinduism's encouragement to diversity of thought. In a sense it is not a religion at all, but a culture.

Gandhi defined Hinduism as "Search after truth through nonviolent means." But pacifism, and its Indian corollary, vegetarianism, apparently did not become important until two great "protestant" revolutions occurred in Hinduism, Jainism and Buddhism, both of which religions arose in the fifth century before Christ.

Shortly after our arrival, the religious leader of the present-day Jains visited Delhi and invited me to see him. Later I met him, but on this first occasion Steb went as my representative. After she took off her shoes, she was ushered into an immaculate room. All around were mops and brushes of various kinds, which made it look like a Fuller Brush showroom. They were used in almost constant sweeping to make sure that no one stepped on an ant or any other living creature.

His Holiness was seated cross-legged on a small platform, and Steb was asked to sit on the floor in front of him. He wore a mask over his mouth and nose to keep from inhaling, and thereby destroying, germs. For half an hour or so he explained to her the fundamentals of Jainism, whose founder, Mahavira, had lived between about 540 and 468 B.C. He likened Mahavira to Christ, and said that his greatest criticism of the modern Christian faith was "the failure of so many people who call themselves Christians to practice it."

At the age of thirty, Mahavira had left the luxury of a distinguished family to become a wanderer. After thirteen years of self-mortification, fasting and meditation, he took these vows: not to injure life in any form; to speak the truth; not to steal; to live in self-imposed poverty; and to practice chastity.

In connection with the Jain principle of nonpossession, His Holiness, who owned only a small wooden bowl with which he begs his food, teased Steb a little about the wealth of America. Later she discovered that she could have reciprocated by teasing him about the many wealthy Jains, who are one of India's richest communities. She also decided to practice sitting cross-legged so that the next time she could maintain that position for an hour without becoming almost paralyzed.

The Jain conviction that all things have a soul has entered deeply into the Indian mind. Gandhi's mother, who was a devout believer in Jainism, imbued him with this faith. But today only some three million Indians still follow the Jain religion.

Buddhism also has had a profound effect on Hinduism, although today it has practically no organized following left in India. Gautama Buddha, born the son of a minor prince in the foothills of the Himalayas, probably in what is now Nepal, was a contemporary of the founder of Jainism.

Like Mahavira he began life in an atmosphere of wealth and privilege. Although not Brahmans, both were of the warrior caste. Both rebelled against what had gradually become a ritualistic, doctrinaire, caste-ridden society. Both disavowed the ancient gods and placed emphasis on personal morality, particularly on nonviolence.

Buddha's approach, which attacked not only the lower superstitions but the higher metaphysical speculations of Hinduism, and which refused to recognize caste, came to the people of India, according to Nehru, "like the breath of the fresh wind."

Legend has it that the young Buddha was protected by his father from all contact with the misery of ordinary life. At the age of twenty-nine he saw for the first time an old man, a sick man, a corpse and an ascetic. This shattered his youthful view that all in life was serene.

When he recalled that only the calm face of the ascetic had shown signs of peace, he renounced his rulership and set forth as a pilgrim in the common yellow robes of a Hindu monk. After six years of fasting, he received "enlightenment" while sitting under the now sacred pipul tree, in the full moon of the month of May, at Gaya, in Bihar.

In the deer park at Benares on the banks of the Ganges, he preached his first sermon on what he believed to be the universal law of life. "Not by birth, but by his conduct does a man become a low caste or a Brahman," he stated. Salvation would not come from formal rites or fasts or prayers, but from good actions and good thoughts. "Not by hatred is hatred quenched. This is an eternal law. Let one overcome anger by love, deceit by truth, evil by good, greed by liberality."

"Go unto all lands," Buddha told his disciples, "and preach this gospel. Tell them that the poor and the lowly, the rich and the high, are all one, and that all castes unite in this religion as do the rivers in the sea."

By the time Alexander entered India 150 years after Buddha's death, Buddhism was a serious competitor of Hinduism. However, despite Asoka's missionary efforts, Buddhism diminished thereafter in the land of its birthplace. Over the years it, too, became rigidly doctrinaire and further and further removed from the day-to-day struggles of ordinary human beings.

When the conquering Muslims swept onto the Indian plains after the ninth century A.D., the remaining Buddhist monasteries were easy targets. Nalanda University was burned to the ground and thousands of Buddhist monks went into exile. But Hinduism, with its insatiable ability to form a synthesis from each new proposition, had already absorbed the remains of the once great faith of Asoka, accepting much of its compassion and nonviolence. And with its patient tolerance, which is part of its great vitality, Hinduism continued its ageless task of absorption, by starting to adapt some of the truths of Islam.

Buddhism has receded from India, but elsewhere in Asia it still prevails, among about one-fourth of the human race. In Ceylon, where Asoka is said to have sent his son and daughter to convert the people, we saw the Buddhist temples and the continuing Buddhism of the people, as we did in Burma, Thailand, Korea and Japan.

Islam overran most of Indonesia in the sixteenth century, and eliminated both Hinduism and Buddhism. But on Java there remains the amazing Borobudur with the whole life story of Buddha magnificently carved in stone.

When Nehru, on travels outside India, sees the statues of Buddha, he feels that they still seem to, ". . . symbolize the whole spirit of Indian thought. . . . Seated on the lotus flower, calm and impassive, above passion and desire, beyond the storm and strife of this world.

so far away he seems, out of reach, unattainable. Yet again we look and behind those still, unmoving features there is a passion and an emotion, strong and more powerful than the passions and emotions we have known. . . . The ages roll by and Buddha seems not so far away after all; his voice whispers in our ears and tells us not to run away from the struggle but, calm-eyed, to face it. . . ."

Buddha's voice and those of innumerable Hindu prophets also whisper in the ears of modern Indians that nothing is all good or all bad. In India's noninvolvement in the Cold War and in her attitude toward the West and Russia, ancient themes are still at work.

The test "of a nation's cultural background," Nehru once suggested several years before he became Prime Minister, is: "to what kind of leaders has it given its allegiance?"

That more than two thousand years ago India turned to such noble men as Buddha, Mahavira and Asoka, that in the twentieth century it followed Gandhi, another non-Brahman "protestant" and champion of nonviolence, certainly gives reassurance for the future.

Today, the flag of Free India carries a wheel which symbolizes both the spinning wheel of Mahatma Gandhi and the Buddhist "wheel of life." The seal of the Indian Republic is the lion pillar of Asoka on which was found one of his first edicts. Every day many documents came across my desk, engraved or stamped with this reminder of the first Buddhist empire.

One day we drove outside Delhi to visit the Kutab Minar, a tall "tower of victory" erected in the twelfth century by one of the early Mohammedan conquerors. In the courtyard we saw one of the iron pillars of the fourth century A.D., on which is a Sanskrit inscription describing the military feats of one of the Gupta kings who conquered Bengal and later crossed the seven tributaries of the river Indus.

The column, which is twenty-three feet high and estimated to weigh not less than six tons, is forged in a single piece of pure rustless iron, unaffected after 1600 years of exposure, a feat of the forger's art which the West did not equal until the nineteenth century.

When we climbed the tower and looked out over the flat lands and the slowly winding Jumna River, we felt very humble before all the triumphs and all the sorrows which these plains had witnessed. Before our eyes seemed to pass the myriad invaders, the

Aryans, the Huns, the Pathans, the Moguls, the civilizations and emperors which had come and faded away, the saints and monks on their pilgrimages. All this had taken place before Columbus had set sail for India, and, miscalculating, had discovered America.

India, we thought, was a land where history cannot be lightly brushed aside.

6. Rise and Fall of the British Empire

COLONIALISM IS a fighting word today in Asia, as it once was among the thirteen rebellious American colonies. It is colonialism "in all its forms" against which Nehru in India, U Nu in Burma and Soekarno in Indonesia constantly vow eternal hostility. It is a subject full of emotion and resentment. Asians want no more white Western occupation, domination or exploitation.

A thorough appreciation of this passionate hatred of anything that smacks of colonialism, and of its roots in Asian history during the last two centuries, is essential to any understanding of the mind of Asians today.

The colonial experience was the central theme of that history in every one of the newly independent Asian countries as well as those in Asia and Africa still struggling to be free. By the middle of the eighteenth century the European colonial powers had pretty well divided the world among themselves. England, France, Portugal, Spain and Holland fought over the spoils of North and South America and of South Asia. Later Germany, Italy and Belgium entered the competition for control of Africa. The inhabitants of all these continents were governed by foreigners for the profit of foreigners, and it so happened that all the foreigners were white and Western.

No country profited more than England, whose empire, on which "the sun never set," stretched from the Atlantic seaboard of America to the island continent of Australia. Its "brightest jewel," in Winston Churchill's words, was India. Without India's enormous annual "contribution" to the British economy, Churchill believed as late as 1935 that "one-third" of the British population "would have to go down, out or under." "India," he said, "was England's daily bread, that's all."

Yet by the middle of the twentieth century India was free, and the British Empire had been largely converted into a Commonwealth of entirely independent nations. South America and most of South Asia were also free. If the war in Indo-China had not turned into a battlefield in the struggle against world communism, the French would long since have been driven from that rich colonial possession as completely as the Dutch had been driven from Indonesia. Only in Africa were the European powers still able to cling desperately to their old colonies. On most of the nineteenth-century empires the sun had already set.

We sometimes forget that this world-wide rebellion against colonialism, which has already lasted for two centuries and has yet to be completed, was begun by the people of the United States. Until I went to Asia I did not realize the extent to which our example has been a challenge to the world, and how closely our history has been read. A Ceylonese cabinet minister once said to me, "Your Boston Tea Party, your Continental Congress, your Declaration of Independence, your Bill of Rights, even your Constitution, these have been our models."

The contrast between America's great development under freedom and Asia's lack of development under colonialism rankles in the minds of most Asian leaders. "You won your independence at about the time we lost ours," an Indian said to me sadly.

Just as England is the leading example of empire in the last two centuries of world history, just as America is the leading example of free, democratic development, so India epitomizes the experience of the colonial nations in Asia and Africa. The story of the evolving relations between England and India over many generations, and the stark contrasts between the development of the United States and India during this same period have been burned into the hearts of the people of two continents.

The English arrived in 1600, seven years before the settlement of Jamestown, while Shakespeare was alive and writing. In that year Queen Elizabeth gave a charter to the East India Company. By the time the pilgrims were landing at Plymouth, the English, the Dutch and the Portuguese were fighting for footholds in India, and soon the French joined the fray.

None of the European powers wished to pay in gold or silver for the raw materials they desired from India, a policy ironically described at the time as "bleeding Europe to enrich Asia." So when barter on strictly European terms failed, outright warfare and annexation were adopted. Since the Mogul Empire had disintegrated into dozens of petty, rival principalities, the European conquest was not difficult.

As the American colonies impatiently moved closer to independence, the British were consolidating their colonial grip on India. Portugal and France were driven out except for Goa and Pondichéry and a few other small settlements. Lord Clive had conquered Bengal. The remaining Muslim and Hindu states were at the mercy of the British crown, to be played against each other or to be taken one by one.

In America, the British had established policies designed to make the thirteen colonies permanent sources of raw materials for British industry. But instead, these policies were a major factor in bringing on our own revolution. The success of that revolution and the failure of the British colonial policy in America led to redoubled efforts to establish the self-same policies in the great new imperial possession of India on the other side of the world.

By an extraordinary coincidence, while the Americans, who had defeated Lord Cornwallis at Yorktown, were meeting in Philadelphia to draft a constitution, the very same Cornwallis was taking up his new duties as the British Governor-General of India. Cornwallis did his best to make up, by the thorough subjugation of India, for his military failure in America. He arrived to face mounting Indian resentment against Clive's plunder of the previously wealthy Bengal. (Nehru says that "loot" is one of the few Hindustani words which the English added to the language.) Not only were Indian treasures shipped directly to London, but the British land revenue system squeezed so much out of the peasants that despair, and then famine, swept North India.

The land revenue system, established by Cornwallis to solidify his regime, and perhaps the most far-reaching of his economic measures, was known as the "Permanent Settlement." The heart of the Settlement was the creation of hereditary tax collectors known as Zamindars. Each Zamindar was given the responsibility of collecting the revenue quota established by the British for a particular area.

The important feature of the system was that, while this revenue quota was relatively small, anything over and above the quota which the Zamindar could collect was his to keep. This system insured a regular income to the government, but far more important was the fact that it created a powerful class of Indian "landowners" with a stake in continuing British rule.

Indian scholars claim that when the British conquered India, manufacturing was actually further advanced than in Lancaster, Manchester and London. They remind us that Indian textiles were so admired that to this day we have cloths called "Madras" and "Calico" (derived from Calicut). And they find statistical confirmation of the destruction of these industrial beginnings in figures which indicate that despite the rise of the new British cities of Calcutta, Madras and Bombay, the proportion of the Indian population dependent on agriculture for a bare living steadily rose throughout the subcontinent.

These statistics reflect the success of the deliberate British effort to crush Indian industry. Indian textiles were excluded from British markets by every conceivable device. As late as 1860 fines were levied against any Englishman who wore a shirt made of Indian cloth. In India internal levies discriminated against local manufacturers, while English goods, free of tariff, swamped the Indian market. The economic result in India was catastrophic. "The bones of the cotton-weavers are bleaching the plains of India," reported an English Governor-General in 1834. "The misery hardly finds a parallel in the history of commerce."

"It was all in the cause of progress," Nehru says generously in his *Discovery of India*, and India "can take pride in the fact that she helped greatly in giving birth to the Industrial Revolution in England." He cites English and American economists who believe that the influx of wealth from India provided the crucial source of capital which made possible the major British industrial development. According to these economists, it was British fortunes, largely made in India, which supplied the capital to translate the inventions of the eighteenth century, the flying shuttle, spinning jenny, power loom and steam engine, into the mass industries of the nineteenth century employing hundreds of thousands of skilled workers.

Thus India became the classic example of colonialism: a vast agricultural appendage of industrial England, supplying cheap raw materials and providing a readily profitable market for England's products.

Almost all Asians with whom I have talked on this subject believe, with unshakable conviction and with considerable logic, that the price of Western Europe's transition to industrialism, which was inevitably a costly and painful process, was paid, to a large extent, by the colonial peoples of India, China, South Asia and Africa. European workers labored long hours and for pitiful wages and under poor conditions. But at least their sacrifices enriched and strengthened their own country, and their descendants reaped the benefits. Asia's contribution in human cost was much greater, and the benefits went almost entirely to foreigners.

"Let's clear our minds of cant," a British Cabinet Minister, Lord Brentford, once said. "We are in India, not for any love of the Indians, but for what we can make out of it."

Naturally many Indians like to contemplate what India might have achieved if she, too, had been free since 1783. "Surveying the past century and a half," Nehru writes, "an Indian looks somewhat wistfully and longingly at the vast progress made by the United States during this period and compares it with what has been done and what has not been done in his own country."

What embittered the Indians even more than British ruthlessness in economic affairs was their Anglo-Saxon sense of racial superiority. In 1818 Sir Thomas Munro wrote, "Foreign conquerors have treated the natives with violence, and often with great cruelty, but none has treated them with so much scorn as we. . . ."

"India as a nation and Indians as individuals," Nehru once wrote, "were subjected to insult, humiliation, and contemptuous treatment. As an Indian, I am ashamed to write all this, for the memory of it hurts, and what hurts still more is the fact that we submitted for so long to this degradation."

As late as 1947 the most desirable benches in many Indian parks still carried signs "For Europeans Only" and Indians were excluded from British clubs except as servants. Even today the American Club is the only "white" club in Singapore which will accept "natives" as members or even as guests. I came to realize that this attitude of white superiority was the aspect of colonialism which is most hated by the colored peoples of Asia and Africa.

The most skillful technique in maintaining Britain's grip on India was her policy of divide and rule. At first the British threw their weight against the former Muslim rulers, whose power had to be broken. Then when Hindu nationalism began to appear as a serious threat at the turn of the twentieth century, the British began to encourage the forgotten Muslim minorities.

With British support the Anglicized Aga Khan organized the Muslim League as a counterbalance to the Indian National Congress. And the British introduced a separate election system, by which Muslims were permitted to vote only in contests limited to Muslim candidates.

"Wouldn't religious divisions in America have become serious if in your elections Protestants could vote only for Protestant candidates, Catholics only for Catholics, and Jews only for Jews?" asked a bitter Indian professor. He was a Muslim who did not want to see his country divided on religious lines, and who still primarily blames the British. Although his example may be unfair to the British, it is easy to see how the communal electorate system acted like a wedge, splitting the religious groups into competing political camps.

Zamindars, economic repression, racial discrimination and divide-and-rule were powerful weapons. But the tide of nationalism could not be easily stopped. In Europe, the revolution of 1848 and the Communist Manifesto of Karl Marx marked the midway point between the French and the Russian revolutions. Asia too had reached a turning point by the mid-nineteenth century.

In China the fanatic and complex Christian leader Hung Hsiu-ch'üan, who had never heard of Marx, led half a million men against the Manchus in the Taiping Rebellion of 1851 to establish a kind of Communist Utopia. In India the world-wide popular awakening was reflected in what the British called the "Mutiny" of 1857, but which Indian nationalists more properly named the "First War of Independence."

Indian troops of the British army sent to put down Hindu and Muslim princes who were rising against the British joined the rebellion, killed their English officers and captured Delhi. At the Red Fort the ex-Mogul king was proclaimed as the new sovereign of India.

Although the revolt was widespread in the North, and for a long time various British units were isolated, many princes remained loyal to the crown. Reinforcements, including Gurkhas from Nepal, finally arrived in time to save the day. Then the victorious British savagely let loose their fury. "Every Indian who was not actually fighting for the British became a 'murderer of women and children,'" writes one English historian. "Soldiers and civilians alike were holding Bloody Assize, or slaying natives without any assize at all regardless of age or sex."

One would like to forget all this now, but as Nehru writes, "Psychology counts and racial memories are long." In his own district of Allahabad, Nehru says, it is still told how volunteer hanging parties went into the countryside, and women and children were burned to death in the villages.

Mounting anger was the main Indian reaction to the suppression which followed the "Mutiny." And many Indians began to plot forms of resistance as violent and terrible as British vengeance. The legendary Rani of Jhansi, a twenty-year-old princess who died fighting the British in guerrilla warfare during the Mutiny, considered by the English general as the "bravest and the best" of the rebel leaders, became the national symbol. We saw her heroic story retold in a long dramatic movie which drew huge audiences throughout the country in 1953.

By the turn of the century, revolutionary passions reached new extremes of violence all over the Asian world. In 1900 China witnessed the bloody Boxer Rebellion, and in 1905 came the first revolutionary uprising in Russia. India, too, was seething with unrest. Secret terrorist societies were growing in Bengal in the image of the Russian and Irish revolutionaries.

In 1912 the Viceroy barely escaped assassination by a bomb hurled as he entered Delhi on a regal elephant. "It looked as if India was going to blow up in hatred and warfare," a veteran American observer who knew this period told me.

In China, by 1923, Dr. Sun Yat-sen, disheartened by the success of the war lords in capturing his revolution of 1911, and by lack of support from the Western powers, had decided to turn the Kuomintang into a para-military party based on the Communist experience. The young and promising Chiang Kai-shek went to Moscow for military training and Borodin, an experienced Russian revolutionary, was sent as head of an advisory mission to Peking.

Lenin and his comrades were already unleashing the gospel of world-wide class warfare. Everywhere the Communists were seeking to win control of the anticolonial revolutions. The world seemed headed toward the catastrophe of endless civil wars, bloody revolutions and totalitarianism, and India seemed the easiest target.

Then something strange and dramatic occurred. A frail little man, Mohandas K. Gandhi, demonstrated a new kind of resistance, and a great empire showed a new kind of response. Instead of the final terrible explosion that most people expected, the Indian revolution became nonviolent, and after a unique struggle extending over thirty years, the British withdrew from India suddenly, peacefully and with dignity, and most extraordinary of all, with the friendship of the Indian people.

One of the Viceroy's most frequent political prisoners, Jawaharlal Nehru, who had willingly sought jail as a way to win freedom for his country, became the Prime Minister of the Indian Republic. And although India refused any longer to acknowledge obedience to the British crown, it joined the reconstituted Commonwealth of Nations of its free will, accepting the crown as a symbol of friendly association. Mr. Nehru, Prime Minister of the world's largest republic may have felt out of place at the coronation of Queen Elizabeth, but there he was in the royal procession for all the television world to see.

What a startling contrast to Indonesia, where so much bitterness is still shown toward the Dutch who attempted to destroy the new republic by force, and who left in shreds and tatters because they did not understand that colonialism was doomed in Asia.

And what a contrast, too, with Vietnam, Cambodia and Laos where even the most ardent anti-Communists insist that French rule is no more welcome than Chinese, and who resent the proposal that they must negotiate in Paris for the freedom which they feel is theirs by right.

In Djakarta, capital of Indonesia, I saw workmen busily engaged in tearing down statues of Dutch governor-generals, and removing every last vestige of Dutch rule from the parks. Yet today in New Delhi there are still many streets named after English viceroys and generals, and I have never heard an Indian suggest that they be changed. Even a statue of Nicholson, who led the British against Indians during the "Mutiny," still stands, sword in hand. In Government House, now presided over by President Prasad, we often passed through the corridors still lined with paintings of former viceroys.

No viceroy was ever more popular than the last one, Lord Mountbatten, who announced clearly that his purpose was to be the *last* one. Sir Archibald Nye, British High Commissioner in India at the time of our arrival, who was the last British Governor of Madras, told us how, on the day of independence, August 15, 1947, he and his wife drove through the streets with the crowds cheering and showering them with flowers.

Foreign lecturers in India who seek to win the applause of their audience by unbalanced criticism of the British, or even of British rule, are often startled to find themselves faced with a barrage of rebuttal. Only in the Philippines, where the United States kept its promise of independence, and where, in the face of many political obstacles, a genuine effort has been made by the United States to ease the economic difficulties of the people, and perhaps in Pakistan, is there such genuine warmth between an Asian and Western people as there is now between the Indians and the British.

The explanation, it seems to me, involves many complex factors, many of which stem from a strength which lies deep in the British people.

The first of these factors is the vitality of the democratic tradition within Britain itself. Even when the colonial administration in India was at its ruthless worst, there were always voices raised in the House of Commons, and throughout Britain, protesting the outrages and demanding a more moderate policy. When the first stories reached England of the brutal terror following the suppression of the "Mutiny" in 1857, a wave of resentment ran through the country. Later, when an investigation showed how the excesses of the British East India Company had led up to the desperate revolt, there was an immediate and successful demand for reforms.

All over England, and often in high places, the cause of Indian independence always had many staunch supporters, and Indians who visited Britain found in them a source of constant encouragement. It was an English civil servant, Allan Octavian Hume, who organized, in 1885, the Indian National Congress, which later became the instrument for Indian freedom.

Secondly, there was the influence of missionaries, largely from

Great Britain and the U.S. Although the early Christian missionaries promised not to engage in politics, their gospel of equality under God had profound political implications. British colonial administrators banned the use of modern printing methods among the Indians, but still the missionaries pioneered the development of many Indian languages into written form, and eventually managed to set up the first necessary printing presses.

Third were the schools which the colonial administrators established to train English-speaking Indian clerks for government offices and for British business establishments. In them the language of Milton, Locke and Mill taught the meaning of freedom and stimulated thousands of young Indians to dream of a day when they would serve, not a colonial government, but their own independent republic.

On his eightieth birthday in 1941 India's great poet Rabindranath Tagore recalled how as a boy in England he had listened to the speeches of John Bright, how he had loved the "mighty literature" of Shakespeare's drama and Byron's poetry and "the large hearted liberalism of 19th century English politics."

Today most Indians remember how the British established a tradition of law and order, and how in spite of their colonial position, as Englishmen they could not help but teach the principles of free speech and self-government, which laid the basis for later Indian independence.

The Indians also recognize the part that Britain played in bringing about the unification of India under one law. By ruling all of India, either directly from New Delhi, or indirectly through the hundreds of princely states owing allegiance to the crown, the British Empire in a sense created the very nationalism which gave birth to the Indian Republic.

But the fourth and I believe most important factor which has made possible the friendship between Britain and India lies in the great heart of Gandhi, who, drawing on India's past, created an atmosphere of tolerance and good will even toward those who brought India so much suffering. Gandhi gave the Indian people confidence in themselves and out of that confidence came their ability to oppose the British without hating them.

And yet to what extent did British respect for democratic law and free speech itself help to pave the way for Gandhi's gigantic victory? On this point Gandhians will argue until the end of time.

One night I heard one of them say, "British terror was never relentless enough to succeed. At the crucial moments it always found itself troubled with a bad conscience, and suddenly, when least expected, even with respect for the individual Indian as a human being. A terror that never relented, that never compromised, that was always free of doubts, might have crushed us."

I have heard other Indians describe the way in which British respect for law enabled Gandhi, Nehru and other leaders of the independence movement to turn the very courts which sent them to prison into effective public platforms.

The British people have often achieved greatness, but never were they greater than in the time and manner of their leaving India, Pakistan, Burma and Ceylon.

Today they have an opportunity to respond with equal greatness and imagination in British Africa. Perhaps it will be possible for them to mobilize the good will they have won from their former colonial peoples in Asia in dealing with this new problem. Why could they not invite the Commonwealth nations, including India, Pakistan and Ceylon, with their 500 million free nonwhite citizens, to act as a trusteeship organization for the African peoples in the twilight phase between colonialism and freedom?

Throughout Asia I have met a new generation of Britons who see clearly the aspirations of the Asian and African peoples, and who see with equal clarity their implications for the West. Among these, the man who will always stand out in my mind most vividly is Malcolm MacDonald (son of Ramsay MacDonald, the former British Labour Prime Minister) who as the British High Commissioner for Southeast Asia is the co-ordinator of British policy in an area with a population running into hundreds of millions. Throughout all Asia, where his deep dedication to democratic principles is well known, MacDonald's name today is legend, and few Westerners have ever been more beloved or respected.

Although I had heard much about him and had corresponded with him on numerous occasions, we did not meet until an April night in 1953 at his home in Singapore. We talked for many hours about the urgent need for a new kind of understanding and respect on the part of the West for the people of Asia.

Two hundred years ago Clive in India reflected Western imperialism at its worst. Does MacDonald in Singapore represent a new kind of Western viewpoint which can build a bridge between East and West? Or is his simply another voice crying in the wilderness?

7. Gandhi Also Shakes the World

ONE of the first things that I wanted to do as ambassador to India was to visit Rajghat, the memorial park on the banks of the Jumna River where Mahatma Gandhi was cremated. Soon after our arrival I went there to lay a wreath alongside the simple floral offerings of countless men, women and children who daily pass by the cement slab inscribed with Gandhi's last words, "He Ram"—"Oh, God."

We walked through the garden to the memorial; later we planted a cypress tree from Arkansas in a grove nearby. It was more than a diplomatic act on my part, for the murder of this extraordinary man of peace had brought grief even to faraway America.

"To understand India today you will need to know the India of the Gandhian age," an Indian friend had told me years ago in America. In my first two weeks in India I had seen enough pictures of Gandhi hanging in little mud huts, decorated with a string of flowers like a Hindu god, and I had noticed enough reverence and melancholy in Nehru's voice whenever he mentioned the leader of India's great nonviolent revolution, to guess that this was true.

Gandhi was also a key to the revolutions of our time. Of all the revolutionaries who have dominated this century's stage—Lenin, Mussolini, Hitler, Stalin and Mao—Gandhi alone offered hope for reform without destruction. It seems no less important to understand his history than to study the course of fascism and communism.

Our five-mile drive from New Delhi to the Jumna River followed the route traveled by Gandhi's funeral procession almost four years before. "More people probably came to say farewell to Gandhi than ever assembled before in the world's history," an Indian newspaperman once told me. Millions lined the road, weeping, as the body slowly passed on a flower-decked motor vehicle, on which Nehru and his chief ministers were sitting.

That fateful night on the All-India radio Nehru had said, "Friends and comrades, the light has gone out of our lives and there is darkness everywhere. I do not know what to tell you and how to say it. Our beloved leader, Bapu, as we called him, the father of the nation, is no more."

On the ground in front of the funeral pyre were not only the leaders of the Indian National Congress but also the Governor-General of Free India, Lord Mountbatten, and his wife. Photographs of the scene taken while flames were shooting skyward show the Mountbattens with comforting arms around the forlorn Nehru. After the ashes cooled, the Prime Minister wept openly: "Bapuji, here are flowers. Today at least, I can offer them to your bones and ashes. Where will I offer them tomorrow and to whom?"

When Gandhi had set out to conquer his enemies by nonviolent action the world had laughed. The Viceroy in 1920 had denounced the Gandhian campaign of nonviolent direct action as the "most foolish of all foolish schemes." In those early days in America the homespun dhoti which Gandhi always wore had been dubbed his "diaper" and had become a national joke.

And yet in his lifetime and largely because of his genius, the British had transferred all their powers to a free Indian government and in his death Mountbatten, the final Viceroy, a cousin of King George VI, the last British "Emperor of India," sat at his feet in homage. The King himself spoke of the "irreparable loss" which Indians "and, indeed, mankind have suffered."

Gandhi was born just six months before Lenin, and within two years of Sun Yat-sen, and his career paralleled theirs in many respects. Lenin, too, was a lawyer, who was to spend years in jail for violating laws. All three were to live and work abroad during the formative years of their program.

While Lenin in Russia was encouraging the unsuccessful armed uprising of 1905 and Sun Yat-sen was organizing the secret Chinese Revolutionary League, Gandhi was in South Africa conducting his first great "experiment with Truth."

He had gone to South Africa in 1893 to settle a legal dispute between two Indian trading families. This had finally brought him face to face with rampant racial discrimination. The 100,000 Indians whose migration had been solicited by white employers seeking cheap labor were treated as inferiors, only slightly above the more than five million Negroes who were being ruthlessly exploited by the less than a million whites.

For twenty years Gandhi led a nonviolent struggle against the discriminatory laws imposed by South African whites in which his principal weapon was mass civil disobedience. Sentenced in 1902 to his first term in jail, two months, Gandhi chose to wear the same prison garb as the Negro inmates. This is said to have included a plain white cap which later became famous in India as the "Gandhi cap," the badge of the independence struggle.

When the jails finally began to overflow, General Smuts, Prime Minister of South Africa, summoned Gandhi from jail, and proposed a compromise which included a promise to repeal the discriminatory "Asiatic Act," and the release of all Indian prisoners. For this settlement, Gandhi was criticized by militant Indians, and was even struck unconscious by one aroused assailant who insisted that Smuts would betray them.

Under angry white pressure, Smuts did betray the agreement and Gandhi promptly reopened the struggle, again filling the jails. After a year of struggle, Smuts yielded and the specific limited demands made by Gandhi were granted. One of Smuts' assistants told Gandhi jokingly: "I do not like your people but what am I to do? . . . I often wish you took to violence like the English strikers, and then we would know at once how to dispose of you. But you will not injure even the enemy . . . and that is what reduces us to sheer helplessness."

In the midst of the struggle Gandhi sent a pair of sandals as a present to his opponent, General Smuts. Many years later on Gandhi's seventieth birthday, Smuts returned those same sandals, saying, "I am not worthy to stand in the shoes of so great a man." On Gandhi's death, this first statesman to jail him called him "a prince among men."

Before Gandhi sailed home for India in 1915, he warned that the limited rights which had been won must be guarded vigilantly, and that "complete satisfaction cannot be expected until full civil rights have been conceded." In 1952, while I was at Sevagram, the Indians in South Africa, led by Gandhi's son, Manilal, were joining with hundreds of thousands of Africans in a new campaign of civil disobedience against the new "apartheid" (pronounced "apart-hate") segregation program of the Malan government.

When Gandhi returned to India in 1915 his new revolutionary methods were engaged in a historic race with the violent revolutions underway in China and Russia. During Lenin's bloody "ten days that shook the world" in October, 1917, Gandhi was quietly presenting his people, particularly the Western-educated leaders of the Indian National Congress, a disturbing challenge. "Look at the history of the British empire and the British nation," he said, "freedom-loving as it is, it will not be a party to give freedom to a people who will not take it themselves. . . ."

In 1919, instead of the promised steps toward self-government as a reward for Indian co-operation in World War I, the British introduced new restrictions on civil liberties. Gandhi invited Indians to join him in this pledge: ". . . we shall refuse civilly to obey these laws . . . and we further affirm that in the struggle we will faithfully follow truth and refrain from violence to life, person or property."

Not only did people respond throughout the country but the Congress Party itself decided to join the experiment. The official British report, "India 1919," told of another victory for Gandhi: "One noticeable feature of the general excitement was the unprecedented fraternization between Hindus and Moslems. . . . Hindu-Moslem unity was the watchword of the processions."

Nonviolence, however, was not everywhere maintained. When Gandhi learned that even his home town Ahmedabad had rioted and killed several British officers, he suspended the struggle, confessed that he had made a "Himalayan miscalculation" in beginning before the people were trained in self-restraint, and started a three-day fast of penance.

On that very day in Amritsar a British general ordered his troops to open fire on an enclosed meeting of 20,000 unarmed Indians who refused to disperse. Gandhi's later investigation reported 1,200 dead and 3,600 wounded. The general stated that he might "have dispersed the crowd without firing, but they would have come back again and laughed and I should have made what I consider to be a fool of myself."

Up to this time Gandhi had been seeking only dominion status for India. But the massacre and the days of wild British violence which followed Amritsar, including public floggings of naked men and aerial strafing of unarmed villages, convinced him that complete independence from the British must be the only goal. At the 1920 session of Congress, attended by over 14,000 delegates, the Gandhian program was adopted in full: nonco-operation with the British Viceroy; boycott of British titles, jobs and goods; a constructive work program based on hand spinning. The poet Tagore led the way by giving up his British knighthood.

"I invite even the school of violence to give this peaceful nonco-operation a trial," Gandhi said to the fiery young Indians thirsting for vengeance, and eager to follow the current examples of bloody rebellions in China and Russia. He pleaded that India had "a better mission to deliver the world."

"We in India," argued Gandhi, "may in a moment realize that one hundred thousand Englishmen now in India need not frighten three hundred million other human beings." He knew that foreign rule would become impossible if Indians learned simply and peacefully to say "no."

As a test of the people's readiness for nonviolence, Gandhi in 1921 had asked that the Congress members purchase and put in operation two million hand spinning wheels, and that each member spin daily and dress only in homespun cloth, called "khaddar" or "khadi."

No item in this program has been more ridiculed by Indian and Western intellectuals, but with the advantage of hindsight, it is easy to see its value. It focused attention on the poverty of the ill-clothed and ill-nourished people, which was the real problem which free India must face. It forced upper-caste Indians to do manual labor.

It brought Brahmans and untouchables, Hindus and Muslims and Christians together in a common task. It gave Westernized city Indians a chance to cross the gap isolating them from the people. It taught habits of self-discipline. It was also an antidote to too much idle talk. Serving mankind requires drudgery, Gandhi believed.

What a contrast in revolutions! While Mao Tse-tung in China was collecting weapons for civil war Gandhi in India was distributing spinning wheels. While the Bolsheviks in Russia were killing the Czar's family and liquidating whole classes of people, Gandhi was inviting the rich to give up their gains, take up their spinning wheels and follow him. To follow him meant to go to jail, which Gandhi said they must learn to enter "as a bridegroom enters the bride's chamber."

By 1922, there were already twenty thousand individual civil resisters throughout India who had pledged to be nonviolent in word, deed and intent, and who had courted prison. Another ten thousand volunteers went to jail, but still the British Viceroy refrained from arresting Gandhi.

Then on the eve of nationwide mass action, news came that a Congress procession in the small town of Chauri Chaura had suddenly turned into a riot, in which twenty-two policemen were killed. Gandhi stunned the country by immediately calling off the campaign and directing the Congress back to the constructive program of spinning, village service and removal of untouchability. "We were angry," Nehru writes of his feeling in the prison cell, "when we learned of this stoppage of our struggle when we seemed to be consolidating our position and advancing on all fronts."

Now the government released its thousands of prisoners, arrested the little man in loincloth and tried him for "exciting disaffection toward His Majesty's Government."

"I am here," Gandhi told the court, "to invite and submit to the highest penalty that can be inflicted upon me for what, in Law, is a deliberate crime and what appears to me to be the highest duty of a citizen. I knew I was playing with fire. I ran the risk, and if I am set free, I will still do the same again."

From his cell, where he was sent for a six-year sentence, he gaily reported to friends, "I am happy as a bird—M. K. Gandhi #827."

Although Gandhi's revolution during the 1920's seemed to be falling behind Lenin's in material accomplishment, it had accomplished one thing which did not happen in the Soviet Union: because of Gandhi, according to Nehru, the "black pall of fear was lifted from the people's shoulders; fear of the army, the police, the widespread secret service; fear of the official class; fear of laws meant to suppress, and of prison."

Like Mao Tse-tung, Gandhi knew that the key to Asia lay in the villages. "I know that I am unable to carry with me the bulk of educated India," he remarked in 1925. But he had the illiterate peasants on his side.

"Go to the villages," Gandhi kept repeating and he always practiced what he preached. He moved ceaselessly through rural India to spread his constructive program. "I do not think that any other human being has ever traveled about India as much as he had done," says Nehru.

When in 1928 tens of thousands of Indians showed Gandhi that they were willing to withstand charges by mounted police who beat them with lathis, wooden clubs tipped with steel, and that they neither ran nor hit back, he sensed the country was ready for its second nonviolent ordeal.

After sending a list of specific demands to the Viceroy, such as a 50 per cent reduction of the land tax, discharge of political prisoners and abolition of the secret police, Gandhi picked a single issue as the symbol for mass struggle: abolition of the salt tax which prevented villagers from making their own salt from local deposits. If the Viceroy did not negotiate, the salt laws were to be broken. "We were bewildered," Nehru writes, "for we could not quite fit in a national struggle with common salt." But when Gandhi announced that he was marching two hundred miles to the sea, where he would make salt from God's ocean in defiance of one of man's greatest empires, Nehru saw that salt had "become a mysterious word, a word of power."

Hundreds of thousands of peasants gathered along the path to watch the Mahatma as he strode by quickly. India was electrified when the news was flashed that he had raised his first handful of salt.

When he was arrested, the signal for nationwide civil disobedience again went out across India. People everywhere bore up under lathi charges of great brutality by mounted police, and nearly 100,000 Indians were soon on their way to jail. But still there was no retaliatory violence against the British.

This time the Viceroy, Lord Irwin, a religious man himself, decided to negotiate. He released Gandhi unconditionally and the two produced the Gandhi-Irwin Pact, which Gandhi described as a victory for both. It provided for the discontinuance of the struggle, release of all prisoners, withdrawal of the ban on salt making, and an invitation to Gandhi to attend a Round Table Conference in London, where self-government would be considered. To Winston Churchill, it was "alarming and also nauseating to see Mr. Gandhi, a seditious Middle Temple lawyer, now posing as a fakir of a type well-known in the East, striding half-naked up the steps of the Viceregal palace . . . to parley on equal terms with the representative of the King Emperor."

Yet that "half-naked lawyer" was on his way to Buckingham Palace itself, where Gandhi reported that "the King had enough on for both of us."

But agreement was impossible, and at the end of the conference Gandhi announced his "utter failure" to convince the British to treat India as a "partner, not held by force but by the silken cord of love." . . . "I find that our sufferings are not vital and real enough to make themselves felt," Gandhi said as he sailed away, "and I shall have to go to India and ask my countrymen to go through the fiery ordeal in a more intense form than last year."

Not only did he return to lead another year-long struggle which filled the jails, but while in prison he learned of a new British effort to divide and rule, by providing separate electorates for the untouchables, a plan which in London he had vowed to resist with his life. Gandhi believed that it would perpetuate their outcaste status in each village, and he said he "would far rather that Hinduism die than that untouchability live."

He announced "a fast unto death," which would be broken only if the leaders of the Hindu community vowed to outlaw untouchability and if the British withdrew the new plan. "Fasting," Gandhi believed, "stirs up sluggish consciences and fires loving hearts to action."

Again Nehru in prison was dismayed: why should he choose "a side issue for his final sacrifice?" But again the news came to his cell of a "tremendous upheaval all over the country, a magic wave of enthusiasm running through Hindu society, and untouchability appeared to be doomed."

On the sixth day of the fast, a pact was signed between high-caste Hindus and untouchables establishing new rights of equality. And finally the British cabinet saved the life of its greatest foe by withdrawing the plan.

Temples and wells were opened to the outcastes in many sections, and intercaste dinners became common. Gandhi called the untouchables "Harijans" or "Children of God," and started a weekly newspaper by that name.

To prod villages everywhere into remedial action he went on walking tours of every province—during the very period when Mao Tse-tung was leading his Communist army on the Long March to Yenan. About the time the "Red Star over China" had found its strategic location in North China, Gandhi settled in the largely untouchable village of Sevagram. Even in 1953, caste prejudice still remains but Gandhi had given it blows from which it is not likely to recover.

The coming of World War II presented another trial for him and for India. After Munich he wrote that "Europe has sold her soul for the sake of a seven days' earthly existence."

To the aggressive, expanding Japanese, who strangely sought his blessing, he wrote, "I do not subscribe to the doctrine of Asia for the Asiatics, if it is meant as an anti-European combination. For Asia to be not for Asia but for the whole world, it has to relearn the message of Buddha."

Gandhi was shocked when immediately following England's entry into the war, the Viceroy declared war on behalf of India, without consulting the Congress or the people. But Gandhi did not hesitate to tell the Viceroy that his "sympathies were with England and France from the purely humanitarian standpoint," and he said that he wept when he contemplated the destruction of the Houses of Parliament or Westminster Abbey.

As the Japanese tide swept into South Asia and the British, taken in the rear, surrendered Singapore without a shot, he decided that only a free India could defend herself, whether violently as Nehru and others suggested, or nonviolently as Gandhi wished. At that time an Indian who believed in violence, a former president of Congress who had been defeated only by Gandhi's opposition, Subhas Chandra Bose, was in Burma organizing an Indian National Army to fight alongside the Japanese.

Gandhi emphatically disagreed. "Better the enemy I know than the one I do not," he said. But everywhere in South Asia the people were welcoming the Japanese in place of the hated white colonialists. In Burma, even in retreat, the British practiced what Gandhi called "wretched discrimination—one route for the whites, another for the blacks!" . . . "What can conquer your unpardonable pride of race?" Gandhi asked of the whole Anglo-Saxon world.

In August, 1942, Gandhi called on the British to "quit India."

"Leave India to God. If that is too much, then leave her to anarchy."

In asking for independence, Gandhi wrestled with the question of Allied troops on Indian soil. "India has not yet demonstrated non-violence of the strong such as would be required to withstand a powerful army of invasion," he admitted. "I could not be guilty of asking the Allies to take a step which would involve certain defeat." Therefore they could continue to use India as a base of operations, and he promised that a free India would "oppose Japan to a man."

Gandhi held great hopes for America. "If my demands are just, America can insist on Indian independence," Gandhi said.

But Gandhi was underestimating the strength and conviction of Winston Churchill, who answered firmly, "No, sir," when asked if the Atlantic Charter applied to Asia. Harry Hopkins reports that every time Roosevelt mentioned India, Churchill, who contributed more than any other one individual to preserving Europe's freedom from Nazi rule, became immediately wrathful. Churchill even declared Roosevelt's special envoy to India, William Phillips, persona non grata, after he asked to visit Gandhi. When in 1942 Willkie set out to see "One World," he was asked by timid diplomats to bypass India.

On August 8, 1942 the Indian National Congress began what was to be the greatest campaign of all. Already twenty thousand individually selected volunteers had gone to jail. This time Gandhi was prepared to call a general strike. The Viceroy struck first, arresting the seventy-three-year-old rebel and almost every leading Congressman.

The 630 days of Gandhi's last incarceration were days of agony. His wife died, and then his devoted secretary. In 1943 over a million of his countrymen died in a Bengal famine which he believed a free Indian government could have avoided.

And when nonviolent resistance seemed to be failing, the younger members led by Jayaprakash Narayan organized an armed underground which, although pledged to refrain from killing, sought to destroy British property and to prevent communication by cutting railway lines and blowing up bridges. In whole sections of the country British rule ceased for months. In 1946 the Royal Indian navy mutinied in Bombay.

Although the quick timing of the British departure may have been precipitated by these signs of a violent explosion, the decision in favor of Indian freedom seems to have been a genuine conviction of the new Labour Government. Certainly the generous manner of their withdrawal was made possible by Gandhi, whose insistence on nonviolent methods paved the way to a real partnership. And no small credit must go to Lord Mountbatten, who with royal drama and dedicated respect for the Indian people accomplished his mission of establishing independence and equality.

Nevertheless, because independence brought with it the partition of India, there were soon new tragedies to be faced. "Vivisect me before you vivisect India," Gandhi said as he begged Jinnah, the creator of Pakistan, to pick his own cabinet for a united India.

But religious differences had been enflamed and forces were loose which could not be contained. Maulana Azad, now the Indian Minister of Education, and a devout Muslim, told me that until the very last minute he did not believe that his close friend Jinnah actually intended to insist that Pakistan be a separate nation. He assumed that his demands were simply a way of bargaining for greater autonomy for the provinces where Muslims were in a majority. Jinnah's sister herself says, "We never expected to get it in our lifetime."

"We shall either have a divided India or a destroyed India," insisted Jinnah, and he called for "Direct Action Day."

In Calcutta, "Direct Action Day" led to terrible riots. To prevent further bloodshed, Nehru and the leaders of Congress reluctantly agreed to partition. Muslims like Azad who saw this as a tragic division of a historic nation could do nothing but throw in their lot with India, which thousands of them did.

In his heart Gandhi never accepted a separate Pakistan. "Shall I ask the country to rebel against the decision for partition?" he asked at his daily prayer meeting. Reluctantly he agreed not to upset the decision, but first to stop the riots; then he would seek to reunite the country. He declared himself a citizen of both the land ruled by India and that ruled by Pakistan. On Independence Day, August 15, 1947, while Lord Mountbatten was installing Nehru as Prime Minister, Gandhi was on a third-class railway coach, heading for the riot areas of Bengal where he spent the day in mourning, fasting, prayer and spinning.

Most of his seventy-seventh year was taken up with a walking pilgrimage through riot-stricken areas. I shall never forget the wonderful pictures of the Mahatma, walking barefoot, through the remote Muslim district of Noakhali, tending the wounded from the recent riots, preaching peace between Hindus and Muslims.

Instead of preventing bloodshed, the partition of Pakistan from India, by cutting through whole communities, and by leaving millions of Hindus and Muslims isolated on the wrong side of a necessarily artificial line, led to vast, unorganized civil war. The miracle was that such a conflagration was stopped before it consumed the country.

. . .

On January 12, 1948, Gandhi told his countrymen that the time had come when, as a believer in nonviolence, he had no remedy for the disorder sweeping India but a fast unto death. "My fast," he explained, "in plain language is on behalf of the Muslim minority in the Union and, therefore, it is necessarily against the Hindus and Sikhs. . . ." It was also against his friends in the Cabinet of free India who, because of the attack on Kashmir, were holding back on their agreed division of the treasury with Pakistan. The fast would end "when and if I am satisfied that there is a reunion of hearts of all the communities brought about without any outside pressure, and from an awakened sense of duty." Fasting was his "last resort in the place of the sword."

On the third night, the Indian Cabinet reversed itself and promised an immediate transferral of the remaining 550 million rupees owed Pakistan. On the sixth day, leaders of the Hindu and Sikh communities, including even the fanatics who had been fanning the flames toward a war between the two new nations, signed a pact of communal peace at Gandhi's bedside. Only then did he break his fast.

But Gandhi's success only drove the fanatics into plotting his removal. Nehru found a group outside Gandhi's room shouting "Gandhi Murdabad!"—"Death to Gandhi." He jumped from his car and rushed to the crowd in a rage: "Kill me first!" They shuffled away sullenly.

On January 20, a young man threw a bomb during Gandhi's daily prayer meeting, but missed. The next day he asked no one to look down upon the misguided youth who thought he was doing right.

On January 30, as Gandhi was walking out to the prayer meeting, another young man, an intellectual Brahman named Nathuram Godse, member of an extremist militant Hindu group known as the R.S.S., bowed low before him, then suddenly pulled out his revolver. Observers report that as Gandhi fell he raised his hands into the folded gesture of greeting, and said "He Ram"—"Oh God."

By his own tests Gandhi's works could only be tested by his death. "The means may be likened to a seed, the end to a tree," he once said, "and there is just the same inviolable connection between the means and the ends as there is between the seed and the tree." But great trees take a long time growing.

Today more than any place in India Gandhi's spirit lives in Sevagram. "Find me the poorest village in the poorest part of India," Gandhi once said to his followers. There he would make his home and prove that he could bring about a new life for the villagers. He found a miserable malarial spot, where untouchables predominated, and there he built his hut, established a "basic education" school for neighboring children, and named the place Sevagram—"Village of Service."

Independence for India, he often said, meant primarily independence for the villager, which required that "even the poorest Indian should get enough milk, vegetables and fruit. Today the villages of India are dung heaps. Tomorrow they will be like tiny gardens of Eden where dwell highly intelligent folk whom no one can deceive or exploit."

For all his determination not to live better than the masses of his people, for all his opposition to what he called the West's "craze" for material luxuries, he always added, "But neither do I want poverty, penury, misery, dirt and dust in India."

Sevagram is not yet a garden of Eden, but it is clean, healthful and full of purpose, and I always came away refreshed and invigorated. It is a place where peace is natural and human dignity is fully recognized. Above all, human labor has become dignified and creative.

Steb and I visited Sevagram several times, observing the Gandhian institutions at work, and it is a place we hope to return to one day. It was hard to realize that our friends the Aryanayakams, who direct the school, and live cheerfully in utter austerity, had come from the world of city wealth.

The food was simple, strictly vegetarian and uninspired. Nor did the flat wooden tables which go under the name of beds encourage one to sleep long after dawn. Steb confesses that on her second visit she fortified herself for those bed tables with a sleeping pill.

The simplicity of Sevagram made complete sense in the light of Indian conditions. After walking through miserable villages and seeing the faces of emaciated hungry children, I knew what Gandhi meant when he said that "to partake of sweetmeats and other delicacies, in a country where the millions do not even get an ordinary full meal, is equivalent to robbery." And after observing the frightening gap almost everywhere in the country between the educated rich and the village poor, which is so similar to that which existed in Czarist Russia, I was able to appreciate Gandhi's grim prophecy that "a violent and bloody revolution is a certainty one day unless there is a voluntary abdication of riches and the power that riches give, and sharing them for the common good."

Not only did I admire the Gandhian volunteers, who had abdicated their soft city life, but I also sensed that they were happier than most of their countrymen. Gandhi said, "The real secret of my health" was "that my body happens to be where I have set my heart."

Gandhi's hut of mud and bamboo, which is preserved just as he left it, is now a shrine. With Sally, Sam and my married daughter, Barbara Coolidge, I stood silently in the tiny room. "This was the unofficial capital of India," a friend remarked. Although Sevagram was in the very center of the subcontinent, and a long journey from any of the great cities, this was the place to which the leaders of India, including a British Viceroy, came for consultation. This was the spot where historic decisions were announced.

Gandhi's bed was a straw mat with a board which he propped behind his back when he worked. Beside the mat was a small writing table, a waste basket and a spinning wheel. There was a paperweight with the inscription "God is Love." And the three familiar monkeys, "Hear no evil; see no evil; speak no evil."

On two shelves were a few books, including the *Bhagavad-Gita*, *Life and Teachings of Jesus Christ* and the Gospel of St. John. On the wall hung a sign: "When you are in the right you can afford to keep your temper, and when you are in the wrong, you cannot afford to lose it."

At first I thought how uniquely Indian, or Asian, all this was. Gandhi was a "Mahatma"—"Great Soul"—in the line of Buddha, in the Eastern tradition of worldly renunciation. In India the route of a leader was not log cabin to White House but mansion to mud hut.

Yet worldly renunciation, fasting and poverty were also in the tradition of Christian saints. And although nonviolence and nonpossession were mainstays of Jainism which Gandhi learned from his mother, he himself credits Tolstoy and the New Testament with his conversion to nonviolence. Nor was he at all otherworldly. Coming from the caste engaged in business, he above all prided himself on being a practical man.

Gandhi said that from the English he learned among other things, "punctuality, reticence, public hygiene, independent thinking and exercise of judgment. . . ." His punctuality alone, in a land which boasts of timelessness, gave a new efficiency and drive to Indian politics. Once when a political meeting commenced forty-five minutes late, Gandhi consulted his dime-store watch sternly and remarked that independence would also be delayed by forty-five minutes.

The prayers we heard at Sevagram reminded me how universal was Gandhi's religion. At dawn and at sunset the community, made up of Muslims, Christians, and Hindus, high caste and untouchables, assembles to meditate, to sing a hymn from the *Gita,* to read the Christian Lord's Prayer in Indian language and a section from the Koran.

"All faiths constitute a revelation of Truth, but all are imperfect and liable to error," Gandhi said; yet who has lived a more Christian life? He said that he looked upon his life as an attempt to live the Sermon on the Mount.

Far from accepting some Asian concepts of an inevitable fate, he believed that "it is possible for a single individual to defy the whole might of an unjust empire to save his honor, his religion, his soul, and lay the foundation for that empire's fall or its regeneration."

Gandhi was never passive in the usual meaning of the word, as the dynamic nature of his Salt March demonstrates. He did not lie down and let things happen to him; on the contrary he always tried to seize the initiative from his opponent. Nor did his nonviolence "mean meek submission to the will of the evil doer." On the contrary, "it means putting one's whole soul against the will of the tyrant." He believed that his nonviolent method was "a more active and more real fighting against wickedness than retaliation whose very nature is to increase wickedness."

"Truth and Nonviolence" was his creed, but Truth was first—the courageous pursuit of Truth as one saw it. "Cowardice is a thing even more hateful than violence," he repeated time and again. "Far better than cowardice would be meeting one's death fighting," he said. "The golden rule is to dare to do the right at any cost." It was a faith in militant individualism which told every man to look solely to his own conscience and his own reason as a guide, and not to any party or state.

Rather than accept the designation "passive resistance" Gandhi coined a new word "Satyagraha," from "Satya," meaning truth and from "agraha," meaning firmness. "That is to say, the Force which is born of Truth"—"soul force." In English he called his campaigns civil disobedience, after Thoreau's essay by that name.

Gandhi was a London-trained lawyer, and it was as an advocate of law that he arrived at the theory of nonviolent civil disobedience. Instead of undermining the basis for law, Gandhi was convinced that his way reinforces law. He believed in law so much that when a particular law or set of laws violated his conscience he willingly went to jail, as if to say to the state, "You have the right to pass such a law and I have the right to accept its penalty rather than obey it; I hope you will decide to change it but until you do, I respectfully insist that I belong in your jail." Far from anarchy, he believed that such a position taught the highest possible respect for law.

I began to see that Gandhi's revolt had not only overthrown an empire but had laid the foundations, in the mind and habits of the people, for democracy. A faith in the possibility of persuasion and confidence in the judgment of the people is the precondition for democratic politics, and such a faith was the very cornerstone of Gandhi's philosophy.

"A superficial study of British history has made us think that all power percolates to the people from parliaments," Gandhi had written. "The truth is that power resides in the people." Could this truth produce democratic power, particularly in Asia, where in so many countries parliaments were either nonexistent or powerless?

Communists, of course, ridiculed Gandhi as a compromiser, who would never change the status quo. Gandhi replied, "I believe myself to be a revolutionary, a nonviolent revolutionary."

"Have you heard of the time when a militant young Communist came to Sevagram to convert the 'old man' to a more 'radical' program?" I was asked by a friend, who told me the story. After this young man had spent an hour with Gandhi he came out of his mud hut and said somewhat sheepishly to his waiting friend, "What fools we can be!"

They inquired what had gone wrong. "Nothing," the young Marxist replied, "but that little man is the only true revolutionary in our country. We spend ourselves in talking and shouting, and he acts."

Gandhi had probably suggested that if the young man wanted revolution he could begin by revolutionizing his own life; by going to the villages, by undertaking constructive work, by doing the scavenging work of the untouchables.

Gandhi welcomed the revolutionary age in which he lived and sought to turn it into constructive and nonviolent channels. "The cataclysm that is sweeping over the earth today is a great sign," he said. "As a chaotic force it is pernicious, but it has at its back a noble object . . . it desires reform, it seeks the reign of equity and justice."

Yet to believe that out of concentration camps and secret police could ever come equality or brotherhood seemed to him like "saying that we can get a rose through planting a noxious weed."

"Some say that there is ruthlessness in Russia but that it is exercised for the lowest and the poorest and it is good for that reason," he wrote many years ago. "For me it has very little good in it. Some day this ruthlessness will create an anarchy worse than we have ever seen."

One hot night at Sevagram I could not sleep and I walked out into the moonlight glistening over the rice paddies in the fields beyond Gandhi's hut. I wondered again what would be the ultimate fruit of this amazing man who had created a free nation, armed only with a deep faith in mankind. The seed he planted was surely not a noxious weed, but would it produce the "rose" that Gandhi wanted?

His hut was not watched by the powerful searchlights which guard the Kremlin walls, and it lacked the shining splendor of the Viceregal Palace, but was there not a kind of light radiating from Sevagram?

On the night of Gandhi's death, Nehru said that he was wrong to say "the light has gone out." Rather he predicted, and from Sevagram it seems like a safe prediction, that "a thousand years later that light will still be seen in this country and the world will see it and it will give solace to innumerable hearts."

8. A New India Emerging

AS I NOW look back on our many months of traveling around India, totaling more than sixty thousand miles, I confess that we did not see enough of the old India. For instance, I never visited Benares, which is supposed to be the oldest city in the world and where are concentrated the beauties, superstitions and strange rites of many centuries.

I think I must have had a subconscious prejudice against looking backward in a nation which is struggling so hard to move ahead. I wanted to understand the people and their problems as they are today, and I had known many Westerners who spent so much of their time in India examining the vestiges of the past that they found it impossible to believe that a modern nation is slowly emerging.

Nearly thirty years ago an American writer, Miss Katherine Mayo, gathered together all the worst things that she could find and put them into a book called *Mother India,* which Gandhi described as "a drainage inspector's report." "If I went to your country and wrote only of what I found in your slums, your night club dives, and your divorce courts, it would also be a shocking story, wouldn't it?" asked an Indian professor who was still seething over Miss Mayo's one-sidedness.

I do not think I was blind to any of the obstacles to India's progress which I came upon as I crossed and recrossed the subcontinent, and if I did not find the average Indian any worse than other people, I did not find him any better. "Murders are committed in India about as frequently as in other parts of the globe," an Indian writer told me. "There are saintly Indians and there are devilish Indians. Bombay's red light district is as full of vice as that of New Orleans."

But as I think back on all the thousands of individual Indians, with all their castes and classes, as well as the innumerable Burmans, Pakistanis, Ceylonese, Thais, Vietnamese, Indonesians, Filipinos, Chinese and Japanese whom we got to know during our visits to their countries, my dominant feeling is that people are pretty good everywhere, in Asia as in Europe and America, and not nearly as different as most of them like to assume.

When most Americans think of India they probably still think of rich, fabulous, useless Maharajas or of miserable untouchables and caste prejudices, just as most Indians still think of America in terms of lush Hollywood movies or racial discrimination against Negroes. Even in the age of supersonic flight, good seems to travel at a snail's pace, while the lurid and the bad alone take wings.

Most of the old princes are now sitting on the sidelines. A number hold a warm place in the hearts of their former subjects, and a few have successfully run for office.

Though they no longer rule, with some exceptions they continue to live in luxury. As part of the amazing agreement by which they abdicated voluntarily and merged their states voluntarily in the Indian Union, they have been allowed to keep their jewels and most of their palaces, and have been granted lifelong pensions from the government.

This must rank as one of the great peaceful revolutions of all times. The 584 princes, ruling over more than 100 million people, were all called to Delhi to meet with the departing British Governor General, Lord Mountbatten, with Prime Minister Nehru and with shrewd old Deputy Prime Minister Sardar Patel, the "strong man" of Congress until his death in 1950. They were asked peacefully to cede their territories to the new Indian Republic, in return for which they would be permitted to keep their present properties and income. After long deliberation, they agreed.

One of free India's first great laws, written into the constitution, outlawed the practice of discrimination against untouchables. The former Minister of Law, Dr. Ambedkar, who drafted the Constitution, is himself an untouchable, as well as a graduate of Columbia University. "When an outcaste violates community practices of segregation, or an upper caste man crosses the caste line himself, he now finds the local government officer on his side," a young village worker proudly told me. We in America know that while legislation is often necessary and helpful, race prejudices, like caste prejudice, cannot be destroyed by legislation alone, as long as it remains in people's hearts.

A 1953 report to the Indian Parliament by L. M. Shrikant, the Commissioner for Scheduled Castes (the British name for the untouchables), concludes that it will be a long-term task because of "deep-rooted prejudices, deeper than the ones against the Negroes in America." Yet in full participation of untouchables in elections, and the election of a number of them to office, the Commissioner saw "hopeful signs of a silent revolution in Hindu society."

In our New Delhi home we had an outcaste sweeper named Madan who we soon found was expected by the other servants to handle all the menial chores. For instance, in the process of housebreaking Tichat some unpleasant clean-up tasks were inevitable. The servant who discovered her latest mistake would invariably shout for Madan. This system finally broke down, however, when Steb in sight of the servants made a point of cleaning up after Tichat herself.

It was exciting to see Madan's self-respect grow over a period of many months. At first he avoided shaking hands with us, but gradually he came to put out his hand as surely and firmly as anyone. He even started going to night literacy school. The others accepted his changed status, which I think will happen wherever people act with determination to end the old ways.

Christianity and Islam both made many converts among the outcastes, but I was sorry to see that even in some South Indian Christian communities a kind of caste system still prevails. "Only sweeping land reforms and new jobs will end the economic basis for these prejudices," a prominent Indian Christian told me.

In many cities, caste barriers tend to lessen and disappear, although some factories still have "untouchable jobs." Caste is also waning quite rapidly among the 280,000 university students. A specially important sore point among them was family-arranged marriages usually along strictly drawn caste lines. However, even among family-made arrangements, often brought about by newspaper advertisements, we noticed that over half the ads for wives or for husbands included a phrase such as "caste restrictions are no object."

Students are increasingly marrying whom and when they choose. At one such wedding in New Delhi, which a close friend attended, a Brahman priest asked the girl her caste, and she told him. But when he asked the groom his caste, the boy said he did not know. "That's the trouble with modern young people," said the priest. "They don't even know what caste they are in."

That is an extreme case, but the essential caste taboos against intermarriage and eating together are gradually on their way out, and there is no doubt that the basic structure of the so-called "joint family system," which for thousands of years has been the foundation of the Indian social system, is gradually becoming weaker except perhaps in the more remote villages. Under the joint family, in most cases the oldest male member of the family and his wife are accepted as the heads of the family. If the grandfather is dead his oldest son usually takes over the responsibility, although the grandmother continues to exert great influence and often shares authority with her oldest son and his wife. The sons, their wives and children all live in the same compound or nearby houses.

All family property is held in trust by the head of the family for the benefit of all of the members. In most instances money earned by the individual members goes into a central account which is used to cover all family needs. Those who are old or unable to work, the sick, and orphan children are cared for by the whole family organization as a matter of course. Since the beginning of time this joint family system has been the social security system of all India.

Relations among members of a joint family are very close. All the children of the various sons play together almost as brothers and sisters, with the grandmother often the final disciplinary "court of appeals." Thus when a child is left as an orphan it is not nearly as much an emotional and psychological shock as in America. Already they are closely tied to all of the cousins, uncles, aunts and grandparents.

In its traditional form, only the oldest son and his wife are likely to be consulted on family decisions, with the younger wives rarely consulted on even household matters. But is is difficult to generalize about the joint family system, because there are literally hundreds of variations.

Most city Indians maintain surprisingly close ties with their family in the village. If you ask an Indian where his home is he will almost invariably give you the name of the village where he was born. Each year many factory workers, after nine or ten months at their city jobs, return to their villages for the harvest season, bringing with them their savings to put into the family coffers. Moreover, the bonds persist even with those who have been cut off from the family for years.

One day a young Indian working at the Embassy asked me if he could borrow three months' salary in advance to contribute toward the wedding of a member of his family. After some discussion I discovered that it was for a fifth cousin whom he had not seen since she was a child.

Those young people who drift away from the restrictions and the security of the joint family are likely to demand an equivalent security from some other source. Thus as the system weakens, we can expect, for a time at least, to see more popular discontent and unrest. In India and indeed throughout Asia the disappearance of old ways and progress toward a better future will be marked generally by demands that the pace of progress be still further increased.

And yet, I believe, it would be wrong to mistake modification in traditional religious and cultural forms for the weakening of Hinduism itself. Hinduism was challenged by Buddhism and Jainism but eventually absorbed them both, borrowing generously from each in the process. Westernism is unlikely to be any different. Hinduism would absorb communism too, if it could, but communism, recognizing its powers of spiritual resistance, would not permit Hinduism to exist.

. . .

Actually, looking back on our Indian experiences, the princes at one extreme and untouchables at the other were not the first to catch our attention. First were the refugees, more than eight million of whom, approximately the total population of Australia or of Norway and Denmark put together, had fled from Pakistan to India, and about the same number from India to Pakistan, after the partition in 1947.

Without a penny of foreign assistance, both of the newly formed governments courageously took over the support and resettling of these tragic people, who far outnumbered the postwar European displaced persons or the Arab refugees in Palestine.

The handling of this vast problem in India has been little short of miraculous. Of the 2.5 million rural refugees from West Pakistan 98 per cent have been given land with a total acreage larger than the land area of Connecticut. The 2.7 million urban refugees from West Pakistan have been partly housed in homes vacated by Muslims who fled to Pakistan. In addition ten new townships and innumerable colonies have been or are being built which provide a total of 150,000 new homes.

There have been $23 million in loans to refugees to help set them up in business, and nearly one million heads of families have been trained in various crafts in more than two hundred schools. The story of the care and rehabilitation of refugees from East Pakistan, most of whom settled in and around Calcutta is also remarkable. The total cost to Indian taxpayers so far is $500 million, a crushing sum for an impoverished people with a nation to build. And Pakistan had the same kind of burden handling the Muslim refugees from India.

In spite of the progress which has been made, the poverty of these people was still all around us, and we could understand their bitterness at losing their homes and lands. Their counterparts in Pakistan must be just as unhappy and just as bitter.

"Have you any news of my daughter?" asked an old man from the Punjab, who came to the house of the lady in charge of the work for refugee women and children, while Steb was there visiting. After all these years he had heard a report that his little girl had managed to get to Delhi from Pakistan and he wanted help in finding her. In the newspapers there were often notices requesting information about someone lost during those awful days.

One of the many bright spots was the city of Faridabad, one of the ten new townships. It was built by the refugees themselves with the leadership of the Indian Co-operative Union and other followers of Gandhi, under young Sudhir Ghosh. After our drive through the dusty countryside, Faridabad appeared like an oasis under construction. Instead of tents, there were now eight thousand neat brick houses, with an average of two rooms and a lavatory for each family, grouped in four development sections with modern buildings for schools, hospitals and social services. There were thirty miles of good roads with a newly planted young tree every hundred feet.

"We have built all this ourselves," a now self-reliant refugee proudly told us. "You do not know how hard it was for these shopkeepers to take up manual work," explained one of the Gandhi workers whose example had been a constant inspiration and guide to the refugees. "All their caste prejudices were against it, and yet they have molded millions of bricks, burned them in simple kilns and made them into a city."

The government had given a $5 million loan to the autonomous Faridabad Development Board, to be repaid over thirty years; but most of the capital had come from the people's own labor.

To provide industrial jobs for this refugee city, the Development Board had erected several factories including a power plant. The heavy machinery was installed by the willing hands of the townsmen without cranes, methods much like those that built the Egyptian pyramids five thousand years ago. Several private factories were locating there, including a shoe factory employing more than one thousand workers. In addition the refugees were counting on the growth of industrial co-operatives. It was to be a democratic community, planned and run by the people themselves, with its economy largely based on the co-operative principle.

More and more Indians are beginning to feel the influence of the government in their lives and to realize that now it is their own government. Every time Steb or I visited Parliament we noticed people from faraway provinces sitting in the galleries. Often village head men and illiterate peasants came to listen to their representatives, who maintain a high level of public debate. I have seen the same scenes in the galleries of the state assemblies.

The Constitution of the Republic of India draws heavily from the experience of the Western democracies. Its parliamentary system, with most power concentrated in a directly elected House of the People similar to the House of Commons, with a Prime Minister responsible to the Parliament, is British. Its President is the same kind of symbolic head of state as the President of France. Its federal structure, with twenty-nine state governments, is much like ours. Its able judiciary is trained in English procedures and precedents, but its court system has borrowed heavily from American patterns of jurisdiction.

Its preamble has a familiar ring: "We, the people of India . . . to secure to all the citizens: justice, social, economic and political:

liberty of thought, expression, belief, faith and worship: equality of status and of opportunity; and to promote among them all fraternity assuring the dignity of the individual and the unity of the nations . . . do hereby adopt, enact and give to ourselves this Constitution."

Nehru once said that this was "an echo of the great voices of the founders of the American Republic."

One reason the new Congress party government took up the reins of office so smoothly in 1947 was the Indian Civil Service inherited from the British. "Our government is operated by the very agents of the Viceroy who put us in jail," complained one Congress worker. But the highly educated, disciplined members of the Indian Civil Service, which Dean Paul Appleby of the Maxwell School of Public Administration at Syracuse University described as "one of the eight most efficient in the world," soon became recognized as indispensable to the new government. Today this civil service is one of India's great assets, although in my opinion not an unadulterated asset.

Because of their British training, standards of administration for mass development programs are often too high for the pace required in an Asian mass development program. Some civil servants, for instance, insist that teachers and public health workers must have more years of training than a new country like India can afford. Free Asia's first priority, it seems to me, must be to touch as many people as possible in the next few years with a sense of progress, even at the expense of quality.

"You know too many things that can't be done," I suggested half-jokingly to a good friend in the Indian Civil Service. "If you experimented more boldly you might find that many things can now be done which were impossible under foreign rule." He and many others, particularly among the 360 so-called "district collectors," who are the chief executive officers of the country's 360 administrative districts, are keenly aware of these problems and anxious to adapt their methods to new circumstances.

In contrast to India's highly trained Civil Service is the makeshift, unskilled but energetic administrative service in Indonesia which we saw during our later stay in Indonesia. In colonial days, the principal government jobs were held by Dutch or by citizens of mixed ancestry, and there was little effort to train

Indonesians. As a result the newly independent Republic of Indonesia lacks an experienced civil service.

Yet this has brought certain compensating advantages. Although there were hurdles that might have discouraged more sophisticated government administrators, there has been a willingness to tackle any task, no matter how formidable; a "go ahead" spirit which has already accomplished a spectacular improvement in literacy and public health. I have seen young Indonesians and Burmans, too, whose lack of training and experience would send a chill down the spine of some Indian professionals, achieving near miracles.

If the Indian Civil Service has been a little too cautious or conservative at times, it is nevertheless one of the main factors for stability. Another such factor also inherited from the British is the Indian military. "India has one of the finest professional armies in the world," an American army colonel who had fought side by side with them in North Africa told me. Others who have seen the remarkable discipline and competence with which Indian troops have handled their difficult assignments during the prisoner repatriation in Korea have been equally generous in their praise.

I got to know many Indian army, navy and air force officers and found them to be dedicated in the best tradition of a democratic military service.

Above all, the great parade I watched in New Delhi on Republic Day, January 26, 1953, will always stand out in my memory. At 10:00 A.M. the President drove down Kingsway to the reviewing stand near India Gate in a great coach pulled by a string of horses, with his magnificent bodyguard of crimson-uniformed mounted lancers in attendance. As hundreds of thousands of onlookers cheered, he was welcomed by Prime Minister Nehru.

Then a squadron of trainer aircraft, the first that had been completely manufactured in India, flew overhead, followed by four squadrons of bombers, fighter bombers and jet fighters. In front of us rolled light and medium tanks, artillery, including heavy antiaircraft guns, and the famous Indian camel corps. Regiment after regiment of infantry, their arms swinging high in the British army style, marched by, including such historic units as the

Gwalior Lancers, the Mahratta Light Infantry and the Rajputana Rifles.

Today the Indian army is largely integrated, with Sikhs, Muslims, Hindus and Christians serving side by side, but we could tell the Sikhs by their turbans and their beards. A capable-looking parachute regiment and ski troops trained for winter warfare in the high Himalayas came past, then trim naval and air force marching contingents and the Corps of Engineers, all to the tune of a score of military bands.

India's army, although not large in European terms, is a major deterrent to any aggression against India itself. Since its proportion of noncommissioned and junior officers is high, it could be rapidly increased if need be.

After the troops in the Republic Day parade had passed, a procession of thousands of school children came by, and then a remarkable pageant of tableaux-on-wheels contributed by each state, portraying folk dances, special crafts or river development projects important in the life of its people.

This was a prelude to a two-day festival of folk dances to which had come thousands of specially selected villagers from every corner of the land, including the most remote tribal and mountain areas. They had arrived a week in advance for rehearsal,—and were housed in camps in Talkatora Park by the Ministry of Defense.

Arrangements were made for the special foods they were used to, and for performing their own customs. "When our countrymen come here from the frontier areas of India," Nehru said to the people of Delhi, "we should welcome them and make them feel at home in the capital of India which is theirs as much as ours."

What diversity there is in India! These people were of every imaginable type and wore every imaginable kind of clothes. From Hyderabad came the Sidis, black African Muslims who had entered India in the fourteenth century as special elite troops during the Muslim invasion and who, from the breakup of the Mogul Empire until the birth of the Indian Republic in 1947, had served as the bodyguard for the feudal Nizam of Hyderabad.

"Where have you heard that music before?" Steb had asked when we first listened to the Sidis sing their ancient songs. Suddenly I remembered some very early Mississippi spirituals which were produced by the Library of Congress as music believed to be actually brought from Africa, and Steb nodded in agreement. Sam thought their rhythm came right out of Cab Calloway.

Certainly the dances in the festival showed a vast mosaic of cultures. Steb found them so exciting that she went back twice. The second time she went with Ashadevi of Sevagram and took the two little sons of the *dhobi*, who did our washing. Ashadevi said that this festival was the first time that she had felt that New Delhi was really the capital of her country.

The festival also dramatized the ever-present question whether a country with so many factors making for disunity can be held together. Not the least of these is language. Many of the dance delegations could not converse with each other, or even understand their Prime Minister, because Hindi was as foreign to them as it would be to Americans.

Of the hundred-odd tongues and dialects, there are twelve major languages which account for most of the people: Bengali, Punjabi, Urdu, Gujarati, Marathi, Assamese, Oriya, Telegu, Tamil, Malayalam and Kanarese, which are spoken by from ten to forty million each, and Hindustani, or Hindi, by perhaps 150 million. The first seven and Hindustani have a common Sanskrit origin, while the latter four are South Indian languages based on the early Dravidian, and wholly unintelligible to a North Indian.

To make himself even partially understood to South Indian crowds, Nehru is forced to speak in English, which is more widely known than the northern Hindi in the states of Madras, Mysore and Travancore-Cochin.

However, when Steb and I sailed a small boat along the Maharashtra coast on the Arabian Sea, we found that we could get by successfully on Steb's Hindi. Similarly, after Cynthia had mastered Hindustani and Urdu, it was much easier for her to pick up Bengali, with its Sanskrit similarities.

Most people in South India were not happy to see Hindi adopted as the national language, to go into effect in 1960. Frequently Hindi signs are torn down and defaced in Madras. Most educated South Indians have English as their second language, and would prefer their children to continue in that tradition. "After all, India is the fourth largest English-speaking country in the world," a Madrasi said to me.

There is one good argument for English, exemplified by a young couple we knew, who did not understand each other's respective Bengali and Tamil, but fell in love in English and are now happily married. The several million Indians who speak English, and who include practically all Indian leaders, provide at least a unique opportunity for America and India to understand each other.

Yet ultimately India's intellectuals must learn the language of most of the people, rather than vice versa. Perhaps, as has been done in Indonesia, the Roman script could be adopted by all the Indian languages, even though their alphabets and sounds are more numerous than ours. This would not only make it easier for poor linguists like most Americans, but would bring out the similarities between the tongues and make the learning easier. Meanwhile the government gets along primarily in English, which at least makes life simpler for an American Ambassador!

It is not hard to understand why one wishes to stick by his own language. Nor is it hard to see why the Congress government fears the move toward states organized along tight linguistic lines. Although for many years it championed the idea of state lines being drawn to comprise homogeneous language areas, it now has considerable ground to worry that this might lead to state loyalties overshadowing national loyalties.

Yet the popular demand is strong. In 1952 among the Telegu-speaking people in Madras an old Gandhi follower, Sriramula, finally started a "fast unto death" to force the government into granting the long-sought Telegu state of Andhra. Since the area covered by the proposed state is a stronghold of the Communists, the national government was particularly reluctant to see them united in one area.

Sriramula did fast unto death, widespread riots resulted throughout the whole area and the central government at last agreed to the formation of Andhra out of the northeastern part of Madras. Some members of the Madras state government heaved a sigh of relief at their good fortune in getting rid of their main Communist section, but most thoughtful Indians were apprehensive.

. . .

Perhaps the greatest immediate force for unrest in India, as we shall see in our discussion of the Communist movement, is her youth, particularly the university students and graduates. After an intensive year studying the Indian situation, a shrewd American observer remarked, "If revolution comes here it will not be because factory workers are exploited, nor even because peasants are hungry. If left alone most Indians might continue in the same old channels for a thousand more years. The people who are unhappy and likely to do something about it are the educated and the semieducated. It is this small literate minority, not more than 10 per cent, which will make or break India."

I have visited most of India's thirty main universities and nearly one hundred of her eight hundred-odd affiliated colleges. The cross section I have seen of the quarter of a million students now studying for a degree in many ways makes me frightened and sad.

"The acid of Western modernity has dissolved their faith in traditional values and patterns," an Indian Christian explained about his fellow students to the non-Asian delegates of an Indian session of the World Student Christian Federation. He was speaking about the educated younger generation in every land from Suez to the Sea of Japan when he went on to say: "We tend to live with one leg in the world of the ancients and the other in the rational scientific world of the modern, with the feeling that both these worlds are breaking to pieces under our feet."

Earnestly he asked the Western delegates to try to understand "the moral chaos inherent in a cultural and religious crisis, the hopes and fear, the promises and frustrations, the skepticisms and uncertainties in which young Asians find themselves," and the resulting "superficiality or self-seeking" or political extremism.

This attempt to find new roots and to create a new synthesis of old and new ideas leads many young students into communism, while others, unable to find satisfying answers anywhere, retreat into reactionary communalism, into arch opposition to change and the glorification of the past.

The limited education provided under British rule was designed to build a class of "Indian gentlemen" who, it was assumed, would associate themselves with the imperial rule. But it produced more awakened nationalists than the expected "brown Englishmen."

Many Indians learned flawless English, which is still the language of all university and most secondary instruction, but having turned away from their own tongue and from their old town or village in favor of a Westernized Indian city, they found no new roots to replace the old. When we discovered how completely most of these educated Indians are disconnected from the main body of people, we understood the evils of transplanting English schools, or any other kind of foreign schools, into a land where they do not fit.

As a result of the long independence struggle, it became a patriotic custom many years ago for students to strike against the alien or aloof authorities. Even now this habit continues, and newspapers frequently tell of violent university strikes on issues such as tuition or unfair exams. In the Delhi school, Sally found herself inevitably involved in one flurry, in which her class unanimously handed in a blank examination in protest over something or other. One day they refused to go to classes until the authorities agreed to honor the anniversary of Gandhi's death as a holiday.

Of course, many indigenous educational efforts do exist, such as the cultural center established by Rabindranath Tagore at Santiniketan, just recently recognized as an accredited university. Cynthia studied there for nearly a year, living in a girls' dormitory, sleeping on a wooden table plus a thin pad, and particularly loving the "Rabindra studies" of Tagore's own great Bengali poetry. Yet even Santiniketan, dedicated to Indian history, beauty and art, is to some extent disconnected from village India.

The Gandhians have taken the lead in developing an educational program designed for present-day rural living in free India. At Sevagram's "basic school" and at many other centers throughout India they have applied some principles of learning by doing which are quite reminiscent of those sponsored by our own John Dewey. For instance, they learn village crafts such as spinning and weaving, and in connection with it do their arithmetic. "How many threads will make the pattern?" leads them into multiplication. They study where cotton comes from, and thus into geography and history. From folk dancing they learn the religion and culture of their country. They are taught to return to their village and to work to transform it into "the little republics" of Gandhi's vision.

In many parts of India I have visited such schools, modeled on Sevagram, and I was always impressed with the boys and girls who smiled cordially when I came into the room, *namasted* in Indian greeting and then plunged earnestly back to their work, oblivious of our presence. Steb, who has always been keenly interested in education and who served as chairman of our school board in Essex, was particularly impressed with the Gandhian work she saw in Bihar. Now at Sevagram Gandhi's followers are experimenting with a "rural university," where they will apply the same principles to higher education.

Despite the good work at Sevagram, the development of Gandhian educational programs in many states and the almost universal complaints about Anglicized schools, the main line of higher education continues in its distorted British direction. The system continues to turn out a high proportion of liberal arts students and all too few engineers, teachers, agricultural experts or workers in public health. The technicians and doctors India does train are excellent, but the majority of young people leave their universities with almost no practical training for the battle of building a new nation.

If there was a reasonably constructive future for the average graduate with a British-style B.A., it would not be so bad. But, except for a few, the brilliant, the lucky and the more aggressive, most graduates find no jobs or at least no jobs in line with what too many still consider their "station."

To build up their confidence, some of them even have calling cards engraved with their degrees, but to earn enough to live they take any work they can find. I have seen college graduates in Trivandrum collecting tickets on buses for twelve dollars a month. When a professional opening occurs in a large concern there are often a thousand frantic applicants.

"The real downfall of the Nationalist Government in China," Pearl Buck wrote to Steb, "was basically because the young Chinese men and women who flocked to Chiang's government after 1927 could not, or at least did not, understand the necessity of living at the level of those who needed to be taught." She added that "the brilliant, self-confident Chinese graduates of our American universities and those of England and Europe, wearing all sorts of degrees" refused to go to the villages.

When I made this point to an Indian student, he replied, "But how do we go to the villages? Where do we start, who pays us enough to live on, what do we do there?" His questions were real. He may have only visited a village once or twice in his life, and he may have no income of his own on which to experiment.

I am convinced that most young Indians will rally to a national program of development as the momentum of the promising new effort begins to be felt. I believe that all their frustration and bitterness, their explosiveness and even their radicalism, is a sign of their eagerness to be summoned to a great democratic task of nation building.

"In China we hear that every student is drafted into national service in the villages or the city slums," said a young man who explained why he wanted communism to come to India. "I want to be put to work to help my country."

What can democracy offer this young college graduate to fill his life and consume his energies? In America the easy answer would be to go into private business. But in India not only is there little opportunity for this, but most of the students consider themselves socialists of one kind or other.

I soon discovered why this was so. Indian capitalism is hardly recognizable as capitalism to an American accustomed to an expanding economy based on mass production, huge consumer purchasing power and ever rising living standards. Long held back by the British, the Indian industry which did finally develop often outdid even the European example of monopoly. For the most part ownership is in the hands of a small group in the cities, who squeeze it for all it is worth.

"There are only three ways to make money," an Indian manufacturer explained to me. "You lower the quality of the product, you raise the price or you reduce the wages."

He could not conceive of broadening the market by higher wages and cheaper products of good quality, with a small margin of profit which would multiply under mass consumption. Too much of Indian capitalism is of the nature of quick speculation to the detriment of the long-range development problem facing the country. That helped explain why "capitalism," which to Americans means development and expanding opportunities for everyone, is considered a horrid word in much of Asia.

Of course, one thing the young frustrated college graduates can do while they are drifting is to go to the movies. And this many of them do, if 600 million paid admissions last year means anything. Most of these are not Hollywood films, although many

American movies are popular. India has the second largest movie industry in the world, surpassed only by the United States.

Although the technical competence of Indian films is developing rapidly, the producers are still inclined to borrow the most lurid dramatic techniques from Hollywood. A long technicolor film, *Aan,* was unfortunately typical. Its theme was a love triangle in which a Maharaja and a bullock cart driver struggled for the affections of a girl. Of course, the bullock cart driver won. Almost every melodramatic event Hollywood has ever imagined was crowded into this single film. There were battles, murders, sex appeal Indian fashion (kissing is taboo) and a series of happenings that rivaled the *Perils of Pauline.*

Both Indian and Hollywood pictures, with their portrayal of exaggerated plush living, serve to whet the appetites of the viewers, many of whom go home to drab slums, with six people jammed into one tenement room and scores to one outside latrine. Is there any wonder that so many of the city-dwelling young people feel rebellious?

. . .

But what is happening among the 80 per cent of the people living on the land? When anyone looks at the Indian scene the villages are everywhere in the background. Unlike a sprawled-out American rural community, with a house in the middle of each farm, the Indian village is a crowded cluster of perhaps a hundred mud and thatched huts, with perhaps one thousand acres of farm plots, usually divided into a hundred or more tiny holdings, all lying within a short radius. Every day the peasants walk to their fields over ridges which dam up the water lying in the wet rice paddy fields. From an airplane at night their dimly lit villages often look almost like endless army camps encircling the cities and towns.

These 500,000 villages are still the centers of caste, of feudalism and of poverty. Most of the villagers, as we shall see in a later chapter, rent their land at exorbitant rates or work as laborers for a large landlord. Most of them are heavily in debt to the village money lenders to whom they often pay annual interest as high as 25 per cent.

I could appreciate how distant the village problems must seem to the city Indian, because to a small town American, like myself, the villages of India were a new world. I made it a point to spend a lot of my time visiting scores of villages and talking with hundreds of villagers in almost every state in India, and so did Steb.

But Cynthia really came to know them at first hand. In the spring of 1952 she went to stay and work with some Indian girls from the Delhi College of Nursing, who were doing public health work in the village of Chawla, twenty miles from Delhi. A year later she lived for six weeks in villages in Punjab and Uttar Pradesh. Her diary of the first of many subsequent adventures in village India was exciting to read.

She tended a sick baby girl, whom she discovered was unwanted because of her sex, and because of the expensive dowry a girl requires. She helped with the two typhoid cases in the village. She also participated in a wedding, watching the gay procession of the groom's decorated bullock carts from a nearby village, listening to the band which escorted him to the bride's home, talking to the bride when the day-long feast and festival was over, and the groom had gone back to his own family, as was the custom. She saw face to face the caste discriminations, and the shocking differences in land holding.

Each year these villages produce new millions of Indians and then see millions die. One-fourth of all the babies die before their first birthday, and half the children never reach the age of twelve.

Some Americans still consider the "holy cow" of Hinduism the symbol of all that is wrong in India. Actually, without their tens of millions of cattle, the people of India would perish. To an Indian villager his cow provides milk for his children, his ox or bullock is his source of power for plowing and transportation, and the cow dung, carefully dried in the sun, is his fuel for cooking.

In this light, it is not hard to see why our word "capital" comes from an ancient Latin word for "cattle." India's cattle population can be, if properly used, one of her main capital assets. That was a practical reason why Gandhi placed so much emphasis on "cow improvement."

"You will never get us to kill our cows," explained an Indian. "Would you kill and eat your favorite dog?" he asked me. "Our cows mean even more to us than your dogs mean to you," he asserted, telling about their place in Hindu mythology. But Hinduism apparently presents no obstacle to castrating bulls, and sending useless worn-out cattle to semijungle areas where they die off and where their bones and hides can be secured for commercial use.

Several American Congressmen, during the debate on the wheat loan, seemed to be convinced that if it was not "sacred cows" it must be "sacred monkeys" which were at the root of India's problems. In India I saw many monkeys, perhaps a total of five or ten thousand, but I doubt if they and the cattle together consume a fraction of one per cent of India's human food.

Whenever the monkeys do become a menace, the villagers invariably find ways to get rid of them. In the state of Orissa, where they were beginning to threaten the crops, the government offered one rupee (about twenty cents) for every three tails. In two years more than half a million were turned in.

Almost every American who has been living and working in villages agrees that the old structure of village society is crumbling faster than it seems on the surface. The main thing an impatient Indian reformer still sees is lethargy; but the main thing an impartial and practical foreign observer sees is change.

In many states the government has organized new village governing *panchayats*, with local councils elected. Often members of the lower castes have won in these elections. The result may be a tug of war between the landowners and the majority of the village. In one village which an American anthropologist was studying a low-caste refused to work for the landlord and succeeded in organizing one thousand fellow villagers behind him. Eventually he was murdered by the landlord's son but now he is remembered as a saint by many of the villagers.

The government, all the political parties and world events are coming to village doorsteps. Enough new deep "tube" wells have been drilled, for instance, to let the villagers of North India know that means now exist for finding water. An American girl working with the Gandhians writes how the villagers "live through the wells." "When the wells go dry, they go to the dry river beds and dig for water; if there's no river or they're unsuccessful, they seek out small slimy pools which may have survived the heat."

She described taking a bath in a little pit of water after twenty or more other people had taken baths and washed clothes and drank from the same water. "Do you think that such people will be satisfied much longer," she asked, "when they hear that elsewhere people are getting water by modern methods from just such parched lands as theirs?"

We of the West are irrevocably a part of this picture of New India, not just because we invented the tools to dig the deeper wells, but because Western colonialism has been the primary factor shaping the new Indian mind. The wound which the West has inflicted goes deep, and it will take long years to mend. It makes the relationship between India and America complicated and sensitive, in spite of the fact that our position has traditionally been opposed to the colonialism with which, in Asia's eyes, all of the West is identified.

A Westerner who is so uninformed or insensitive as to refer to an Indian in the colonial vocabulary of "native," will in all likelihood find that he is faced with a stone wall of resentment. Even the word "Asiatic" is now taken as a kind of insult. The proper word is "Asian." Small things can be salt in an open wound.

The new Indians may still talk proudly of their spiritual heritage and pucker their lips at our materialism and too rapid tempo of life. Yet the same champions of Indian timelessness are in a hurry, a terrible hurry, to develop and to catch up. They are thirsting after the material progress of the West and are determined that in India and in Asia it will be shared more broadly among all men.

Although they generally cannot bring themselves to be pro-Western, however much they are attached to many of the values of the West, they are as we shall see, even less likely to be pro-Russian, however much they may sometimes seem to be blind to Russian transgressions. Primarily they are passionately pro-Indian, and after that, pro-Asian.

Some of the spirit of this awakening, complex New India came through in the news dispatches in the Spring of 1953, after Hillary, the New Zealander, and Tenzing, the Asian, reached the summit of Mt. Everest. There developed an angry debate between their partisans over who got there first. "That make much trouble," said Tenzing. "If I say Hillary first, Indian and Nepali people unhappy. If I say I first, European people unhappy. If you agree, I like say both got top together almost same time."

But there was even more trouble when Queen Elizabeth knighted Hillary, the white man, and only gave a civilian medal to Tenzing, the brown man from Asia. And in the very response of the two men to the joint achievement, the ancient differences of East and West seemed vast.

"Damn good" was the way the Westerner from New Zealand described his feeling while on top of the world's highest peak. "I thought of God and the greatness of His work," said Tenzing. "I have feeling for climbing to top and making worship more close to Buddha god. Not same feeling like English sahibs who say they want 'conquer' mountain. I feel more like making pilgrimage."

Yet just when one is about to conclude that "never the twain shall meet," the news comes that the Indian public is contributing to a subscription to build Tenzing a modern home, and that above all Tenzing wants an American-style kitchen, including an electric refrigerator. In the New India, West and East will surely meet, but only God knows the result.

III. THE POLITICS OF INDIA

9. Nehru and the Mind of Asia

WHEN THE Communists speak of Asia they see the great land mass of China and its 500 million people under the leadership of Mao Tse-tung. Some Americans, although very few Asians or Europeans, still think of Asia in terms of Chiang Kai-shek on Formosa and Syngman Rhee in South Korea. But I believe that the heart of Asia and the key to her future lies in the billion or more peoples who live in the largely uncommitted nations, which stretch along the periphery of Communist China and the Soviet Union from Cairo to Tokyo.

The strategic, geographic and political center of this area is India, and more often than not its chief spokesman is Jawaharlal Nehru. An understanding of this complex, controversial and attractive personality is essential to an understanding of Asia itself.

Jawaharlal Nehru *is* the politics of India. "Our government is strong today," a leading figure of the Congress party told me in 1952 shortly after the Indian election, "for one reason, Nehru." No less candid was the more recent "concession" of a leader of the Socialist opposition to Congress: "Nehru is undoubtedly the only man in Indian politics."

When I made my round of visits to ambassadors from other countries shortly after my arrival in India, my repeated question, "Who is likely to be Nehru's successor?" was met, as often as not, by an expressive shrug or an abrupt, "God knows."

Wherever he goes, enormous crowds of peasants and workers from miles around come by the hundreds of thousands, to see him, to sit silently on their haunches as long as he will talk. Even with many loudspeakers, it is frequently impossible to carry his voice and words to the outer edges of these vast assemblies. Yet those who cannot hear or who are shut off by the barrier of language seem satisfied simply to watch every motion of the distant graceful figure.

Such receptions do not mean that the people of India are satisfied with their lot or even with their leaders. On the contrary, most reports tell of growing dissatisfaction—of grumbling about delay in land reform and other social improvements, and about bungling and bureaucracy in the lower layers of government. Thus far, however, except for some of the militant younger people, this criticism is directed principally at the provincial governments or at the Congress party. Nehru's personal popularity has remained largely undimmed.

Nehru's dominant position is not based, as is that of many other leaders in the new Arab-Asian world, on control of the army or of a well-disciplined party or of an unruly mob which may be flushed at will through the streets of the capital and other important cities. His grip is based on his personal hold on the affection and loyalties of the two great forces in the fifty-year struggle for Indian independence: the educated, governing minority and the illiterate peasant and working masses.

It is easy to see how Nehru has captured the imagination of the Indian intellectual groups which are largely British educated and imbued with the traditions of Western liberalism. In many respects his experience paralleled theirs but in a heightened degree.

Although some kind of English-style education was almost universal for educated Indians, Nehru went to one of the most exclusive schools in all England, Winston Churchill's old school, Harrow, and then on to Cambridge. Like other educated Indians of his time, Nehru has felt and grappled with the conflicting pulls of East and West, of England and India, and he has expressed this schism in the Indian soul in terms that evoked a sense of recognition and kinship.

"I have become a queer mixture of the East and the West," he wrote. "Out of place everywhere, at home nowhere. Perhaps my thoughts and approach to life are more akin to what is called Western than Eastern, but India clings to me, as she does to all her children, in innumerable ways . . . I am a stranger and alien in the West. I cannot be of it. But in my own country also, sometimes I have an exile's feeling." Gandhi said that when Nehru talked in his sleep, he talked in English.

Finally, when the long fight for independence began, Nehru threw himself into it with a daring and passion that pointed the way for the Indian intellectuals, those aliens in their own land, again to become a part of India and her struggles.

Thus a whole generation of educated young Indians grew up admiring, almost worshiping Nehru. They followed his actions with awe and enthusiasm, and read each of his many books with a kind of intoxication.

Gandhi, with his hard, disciplined asceticism, his mud hut and spinning, went straight to the hearts of the villagers. But Nehru was warm, melancholy, intellectual, sophisticated and glamorous. He had what Gandhi called "the dash and rashness of a warrior." He combined all the qualities of the Byronic hero for whom the British education of Indian intellectuals had built a deep response.

For this large and influential group there was no thought but that Nehru would be the builder of the new India, with or without Gandhi in the background. And even today, in 1953, when a new student generation is emerging which has not known at first hand the courage and charm of the revolutionary Nehru, most of the educated people over thirty-five can think of no one else to whom such allegiance is possible.

While the sources of Nehru's strength among this educated and ruling group are obvious, the basis of his hold upon illiterate India is less clear. Partly it has become his by the grace of Gandhi, who often said, "Jawaharlal is my political heir." And partly it comes from the very legend of his life which is in the tradition of renunciation and service of the great leaders of India's history from Buddha to Gandhi. Born into one of the wealthiest families of the top Kashmiri Brahman caste, Nehru chose instead a life of struggle for his country's freedom, donated his great home to the Congress party and went to jail. Between 1920 and 1945 over half of his time was spent in prison.

Of course, no one can put Nehru in a nutshell. He is many-sided, complex, full of conflicting enthusiasms and burdened by many sorrows. Yet, there has seldom been a public figure who has more fully opened himself, his problems and his thoughts in books, in public print, in speeches and in talk with friends. Analyzing Nehru is a favorite pastime, not confined to India alone, because he is the most important, most attractive and in many ways the most puzzling character on the Asian stage.

I have already described in an earlier chapter the misgivings with which I left my first meeting with Nehru and the relief I felt when his earlier mood of coolness and reserve evaporated at our subsequent meetings. With that change came the beginning of an unusually warm and friendly relationship.

For a year and a half I saw him frequently, sometimes two or three or even four times a week and our visits lasted anywhere from twenty minutes to three hours. Sometimes I would not see him for two weeks at a stretch, and after these absences, he would always have much to talk about.

He is the most articulate man I have ever heard in personal conversation. His flow of flawless English makes it a pleasure simply to sit and listen to him talk, even when one disagrees with what he is saying. He always seemed to me to talk fully and freely, to tell me just what he thought and to make every effort to see that I understood his viewpoint regardless of my opinion of its merit. There was one exception to this, Kashmir, the mountain valley where his ancestors were born and which Nehru loves above all else on the Indian subcontinent. On its beauty and history he had much to say, but on the present conflict with Pakistan, he was always reluctant to talk.

Wearing a long white Indian coat, buttoned up straight to his collar, with a brilliant red rose in his buttonhole, he would by turns walk back and forth impatiently and then fall back thoughtfully into his chair. He seemed to smoke almost continuously, as much as forty cigarettes a day, he said. His one concession to moderation on this score is in sometimes cutting the cigarette in half before putting it in his holder, a unique way of cutting down smoking!

When he touched upon an ancient Asian wound, like colonialism or racial discrimination, his voice sometimes became tense, but for the most part he discussed his beliefs and his doubts in a quiet, temperate, almost questioning way. His conversation often consists literally of thinking aloud, and he explores all sides of a problem until its full complexity is felt. He seems to reach a conclusion almost reluctantly, as though hesitant to give up the good along the other path. For Nehru the world is not painted in harshly contrasting blacks and whites, but in many subtly interwoven shades of gray.

"We find people, nations, statesmen," he said as he inaugurated India's commission for UNESCO, "talking in terms of the greatest certitude about their being right, about their undertaking some moral crusade or other for the benefit of mankind. Sometimes I feel that the world might be far better off if there were a few less of these moral crusaders about. Everyone wants not only to carry on the moral crusade in his own environment but to impose his moral crusade on others."

His avowed skepticism has roots deep in Hinduism's emphasis on the diversity of truth. But it is also fed by the liberals of England and the West, who made tolerance of the beliefs of others the cornerstone of their democratic philosophy. Like them, Nehru has never let his skepticism corrode his deep and abiding belief in democracy.

And yet there are many strains of the aristocrat in Nehru. Once he wrote an anonymous article criticizing himself in which he remarked, "He is far too much of an aristocrat for the crudity and vulgarity of fascism." And in his autobiography he wrote, "Behind me lie, somewhere in the subconscious, racial memories of a hundred, or whatever the number may be, generations of Brahmans."

Sometimes one might think his ancestors were British Brahmans. Some of his closest friends are English, or English-educated Indians of the old Civil Service. And he has all the manner and charm of an English gentleman of the old school.

But his feeling for aristocracy is easily exaggerated. At any rate, it does not prevent him from listening respectfully to whoever happens to be seated opposite him. Once he has made up his mind that he can trust the man with whom he is talking, he seems entirely willing to accept his statements at face value. Except on two or three particularly overcharged subjects, I have never known anyone in public life who seemed more willing to listen objectively and to change his mind when the facts or logic called for it.

I used to spend hours explaining to him the background and motives of American foreign policy. Once in the fall of 1952, when the Korean war was taking an ominous turn, and when the Communists were accusing us of plotting to bring on a third world war, we read together, word for word, two issues of the "News of the Week in Review," the news summary section of the Sunday *New York Times*.

Those particular issues were filled with articles and commentary on American concern over how to end the war and avoid a military entanglement on the mainland of China. I think that these pages, which we read so carefully, did much to reassure him about our peaceful intentions.

. . .

Getting to know Nehru as a person was a fascinating and rewarding adventure. Appraising his success in governing India is another problem.

One of his greatest achievements is the creation of a secular state in which the forty-five million Muslims who chose not to go to Pakistan may live peacefully and worship as they please. Two of the most important cabinet posts, including the Ministry of Education, have been filled by Muslims, and hundreds of other Muslims hold important positions throughout the government.

Several times Nehru told me that if he were to die today this would be his most enduring accomplishment; and most of his critics concede that an India in which freedom of religion is a fact, not a theory, has come about largely through the determined efforts of the Prime Minister, following the principles laid down by Mahatma Gandhi.

Nehru has not confined his work on behalf of religious freedom to exhortation. In the terrible riots at the time of partition, he rushed into the midst of danger zones and ran recklessly into the center of rampaging crowds. Sometimes he would disperse a whole mob by his sudden appearance. "In bravery he is not to be surpassed," Gandhi said.

Later, when passions in Bengal were rising and demands for war against Pakistan were on dangerous increase, Nehru disregarded the pleas and warnings of his friends and colleagues. Traveling to the storm centers in Calcutta, he rode through jammed streets in an open car, addressing half a million rebellious citizens.

Bombs were thrown. A policeman guarding the route was killed. Young men hurled stones and rotten eggs toward the platform where the handsome Prime Minister stood. As though bearing some charm, he was untouched. Almost magical, too, was the way his eloquence gradually won the sullen and grumbling audience.

Earnestly preaching the need for unity regardless of religion or race, and particularly the need for peace and understanding between India and Pakistan, he turned back the ugly tide of religious fanaticism that seemed again about to explode into mob violence.

Today the task of keeping the hard-won communal peace between Hindus, Muslims, Sikhs, Jains and Christians presents few physical risks, but until the Indian election, the political strength of the Hindu extremist parties, several of which included certain fascist trappings, was an unknown and potentially large quantity. Yet Nehru would have no truck with them. "No one has a right to bring religion into politics," he insisted sternly.

Once to a great election crowd of extremist Hindus which he had been urged to pass by as hopeless prospects for the Congress party, he cried, "Put your arm around your Muslim brother, your Christian brother, your Buddhist brother. Take their hands and work together for a better India." When he left they cheered him. The unexpected weakness of the orthodox Hindu parties in the national election bore eloquent testimony to the success of his campaign against religious fanaticism.

Along with this insistence upon freedom of religion, goes an equally strong devotion to the other forms of Western parliamentary democracy. It is this devotion that India must thank for the stirring success of her national election in 1951. Although many of his advisors argued that an early election would be dangerous, Nehru insisted that India's government could never be fully effective without the freely given support of the people at the polls. Thus within four years after independence India followed Japan and the Philippines and became the third nation in the long history of Asia to hold free elections. Every man and woman over twenty-one was eligible to vote.

So, too, the Indian Parliament, organized along British lines, is almost a model democratic legislature. Debate is open and public. Daily the Congress party ministers face a barrage of questions on every detail of government policy from an array of opposition spokesmen.

Nehru himself will often take the floor, frequently to answer an attack by a Communist member. He is a master of parliamentary tactics. But whether the questioned minister is successful in defending his policy or not, the debate is fully reported in the Indian press. Thus the democratic process of constant molding of public opinion by events, and of policy by opinion, is actively at work in Nehru's new India.

What kind of economic organization does Nehru want for India? In his younger days he read Marx thoroughly and found the Marxian analysis of imperialism a useful tool during the long struggle against the British. But he dislikes dogmatism of all kinds, and has never really accepted any rigid economic doctrine. Socialism, today, he considers too narrow to be workable. He always seemed to me to be a thorough pragmatist on the question of economic development. He has announced himself in favor of private ownership wherever it will work, government ownership where that will work, and the use of co-operatives in other fields. While I was in India a great debate was waged about the effectiveness of rationing and price controls in the present Indian economic climate. Finally with Nehru's full agreement practically all controls were abandoned in the hope of encouraging more production.

Although under British rule India's transportation system, communications and utilities, and major water resource developments, had been placed under government ownership, Nehru has undertaken no new major program of nationalization since independence, with the exception of the air transport industry which was later let out to private management on a contract basis. While I was in India, a contract with two American oil companies for the construction of large refineries near Bombay included a thirty-year guarantee against nationalization.

Like that of most Indians, and Asians generally, Nehru's impression of capitalism has been distorted by the irresponsible speculation, wild profiteering and monopoly control which characterized much of private business in colonial Asia. We had many long talks about the totally different course that free enterprise has taken in America. Over the months, I believe I made considerable progress in convincing him that our economic structure has resulted not only in continuing expansion of industry and higher profits for businessmen, but in higher living standards for wage earners, farmers and the general consuming public as well.

Still, Nehru remained skeptical of the adaptability of the American system to India and other underdeveloped economies. But upon close examination his concept of a mixed economy and welfare state turns out to be hardly more radical than the economic program of Winston Churchill's Conservative government in England.

. . .

The sixty-four-dollar question for most Americans is "What about Nehru and communism?" Anyone who reads his books, overflowing with an irrepressible faith in Western liberalism, law and the rationalism of the Renaissance, must recognize at once that the dogma and oppression of communism can have no appeal for him. This basic hostility has led him to take ruthless action against the domestic Indian Communist party when he saw that it clearly threatened the new Indian Republic.

When the Communist rebellion broke out in Hyderabad in 1948 and 1949, Nehru did not hesitate a moment in sending the Indian army to the scene with instructions to stamp out the uprisings and to arrest the Communist leaders. In the fighting that followed, hundreds were killed and thousands were imprisoned.

His government then put through a Detention Act which permits it to imprison anyone charged with subversion for six months without trial. "We detest the need for such arbitrary power," the Congress party minister in charge said in presenting this bill in the House of the People. "But a young democracy can accomplish nothing unless it is competent to defend itself against the enemies within who would use the very cloak of democracy to destroy it."

When I reached India, I was told that 8,500 Communist and fellow-traveling agitators had been imprisoned under this Act, a much harsher Communist control measure than any we have in the United States. Even though the Communist tactics had changed for the moment to "peaceful co-operation," Nehru insisted that this act be renewed in 1952 for use in future emergencies.

Actually, the suspension of habeas corpus is a measure so extreme that many Indian champions of civil liberties bitterly oppose it, but there can be no doubt about the government's determination to take any steps necessary to defeat communism *in India.*

In September, 1953, a few months after Mr. Dulles's trip to New Delhi, the State Department issued a report entitled "India; a Pattern for Democracy in Asia," which stressed that until 1951 when the Communists abandoned violence "India had more Communists in prison than any other country, except perhaps the Soviet Union."

Nehru's unequivocal opposition to the Communists is in terms as harsh as those he used against religious bigots. He calls them a "foul conspiracy based on fraud and deceit and violence to produce chaos in India."

Because of his very success in checking the Communists, he underestimates, in my view, not only the problems of world communism, but also the real dimensions of the Communist threat in India over the coming years. One reason that Nehru may tend to minimize the danger is that he mainly sees the party in Parliament, where they appear as an embittered and ineffectual group, hopelessly in the minority. In this forum, where the Communists show up so badly, Nehru is in his element.

Often the Communist members will have worked out a plan to discredit some government department, and they toss the oratorical ball glibly from one to the other. Nehru delights in breaking up their routine by taking over from the cabinet minister under attack and scathingly answering the criticism himself.

In Parliament on February 18, 1953, for instance, Nehru took up the Communist claim that 1,200 landings had been made in October by American military aircraft at a single Indian airport. A complete master of the facts, Nehru proved that in the whole year only 459 military planes, Indian and foreign, had landed. If the Communist members' figures were correct, he said, everyone would have known about it, for a large-scale invasion of India would have been under way.

Having thus disposed of the immediate issue, Nehru went on in a broader vein. "Some members on the other side are constantly saying, and repeating like some *mantram* which they have learned by heart without understanding what it is, that we are stooges of the Americans, that we are part of the Anglo-American bloc, and so on. Persons who are less restrained than I am might retort in kind, but I do not wish to do so. I should, however, like them and others to try to get out of their habit of learning slogans and phrases and repeating them again and again. It becomes rather stale work."

At some such climactic point, Nehru will turn on his heel and leave the floor, with the cheers of the overwhelming Congress party majority ringing in his ears. No wonder he feels confident. Yet the honest devotion of his own party and the exhilaration which he feels from his contacts with the people may lead him to overlook some of the real soft spots.

In 1953, on a trip through Hyderabad and Madras, I became alarmed at the seriousness of the crop failures and the dissatisfaction that was evident among the people. It was what is called a "hunger area," a notch or so above famine. People were not starving, but thousands were dying from other diseases because of undernourishment. Land reform had been ineffective or nonexistent and Communist strength seemed to be growing. When I told him of my impressions, Nehru assured me that he was going to visit the same area in a few weeks and would examine things for himself.

On his return he said that we must have visited two different places. Everywhere he had gone the people had thronged to show him their affection. They greeted him joyously. Nehru knew that the situation was bad; but the villagers were at their happiest and most hopeful because of his presence. Seeing only this, he was inclined to think that it was not as dangerous as it had seemed to others.

It is in the broader area of communism in world politics and the Cold War that the differences between Nehru and his American critics become sharpest. Unlike his clear understanding of the threat of domestic communism to democracy in India, I think he does not yet fully appreciate the menace of aggressive Soviet and Chinese communism to peace in the world. My many talks with him left no doubt that he was fully aware of the hate and tyranny that pervade the Communist regimes within Russia and China. In fact, he knows more in detail about China than the vast majority of Americans because he has many more sources of information. Nor is there any doubt that the inhumanity and ruthlessness of communism in the countries where it has come to power is abhorrent and disgusting to him.

But he has not yet drawn the conclusion from these observations that the whole world must finally choose up sides. He remains convinced that there is some middle way, involving allegiance neither to Moscow nor to Washington, by which India and other states may contribute more fully to peace.

We should not be blind to this disagreement, which I shall deal with more fully later on. But we should also be aware of some factors which I believe lead us to exaggerate the differences which do exist. The first of these is the circumstances under which most of Nehru's statements are made.

Nehru speaks as the head of the largest and most stable of the free Asian nations. He is one of the few statesmen in the whole underdeveloped world of more than a billion people who has really powerful mass support among his people. He is one of the few non-Western statesmen who has to speak almost daily on a wide range of subjects to a freely elected Parliament.

These speeches are in flawless, beautiful English in an assembly which is conducted in English. He prides himself on saying everything he thinks regardless of what others may think. Competent, alert American newsmen sit in the galleries, follow the debates without translation and pick up his quotable phrases to flash to this country.

Although he criticizes the Russians far more sharply, he frequently expresses his doubts and criticisms of particular American attitudes and actions. These references to American policy are inevitably the ones that make news here. It is understandable that, reading them as we do, out of context, we, who are making such sacrifices in defense of the free world, should feel hurt and misunderstood. But it is immature and indeed ridiculous for us to jump to the conclusion that because he is not 100 per cent for us, he must be against us.

. . .

For his part, Nehru hears of the arrest of the independence leaders in Morocco by the French, he remembers his own struggle against the British and he cannot comprehend what he sees as American support of French colonialism. He remembers thirteen years of his life "buried within British prison walls"—"sitting alone, wrapped in my thoughts, how many seasons I have seen go by, following one another into oblivion!"

He remembers his wife, Kamala, from whom Gandhi summoned him to the struggle that led to jail. "We lived for a while on the edge of life," he writes of his one and only holiday with her, and then again to jail for "two long prison terms of two years each. . . . Before the second of these was over, Kamala lay dying."

When his blood boils at the thought of others like himself in other Asian and African lands, still imprisoned by foreign colonial rulers in the second half of the twentieth century, because they dared to stand for freedom, it should be easy for Americans, of all people, to understand. When he grows impatient when we tell him that, of course, we favor self-determination for all people, but that communism must be stopped first, we might do well to stop for a moment and think what we might feel if we stood in his shoes.

With these experiences so immediate and vivid for him, he feels that Americans are inclined to ignore the very existence of democratic free India and the burning aspirations of the Asian half of the world. In exasperation he tells us that we have "no understanding of the mind and heart of Asia." Are we so far from our own struggle for independence and freedom that we must say and do the very things that seem to prove him right?

For we must make no mistake about it, when Nehru speaks on world issues, right or wrong, he expresses not only his own convictions but also the yearnings and the attitudes of the vast majority in free Asia and in Africa. The attitudes which come to us in his words, and which sometimes disturb us so deeply, are shared generally by the leaders and the people of non-Communist countries from Morocco to Japan. I have talked with statesmen and with students, with villagers and businessmen, throughout this great stretch of the world, and I am convinced that what Nehru says, most free Asians think.

Whether we agree with it or not, there is no doubt in my mind that there is a free Asian way of looking at the world which Nehru happens to express most eloquently. We will have to come to terms with this Asian mind if we are to avoid adding dangerously to our already long series of failures in that part of the world.

To see the Asian mind in action, one need only follow the debates in the United Nations. On issue after issue, the so-called Arab-Asian bloc, representing over one-fourth of the world's people, stands solidly together.

Even if India never took the lead, the delegates of Egypt and Burma, of Pakistan and Indonesia would continue to find themselves reacting in the same way to the many issues arising directly or indirectly out of colonialism, which was the common experience, in one form or another, of the whole area. The memory of the political domination and economic exploitation by the European colonial powers, creates bonds among the former victims and leads them to a common and often distorted view of the West, the world and the Cold War. But their sense of unity is not confined to world political questions. Their common status as economically underdeveloped countries gives them much the same problems and needs and attitudes.

The most powerful thread running through the Asian attitude on all these issues is nationalism. Because it is often anti-Western, we are sometimes irritated and hurt. But the very strength of Asian nationalism is one of the region's most effective defenses against the new Soviet-directed imperialism of world communism.

I was happy to see that Secretary of State Dulles, in his talks with Nehru shortly after my departure, came to much the same conclusion. Speaking about all of the nations of South Asia and the Middle East, he said they were "proud peoples," and that "we in the United States are better off if we respect and honor them, and learn the thoughts and aspirations which move them."

Of Nehru, whom Mr. Dulles called "one of the great leaders of our time," and whose "calm demeanor and lofty idealism" impressed him, he reported, "We did not always agree, but we did clear up some misunderstandings and, I felt, gained respect for the integrity of our respective purposes."

Beginning with his trip to the United States in 1949 and continuing through the many fruitful months Nehru and I worked together, I believe he grew to have a far more sympathetic feeling for America's complicated problems and responsibilities. I am confident that if we are really willing to offer understanding in our turn, he will prove, in his own way and within the strict political limitations under which he works, a stalwart associate in the struggle for a world of expanding freedom and opportunity for all men.

In many ways Nehru was unprepared for what he found on his first trip to the United States in 1949. Perhaps his lingering identification with England had left a residue of the upper-class Briton's attitude toward America, that we are brash and uncouth and slightly barbarian. On the other hand, during his fight for independence, he had turned for inspiration to our own revolution, and he has come to know early American history better than do most Americans. I found that he has very high standards for America which he earnestly hopes we will live up to.

There was much that impressed him favorably on his trip here. He enjoyed the vitality and informal friendliness of the people, from taxicab drivers in New York to farmers in Illinois. He spent one whole day just walking around a typical farming community, winding it up by sitting down to a big, family-style dinner.

But though there was much to please him, some of the attitudes he found were not so congenial. He was particularly irritated by the insistent assumption of many Americans, both in and out of public life, that if he was unwilling to accept completely the American analysis of the world situation, he must be pro-Communist. In such company he would raise his guard and become distant and difficult.

Other things astonished Nehru, some of them quite casual and unimportant. One night at a dinner in New York City with a group of business leaders, someone, on the spur of the moment, said to him, "Mr. Prime Minister, do you realize how much money is represented at this table? I just added it up, and you are eating dinner with at least 20 billion dollars."

Nehru attached an extraordinary amount of significance to this remark. It fitted in so neatly with his own preconceptions about modern American culture that he frequently cited it as an example of our preoccupation with materialism. Whenever he did so in my presence, I would always reply that it was simply a lighthearted bit of dinner table small talk from which it was grossly unfair to draw such conclusions.

As was the case when he explained Indian policy to me, my effort was not to convince him that we were always right. Rather it was to assure him of the complete sincerity of our aims and objectives, and to give him an understanding of the political, economic and military analysis which, as we saw it, determined our decisions. In a discussion with Nehru, it does not do to try to cover up one's own mistakes, and I was always careful to admit ours quite frankly, before he had a chance to bring them up himself. For instance, I often deplored our failure to support the League of Nations after the First World War, and our slowness in the 1930's in recognizing the threat of Nazism and fascism to the peace of Europe. The long process of self-education about America which Nehru has undergone has left him, I think, convinced that, on the whole, America is striving for the kind of peaceful and productive world he himself would like to see.

What of the future of Nehru within India? When the American *Life* photographer, Margaret Bourke-White asked him what was now to be done in India, he replied, "That is the difference between the Indian and the Western mind. The Indian would not ask what he should *do*, but what he should *be*." But then he added, "I think that now in the new free India the time has come to ask ourselves the new question: 'What should we do?' "

For Nehru this is a specially pertinent question. Like other great leaders, Nehru has only a limited period when he can summon the wave of enthusiasm, which brought him to power, to the task of shaping the future. The political iron is still hot for him now.

The danger of ruthless action by Nehru is slim. Much more important is his quality which sees all around the problem, recognizes its difficulties and complexities, admits the possible validity of competing solutions and sometimes hesitates to act decisively. He himself wrote in 1946: "No longer can I function as I did in my younger days, as an arrow flying automatically to the target of my choice, ignoring all else but that target."

One of the most important weaknesses in the Nehru government is the inadequacy in land reform. The problem throughout Asia of meeting the age-old cry of the villagers for land of their own is discussed in detail in a later chapter. It is sufficient to say here that, despite the fact that land reform has been a long-standing plank in the Congress Party platform and that it is one of the single most critical issues for the success of Indian democracy, progress has been disappointingly slow. On such questions, it sometimes seemed to me Nehru's very dedication to the legal and constitutional principles of the West have prevented him from acting decisively to strengthen democracy at its roots.

Nehru is essentially a conservative, in the good sense of desiring continuity of law and order and the preservation of worth-while traditions. The terrible riots of partition, the murder of Gandhi, the corruption of people he trusted have left deep marks upon him. He began to question whether new struggles for quick reform were worth in achievement what they cost in pain and blood and violence.

He once asked the question that has made many men conservatives: "Was human nature so essentially bad that it would take ages of training, through suffering and misfortune, before it could behave reasonably and raise man above the creature of lust and violence and deceit that he now was? And meanwhile was every effort to change it radically in the present or the near future doomed to failure?"

A well-known American businessman who was visiting India said to me after a talk with the Prime Minister: "I came to India thinking that Nehru was a rip-snorting Marxist radical. Yet in some ways, I believe he is actually too conservative in his ideas of what needs to be done and the time that he has left to do it."

Nehru would perhaps not be happy to be described as a conservative in revolutionary Asia. Nevertheless I think that one of the important reasons for his reluctance to act decisively on some issues is his desire at almost any cost to avoid another descent into chaos, irrationality and bloodshed.

One cannot even make this fundamental point, however, without being brought up short by the complexity and paradoxes of the man. For instance in August, 1953, he appears to have acted boldly, if on the basis of pure expediency, in approving the sudden deposition and arrest of his old associate, Sheik Abdullah, Chief Minister of Kashmir state.

In one respect, at least, this view of Nehru as a conservative does not hold up. Just as he ignored his own safety in dealing with the mobs of the partition period, so he remains to this day oblivious to the dangers inherent in his position. Often I have seen him brush aside the police arrangements for his protection, and move off unexpectedly into a crowd at the sight of a familiar face. The people fall back to make way for him, and then promptly close in behind him. His bodyguards are left far behind, until finally some young policeman manages to push frantically through the mass to reach his side.

One occasion when Nehru always exposes himself freely is Holi, the ancient Indian holiday in early March which celebrates Spring. This holiday has a Halloween-like quality and every passerby is likely to have colored waters and powders thrown on him by crowds of laughing children. On such occasions the Bowles family returned from the streets dyed a hundred hues. Nehru has a genuine feeling for children and always invites large numbers to the gardens outside his house on holidays in which they have a special interest. But on Holi, he himself walks through the streets, while children put colored chalk on his face and spray him with colored water from head to foot.

This casual unconcern of Nehru has its political implications, for a number of fanatical groups in India, particularly the Communists, would stand to gain much if he were removed from the scene. The loss of Nehru could be catastrophic for India. With another decade of active and vigorous life after his sixty-fifth birthday in 1954, he could spell the difference between success and failure for Indian democracy.

Today the foremost leaders in the Congress party, in addition to Nehru and President Prasad, are Rajagopalachari in Madras, Morarji Desai in Bombay, Pant in Uttar Pradesh, B. C. Roy in Bengal and Shukla in Madhya Pradesh, whom the Communists describe as "Nehru's five war lords." These are able men but only Prasad and Rajagopalachari are really national figures, and their average age is seventy.

One of the most able members of the Congress party is Chintaman Deshmukh, the present Minister of Finance, who many observers believe is one of the most competent financial experts of his time. He is fifty years of age, with a penetrating analytical mind, rare courage, and growing prestige within the Congress party and the nation.

His background in the Civil Service under the British, for which he was knighted, is a political handicap in a nation where almost every other leader has served at least one term in a British prison. Nevertheless, Deshmukh is one of the most important figures in the central government, and is largely responsible for all economic matters.

In the democratic opposition outside the Congress party, the Praja Socialists have a nationally respected leader in Jayaprakash Narayan. He was educated in the United States, and served with Nehru as one of the young and brilliant leaders of the Congress party during the fight against the British. He was the chief hero of the 1942 struggle, and left Congress only in 1948 when he became convinced that conservative interests within the party were blocking full-scale land reform. He is a remarkably competent man, of great charm.

Narayan and his party are determinedly anti-Communist, and indeed seemed to me often more aware of the world Communist danger than many of the more conservative Congress party members. Although the Socialists still advocate nationalization of some big industries, they have moved a long way toward the Gandhian concept of a decentralized economy of village industries.

This position is not popular among many Indian leaders who want large-scale industrialization in a hurry. But Jayaprakash Narayan's ability and personality, plus his devotion to Gandhism, as manifested by a twenty-one-day self-purifying fast in 1952, the first such fast by a major political leader since Gandhi's death, is steadily increasing his popularity among the people.

Many believe that Nehru wants Narayan to be his successor. In any case, in the spring of 1953, just before I left India, the Prime Minister worked hard to bring the Praja Socialists into a coalition government. Probably he hoped this would add support to the younger and more progressive element in the Congress party itself.

The Socialists presented a fourteen-point minimum program as the basis for any such coalition. It included proposals for the nationalization of banking, insurance and mining. But these were not as important to the Socialists as their first point, a constitutional change to permit sweeping land reforms with only small compensation for the large land owners.

Nehru could not accept these fourteen points, and eventually the talks were suspended. Narayan promised to continue to meet with Nehru, whose offer he called "a statesmanlike step . . . a bold and unusual one because the Congress party stood in no need of a coalition either at the Center or in most of the states." Both agreed that they had much in common, and that "a joint effort to build a new India" was desired by the people.

This then is Jawaharlal Nehru. He is loved by the Indian people for his courage and devotion to their future, and they have elected his government to power because of that. He knows well, and indeed often says, that neither he nor his party can live long on the capital of their past achievements.

For those in the West who believe deeply that political stability and democratic progress in Asia are essential to the peace of the world, I can think of no better path to an understanding of the new free Asia than an effort at sympathetic understanding of the mind and heart of Jawaharlal Nehru.

10. The Zigzags of Indian Communism

FOUR OR FIVE hundred students were furiously chanting something in Bengali, ending in "Bo-less," when I arrived at the University of Calcutta to speak. I walked over to see what was happening.

"What are you shouting?" I asked one of the boys who was waving his fist in unison with the others like a cheer leader. "We are saying, 'Go home, Bo-less' to the war-mongering American Ambassador who is trying to drag us into the Anglo-American imperialist camp," he replied, and again picked up the refrain.

Inside I found several thousand students, two dozen or more faculty members, and the president of the University, who in India usually carries the title of Vice-Chancellor, the Governor or Chief Minister of the state acting in the somewhat honorary capacity of Chancellor.

After greeting me the Vice-Chancellor rather nervously said that he could not allow the Communist-led students into the meeting because clearly they only wanted to start a riot. I said I thought they had a right to hear what I had to say, whether they opposed me or not, and after some discussion he agreed to admit them. In they came, looking rather fierce, with anti-American placards on big sticks which they waved ominously.

For forty minutes I talked to the tightly packed auditorium about three phases of American history: first, the struggle for full political democracy from Jefferson and Lincoln to the fight for woman suffrage and the continuing one against racial discrimination; second, our efforts to secure a broader share of economic justice, from Jackson to the two Roosevelts; and third, our progress toward international co-operation, from the old isolationism through Woodrow Wilson to the United Nations.

When I sat down the Communist delegation remained silent, but the rest of the audience applauded generously. I then turned to the Chairman of the meeting, a history professor at the University, and said that I was ready for the question period.

"That is impossible," he said. Again he predicted a riot, but encouraged by the friendly response of most of the audience I insisted on an open question period.

Immediately the Communist contingent went into action. One student with a banner jumped up, shouted a question, and before I could begin to answer he started bellowing the answer he thought an American "imperialist" should give.

At first I waited patiently until he was through, but by then another had started screaming a new question, again with his own self-provided answer. Finally I decided that with all the advantage of a big voice and a microphone, I might as well join the fray.

By turning their questions around and copying their technique it was easy to get the rest of the audience laughing. When they kept asking me why Communist China was not allowed in the United Nations, I asked them why the Soviet Union had vetoed the admission of Japan, Nepal and Ceylon, all good friends of India, and I gave my own uncomplimentary explanation, as they had done.

Soon I found that a firm, factual, good-humored, reasonable answer was appreciated by most of the students, although the Communists kept things fairly uproarious for nearly three hours. Afterward arguments among the audience led to street fights.

The memory of the flashing, bitter, hating eyes of those young Communists, who seemed drained of human decency and packed with venom, remains with me even now. This experience was my first encounter anywhere with militant communism, and it was a fitting introduction to the Indian Communist party.

Most of the fifty to one hundred thousand Indian Communists are young, and most of them are not poor, illiterate peasants, but frustrated, educated city folks. And as I came to see the party in action I found that its main features are hate, fanaticism and discipline, which were all so vividly portrayed at that fracas in Calcutta.

Of course, most Communists, at least at the beginning, must genuinely believe that communism is the way to rid mankind of its social ills. But as Gandhi said "their remedy is worse than the disease." Soon the idealistic young convert, who desires to "serve" his people, either quits in disillusionment or is caught up in the web of hate, fanaticism and discipline which are the organizing principles of the party.

Stalin once said, "It is impossible to conquer an enemy without having learned to hate him with all the might of one's soul." And that is precisely what Indian Communists have learned to do, whether against the "Hitlerite dogs of Wall Street" or the "fascistic Indian plutocrats." Their avowed purpose is to help "downtrodden peasants . . . demand a tooth for a tooth."

Fanaticism, too, is a powerful force. Into an empty, unemployed life, recently cut loose from age-old cultural and religious systems, communism comes like a mighty purpose: It is a complete ideology, which purports to answer every question. It demands total service, sacrifice and secrecy. For the rigid concepts of caste and family restrictions communism substitutes an entire new pattern of existence with equally rigid loyalties, with clear-cut day-to-day objectives and with ready-made enemies marked for extinction.

Western concepts, long taught in Indian universities and in other nations in the East, have done much to undermine the old way, and in its place, instead of an easily understood formula for existence they offer this infinitely more complex concept of individualism, the right to speak one's own mind and to act according to one's own judgment as long as there is no interference with the rights of others.

Many young Indians, suddenly breaking loose from caste and family find in this new individualism only uncertainties, frustrations and a never-ending series of decisions for which there are no ready-made guide posts. They become bewildered, powerless to act, and often easy targets for the Communist agent.

Once caught up in communism they find it difficult to break away. Three or four years ago a young Russian aviator flew into Western Germany seeking freedom from Soviet rule. He was invited to the United States, greeted warmly, entertained and offered a series of jobs and other opportunities.

But he had grown up in the tight pattern of Communist conformity and he felt suddenly strange and alone. Eventually his bewilderment became overpowering, and knowing full well that a firing squad might be waiting for him behind the Iron Curtain he asked to be returned to Russia where at least life was clear and familiar.

The fanatical discipline of the Communists is a formidable force.

"I, too, am willing to struggle on behalf of the peasants and to go to jail against injustice," said an anti-Communist member of one of the democratic parties. "But I am not willing to look at everything, even at art and at family life, from a party viewpoint. I am not willing to spend every waking moment working for my party. I like to play with my little boy too." And he expressed the fear that tolerant believers in democracy such as he, who stopped to enjoy daily living, would over the years be no match for the fanatic Communists, who were consumed by their conspiracy.

Because the Communist considers himself in a state of war with society in every non-Communist land until the "dictatorship of the proletariat" has been everywhere established, he joins the party as if joining an army, to obey and to fight for the duration of the "world revolution."

Lenin's essential organizational principle is "democratic centralism," under which the local Communist and his cell of three or more comrades participate in deliberation when there is time for it, but at all times accept the decisions of the central command which fits each move into a world-wide picture. At the center of that picture is the Soviet Union which, in Vyshinsky's words, as "the motherland of the world proletariat" is the "sole criterion for a Communist."

The national affairs of the Indian Communist party are in the hands of a Central Committee, a Political Bureau and a Secretariat, but it is the Kremlin in faraway Moscow which co-ordinates and determines the global strategy. With this theory and kind of organization, the dedicated Communist becomes able to adjust himself to overnight switches in the party line which seem confusing or amusing to the public. "The strictest loyalty to the ideas of communism," Lenin warned, "must be combined with the ability to make all necessary compromises, to 'tack,' to make agreements, zigzags, retreats, and so on, in order to accelerate the coming into power of the Communists."

Certainly the history of the Indian Communists is an amazing story of zigzags.

• • •

Like so many things in present-day India, communism came from Britain. In the early 1920's several English Communists were sent to organize an Indian party. They came with the usual European Marxist concept of the city factory workers as the key to revolution, and ridiculed Gandhi's organization of villagers.

They made enough progress organizing the labor unions for the British imperial government to arrest them and a number of trade union leaders in 1929 and hold them for the long drawn-out Meerut Conspiracy Trial. The real birth of an all-India party is said to have come during the several years these leaders were planning together in the Meerut Detention Camp.

Although the party was outlawed in 1933, it made some headway among the workers. During the United Front days of the mid-1930's Communists were instructed to join the Congress party and the Socialist section in the Congress, while continuing their opposition to the tactics and village emphasis of Gandhi, whom they called "reactionary."

Jayaprakash Narayan had become a Communist in the United States during the depression, but on his return to India, finding the party wedded to Moscow and blind to Indian realities, he had abandoned the Communist faith, enlisted with Gandhi and organized the Congress Socialists. When the Communists sought to join the Socialists in 1937 following Moscow's directive to Communist parties everywhere to attempt to establish "united fronts," he accepted them in an experimental attempt to woo them away from Soviet domination.

Instead, the Communists secretly infiltrated his own organization, took over most of the Socialist party in South India, and by their deception were able to do great damage before they were expelled. "We were badly burned," a veteran Socialist told me, explaining why he and his associates are now among the most confirmed anti-Communists in India.

What did more than anything else to cause the gulf between the Communists on the one side and the Congress and Socialist leaders on the other, a gulf, in my opinion, which can never be closed, was the Communist about-face in World War II.

In 1939 and 1940 the Communists called it an "imperialist war" and opposed the offer of Congress to support the British against the Nazis if given independence. Then suddenly on June 21, 1941, the Nazi panzer divisions invaded Russia and the very next morning the self-same Communists were fanatically demanding all-out, unconditional support to Britain in what had become overnight a "people's war."

"While Gandhi was leading us into the Quit India campaign against the British, the Communists were making love to our opponents," a Congress leader told me bitterly. Nehru describes how the Communists on repeated occasions broke up strikes which the Congress had called as part of the struggle for independence.

All the national democratic leaders who said they would oppose the Germans and Japanese only as citizens of a free India crowded the Viceroy's jails, while the Communists, whose only criterion was the interest of the Soviet Union, co-operated with the British and won the Viceroy's blessings. Legalized as a party by the British in order to promote the war effort, the Communists were able to take over the All-India Trade Union Congress and the All-India Student Federation, and to increase party membership from about six thousand to over fifty thousand.

When the Congress leaders were released from prison after the war they promptly launched an all-out campaign to clean the Communists out of the labor movement. Nehru angrily scoffed that "the Communist party is completely divorced from, and is ignorant of, the national traditions that fill the minds of the people." This drive was successful in the majority of cases but a hard core managed to survive.

For a time the Communists laid low. But soon Soviet policy shifted to the Cold War offensive, the Cominform was organized as a world revolutionary force, and new directives for militant action began to reach India and other South Asian countries. In 1948 the so-called "moderate" Communist leader, P. C. Joshi, was removed, for much the same reason and in much the same way as Earl Browder was dismissed in the American party.

Adopting this new "line" in an official convention, the Indian party accused Joshi of "right deviationism," stated that his "estimate of Nehru is anti-Marxist and serves to tie down the masses to the bourgeois leadership" and embarked on a widespread campaign of violence under a new leader, Ranadive. In approved Communist fashion, Joshi gave an hour-long speech of self-accusation, confessing his "reformist" errors and his "backsliding and retreat."

Simultaneously with this shift in Indian leadership and tactics

Communist violence flared up throughout all of Southeast Asia, led in many countries by wartime leaders of guerrilla resistance to the Japanese.

In the Philippines the Communist-led Huks redoubled their efforts to overturn the newly independent nation.

In Indo-China the ex-guerrilla leader, Ho Chi Minh, launched an all-out war against the French with full Communist support.

In Burma the Communists attacked the new government which already had its back to the wall in a struggle against the Karens of southeastern Burma, who were demanding independence.

In Indonesia the army of the new republican government, preparing for a final struggle against Dutch troops, was suddenly and treacherously attacked by thousands of well-organized and well-armed Communists.

In British-held Malaya the slumbering guerrilla fighting exploded into widespread murders of planters and government officials, destruction of rubber trees, and anarchy.

India was no exception to this new Moscow-directed outburst of Asian civil war. Violent strikes, sabotage, riots and guerrilla warfare occurred in the centers of Communist strength in Bengal, parts of Maharashtra and the Punjab, central Tamilnad, Malabar and Andhra. Ranadive's Communist program concentrated on inflaming the city "proletariat," a strategy described by his opponents as the "acid-bomb-in-city" phase. Young Communists were ordered to throw homemade acid bombs into police stations or in the midst of crowds, hoping that riots would ensue.

Nehru announced that he had in his possession Communist instructions "containing open incitement to murder, violence and sabotage." In several provinces the party was banned, thousands of agitators were arrested, and many Communist plots were nipped in the bud.

Because of their violent extremism the Communists during this period lost control over many of their unions to the Congress and Socialist labor organizations. Many disillusioned intellectuals resigned from the party or were expelled for criticizing Ranadive. By the end of 1949 Communist organization was shattered everywhere and morale was low except in the Telegu-speaking areas of North Madras and of South Hyderabad, known as Andhra.

There a new kind of Communist leadership with a new kind of

strategy under Rajeshwar Rao and Narayan Reddy had succeeded in digging deep roots. Rather than the "acid-bomb-in-city" approach, based on factory workers, the Andhra party believed in the "revolver-in-village" strategy of Mao Tse-tung. As in China it had been the agrarian revolution on which the Communists rode to power, so, the Andhra Communists argued, in India the villagers must become the base of the revolution.

"Land to the tiller" had become the slogan of the Andhra party, and for the first time Indian Communists began to find themselves with a mass following. The Telegu-speaking areas of Hyderabad, where they first put into effect their new techniques, fitted Lenin's prescription for the place to start a revolution: "the weakest link" of the old order.

If land ownership is shockingly unjust in much of India, it was incredibly worse in the state of Hyderabad. The ex-ruler himself, known as the Nizam, owned some five million acres, roughly equal to our state of New Jersey, on which more than a million poverty-stricken serfs earned for him millions of dollars every year.

Other rich landlords owned 100,000 acres or more. A feudal structure of no more than a thousand families controlled almost all the wealth of Hyderabad. The peasants lived under inhuman conditions, born into debt and paying most of their crops in rent.

It was in this explosive economic and political soft spot that the Communists struck in 1948, while the Nizam, a Muslim, was still trying to establish the independence of his state from the new Indian Republic, and most of the people, who were Hindus, were opposing him. Since 1944 the Communists had conducted ever-increasing peasant protests in the area, but this time the struggle broke into bitter violent rebellion.

Into the villages in armed bands went the young Communist intellectuals. They assembled the land-hungry peasants and announced that henceforth the land was theirs, that no rent should be paid to the landlords, that all debts were erased, that the landless families should be given the land of the rich and that the villages should resist all efforts to re-establish the old order.

In over a thousand villages of the Telingana district among a million or more people, this happened, and the landlords and officials of the Nizam who did not flee were murdered. At this point the Indian army crossed the border, the Nizam agreed that the state of Hyderabad would become part of the Indian Union, and the Indian army moved against the Communists in Telingana.

"The armed revolt can continue only through guerrilla tactics," the Communist circulars now stated. "When the police visit the villages go quietly and throw hand bombs. Enemies will be finished when they explode." Villagers were ordered to kill anyone who took their newly distributed land, and to "hide the party leaders and guerrilla members very secretly."

Despite firm Indian army occupation, newly built roads which for the first time permitted rapid patrolling by armored cars, concentration camps filled with captured Communists, police outposts every few miles and in some places very ruthless suppression, guerrilla fighting continued spasmodically until the Communists themselves changed their program of violence two years later.

Even under military law over five hundred returning landlords or government officials were murdered in nine months. Actually, few landlords have tried to return, and the Indian government finally forced the Nizam to part with most of his land which was then distributed among the former tenants. Only in the last year of my stay in India, when the Communists themselves had switched their tactics to "peace and collaboration," was it safe for a government supporter to travel through this strife-torn district.

The lessons learned from this revolutionary upheaval are far reaching. "Do you really know what guerrilla warfare is like?" an Indian army officer asked me. "I can understand why the French have not won in Indo-China," he said. "We could not *completely* win even in that one section of Hyderabad, and we were Indians, not white foreigners."

He described how difficult it was to find a Communist leader who dressed and lived like the other peasants during the day. At night the Red bands would dig up their arms and strike against an isolated outpost. Once a Communist leader was detected when a suspicious army patrol caught him doing an unusual thing in a village: reading a book.

The Hyderabad Communists skillfully operated under Mao Tse-tung's description of guerrilla tactics: they were the fish, the villagers were the sea; when the sea is warm and friendly the fish can multiply and swim where they wish.

In villages where people were given their own land for the first time the sea was ready to receive them. Between 1923 and 1927 Mao Tse-tung in China had watched the city-oriented policy laid down by Borodin's mission from Moscow with profound skepticism. Sun Yat-sen, although anti-communist, had thought it possible to borrow Communist techniques to bolster his Kuomintang party organization and had invited Lenin to send Borodin to China. But Borodin failed, not only in his efforts to capture the Kuomintang by subversion, but also in his doctrinaire attempt to prepare a revolution by organizing workers in the cities.

Mao concluded that the only successful road for an Asian revolution was through the villages, where the food was produced, where the bulk of the people lived, where the injustices were greatest and where the ultimate power rested. However, his early refusal to accept the dogma of Moscow laid down by Borodin placed him temporarily in disrepute, and similarly the Hyderabad Communist followers of Rajeshwar Rao soon found themselves in disagreement with their national party leaders.

They argued persuasively that Ranadive's tactics of city worker agitation were too narrow and instead proposed Mao's broad-based, rural, "land for the tiller" program, which had won over even many of the middle-sized Chinese farmers. For daring to disagree, they were denounced by the central leadership which refused to accept Mao as a prophet. "The Communist party of India has accepted Marx, Engels, Lenin and Stalin as the authoritative sources of Marxism," said an official letter published in the party organ in June, 1949. "It has not discovered new sources of Marxism beyond these."

In China Mao came out on top only because his village-to-village strategy succeeded, while the Kremlin's earlier effort failed. But in India the Hyderabad Communists came to the top primarily because the Kremlin directed it.

On January 27, 1950, the official Cominform journal, *For Lasting Peace, For a People's Democracy*, published in Bucharest, abruptly changed its views about Mao, praised the victory of the Chinese Communists and advised Asian Communists to follow the path blazed by Mao.

"The task of the Indian Communists," the editorial specifically stated, "drawing on the experience of the national liberation movement in China and other countries, is, naturally, to strengthen the alliance of the working class with all the peasantry, to fight for the introduction of the urgently needed agrarian reform. . . ."

Obediently the Indian Communist party reversed itself and accused Ranadive of "Trotskyite-Titoist" mistakes and "left adventurism." On June 8, 1950, it was reported that the Cominform had ordered Ranadive to resign, and on July 19 party headquarters announced that Rajeshwar Rao of Hyderabad was the new General Secretary of the Indian Communist party. A policy statement proclaimed that "the path followed by China . . . is the only correct path before the Indian people."

For a time guerrilla struggle was continued in Hyderabad and was attempted on a modified scale in parts of the states of PEPSU, Assam and Tripura. But the New India was already too strong for such a strategy to succeed. These tactics led many Indians to agree with the conclusion of Nehru: "Communists in South Asia have, firstly, by their extreme violence and terrorist methods, and secondly, by going against one of the dominant urges of these countries, that is, nationalism, performed a counter-revolutionary act."

While Nehru repeated that "as a government which tries to respect civil liberties, India was prepared to allow any kind of discussion or propagation of the philosophy of Communism, peacefully," he firmly carried out his threat that "if communism, or any other ism, becomes violent, then any state has to suppress it."

When it became clear that both the "acid-bomb-in-city" and "revolver-in-village" approaches had failed to destroy the Nehru government the Communists tried a new stratagem. With the national and state elections approaching, old-time Communist leader Dange in Bombay and Ajoy Ghosh of the Punjab took over the leadership with a policy of "peace for the time being."

The new policy had the solid support of Moscow. "As long as you are unable to disperse the bourgeois parliament and every other type of reactionary institution, you *must* work inside them," Lenin had written. Thus in 1951, on the eve of the election, the Indian Communists adopted a course of "constitutionalism" and "United Front," in order to obey the command of Lenin that Communists should seek election to parliament "to *prove* to the backward masses why such parliaments deserve to be dispersed."

In this intricate story of foreign direction of an Indian party, there is more to be said than that Indian Communists dance to the

Kremlin's tune. Not only do they listen to Moscow for instructions but they look to Russia and China for substantial assistance of many kinds.

In Communist bookstalls throughout the country, and in general bookstores, I saw the vast quantity of cheap literature, printed in the Soviet Union, which supplies the intellectual training for an Indian Communist. "Not one of the books we studied to become party members was written by an Indian or published in India," an ex-Communist student once told me.

Marx, Engels, Lenin, Stalin, Gorky, some Russians of whom I had never heard, some British Communists, books by all these are widely used, particularly Lenin, but no basic works by Indian Communists. I have a list of forty-eight books, printed by the Foreign Languages Publishing House in Moscow, which were found on sale in India at fantastically cheap prices. Lenin's *Marxism*, 580 pages cloth bound, sold for about forty cents; a 176-page book by Stalin, paper bound, sold for less than five cents.

"Buy enough of the Communist literature in India and you will eventually break the Soviet budget," was a common joke among anti-communists. But in fact, it is no joking matter. This literature is used by Moscow, not only for propaganda purposes, but to subsidize the Indian Communist party itself. The literature is sent free by the Russian government and the proceeds from its sale go directly into the treasury of the Indian party. This provides the largest single source of party funds.

In 1952 the Indian government attempted to cut off this flow of Soviet money which it knew was largely financing the Communist effort to undermine the Indian democracy. Although blocked by Indian law from barring this Soviet-subsidized literature from private newsstands it was able to prohibit its sale on government property throughout India, which included the thousands of railway newsstands.

For years Moscow has also been a center for training future Indian party leaders. To the Lenin Institute in Moscow many promising young Indian radicals have been sent, to return dedicated Communists. Happily, the totalitarian atmosphere sometimes repels sensitive Indians who stay long enough to see through the façade. Still others are eliminated in periodic purges.

India's most famous early Communist, M. N. Roy, who became

an officer of the Communist International and its representative in China as a member of the Borodin Mission during the 1920's, got caught in the web of purges, was expelled as a "Trotskyite" and barely escaped with his life. Roy now lives in Dehra Dun, in North India, writing articles which seek to show India the brutal results of communism which he saw firsthand in China and Russia.

If the despotic character of the Russian regime is becoming better known, the Communists, as we have seen, now have a new attraction, with far greater Asian appeal in the "New China."

"In India the Communists made nothing but mistakes," said an anti-Communist political leader, "but their smashing victory in China gave them higher morale than those of us with the right democratic answers." He complained that the Communist has "two shrines of worship," China and the Soviet Union, while the Indian democrat has only his hopes for his own country and so far little to show. "I know the Communist is offering false gods," he said, "but how can we convince people of that when they want so desperately to believe in something?"

Yet even with considerable outside aid and direction, the test of Indian communism will probably come in its day-to-day operation on the Indian scene. From former Communists and from direct intensive study and observation I began to get an increasingly full picture of how the party goes about its work.

For instance, in 1952 the Communists picked the state of PEPSU (Patiala and East Punjab States Union) as an area for concentrated organizing. Formerly ruled by princes, this section had no tradition of democratic struggle, and law and order had not yet been firmly established.

First the Communists focused on the Sikhs, whose community had been devastated by the partition struggle and whose bitterness is still smoldering. They threw their support behind demands by the extreme Sikh communal organization, Akali Dal, for a separate Punjabi-speaking province.

"For their base they chose the village of Kishangarh," a local government observer told me. There the Sikhs were in a majority, and the Communists had been active off and on since 1926. The organizer assigned to the village formed a branch of the Communist Peasant Movement, the *Kisan Sabha*, to start a struggle against the *Bisawadars*, or the local landlords.

The Communist representative promised that not only would the people own the land they till, when the Communists came to power, but that prices would come down and that they would be able to buy two dhotis for the price of one, the observer explained. The most ardent converts came from unemployed young men who were psychologically suffering from being useless. The party work gave them a new, important function in the village.

"When more than fifty villagers had paid the membership fee of one anna (two cents) a year, the elders and leaders of the community were approached and most of them won over," he continued. Then a big conference was called, with Communist speakers from New Delhi and other centers, and it was resolved to stop paying rent to the landlords.

"The Communist organizer knew this move would invite repression," my observer friend continued. "He wanted it and welcomed it when it came. Such a repression makes the government unpopular and creates heroes of those who go to jail and suffer on behalf of the peasants." This is particularly true in India when so many thousands of leaders suffered prison sentences to help win independence from the British.

Once arrests began, other Communist organizers started a campaign to release the prisoners, which naturally the families and friends supported. Inside the jail, Communist leaders promptly set up indoctrination courses for the nonparty inmates whom they found there. On release they would be ready with new and apparently reasonable demands, such as for the cancellation of excessive debts to money lenders, or the building of a village school and health dispensary by the government.

"Their effort is to prove that they are the most active party, and that they alone are interested in the people's problems," my friend said. "When any democratic party tries to work in the village the Communists go to any length to discredit it, with unbelieveably vile lies when it is necessary."

. . .

Throughout India it is the practice of Communists to ally themselves with antisocial elements which can aid in the creation of chaos and lawlessness.

Near Kishangarh lived some of what are called the "Criminal Tribes," whose profession for many generations was thieving or other law-breaking activities. Therefore, when the organizer at Kishangarh village discovered that the current complaint of the Criminal Tribes was the government campaign against their country-made alcoholic beverages, he immediately went to them with the promise that if they helped to overthrow the government, the Communists would permit them to produce as much liquor as they liked.

"Do not underestimate the cultural activities of the party," another sophisticated Indian once said to me. The Communist "People's Theater," consisting of wandering actors, who sing simple new revolutionary texts to the old folk tunes, and put on skits portraying the Russian and Chinese revolutions, moves from village to village with great effectiveness. Thirsty for a change in the monotony of daily life, the peasants attend the performances in large numbers and quickly pick up some of the catchy refrains.

In South India and other areas where untouchability and other caste prejudices are particularly strong, the Communists make a point of brushing aside all restrictions. They go from house to house casually asking for water from outcastes. "I cannot give you water. I am an untouchable," the peasant will usually say. "There are no untouchables for Communists, you are my comrade," the organizer will explain.

Of course, many untouchables and low-castes still willingly accept their status as the inevitable result of their present incarnation. To break the hold of Hinduism on this orthodox group, the Communists use the Marxian argument that "religion is the opiate of the people."

With factory workers the Communists apply equivalent techniques. In the cities and towns even the many party members from wealthy families adopt as their dress the khaki shorts and undershirt of the unskilled laborer. "It is the party of the short pants," said an Indian who lived in a miserable slum. There is no doubt that the Communists understand the worker's psychology.

Today the Congress and Socialist parties as well as the Communist all have their own labor unions, most of which are affiliated with one of the political parties. Even the leaders of the local unions are usually supplied from the ranks of educated party workers.

Now that the Communists again, for the time being at least, are on a less violent tack, they are trying desperately to regain their old labor leadership. They are energetically following Lenin's advice to "resort to all sorts of stratagems, maneuvers, illegal methods, evasions and subterfuges, only so as to get into the trade unions, to remain in them and to carry on Communist work within them at all costs."

One stratagem, not unusual in labor history, which they have used successfully when they are in danger of being defeated by a rival union, is to make a deal with the employer. "If you will continue to recognize us and negotiate with us," they say to the manufacturer, "we will promise not to ask for a raise in wages during the next two years."

Thus the manufacturer is relieved of labor troubles and the Communists gain time to further strengthen their organization. Such nefarious arrangements have occasionally been exposed. In one area the resulting anti-Communist bitterness actually led to the assassination of several Communist organizers.

A more common problem is the political strike called to dramatize some political demand. In other cases when a Congress union asks for a raise from, say, four to five rupees a day, a 25 per cent increase (eighty cents to a dollar), the Communist union may promptly demand ten or even fifteen rupees. The Communist organizer knows that the employer cannot grant the request, and that the strike may be crushed; but by making such demands he appears to be the only militant champion of the workers.

The Communists who organize these unions and who go into the villages are drawn largely from the students and young teachers in the universities. The vigorous, sensationalist Communist party press, particularly *Crossroads*, the official party organ, and *Blitz*, the unofficial but more effective party mouthpiece, reaches a wide audience. All members are required to peddle the party literature, which includes the full Marxist-Lenin-Stalinist library and is avidly read on university campuses. Study groups are organized for those who show interest. And above all young intellectuals are caught in the network of party fronts, the All-India Students Federation, All-India Peace Congress, Progressive Writers Association, India-China Friendship Association, Indo-Soviet Cultural Society.

"They seem ever to seek devious ways for catching fish," commented Chief Minister Rajagopalachari of Madras. "Why are they so shy of daylight?" he asked.

The explanation is probably clear enough. Young Indian intellectuals are idealists and to win them the Communists must appear to champion idealistic causes rather than openly present themselves as revolutionary agents of a foreign nation and a world party committed to violence and dictatorship.

Thus it is the duty of every Communist to work in the various mass front organizations under strict party discipline. When the nonpolitical institutions do not suffice, the Communists hold their own "peace congresses" or start a petition campaign to ban atomic weapons.

In their student front they carry out very effective "relief work" for needy people, such as the supply of costly textbooks, and campaign for lower tuition fees. For frustrated, low-paid teachers who desire recognition and an audience for their talents they offer a place on the program of pro-Communist conferences.

"The Communists in India and most other Asian countries are a party of rich men's sons," a shrewd Indian said. Communist leaders come largely from the upper classes and upper castes, and a great many of the party members are well-to-do young people whose conscience is bothering them in the midst of poverty, and whose desire is to do something to help the misery of people all around them.

Others are from middle or lower class families for whom job prospects are dim and to whom communism is painted as a rosy society of complete equality and full employment. And many converts are girls, who wish to escape the traditional restrictions on their sex. In the university coffee houses these young people talk and talk, and many finally come to communism.

Probably the Communists have a higher proportion of female members than any other party. Perhaps the total commitment to the party and its policies makes it easier for both men and women to break out of the old habits, but in any case the Communists not only preach equality for women but send their women members out on all kinds of tough organizing missions.

"The Communists are evil because they teach our girls to ride bicycles through the countryside," an old villager in Bengal told me. I have not seen their bicycle brigades, but I will never forget the thousands of fanatic young girls I have seen marching in Communist processions, with fire in their eyes and bitter slogans on their lips.

Western visitors to India and other Asian countries find the situation further confused by the large number of anti-Communist students who still consider themselves Marxists.

"India is a country of Marxists," an outspoken pro-American student told me in Trivandrum. He explained that the background of most intellectuals in India was Marxist. "It just happens," he said with assurance, "that Marx was not only the greatest economic thinker of the last century but was the one who first analyzed the process of economic development, and his theories are relevant to a country in need of an accumulation of capital. Unfortunately, Lenin picked up some of those theories, gave them his own twist, put an army and a revolutionary movement behind them, and now the world is plagued with the Communist party."

The widespread assumption of Marxism among the intellectuals makes it an easier step to slip into Communist vocabulary, fellow traveling in the Communist fronts and finally into the party itself. Doubts remain, of course, and occasionally come to the surface. One troubled young leader of an important Communist front, who was getting ever deeper into party activity, had two questions on his mind which he asked a visiting young American during a long, private and exceedingly candid conversation. What did he actually know about the purges and confessions of Communist leaders and is there really no free movement and communication inside the Soviet Union?

However, he made it clear that he would not fully trust the information of an American whom he assumed to be biased. "And even if Russian communism had been corrupted," the young man contended, "Asian communism would be different."

. . .

Whatever happens in China, the immediate question now is whether India will, as the Communists predict, follow the path of China. An objective picture of Indian communism shows a party with powerful potential, but on the other side of the ledger are certain other considerations necessary for even a balanced guess on whether the Communists will ever win India.

So far, Communists have succeeded in coming to power only

under two conditions: either through an invasion, or threat of invasion by the Red army, as in Eastern Europe; or through the genius of an indigenous master revolutionary who finds himself in a society ripe for armed rebellion, such as Lenin in Russia, Mao in China and to some extent Tito in Yugoslavia. Fortunately, in my opinion, neither of these conditions now exists in India although the situation could change sharply within a few years.

Although the Chinese invasion of Tibet caused considerable alarm in New Delhi, the fact remains that the Himalayas present a mammoth barrier to armed attack, and behind the Himalayas for a thousand miles stretches a vast barren plateau with an average height of twelve thousand feet. The twenty thousand or so Chinese troops now in Tibet are having difficulty even supplying themselves. Some of their food actually has to be sent by sea to Calcutta and then up through the mountain passes.

Indian Communists are busily trying to organize units in the border areas, and may thus have a direct route for smuggled arms and money from China, and Chinese Communist agents are often moving in and out. But the conquest of India by a Red army of Russians or Chinese seems most unlikely from the north. The Tibetan route is almost impassable for any large-scale invasion, and at present the superbly trained Indian army appears able to hold its own against any intruder from this direction.

If Communist China should invade Southeast Asia through Burma this situation would change drastically. A Chinese army in Burma or Indo-China would bring heavy pressures to bear on Thailand, spread chaos and fear throughout Indonesia and Malaya and put a strong Chinese military threat on the long eastern boundary of India.

Is there an Indian Lenin or Mao on the horizon? No one can say that there is not, but no Indian Communist who has yet hit the public eye seems able to master the materials of Indian social change. The whole history of the party is a series of major mistakes and somersaults.

While Mao, from the earliest days, threw himself into the forefront of the nationalist struggle, Indian Communists have still to live down their days of collaboration with the British against the independence movement. For all its efficiency as a rigid paramilitary organization, under a world command, the Communist party is at present so dominated by Moscow that the development of independent, indigenous strategists and leaders of the ability and authority of Lenin and Mao seems rather unlikely. Would Mao have ever undertaken the Long March or developed his system of peasant revolt if he had felt obliged to accept the Kremlin's dogma about the city proletariat? How much could Lenin himself have accomplished in Russia if he had been operating under strict directions from a Cominform made up of foreigners located in Calcutta?

It is reassuring to know that so far, at least, the Communist drive in Asia, with the single exception of China, has fallen far short of its objectives. In the years following the war when first the Philippines, and then India, Pakistan, Burma, Ceylon and Indonesia finally won their freedom from Western rule, the predictions of the pessimists were dire indeed.

"What could be an easier target for the Communists than 600 million largely illiterate, impoverished people, with no experience in self-government, with ineffective government services, split every which way by jealousies, ambitions and religious differences?" a British Member of Parliament suggested to me in the winter of 1948. "They may be free for the moment but they'll all be down the Communist drain within five years."

Those five years have come and gone and today these six nations not only remain free but the record shows that they have dealt far more effectively and decisively with their native Communists than have the two remaining major colonial powers of Asia, France and Britain, with all their wealth and power.

In the Philippines, the Communist-led Huks have been driven into the hills under the brave and imaginative campaign of Magsaysay. In the summer of 1952 Steb and I drove for 180 miles through sections of Luzon north of Manila, which had been largely under Huk control until Magsaysay began a new kind of campaign, combining reform and force, land to the peasants and an armed offensive against the Huk troops.

In free Indonesia the Communist rebellion in September of 1948 was crushed by the new Republican army which placed twenty thousand Communists in concentration camps and executed more than two hundred leaders.

In Burma the Communist party split into two violent factions, the "White Flag," which followed a Trotskyist line and the "Red Flag," which took directions from Moscow, both of which conducted an open revolt. Gradually the young democratic Burman government mustered its resources, trained a new army, carried out reforms which won the support of the people and, as I write this, has succeeded in breaking the backs not only of the Communist rebellions but of the Karens, while at the same time holding in check the Nationalist Chinese in the north.

In Japan there was no armed rebellion, but immediately following the war the Communist party was strong and effective. Since then the good sense of the Japanese people, aided by the land ownership reform, has driven it steadily back.

Today in Asia the only important Communist rebellions that continue are in the only two remaining nations still under Western domination, Malaya and Indo-China. Here the well-worn Communist cry, "Throw out the white imperialists!" has sufficient reality to convince millions of non-Communists, and thus give the Communists mass support.

For many years our newspapers have told us of the long drawn out struggles against communism waged by the Chinese Nationalists, by the French in Indo-China and by the British in Malaya. But America and the free world have almost completely ignored the victories over communism achieved by the free nations of Asia, which again and again and with few resources have acted vigorously and in time.

So far, at least, free Asia has prevented Communist revolution, Moscow model. What would happen if the label were changed to "made in Peking"?

No one can be certain, but I believe that if the Communist parties in India and other free Asian nations shifted their primary allegiance from Moscow to Peking their prospects would improve dangerously. Mao's guidance would seem less alien, there would probably be more flexibility and greater room for local decisions, and the directives, when they came, would probably be better fitted to Asian conditions.

There is but little question in my mind that Mao is already moving to stake out his claim. In Peking he has established an organization known as the "Peace Liaison Committee of the Asian and Pacific Regions." Will this new committee with its unhandy name be the Chinese counterpart of the Russian Cominform? Its Secretary General is Lin Ning-i, well known in the Chinese Communist movement and with many international connections. Its President, obviously an honorary position, is the famous Mme. Sun Yat-sen, wife of China's hero of the revolution against the Manchus, and sister of Mme. Chiang Kai-shek.

This committee may well be the vehicle through which Mao seeks to exert his control over the Communist parties of Asia. A growing minority of India's Communists would apparently like to make such a shift, but in the autumn of 1953 the majority in India still seems to look first to Moscow. However, with the obvious internal stresses and strains within Russia following Stalin's death, Mao's standing has been steadily moving up, and the emergence of Maoism as the dominant Communist power in Asia seems to me a strong possibility.

Whether this more formidable force might succeed where Stalinism failed may prove to be the most crucial question of our time. In the end the decision may rest, not so much on what the Communists have actually done, but on the estimates of millions of young Indians and other Asians of what they may succeed in doing in the future.

One night in Nagpur a young American-educated Indian engineer said to me earnestly, "You know I hate communism, and desperately want to see India not only remain a democracy, but become stronger and more effective as a free nation.

"But," he continued soberly, "I am only twenty-seven years old. I have a wife and two young children. I have thirty or more active years ahead of me, and I don't want to be a martyr and spend those years in a Communist salt mine. So I suppose that I will watch and see whether the Communists grow stronger. If someday it seems clear that they are going to win I will join them, not because I like dictatorships and dislike democracy but because there will be nothing else for me to do."

His eyes lit up as he added, "Perhaps if communism comes to India it may be different, more tolerant, less bitter, borrowing something from Gandhi. And who knows, perhaps a new kind of communism generated here might eventually soften and modify even the brutal ways of the Russians and Chinese?"

This naïve, anxious young man with his determination never

to grace a Communist salt mine or concentration camp, and his easy rationalization that Indian communism might somehow be different, speaks for more young Asians than I care to think, and his counterpart can be found in most of the countries of Europe.

The final answer over the years will come from within India herself, in her own capacity to draw on her rich past and to interpret the new restless demands of her people into a dynamic effort at national construction in which each individual has an opportunity to contribute his bit to the creation of a new democratic society.

As free Indians pick up the challenge it is clear that they have many advantages. Instead of thirty years of violence as in China the Indians had a generation of nonviolent civil resistance and constructive work. Instead of Japanese military occupation, the last phase of the British Empire stressed law and the parliamentary system.

Indian revolutionary efforts were dominated by the Congress party, democratically organized and with roots deep down in the villages as well as in the cities. Congress was strikingly honest, as political parties go, during the long struggle for independence. There has been some backsliding since, but the contrast with the corrupt bureaucracy of the Kuomintang is great. Above all, India had its own master revolutionary in Gandhi, who may not have achieved all he sought, but who left a heritage which cannot easily be forgotten.

When documents were shown Gandhi about the atrocities committed by the Communists in the Punjab, he said, "I know, I know so well their devastating activities. But remember . . . we can win by constructive methods, by emphasizing the power of love, of respect for individuals so disregarded by them, by working for real freedom, by serving God. Try to do it as I am doing."

When I arrived in India, Gandhi was gone, and the future seemed grim and uncertain. A responsible Congress party member said to me, "The Communists in India are operating with many disadvantages. Their leadership is poor. They cannot hide their foreign control. Their dogmatism and their hate do not come easily for the people of India. However," he frowned and went on, "unless we can prove to the peasant that democracy works in his interest, and give to our educated young people an opportunity to participate in the building of their country, the Communists may be handed a country they could never win."

With apprehension and some excitement I awaited the results of the world's greatest free election. Could it be, I wondered, that India would be the first country where communism could succeed through the voluntary vote of the people? In India that question among many others would be settled at the polls.

11. The World's Largest Free Election

IT IS TEMPTING for newcomers to Asia to say that Asians are not ready for Western-style democracy. Perhaps this is the place for me to confess that when I went to India in 1951 I more or less assumed, reluctantly, that the best solution for most Asian countries would be a benevolent dictatorship like that of Kemal Atatürk in Turkey.

Arriving a few months before India's first general election campaign, I was appalled at the prospect of a poll of 200 million eligible voters, most of whom were illiterate villagers. Few nations in Asia had held any kind of democratic elections. In 1937 and 1946 British India had successfully carried out two small-scale polls with various restrictions on the franchise which limited it to about 10 per cent of the people. But what would happen with universal suffrage on the largest scale ever attempted anywhere in the world? What kind of parliament would result?

Thus, while admiring the courage of the Nehru government in conducting such an experiment, and appreciating its dedication to democracy, I feared a fiasco. My doubts were not lessened by a survey I saw of public opinion in remote Indian villages. Only 50 per cent of the people had ever heard of the United States or Britain, and only 15 per cent of Russia or China. What meaning could political issues have, I wondered, with such lack of information.

My doubts were increased when in November, 1951, a mock vote was taken in Thippagondandhally in Mysore state, as a trial run of the mechanics of voting. The confusion was immense and a high percentage of the ballots had to be thrown out as invalid. "Unless some miracle happens between now and January, the General Elections are bound to be the biggest farce ever staged in the name of democracy anywhere in the world," *The Mail,* a daily Madras newspaper commented in November, 1951.

Yet all over India thousands of election officials persistently worked out the problems one by one, and patiently explained the system to the voters. The country was divided into 497 national parliamentary districts of some 750,000 people, or about 350,000 eligible voters for each representative to be elected, with much smaller districts for the twenty-two state assemblies which were then scheduled to be elected in India's twenty-nine states. Ninety thousand polling stations were established, 224,000 polling booths built, 620 million ballot papers printed.

To enable trained election officials to supervise the balloting in each district it was spread over one hundred days, with the heaviest voting in December and January. It was planned to start in the districts bordering the Himalayas where the early winter snows would later make the roads impassable, then in South India and lastly the great north central plains. By early February the final results would be completed.

Most ingenious of all was the method of voting by party symbols on different colored papers. An illiterate voter would enter an enclosed booth and in complete secrecy pick the symbol of the party he liked and put it in the box. To prevent double voting a mark in indelible ink was stamped on each voter's wrist which remained visible for several days.

Symbols which had religious, caste or superstitious connections were not permitted by the Election Commission. No party was allowed to make use of Gandhi's spinning wheel, or of the national flag. The Congress party chose two bullocks yoked together, the Socialists a spreading banyan tree, the K.M.P.P. a hut, the Hindu Mahasabha a horse and rider, the Jan Sang a lamp, the Communists a sickle around ears of corn.

Soon Delhi was deserted, as most of our friends in the government went back to their home districts to campaign for their own election to the House of the People. It was reassuring to watch some of the Western-educated, English-speaking, city-bred political leaders tramping through village areas, answering questions in their native language, seeking votes in the tiny huts of untouchables.

By the late fall of 1951 over 1,800 candidates were running for the 497 seats in the House of the People, and over 15,000 candidates were campaigning for the 3,283 seats in the twenty-two state assemblies. The small states of Bilaspur, Kutch, Manipur, Tripura and the Andamans voted for representatives in the national Parliament, but since they were still governed directly from Delhi, they did not yet have state assemblies.

As might be expected there was an oversupply of parties: seventy-seven different political organizations. At first I thought the tragedy of French political diffusion was being repeated. But attention quickly focused on half a dozen parties with an all-India basis, along with a few regional parties, and I realized that the large number of independents was a natural phenomenon to be expected before party lines crystallized.

It was largely a four-cornered race in which Nehru's Congress party was being challenged from three sides. There were the extremist religious and reactionary forces represented most successfully by the Jan Sang. There were the totalitarian Moscow-dominated Communists. And as a democratic opposition there were the Socialists, the Kisan Mazdoor Praja Party (Peasants', Workers', People's Party), or K.M.P.P., both of which had broken off from the Congress since independence.

It was a thrilling time to be in India. "All the big parties have already come to our village," a village woman from Bihar told me through a translator. "Congress, Socialists, Communists, they all came, and we listened to them all, under the great tree. For many hours they talked. And then we argued among ourselves. The day will come when we will vote, and then the parties will know what our village thinks."

As in most democratic countries the candidates tried many tricks to get attention. One campaigned on a camel, another on an elephant. A favorite technique was a procession of followers shouting simple slogans. In Delhi the streets were filled with party chants.

Government supporters wearing the white Gandhi caps of the independence struggle, would yell, "Congress party, Gandhi's party! Congress party, Nehru's party!" In retort the opposition would reply, "White Caps' party, Corruption party," or "*Nehru Raj Kya Hai? Nanga, Bukka Hindustan!*" which literally translated means "Nehru rule, what is it? Naked, hungry India."

Congress party workers did not need to shout as loudly as the opposition, because they had Nehru's voice on their side. On a succession of triumphal tours, he crossed and criss-crossed India, east and west, north and south, and millions came to listen.

He traveled a total of seventy thousand miles and sometimes spoke as often as thirty times in a day. As his main target he chose the Hindu communal parties which based their appeals on religion. Tied as they were to the status quo, they were vulnerable to attack in a country thirsting for social change.

The Jan Sang was easy to ridicule for the preoccupation of its platform not with internal Indian problems but with the welfare of the Hindu minority in Pakistan. The Ram Rajya Parishad exposed its prejudices by promising that "untouchables shall be given high posts in the management of the Sanitary Departments, and the leather and hides trades," which were fields traditionally reserved for the outcastes.

Nehru often struck hard at the Communists. Once when he saw a procession of red flags he suggested that the carriers go live in the country whose flag they were carrying. Communist leader Dange replied that the Prime Minister should quit India to reside in New York with the "Wall Street imperialists."

Nehru's greatest weakness was the heterogeneous nature of the Congress party itself. "Congress is like a *dharmashala* [a hostel for any Hindu traveler]," said Dr. Ambedkar, the respected untouchable leader and author of India's new Constitution, who resigned from Nehru's cabinet to run in the opposition. "It is open to all," he snorted, "fools and knaves, friends and foes, communalists and secularists, capitalists and anti-capitalists."

The Communists, for their part, acted as if they wanted to operate a political *dharmashala*, too. Rather than run openly on their own platform they preferred to strive for united fronts. In a few provinces their "new peaceful policy" had been so belated that they were still illegal and therefore other names were necessary, such as the United Front of Leftists in Travancore-Cochin and the People's Democratic Front in Hyderabad.

With an aura of heroism around them, many Communists came up from the underground and out of jail with the ominous but persuasive proposal that all opponents of the "reactionary" Congress party should pull together regardless of their own differences.

The party which the Communists primarily attempted to woo, the Socialists, refused any kind of collaboration, and in this they demonstrated a far higher degree of political sophistication than many of the Socialist parties of Europe in the 1930's. The world Cominform bulletin, in its pre-election survey, noted angrily that "the biggest obstacle in the path" of communism in India "is represented by the right-wing leaders of the Socialist party."

The Socialists are hardly right-wing in any sense we know, but their bitter, determined anticommunism brought on them the brunt of the Communist attack. Now the same Socialists and independents whom the Communists had sought to join suddenly became everything vile, including "American stooges."

Although the Socialists have militantly championed the idea of a "Third Camp" in foreign policy, the Communist press blared constantly that the party was financed by American dollars. In one village a Socialist became so angry about these charges that he asked for a full meeting of the *panchayat*, or local council, before the entire village. He said he could prove that he was not an American stooge and he could also prove that his Communist critic was a Russian agent. Before the village assembly the two were called face to face.

"I will now show my independence of America by criticizing America where I think she is wrong, and I ask only that the Communist representative do the same of Russia," said the Socialist, who then attacked American foreign policy for its apparent support of colonialism in Africa and bitterly criticized American discrimination against the Negro.

When the village council called on the Communist to point out what he believed to be the weaknesses of the Soviet Union, he hesitated and then abruptly left the meeting to the jeers of the people.

Generally, however, the Communists were on the offensive. Their championship of Communist China was aided by the well-timed arrival of a colorful Chinese "cultural mission," which toured the country on the eve of the elections. The Socialists refused to join in the mammoth, politically oriented receptions organized everywhere by fellow travelers, but the myth of an expanding "Peoples" China in which "a new day was dawning" was vigorously promoted during the months of balloting.

The Communists showed no scruples about the political allies they chose or the promises they made, not only in the Sikh areas where they worked with the bigoted communal Akali Dal, but in the South where they supported the Dravida Khazagam, the racialist Dravidian Federation. Throughout the South they played up antagonisms based on language differences.

In Tripura, a tiny former princely state near the Burman frontier, Communists captured the two seats to the central House of the People. "How in the world did they do it?" I asked the government administrator who drove us through ripening rice fields outside the capital city of Agartala. "Believe it or not," he answered, "their main appeal, repeated over and over again, was that they would restore the popular young Maharaja now studying in England to his old preindependence throne."

While I was traveling through Travancore-Cochin in southwest India in December, 1951, just before the election, I heard another story about Communist techniques. Here in village after village two or three days before election they set up what they called "ration booths," and invited people to bring them their ration books.

"How in the world can a family expect to live on such a small ration," the Communist in charge would say to the poor family head. Then he would give him a supposed "ticket" entitling the voter to two or three times as much food at a lower price. "This will be good only if the Communists win the election," he would warn, "so watch carefully how you vote."

On our four-hundred-mile drive along the lush, palm-covered coastal region of Travancore-Cochin which was the first southern state to vote, we saw thousands of Communist flags flying, although the party had been declared illegal and the display of their flag was against the law. Since the Communist front was not allowed to use the hammer and sickle, the Communists instead chose for their symbol an elephant, to the discomfort of some of my Republican friends in Connecticut to whom I reported this substitution.

On our first day we were persuaded to take a side trip into the jungle to see a baby elephant which had just been trapped in a pitfall, and so fell far behind schedule. Well after dark and still several miles from the city of Cochin where we planned to spend the night, we found ourselves on the edge of a huge Communist rally on the very river banks where we had to cross by ferry.

After a long wait, it was nearly midnight when we finally drove onto the wobbly raft which was just big enough to hold the car. As the ferryman poled us across, our way was lighted eerily by great bonfires on both banks, and red flares and fireworks. There was an uproar on the other side when some of the marching, chanting students, with clenched fists, recognized the seal of the United States on the door of our car; but we drove through the crowd without difficulty, blissfully ignorant of the meaning of the epithets which were hurled at us in the Malayalam language of that area.

Our three days in Travancore-Cochin convinced us that the Communists would poll a heavy vote there and this proved to be the case. Voting everywhere was peaceful and orderly, and in large numbers. Over 70 per cent of the eligible citizens of the province went to the polls, a higher proportion than vote in an American presidential election.

The press reported a great Communist triumph, and a defeat for both the Congress and the Socialists. Actually, the Congress party vote of 1.2 million in Travancore-Cochin was greater than the Communist Front and Socialist votes put together.

Communists and Socialists each won about half a million votes, but 200,000 votes received by two non-Communist leftist parties were thrown to the Communist candidates who therefore emerged as the second party with almost 25 per cent of the seats. The Congress found itself with less than a majority in the state assembly. The dramatic news that several Communists were elected while still in jail added to the impact on the rest of the country.

"If it had not been for Nehru's whirlwind campaign through the state," a newspaper publisher in Travancore-Cochin told me, "the Communists might have won a majority. In two days he made seventy-six speeches, covering about every major village and city district. As he spoke we could almost feel the Communist tide recede."

After Travancore-Cochin came the news from Madras and Hyderabad, the heart of South India. In Guntur, and other Andhra districts, which had led the country in Gandhian civil disobedience and had been the stronghold of Congress in the 1920's the Communists defeated almost every regional Congress leader and state cabinet minister.

The Congress vote in Madras was twice that of the Communists, but again Congress did not win quite enough seats to provide a majority in the state assembly. Although the Communists' statewide vote was only about 13 per cent, their victories in the Andhra districts were flashed North to the huge states which had yet to vote. The Communists thus entered the final leg of the northern campaign with an immense psychological headstart.

While the southern elections had left the Congress and the Communists as the two main contestants, in the North the vigorously anti-Communist Socialists and Congress were the chief contenders. Despite their southern success, the Communists won very few footholds in the remaining states. In Bombay state, Bihar and the U.P. the Communists won less than half a million votes compared to 6 million votes for the Socialists.

That the Congress was strong enough throughout India to contest twice as many seats as the Socialists and six times as many as the Communists does not diminish the overwhelming fact that the vote for Congress was four times that of the Socialists and almost ten times that of the Communists.

In terms of votes this is how the leading parties stood in the national House of the People:

	Number of Seats	*Per Cent of Total Vote*
Congress	364	45
Socialists	12	10.5
K.M.P.P. (now merged with Socialists)	10	5.9
Communists	26	5.1
Jan Sang (Hindu right wing)	3	3
Scheduled Castes' Federation (untouchables)	2	2.3
Ram Rajya Parishad (Hindu right wing)	3	2.0

Independents received sixteen million votes, and the rest were scattered among parties receiving less than 2 per cent of the total. A total of 106 million people voted.

The Congress also won over 2,200 state assembly seats, to 173 for the Communists, 128 for the Socialists, 77 for the K.M.P.P., 33 for the Jan Sang, about 300 each for smaller parties and for independents. It had firm control of all but five states, and even in these, Congress soon found enough support from independents to form majority governments.

The returns meant that the Congress party had an unchallenged mandate to rule for five years. The Socialist—K.M.P.P. vote was three times that of the Communists, but so dispersed throughout India that it won them fewer seats.

The Communists emerged strong where they had long been strong: in the contiguous Telegu-speaking areas of Hyderabad and Madras, in Travancore and to a lesser extent in West Bengal. They were still weak where they had always been weak, in the larger states of North and Central India. The Communists did well in sections where landlordism was particularly bad or inequality in land holding was extreme, whereas poverty itself, surprisingly enough, does not seem to have been a determining factor.

Communist districts were often more irrigated, more developed and less poverty-stricken than neighboring districts which remained with Congress. I believe the explanation lies in the fact that poverty, in the poorer districts, was broadly shared, while in the irrigated sections rich landowners had generally grabbed the best land and were exploiting the landless and tenants with a resulting rise in political consciousness.

It was disturbing to see the correlation between areas of militant Communist struggles and areas of harsh military suppression of such struggles, and Communist votes. The Communists swept the polls in almost every village throughout the area of their revolt in Hyderabad.

The Socialists also found that they polled best in the areas where over the years they had conducted nonviolent Gandhian campaigns on social issues, and, on occasion, gone to jail. Perhaps the lesson to be drawn is that the Indian people today will support whoever appears to struggle on their behalf, whether the struggle is peaceful or violent.

In assessing the present strength of Congress, the popular memory of its old days of struggle remains a significant factor. Time and again a voter would tell me, "I am for Congress and for Nehru, not because they have improved things much since the British left, but because they won us our freedom." Another lesser bloc of votes, although in some districts a crucial margin, came from among the forty-five million Indian Muslims, who look on the Congress government, and particularly Nehru, as their friend and protector.

Still the fact remains that fifty-five out of every one hundred voters preferred the opposition candidates, and that Congress won a majority of the popular vote in only the small state of Saurashtra. Congress' tenure in power is firm until the election in late 1956 largely because the opposition is hopelessly divided.

One lesson of the election is the central importance of Nehru. The present position of Congress seems to be a resultant of two forces; on the positive side the abiding popularity of Nehru and Congress' identification with the long fight for freedom; on the negative side the mounting criticism of the Congress party itself as it faces almost overwhelming problems.

Yet Congress can take some pride in the knowledge that even when people turn away from it they turn largely to ex-Congress party members. Together, the Socialists and the K.M.P.P., both only recently separated from the Congress, polled over seventeen million votes. With two other smaller parties led by ex-Congress leaders they comprise a bloc of twenty million.

In addition many of the successful independent candidates were dissident members of the Congress. Thus second to Congress, by far the largest group of voters are former Congress supporters who share the common tradition of the Gandhian struggle, talk much the same language as Nehru and are equally dedicated to the democratic process.

Another result of the election, which shows the direction of Indian politics, is that Congress has emerged clearly as the main conservative party. Of course, Congress did not run on a conservative platform. It promised land reforms and sweeping economic progress through the Five Year Plan, and if the people had not believed those promises, and particularly believed in Nehru who they knew was largely responsible for them, Congress might not be in office today. Without question the popular temper of the Indian people, like that of people everywhere in Asia and the Middle East, is for social change in a hurry.

One of the most encouraging results from the standpoint of Indian's democratic future was the poor showing by the various narrow religious and communalist parties, which together polled only a little more than 5 per cent of the vote, and elected very few candidates.

Actually, the Communist vote of a little more than five million, or another 5 per cent of the total, shows how far they have to go. But this position is strengthened by the concentration of their votes which gave them a few well-placed pockets of strength, which they dream of turning into "little Yenans," following Mao Tse-tung's strategy in China. Over one-third of all seats won by the Communists came from Telegu-speaking areas of Madras and Hyderabad.

The most important spot to watch is the new state of Andhra, which in 1953 was carved out of Madras, and which consists solely of Telegu-speaking people. There is no doubt that the Communists are desperately anxious to come to power in some one state, where they can control and expand the police force with its military equipment which usually includes light and heavy machine guns.

Already the Communists hold a dangerous strategic position, as the second party in several states in addition to Andhra. "A tough, disciplined Communist minority needs no more than 10 per cent of the popular vote to bring about the downfall of any democratic government," wrote Lenin.

"If there are five parties," he continued, "you should work side by side with four to destroy the fifth. When there are four, ally yourself with three to destroy the fourth. When there are three, combine with two to destroy the third. And when there are only two, victory is in your hands."

Immediately after the election when they first took their seats in the assemblies, the Communists seemed formidable indeed. I will never forget one day when I visited the new Madras state assembly. I had been talking with Mr. Rajagopalachari, the respected Chief Minister, a conservative and patriot of unimpeachable integrity. When he was called to the assembly floor to keep his slim majority in line, he invited me to watch the proceedings from the press gallery.

Many of the Congress members seemed old, gray, tired, forlorn and discouraged. In ominous contrast the sixty-two members on the Communist benches were young, aggressive and vigorous. The contrast was startling, and I had a feeling that only Rajagopalachari's political genius stood between order and Communist-sponsored chaos.

At the time the Communists thought that by a united front approach they could muster a majority and form a government for Madras. For a while the K.M.P.P. leaders, to whom the Communists offered the prime ministership and key cabinet posts, were tempted. But because the anti-Communist Socialists refused to support the coalition, it failed to secure a majority, and the shrewd old Rajagopalachari was able to form a ministry.

"I am *your* enemy number one," Rajagopalachari told the Communists in the Madras assembly. "May I say you are *my* enemy number one? That is my policy from A to Z." But for success in the election of 1956 he will also need to show positive economic and social progress.

The most significant trend for the next general election in 1956 is the consolidation now under way among the parties. Some of the smaller conservative parties and independents have gone back to Congress, a few splinter Marxist parties have joined the Communists and the Socialists and K.M.P.P. have merged into the Praja Socialist party. In the past, the weakness of the Socialists has been in organization, and perhaps in being too theoretical. They have now moved away from Marxism and are much closer to the Gandhian position.

As an additional pressure toward party consolidation to avoid the chaos into which French democracy has fallen, the nonpartisan Electoral Commission has decided to recognize only national parties which received more than 4 per cent of the vote; which leaves only four or five in the running. They would have liked to set a higher requirement, such as 10 per cent, but this would have eliminated the Communists as a legal party, driven them underground and probably brought a renewal of violence.

So far the Indian Communists do not seem to have thrived above ground, at least in their parliamentary activities. Signs of frustration and rivalry have increased inside the party, and some members openly yearn for the old days of glory and adventure in the illegal, clandestine movements. Meetings of Communist workers in Telingana and Kerala have already demanded a reversion to the program of armed uprising.

But such a program would run counter to Moscow's current

policy of moderation and "coexistence," and for the moment it seems unlikely. Also with the new-found Indian faith in elections, Communist workers would have difficulty finding an excuse for violence which would be acceptable to public opinion.

For those who think that communism will be stopped by just a little food and education, the Indian election carries a stern lesson. Travancore-Cochin, the scene of the greatest Communist electoral success, testifies that people hunger for something more than literacy and a little economic advancement, for this is the most modern, the most literate and the most Christian state in India.

And for those who think that ruthless force alone will do the trick, Telingana of Hyderabad, the scene of the biggest Communist rebellion, testifies that all the troops and tanks of the Indian army could not wipe out the popular support of Communists who for the first time distributed land among those who had none. Narayan Reddy, the leader of the Telingana Communists, won over 75 per cent of the votes cast in his district, and the largest absolute number of votes of any candidate in India.

There are even wider lessons. For instance, is it not time to revise our pessimistic, and somewhat arrogant, assumption that democracy is practical only for a highly developed, educated people? From what I saw in India, I have changed my own mind about the necessity for a series of Atatürks in Asia as a prelude to democracy. How does any nation prepare itself for self-government except by self-government? The only way to learn to swim is to swim.

I was reminded also that literacy is not a test of intelligence, especially not in Asia where the means to achieve literacy are often wholly lacking. There are hundreds of millions of very wise villagers who have never had a chance to read and write, but who know how to talk intelligently about their problems and to cast a thoughtful vote. The national ballot worked so well in India that the government has extended the electoral system to the local election of hundreds of thousands of village *panchayats.*

This is not to suggest that India's great election was entirely free of corruption or the usual political deals. As in America there were few districts where some politicians of all parties did not promise to get a temple, or a school, or a well, in return for votes.

And also as in America there was the perennial political attempt to make special appeals to religious groups and castes.

But not even the Communists have seriously contested the general honesty of election officials, and there has seldom been a more orderly or peaceful vote of a great nation. The campaign itself was a major education in government, and above all the returns put solid content into Indian politics. Not only did the parties explain to the people where they stood, but the country now knows just how much strength the parties have among the people.

Communists in India and other Asian nations talk incessantly about spectacular material achievements in China, resulting from dictatorship and disciplined labor. I have not been to China; I have not seen the things which may or may not have been constructed there.

But I have seen the spectacle of more than 100 million free Indians going to the polls in the world's largest free election, and I can imagine no achievement greater. I have seen long lines assembled before dozens of polling booths. I have seen women defy old customs and cast their first vote (it is estimated that a higher proportion of women voted than men). I have seen "untouchables" walk for miles to stand in the voting line next to Brahmans.

I have seen Muslims and Christians, Buddhists, Jains and Hindus, half-naked peasants and rich landlords, workers in shorts and undershirts and Western-dressed officials, all waiting their turn to participate in deciding the future of their country.

I saw, too, an old man of eighty on his deathbed who demanded that his fellow villagers carry him to the polls on a stretcher so that he could cast a vote in the New India before he died.

In Asia, as in America, I know no grander vision than this, government by the consent of the governed.

IV. UP BY THEIR OWN BOOTSTRAPS

12. A Democratic Five Year Plan

"AFTER LIVING with Indian villagers for six months, I've come to the conclusion that their problems are insurmountable," an American sociologist, who had been studying the trends in one village in U.P., wrote me shortly before I left India.

"But," he hastened to add in apparent contradiction, he had "developed an immense faith in Indians," and believed that "somehow a people as basically decent and intelligent . . . are going to find a way to overcome their insurmountable problems."

To an American who follows the events in the capital of free India or who surveys what is being done throughout the twenty-nine states, there is that same sense of being appalled by almost impossible problems and yet being impressed and sometimes amazed by the way Indians are trying to overcome those problems through democratic means.

One thing seems certain. A great majority of educated Indians are determined that India will pull itself up out of feudalism into the twentieth century. Enough Indians who know of economic development elsewhere have vowed that their nation, too, shall move ahead. And enough promises have been made to the mass of people to insure that this process will continue, one way or the other.

"Our ability through democracy to surpass, or at least equal, China's development under a dictatorship will determine our ability to survive as a free nation, and if we fail, Asia goes, too," an Indian statesman told me. And he was right, for on the Asian stage, where half the human race is seeking a quick solution to the problem of economic development with Africa and South America looking on, Communist China already serves as the contrast, and in a grim sense, as the criterion, for economic progress in India.

The contest shaping up is no pushover. That the methods used by the Chinese are at odds with our concepts of decency and morality is no guarantee that they will fail. For more than a generation we comforted each other by explaining, quite logically we thought, why communism could never succeed in turning the Soviet Union into an industrial nation. And yet today Russia's steel production is second only to our own and may soon outrun the total of all Europe.

It will be equally dangerous if wishful thinking leads us to underestimate what is now going on behind the so-called "bamboo curtain." There can be no doubt that China is moving ahead with economic construction, however costly it may be in terms of human life and liberty. In the Huai River valley of Central China, for instance, an area where twenty million people from time immemorial have lived in seasonal dread of the inevitable floods, the river has been controlled by great dams and eight million new acres are going under irrigation.

At various times two million Chinese are said to have worked on the project, under the direction of a labor draft and without modern equipment. Indians who have seen it come home in awe. "I saw 800,000 people working with their bare hands," an anti-Communist Indian newspaper man who returned in 1952 told me. That is the competition of Asia.

America and the free world cannot afford to underestimate that competition. Communist China is harnessing the efforts of her 500 million hard-working people to a program of economic development every bit as ambitious as that launched by Stalin and his associates in Russia during the 1920's. Borrowing heavily from the experience of Soviet planners, an all-out drive has begun to telescope a century of economic progress into a generation. When we consider the low standard of living of the Chinese people this means that almost fantastic sacrifices are being called for.

In addition, China is receiving the aid of thousands of Soviet technicians and, it is reported, of over $1.6 billion of outright Soviet credit for industrial equipment, steel, trucks, bulldozers and other capital goods.

India faces the economic challenge of Communist China with

many serious handicaps. America and western Europe created their industrial systems over a period of many generations. We had not only the advantage of time but in America a vast frontier to exploit, and in Europe a steady flow of profits from the colonial possessions of Asia and Africa.

Nor can India resort to the ruthless methods of totalitarianism. As a democracy dedicated to individual freedom she cannot force her people into labor gangs. She cannot dictate which of her young men shall become engineers, doctors or agricultural specialists. She cannot indefinitely withhold higher living standards from her people so that more output can go into the railroads, steel mills and power plants on which a modern industrial system must be based.

Nor, judging from attitudes recently expressed in the administration and in Congress, can India expect from America more than a modest fraction of the aid which the Soviet Union is giving Communist China.

India's Five Year Plan attempts to take these difficulties into account. It offers a courageous program of development which should earn her the admiration of the whole free world.

One Year Plans, Five Year Plans and Seven Year Plans are, of course, not new. What is unique in India is that her Five Year Plan was prepared in a democratic manner, was adopted by a democratic parliament, is administered by a democratic government and is undertaken in the midst of constant democratic criticism.

In March, 1950, the Indian government established a Planning Commission. Nehru served personally as chairman. For fifteen months the Commission studied the country's problems, consulting with various departments of the central and state governments, an Advisory Board and panels set up on a number of special subjects.

In 1951, "The First Five Year Plan: A Draft Outline," a document of about three hundred pages, was distributed throughout the country for discussion and comment. "Planning in a democratic state is a social process in which, in some part, every citizen should have the opportunity to participate," the draft stated. Eighteen months later, after substantial changes were made in response to criticism and discussion from all sources, a revised summary of the Plan designed to strike a practical balance between India's needs and resources was issued to the country.

India's principal resources are her land and natural wealth, her existing productive equipment in the shape of power installations, communications and machinery, and the labor of her people. This last, human labor, is the most important resource available and, in the final analysis, it must provide the main source of all new capital.

India's mineral resources are great and fully capable of supporting a highly productive industrial economy. But they are largely undeveloped. Her present industrial equipment for a nation of her size is probably lower than any nation which has ever embarked on modern development, with the exception of China.

With the equipment India possesses, her trained workers are as good as any in the world. "Look at those steelworkers," an American engineer at Damodar Valley said to me as he pointed at a crew working high up on a great steel structure. "Six months ago they were plowing behind a bullock. Now they are as competent as any workers I have seen anywhere, and that includes both the United States and Germany."

Some eighty million Indians, however, are either unemployed or employed only two or three months a year, and it is to this vast, untapped reservoir of human energy that India must turn for her first effort in lifting herself by her bootstraps. Since most of the people live in the villages and work on the land, the additional capital produced in the beginning must come largely from increased agricultural production and village construction.

To an American the Plan's goals are, in relative terms, modest. Altogether only a little more than $4 billion is to be spent by the Indian federal and state governments over a five-year period ending April 1, 1956. This will increase the national income of $20 billion a year by about 11 per cent. The long range goal is to double the per capita income, that is, to raise it to $100 per year. But for this it is estimated that four additional Five Year Plans will be required following the first.

Yet with a total national income of only about 6 per cent of that of the U.S. and with more than twice as many people, India is undertaking the equivalent of four TVA's.

In this one five-year period she will invest in irrigation and power development as much as had been used for this purpose during the whole preceding century. These river valley projects support the primary purpose of the Five Year Plan, which is to increase agricultural production until India has become self-sufficient in food and cotton. They will also provide the electric power necessary for industrial expansion.

The importance of more agricultural production is obvious. For many years India has been forced to import from 5 to 10 per cent of its food and cotton needs at a cost in 1951 and 1952 of more than $400 million a year. Every year a huge amount of hard-to-earn foreign exchange, instead of being used to buy railroad equipment, machinery and bulldozers has had to go to buy wheat in America, Canada and Australia, and rice in Burma and Thailand.

The encouraging point is that India can easily close that relatively small food deficit and substantially increase the average diet of her people if her crop production can even begin to approach the Asian average. This average is higher than Indian production largely because of more extensive irrigation and the greater use of fertilizer elsewhere in Asia.

India's handicap is not so much lack of rain but the fact that 95 per cent of her rain comes in the two- or three-month period of the monsoon, when most of it rushes off in devastating floods, leaving much of the land parched for the rest of the year. These rains have to be seen to be believed. Once Steb and I were held up at Ahmedabad in Bombay state by fourteen inches of rain in a single day.

Already after the efforts of several hundred years some 50 million of India's 250 million acres are irrigated by one means or another. Some of the irrigation comes from ancient Persian wheels which draw water from shallow wells with the help of an ox or camel, and which provide water for about five acres each. Some of it comes from artificial lakes called tanks which catch and hold the monsoon rains.

In the last two or three generations larger projects were built including low dams across the rivers to hold back the water and divert it to the fields as it is needed through hundreds of miles of canals.

The Five Year Plan by April 1, 1956, calls for an increase of nineteen million acres in the present irrigation system. This is slightly more than all the irrigation in the United States, and roughly equal in area to South Carolina. The major and most dramatic sources for irrigation are the great river valley developments, which will also increase India's electric power capacity by over a million kilowatts by 1956, an increase of 55 per cent.

To see some of the giant projects under way is one of the most thrilling experiences in Asia. I went to the Damodar Valley development shortly before Nehru officially opened the great Tilaiya Dam and the Bokaro Thermal Generating Plant, the biggest in India. They had been completed ahead of schedule by working twenty-four hours a day, in eight-hour shifts, stopping only once a week to repair machinery.

The Damodar, known in Bengal as the "River of Sorrows," is not one of India's major rivers, but during each monsoon it becomes a raging torrent with a terrible capacity for destruction. Now it is being turned into constructive energy in one of India's first attempts to treat a whole river, from source to mouth, as a unit. It will irrigate nearly a million and a half acres. The Damodar Valley Corporation, in charge of the program, is the same kind of autonomous government corporation embodied so successfully in our own TVA.

In the fall of 1952 I went with Sam, who has always been determined to become an engineer, to the Bhakra-Nangal project in the Punjab, another even larger multipurpose valley development. There were 100,000 people working on this entire project including forty-four American technicians, two of whom, G. L. Savage and Harvey Slocum, are responsible for some of our own greatest projects. The salaries of these American engineers are entirely paid by the Indian government.

It is a dramatic setting. The Bhakra dam will rise 690 feet above the river bed to become second highest in the world, next only to our own Boulder Dam, built also by Harvey Slocum. Before the American engineers arrived, Indians had completed two huge tunnels fifty feet in diameter and more than one-half mile long through solid rock through which the river is diverted while the dam itself is being built. They are said to be the biggest such tunnels in the world.

The irrigation canal system for this project, which will be three thousand miles in total length, is now about two-thirds completed.

The main canal is more than one hundred miles long, three or four hundred feet wide and nearly deep enough to float the battleship Missouri. These canals are all lined with concrete and together they will irrigate each year two and one half times the area irrigated by Grand Coulee. It is estimated that the increased production in this one area alone will supply half the cotton which India now has to import each year and about one-third of the wheat now imported.

The three-mile-long Hirakud Dam in Orissa, on the Mahanadi River, on completion early in 1956, will irrigate a million and a half acres of rice land. As a result two crops will be grown instead of one on much of the land, with an estimated increase in production of 600,000 tons of food grains. Of the thirty thousand people who have worked on this project, there were only two full-time foreign experts, both supplied by the British Commonwealth's Colombo Plan.

Several more multipurpose projects of equal size, on the Koyna, Chambal, Kosi and Kistna-Pinar rivers have been authorized, and will probably be commenced during the Five Year Plan. And beside the major national projects there are about seventy state programs of irrigation, fourteen of which include power development.

Another major contribution to India's program of irrigation are the "tube" wells which are now being dug in many parts of North India. These wells go down some 250 feet where they tap an apparently unlimited sheet of water from the Himalayas' melting snows. Four thousand of these wells, each of which will irrigate on the average four hundred acres, are now under construction, many of them with Point Four assistance from America.

But the old ways have not been forgotten and all over India tens of thousands of new tanks and shallow wells are being dug, 25,000 in the state of Mysore alone. In one district which seemed to be almost without water, an American Point Four engineer discovered that by deepening the dried out wells from the usual twenty feet to forty feet, plenty of water could be made available and the food production doubled.

Still more food will be raised on the seven million acres of land which are being reclaimed from the jungle and from the ravages of Kans grass, a devastating, deep-growing weed, which can only be uprooted by huge tractor plows. These were bought with funds loaned by the International Bank. I will never forget the tired-out tractor crews sleeping on the ground, while fresh crews take over to keep the giant machines operating twenty-four hours a day.

If the resources are available to carry out the present plan, it is believed that annual grain production will increase by nine million tons or about 18 per cent by 1956, which will mean that India will not only be self-sufficient in food, but that the diet of the average Indian family can be increased from about 1,700 to 1,850 calories daily. At the same time India's already substantial cotton production will be increased 65 per cent.

The expenditures on irrigation and river control constitute less than one-third of the total outlay under the Plan. Social services, including health, education, housing, refugee rehabilitation, aid to unemployed and to backward castes, altogether comprise less than one-fifth of the Plan, and of this, only about $34 million are for the malaria control program. Yet the antimalaria campaign represents one of the most exciting facts in Asia.

Malaria is recognized as the most formidable of India's health problems. About a million deaths result directly and another million indirectly from the disease. The loss in productivity is inestimable. The Plan aims at no less than the practical elimination of malaria by 1956, the reduction of the present 100 million annual cases to "substantially less than a million." With the virtual elimination of malaria will also go a sharp drop in elephantiasis and other insect-borne diseases.

In several malaria areas I have visited, I have found whole villages so sick that no one had the strength to harvest the crops. The Rockefeller Foundation people who have done splendid work in India, and indeed throughout Southeast Asia, believe, not only that the present program will succeed in relieving this preventable suffering, but that the result will be an increase of at least 5 per cent in food production.

To aid this program, the world's largest effort in malaria control, the United States is now contributing a little over $20 million through Point Four, to pay for the imported DDT, the spray guns and some jeeps.

The remaining costs are paid by the Indians. The four thousand control agents and experts find and check the particular kind of mosquito in each locality, locate and spray its breeding grounds and spray all the houses and outbuildings.

There are few Americans who can possibly imagine the excitement and relief that this program is bringing to the people of India. For the Indian people this is dramatic, tangible evidence that democracy can accomplish in the space of three or four years a public health miracle which few expected to see in their lifetime.

Another effort that is touching millions of Indians for the first time is literacy instruction. Something happens to a man who at last has suddenly learned to read and to write. He stands straighter and he looks you in the eye and a whole new world is opened up.

"Russia, under a dictatorship, taught 100 million people to read and write between 1925 and 1935," an old professor said to me. "India's democratic government must help teach 250 million illiterates by 1972."

Frank Laubach, an American who is probably the world's leading expert on literacy programs, joined our Point Four staff in 1952 and his advice was immediately welcomed by the Indian government. The program prepared by the Ministry of Education with his help calls for the posting of "alphabet charts" in each village through which every Indian can learn the alphabet in his local language.

The classes are organized with the slogan "each one teach one." Instead of the traditional, "The cat is white. The white cat belongs to Mary," their primers are filled with down-to-earth information so that each village may learn as it reads. "Dirt has many germs. Dirty water makes you sick."

In formal education, progress under the Plan will be less dramatic but still quite substantial. In 1951 there were twenty-six million Indian children in some kind of school, primary, secondary, technical or vocational. By 1956 the Plan calls for an increase to thirty-six million.

About one-fourth of the Plan outlay goes into expansion and modernization of transportation and communication, and a little less than 10 per cent to industrial development, including government aid to the Gandhian program for cottage and decentralized industries.

The remaining nearly one-fifth is allocated to agriculture and to the Community Development projects, which may be the most significant single part of the Plan, and which will be discussed in a later chapter. Besides these various government projects, the plan proposes production goals which, it is hoped, will be achieved by forty-two industries under private management.

Steel production will increase about 60 per cent. Cement production will almost double; aluminum will triple; pumps, diesel engines, petroleum refining will all be stepped up substantially. The production of commercial fertilizer, which is probably the most important single factor in Japan's spectacular yields of rice and wheat, will be increased tenfold. We must realize, however, that the present base figures are very low and even after sizable percentage increases, India will have a very long way to go.

. . .

Some Americans have argued that the rapidly growing Indian population will swallow up any increase in agricultural production and thus prevent any general improvement in the standard of living. If you take the present statistics of babies born, subtract the percentage of deaths as they are decreased by the control of diseases, and then place the result alongside the present production of food, you can reach some gloomy conclusions about unprecedented famines in store for India.

But such reasoning does not take into account several crucial unknowns. By what amount, for instance, will India's food grain production be increased? With modern methods Japan produces more than four times as much rice per acre as does India. How about fish as a source of food? The majority of Indians have no religious compunctions about this, but although India is surrounded by oceans teeming with fish, the average Indian eats only two or three pounds annually.

And there is "fish farming" for the irrigated fields. In Indonesia I have seen areas where one hundred pounds of fish per acre are produced each year from the irrigation waters around the rice paddy plants. About four hundred tiny carp grown in hatcheries are "planted" in each acre and left for one hundred days in the eight to twelve inches of water around the rice paddy plants. When "harvested" they weigh about half a pound each. This can be done in much of India.

Then, too, we do not know at what point in Indian industrial development the birth rate will decline, as it declined finally in the West. Nor do we know to what extent family planning will be tried or will be successful. In general it seems that there are fewer obstacles to its adoption in India than elsewhere.

The Indian Planning Commission considered these factors thoroughly and recommended a series of measures designed to relieve the pressures of increasing population. They were careful, however, to place these problems in a reasonable perspective and to avoid the exaggerated and hysterical attitudes that have marked some Western discussions of the subject. For one thing, as they pointed out, the density of population in India is less than half that of Japan, Germany and the United Kingdom. Above all, they emphasize that human beings are born, not only with stomachs with which to consume food but with bodies and brains with which to produce it.

If an upward momentum takes hold of the economy, then improvement in one quarter adds force to progress elsewhere. The confidence of seeing dams go up draws new industries to apply for the cheap electricity. An improvement in public health will create innumerable new initiatives among the people. If this happens, then in succeeding Five Year Plans the Indian government looks forward to the more rapid growth of an industrial economy. Although the government, as in every underdeveloped country, will remain responsible for a large portion of the development program, if Nehru's views on a mixed economy prevail, private industry will have an opportunity to play a larger role.

But if India is to get private capital in these later stages of development she will have to adopt a clear-cut policy toward foreign investors and toward Indian business itself. American businessmen, for example, are generally prepared to work for reasonable profits, but they want to know just what the rules are. They want a sense of security for their investment, in the sense that it will not be subjected to risks other than the normal ones of doing business. They want a feeling of co-operation from the government.

There are many competent and forward-looking Indian businessmen who understand the dynamic role of modern American capitalism. Unfortunately there are a good many others who cling to the old traditions of monopoly, with its patterns of high prices and low wages, who grasp for the quick profits of trading and speculation rather than for long-term productive investment.

The Indian government is certainly justified in being tough with destructive elements of this kind. Indeed it might well go even further by enacting laws which encourage business savings for investment and discourage wild, speculative profiteering. But it should not confuse this type of businessman with those creative-minded corporations, foreign and domestic alike, which are prepared to make substantial investments on fair terms and to share in the building of Indian industry.

This industrialization, when it comes, need not follow the old example of the West, where industries clumped around coal mines and railroad tracks, the only sources of power and transport. With them came the huddled, dispirited industrial slums. Today, electric power and truck transportation mean that industry can be far more broadly distributed.

Already our own country is witnessing some of the beneficial results of the new trend to smaller scale industry. Small towns now support food-processing plants, machine shops, assembly plants and other local factories producing for a regional, or even a national market. The economic basis of these towns is much broader than that of the old manufacturing city. It is usually possible for the factory workers to own their own homes and even to farm several acres. The smaller size of the community makes it easier for people to sink their roots and take a part in its affairs.

No doubt this trend will continue in Western nations. The newly developing countries, however, have the opportunity to guide their industrial growth along these lines without first going through the stage of big-city industrial centralization. Atomic energy, in which field India has many competent research scientists, is opening up new possibilities. Because Indian resources have been entirely devoted to experiments on peacetime uses, India has made considerable progress in plans to harness it for industrial power. Work on an atomic pile in Bombay is well under way and foreign scientists are impressed with the vigorous way in which the Indians are proceeding.

The plan is to convert soil with a high monazite content, which is in plentiful supply in South India, into nuclear fuel. India has enough uranium deposits within her borders to start the reaction in the monazite sands.

All this is a long way in the future. For the present, as Nehru says, "this generation of Indians is sentenced to hard labor." Since the Plan requires that most additions to India's annual output go into industrial expansion and not into more consumer production for the public, the Indian people will have to keep their belts tight for many years.

How can a democracy persuade its people to undergo such a long and painful process? The Plan must be bold enough to challenge the people to their best efforts, sound enough to cope with the nation's problems and adequately explained to the people so as to warrant their understanding. In my opinion, although the Plan represents an imaginative and carefully worked out attack on India's economic problems, there is reason to doubt whether it is sufficient on these three counts.

For one thing, the purpose and the accomplishments of the Plan have not been presented to the people in clear and dramatic terms. The Indians are very poor publicists of their own endeavors. They seem to consider it undignified to blow their own horn, and they believe that one's good works speak for themselves. While this modesty is praiseworthy, it is nevertheless essential that the government let the people know the remarkable things under way to a far greater extent than it has yet done.

To lend assistance our United States Information Service prepared a series of twelve motion pictures entitled "Building the New India." These films simply tried to report the work being done under the Plan, with practically no mention of the United States. Everyone from the Prime Minister down to tens of millions of illiterate village Indians who saw these films in their own language versions seemed to respond. They were probably shown in every theater in India.

But so far there is little evidence that the Indians are prepared to compete effectively with the Chinese, who are ardent and effective propagandists about their achievements, not only among their own people but throughout Asia. The people of non-Communist Asia have heard more of progress in Red China, often in the most exaggerated form, than they have of the remarkable gains being made in free India.

Along with an understanding of the Plan, the Indian people must feel that there is at least an approach to equality of sacrifice if they are asked to contribute their labor and undergo years of austerity. As in all underdeveloped nations, most of the government revenue must ultimately come from the main source of wealth, agriculture, that is from the peasant in the form of land tax and indirect excises. Such taxes do not sit well if the wealthy minority in the cities continue to live in spectacular luxury.

Of course, even if all the wealth of India's rich were redistributed the poor would still be very poor. The primary economic problem is not to confiscate the wealth of the few but to create new wealth for the many. But the necessary psychological climate for building is a community conviction that the sacrifice and the sweat are being shared by everyone.

Recently Finance Minister Deshmukh announced a new system of inheritance taxes which run up to 40 per cent in the top brackets. Over a period of years they will help ease the present dramatic differences.

The direct route to the support of the mass of Indians, who live on the land, during the years of sacrifice and austerity, is thoroughgoing redistribution of land among the villagers, a subject which will be discussed further in the following chapter. In effect, land reform buys time within which the movement toward better living standards can gather the momentum it needs for success. The Plan recognizes that "the future of land ownership and cultivation is perhaps the most fundamental issue of national development."

If measures of reform are adopted that catch the imagination and enthusiasm of the people, there is no doubt in my mind that the targets of the Plan itself should be raised, and that such raised targets could be met. The announced goals of the Chinese Five Year Plan are a good deal higher in terms of percentages than those of India. And though thoughtful Indians have some doubts that China's goals can be met, it will not do for India to lag too far behind.

Even if all these things are done, increased information, equality of sacrifice, land reform and higher targets, India may not be able to lift herself completely by her own bootstraps. Indian taxpayers are already taxed just about to the limit of endurance. With three-fourths of the Indian people living in poverty, and with most of them close to the hunger line, higher taxes and increased savings would result in uprisings and riots and, indeed, this has already occurred in several sections where new taxes were introduced. The fact that out of 360 million people there are only 14,000 with incomes more than $8,500 shows how little there is to tax.

I know of no free government that has shown more political courage than has the Indian in squeezing its people to the very breaking point in order to secure the funds necessary for its own development without depending on others.

In the spring of 1952 it eliminated nearly $100 million of food subsidies which had been used to hold down food prices in the cities in order to speed up the building of the great river valley developments. When opposition members in the House of the People demanded an explanation the government spokesman said, "We must take some bread from the people today so that tomorrow there will be electric power, expanding industry and an end to India's age-old poverty."

Such action makes sound economic sense, but it takes the coolest kind of political guts, which against the background of unrest and agitation some observers feel verges on foolhardiness.

As might be expected, it is the Communists who lead the violent protests over the belt-tightening measures, in spite of the fact that communism would result in a ruthless economic squeeze going far beyond anything proposed by any democratic government. They know, that once in power their police would ride roughshod over any popular protests as did the Soviet police in the mass "liquidations" and planned starvation of the 1920's and early '30's.

With all these efforts, however, India's revenues will finance only about two-thirds of the budgeted expenditures for the Plan.

Of the estimated deficit in the Plan, which is put at $1.2 billion, about $300 million has been secured from the International Bank, the Commonwealth countries and the United States (our contributions through the year 1953 totaled a little less than $200 million).

The missing $900 million dollars must come from some combination of deficit spending beyond what is considered safe, taxing beyond what is considered endurable and a substantial increase in outside assistance. Otherwise the Plan will have to be drastically curtailed, with a resulting frustration of the people's hopes. Failure of the Plan might well start an explosive spiral of disillusionment with the slow pace of democratic progress.

To the extent that Western nations, the UN and the International Bank advance this needed governmental capital, India's chances will be that much improved. As she seeks, by democratic means, to match the achievements of the Chinese dictatorship, which is receiving more and more assistance from the Soviet Union, India is becoming steadily less hopeful of sizable Western assistance. And because India, recently emerged from colonialism, is too proud to seek our assistance in the direct and blunt manner that has been followed by many other nations, only a few Americans are even aware that a crisis exists.

The tragic fact is that if democratic India ever fails, and if a Communist civil war ever breaks out there, the West would spend billions to save India from communism. In defense of tiny, strategic Greece, with 8 million people, the United States in four years contributed more than twice as much as India needs to make a success of her Five Year Plan. One would think that the time to aid India is *now* while she is saving herself, and while her chance for success is good.

When the target date of the Plan is reached in March, 1956, the campaign for India's second general election will commence. Then the Plan will stand or fall, not solely on how many dams were built but on how well it has won the minds and hearts of the people. That is a popular test which the Chinese Communist government does not, at least openly, have to face.

If the people of India feel that the country is on the move in the right direction, if they see that reforms are being carried out and great projects are being built, the democratic way will win their vote of confidence, and India will have another five years of stable government in which to further her economic growth. And thus over the years India may become what Gandhi wanted it to be, "the hope of all the exploited races of the earth."

If the Plan fails for any reason, then it will be the free world which will lose. If, after Gandhi, the democratic way cannot succeed in India, where can it succeed in any of the revolutionary continents? As Gandhi said shortly before his death, "If India fails, Asia dies."

13. Land Reform—by Force, by Law, or by Gandhi?

HE WAS a young villager but his older neighbors were nodding in agreement as he answered an anti-Communist Indian political leader friend of mine who tried to tell him about the evils of the Soviet Union. "I am not concerned about this faraway Stalin against whom you warn us," the young man said to my friend. "We have our own Stalin here in this village—the man who owns the lands we till. First tell us how to get out of his grip."

The village was in the Tanjore district of the state of Madras. In my mind's eye I can still see the green sweep of rice paddy fields disappearing in the horizon, the checkerboard of little plots separated by foot-high ridges to control the irrigation waters, over which one can walk to the village where the farmers live, crowded together in mud-thatched huts.

When I heard that this is one of the best irrigated districts of the whole state of Madras, which sends surplus rice to less fortunate deficit areas, and when I first saw the abundant water and the fertile brown loam, I assumed that this must be a rich country where the people would be better off and happier. And then came the shock of my first visit to the Tanjore villages.

In this particular village there were thirty or so miserable hovels, as usual clustered apart from the other huts, in which the untouchables lived. All were completely without land. In the district as a whole about 35 per cent of the agricultural population were landless laborers, most of them untouchables. When we reached the rest of the village where another seventy families lived, we found two substantial dwellings which seemed empty and dozens of one- or two-room huts full of people squatting around the open cooking fires. "The landlords do not live here any more," one of the villagers explained. "They are in Madras, and one of their sons is studying at a great American university."

"Over half of us are tenant farmers," the village head man explained. "We must pay the cost of cultivation ourselves, and then give 75 or 80 per cent of the crop to the owner, who spends his income in the city." Another farmer said that the villagers had only the value of about 10 per cent of the crop left over after expenses. Counting one-third who were entirely landless, nearly three-fourths of the farm population in Tanjore either leases or works the land of noncultivating owners, and of the 25 per cent who are landowners, 3 per cent own 50 per cent of the irrigated land.

On top of the unfair tenancy terms the villagers were at the mercy of the local moneylender, the sole source of credit and the sole means of marketing their goods. His was a kind of general store, which sold them supplies, and in emergencies, such as weddings or illnesses, provided the needed cash.

Since one of his long-range aims is to secure land, the moneylender often encourages villagers to borrow far above their means, at rates as high as 30 per cent annually. A father with many daughters said to me, "When we go to him for a loan, he tells us, 'Why, that is not a big enough dowery for your daughter, your cousin is giving twice that for the wedding of his daughter,' and we end up borrowing more than we wanted." To marry each daughter this father had borrowed more than his whole year's income, and he fears he will be in debt to the moneylender for his whole lifetime.

In Tanjore the Communists raised two slogans, "Land to the Tiller" and "Five Acres for Me and Mine." By the very arithmetic of landholding this appeals to the majority of the people. The village I visited had joined its untouchables in voting Communist. Tanjore district is a case of exceptionally bad tenancy. But Malabar is just as bad. All of Madras state and much of India have similar inequalities.

The village which I described happens to be a place the Communists picked. But there are many other villages where their appeal would probably be equally effective. In some there are fewer untouchables, but in all there are the landless. In some the landlords are more benevolent, but in others they are even more ruthless. Almost every one of the 500,000 villages which make up most of India is still in the grip of some kind of exploitation.

Before going to Asia I had read much about the impoverished

condition of the peasants who work the land, and the evils of the land systems under which most crops are produced. After first-hand study throughout all of non-Communist Asia I am convinced that the breaking up of huge landholdings is the single most urgently needed reform in most Asian countries.

It is needed, first of all, on its own merits as an indispensable step in establishing democracy in Asia. Only when the peasants own their land can their full enthusiasm be aroused for voluntary labor in creating more irrigation and greater production. I did not have to ask why the tenants in Tanjore did not invest more time and money in improving their output, for I knew that most of the increase would go to the landlord.

The argument that small holdings of land in the hands of individual owners will mean less production is simply not valid. It confuses the *cost* of production per ton in America with the *amount* of production per acre. We have believed this myth because in the United States, where land is plentiful and labor is scarce and costly, we have found large-scale farming with giant machines highly profitable.

But a Long Island farmer with two acres of good land, with plenty of fertilizer and intensive cultivation, could produce more wheat *per acre* than a North Dakota farmer with a tractor combine working a large farm. Of course, on Long Island there are more profitable and productive things for a man to do.

In Japan, where I saw what amounts to "wheat gardening" on tiny terraces all the way up hillsides, the farmer on a two-acre plot, which he plants and weeds and fertilizes by hand, produces half again as much wheat per acre as we do on our vast farms; and between rows of wheat he grows a good crop of potatoes. He tends those two acres with all the tender care that a gardener gives to a rose garden on a millionaire's estate.

In most of Asia this is practical, because labor is plentiful and it is production above all which is wanted. The land is now too crowded for mechanized agriculture, there would be no jobs for the millions of peasants displaced, and in any case there is no money available to purchase the huge machines of the West.

There is another pressing reason for land reform. In the coldest terms of stopping communism, as a strategy in the Cold War, the democratic world simply must carry out these reforms before the Communists can use the lack of them as an excuse to overthrow democracy. At present the high rents demanded by landowners and the pitiful wages paid to the landless laborers represent a ready-made target for Communist agitators from the Philippines to Egypt, as well as throughout most of Africa and South America.

The leaders of the Soviet Union and the world Communist movement claim that their political and economic philosophy is descended directly from Karl Marx, who had little contact with agricultural problems, and who in the mid-nineteenth century visualized the Communist revolution occurring first among the underpaid factory workers of such heavily industrialized nations as Germany and the United Kingdom.

But the Communists' opportunity came first in Russia where industry was poorly developed and where most of the people lived on the land. Although Lenin organized the city proletariat skillfully, his chance to strike successfully came largely because of the slowness of the Kerensky Social-Democratic government in breaking up the vast feudal estates created under the Czars.

"Land to the Tiller" became Lenin's victorious slogan. His decree of November 7, 1917, which distributed the estates to the peasants without compensation to the landowners and in many instances with considerable bloodshed, ensured the massive support of the tens of millions of Russians living in the villages. Without this support the Bolsheviks would have been doomed. "This is the most important achievement of our revolution," Lenin told his associates. "Today," he said, "when we identify ourselves with the peasants" we make the revolution "irrevocable."

Thirty years later Communists were following the same formula in China and in Eastern Europe.

In 1948 on a mission to Europe for the United Nations Children's Fund I saw the first effect of a Communist land reform in a place called Kecskemet, south of Budapest in Hungary. The peasants, who had just been given the land, were tremendously excited. They would pick up the dirt and run it through their fingers. "Mine, mine, the landlords are really gone," an old Hungarian kept saying to himself.

Of course, for the Communists, who actually oppose individual ownership and consider the peasantry reactionary, this is no more than the first stage in their pursuit of absolute power. The second stage is to turn the city workers against the peasants, usually on the ground that the farmers' food prices are too high.

Once the peasants have been thoroughly discredited and intimidated, the third stage is reached; the ruthless revocation of all the newly won rights of individual land ownership, the forcible organization of agricultural production under a system of huge collective farms and the exploitation of these new units under rigid centralized direction.

The Chinese Communists, having come to power almost wholly through peasant support, are already starting to make a mockery of the early land reforms which won them that support. They are establishing a state trading system with tight control over the terms on which farmers must sell their crops and buy their supplies. By this means Mao, in order to secure more capital for industrial development, is now cautiously squeezing the peasants to the point where he feels resistance may become dangerous. His skill in handling this explosive situation may determine the ultimate success or failure of Communist China.

. . .

If the peasants of India and Asia had a way of knowing how the peasants of other lands have been put through the Communist economic wringer they would hesitate to accept their leadership. But they only know that they want more land, that the local Communists promise them that land and seem to fight the landlords in their behalf.

Wherever land inequalities are great or tenancy is high Communists find a fertile field. Inside India itself the correlation is dramatic. In Madhya Pradesh, where the inequities are less, the Communists won not a single seat in the state legislature. Directly to the south in Hyderabad, where most of the good land still belongs to a relatively few large landlords, the Communists remain strong.

In Mysore, just south of Hyderabad, where there is a relatively broad ownership of land, the Communists elected only one member of the legislature. In Madras, immediately to the West, with one of the worst land systems in India, the Communists elected sixty-two members and have a mass following.

I have seen the same close correlation between land ownership and the success of the local Communist parties in country after country, all the way to Japan.

In Burma the government has created legislation which limits land rents to twice the annual taxes, or about 8 per cent of the annual crop. Even though the government of Burma holds the peasants' prices down tightly in order to allow a 60 to 70 per cent profit to the government on all international sales, the peasants feel better off than before, and the Communists have become steadily weaker and their armed revolt is ending in failure.

In Thailand the land system is less unfair than in most parts of India with a majority of the peasants either owning their own land or renting for an average of around 25 per cent of the crop. Even here Communist gains have recently encouraged the right-wing government of Pibul Songgram to put a limit of twenty acres on the ownership of all land used for agriculture.

In Vietnam, in what used to be French Indo-China, we find a less happy situation. Here most of the land is owned by large landlords who extort rents from their tenants of from 50 to 70 per cent, and the peasantry is in the grip of moneylenders many of whom charge 40 per cent interest just for the period between planting and harvesting one crop. This was one of the principal causes for the bitterness against the French colonial occupation which has enabled the Communists, under Ho Chi Minh, to secure mass support for the long drawn-out armed struggle.

At the time of my first visit to Vietnam in August, 1952, the new Prime Minister, Van Tam, told me the slowness of land reforms was one of the main reasons for the failure of the government forces to crush the rebellion.

"When the Communists capture a village," he said, "their first move is to announce that all land now belongs to those who till it, and that all debts are canceled.

"As a result," he continued, "the peasants are wildly enthusiastic." Then with the ebb and flow of battle the French Union forces may again take over the area. Close behind them come the landlords and the moneylenders. "Where are our back rents?" they say. "Where is the money that you owe us?"

"How can we beat the Communists in such a war?" he asked.

Seven months later I was again sitting in Prime Minister Tam's office in Saigon. "Do you remember our last conversation about land reforms?" he asked dryly. "Since then we have made great progress. Now when the French recapture a village they let the peasants keep the land which the Communists gave them. So today throughout Vietnam people are saying, 'The sensible man prays that his village will be conquered by the Communists and then recaptured by the Vietnamese or the French. For only then can he become a small landholder without becoming a Communist.'" Van Tam told me that he was determined to correct Vietnam's feudal land system. I hope he takes action while there is still time.

In most parts of Indonesia, unlike Vietnam, there are few large landlords and correspondingly fewer Communists in the villages, except in a few plantation areas.

During the First World War, when the Dutch were largely cut off from their rich empire in Southeast Asia, the local sultans began to threaten the colonial hold of The Hague. Since the power of these local sultans stemmed largely from their complete control of the land, the Dutch, on their return, sought to end the threat of the sultans by taking their land and giving it to the villagers on a community ownership basis.

This Dutch move did not stop the drive for independence, but it did provide a wide land ownership which is now a life saver for the new Indonesian Republic. On densely populated Java, with fifty million people, the average holdings amount only to two or three acres, but the people all have something. So far this has been a shield against Communist inroads in most of the villages.

In the cities and on the great rubber and tea plantations the Communists can conduct noisy demonstrations, but no revolution in Asia can progress far without deep roots among the millions who till the soil and produce the rice.

In the Philippines the failure of past governments to face up courageously to the land problem permitted the Communist-led Huks to grow such roots in many rural areas. During the war the great landlords moved into Manila and other cities where many of them collaborated with the Japanese. The peasants took over the land, and with this new stake in economic as well as political freedom, many of them fought as guerrillas with great courage, thereby aiding American reoccupation of the islands.

When the war was over and the Philippines became free, the landlords reasserted their ownership of the land and even attempted to collect rents which had been uncollected during the war years. In their bitterness, many of the peasants turned to the Huks. In the Huk stronghold of Pampanga province about 2 per cent of the people owned 98 per cent of the land!

When we visited the Philippines in 1952 we did not see the brave and energetic Secretary of Defense, Rámon Magsaysay, because he was where he should be, in the villages, fighting the Huks and arranging to get land on which to settle the landless peasants. Over and over again Magsaysay stressed that without sweeping land reforms the Huks would continue to find solid support even among a people 90 per cent of whom are Roman Catholics.

In 1953, Magsaysay resigned from the cabinet in order to run as a reform candidate for the Philippine presidency. He explained: "It would be useless for me to continue . . . killing Huks as long as the Administration continues to foster conditions which offer fertile soil for communism." Elected on November 10, he has a great opportunity.

In British-controlled Malaya, the Communists, who have been fighting as guerrillas for seven years, find the same fertile soil. Here, too, the land belongs to large owners who extract exorbitant rentals from the peasants.

In his residence in Kuala Lumpur, capital of the Federated Malay States, Sir Gerald Templer, the British general in charge of the war against the guerrillas, posed the problem in clear terms. "Give me a hundred more divisions and I still couldn't destroy the Communists without the necessary reforms," he said. "My job is only 10 per cent military. The remaining 90 per cent is political and economic."

On Formosa Chiang Kai-shek was faced with some of the same political and economic issues on which he was beaten in China, including land ownership. In the last two or three years, his Nationalist government has put through a land reform program which could well serve as a model for every free nation in Asia.

Under this program no one is allowed to own more than ten acres of land, nor is anyone allowed to own land which he does not till himself. Government officials, with whom I talked in Taipeh, credit these reforms with much of the extraordinary increase in Formosa's output of rice per acre.

How tragic it is that this understanding of peasant problems did not come years ago! The Nationalists turned their backs on

(Above) *Presenting credentials to the President of the Indian Republic, Dr. Rajendra Prasad.* After reviewing an honor guard, I went into the former Viceroy's palace to meet this great follower of Gandhi, who had served many years in British jails. He seemed as uncomfortable in the midst of splendor as I did in my borrowed suit. (Below left) *Meeting the Indian press for the first time.* Their questions were often searching, but except for a few reporters from Communist newspapers they were fair-minded and many became our friends. (Below right) *Steb talking with President Prasad at a party.*

(Above left) *Outside the Khairati Clinic in New Delhi*, run in part by the American Women's Club of Delhi, in which Cynthia worked frequently. This mother is giving her child milk provided by the United Nations Children's Emergency Fund. (Above right) *Cynthia, Sally and Sam in the yard of our home in New Delhi*. Cynthia has on the Punjabi dress which she and Sally wore much of the time. (Below) *Children of the staff in our new home*, who became great friends of our children. The servants included caste Hindus and so-called untouchables, Muslims, Sikhs, Christians and Buddhists

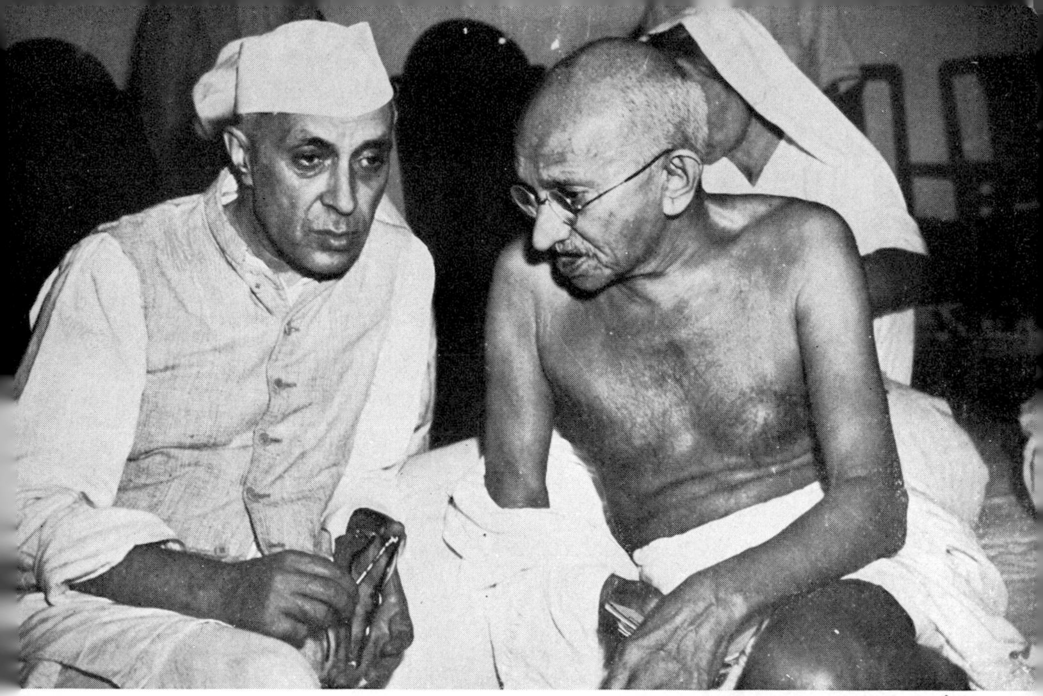

Acme

(Above) *Nehru with Mahatma Gandhi, who taught Indians to fight nonviolently without hating their opponents.* When the British withdrew, India, of its own free will, joined the British Commonwealth of Nations. Today the British are popular in India, and Gandhi is nearly worshiped. (Below) *Steb placing a wreath on Gandhi memorial at Rajghat.* Here Gandhi was cremated after his assassination on January 30, 1948. Perhaps the largest crowd in the history of the world assembled in final homage to the Mahatma. A replica of Gandhi's mud and straw hut is built nearby.

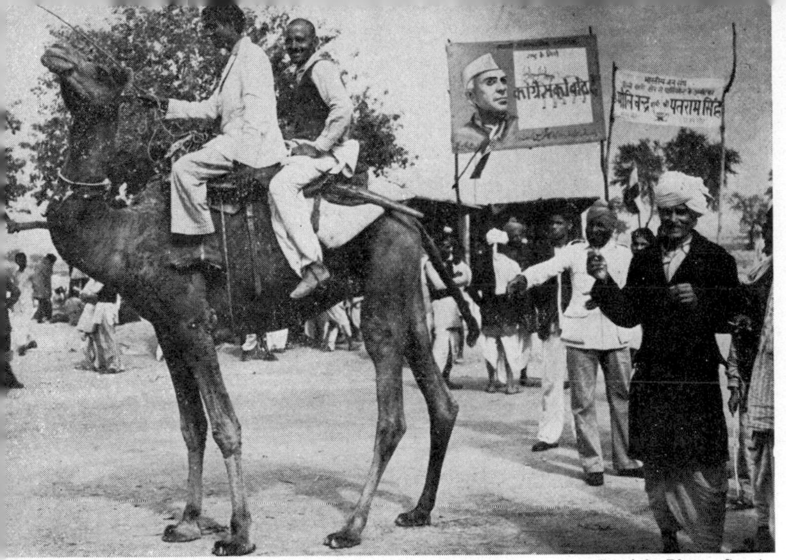

Punjab Photo Service

Punjab Photo Service

(Above) *In the world's largest free election.* This Delhi candidate campaigned on camel back. 60 per cent of the Indian electorate went to the polls. Nehru's party won a large majority of seats in the Central Parliament and in most state legislatures. (Left) *A Muslim woman voting in Delhi.* She is veiled in the custom of purdah. Her hand is being marked to make sure she does not vote twice. India's 45 million Muslims voted in particularly large numbers. (Below) *Mrs Pandit stands for election to the House of the People.* Nehru's sister, the present President of the United Nations General Assembly, spoke to many such election rallies.

Punjab Photo Service

Gopal Chitra Kuteer

(Above) *Mrs Roosevelt at the New Delhi airport.* "I have come to learn," she said. Mrs. Pandit and the Prime Minister are on either side of her. Next to Steb is the Minister of Health, Amrit Kaur, a princess who followed Gandhi. (Right) *Movie stars off to America.* India's movie industry is second in size only to that of the United States. (Below) *Nehru presents prizes for American children.* In a children's competition, arranged by *Shankar's Weekly,* 30,000 poems, essays and paintings from thirty countries were submitted. The United States won the most prizes, with Japan a close second.

Gopal Chitra Kuteer

Punjab Photo Service

Punjab Photo Serv

(Above) *Addressing the New Delhi Rotar Club.* With Indian business groups I stresse the need for private enterprise to adopt as it goal expanding production at lower price instead of the old monopolistic ways. Befor the British came, Indian manufacturing is sai to have equaled Europe's. Today it is trying t catch up after centuries of stagnation unde colonialism. India's need for new capital almost without limit. (Left) *In a fishing villag on the South Malabar coast.* On an inspectio trip of development projects we stop to hel pull in a net, much to the entertainment of crowd of men and boys. Here, in this beautifu lush country which reminded us so much Puerto Rico, American Point Four, Norwegia Technical Assistance and the UN are helpir the Indian government to develop the almo inexhaustible fisheries that surround India, ar which so far have scarcely been touched.

(Above) *In the office of Sudhir Ghosh.* He led thousands of refugees from Pakistan in building their own city, Faridabad, by voluntary labor. (Below left) *Chief Minister Shukla welcomes us to Madhya Pradesh.* A grand old man of the struggle for freedom who spent several years in British prisons. (Below right) *Ashadevi of Sevagram, with Steb and Evelyn Hersey, the Embassy's Social Welfare attaché.* One of our warmest friends was this Indian lady who, with her husband, now runs the ashram and basic education school which Gandhi started at Sevagram.

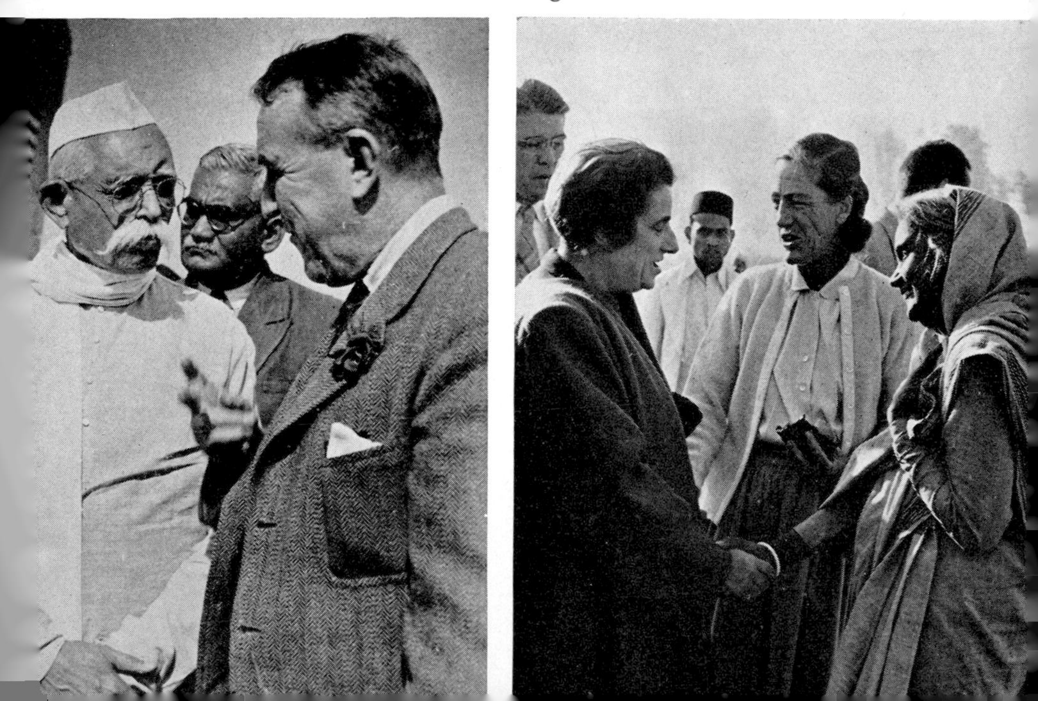

Courtesy Life (c) Time

(Above) *Our children arrive at school.* All classes of the Delhi Public School with its 1,300 students were held in tents. (Below left) *Education in the village.* Everywhere villagers are setting up schools and literacy campaigns. Reading and lessons in public health are taught. India hopes to be fully literate by 1972. (Below right) *At last he can write his name.* Anatram is the first of his family to read and write. The pride he shows before his sister, Basanta, is a pride I have seen in countless villagers. This picture was taken in Bhirlinga Village in Madhya Pradesh.

FOA by Chapelles

FOA by Chap

United Nations

(Above) *The ABC's of good health.* A nurse at Najafgarh explains need for fresh fruit. The UN World Health Organization assists this project. The Indian government matches WHO funds. (Below left) *Extra inches are a sign of health.* The student nurses come from the College of Nursing in New Delhi. One project undertaken by the government, with Point Four Aid, is the elimination, by 1956, of malaria, from which 100 million Indians suffer each year. (Below right) *Under the banyan tree.* Cynthia, second from right, with student nurses, with whom she worked at the Najafgarh Health Center.

United Nations

FOA by Chapelles

(Above) *Dams for the Five Year Plan.* Women carry concrete mix to top of this section of the Hirakud Dam. Similar to TVA, it will irrigate a million and a half acres, nearly as much as Grand Coulee. (Left) *Water and Caste.* This well—now given to untouchables and Muslims by the antidiscrimination laws of free India—is a symbol of India's progress. (Below) *Indo-American Agreement is signed.* To administer Point Four funds an agreement is signed by the Prime Minister and me. To show that no strings were attached, the agreement was given full publicity. Our aim, I said, was solely to help India succeed.

FOA by Chapelles

FOA by Chapelles

(Above left) *These leader-trainees live at Sindewahi school for Community Projects in Central India.* These men are later assigned to village projects, financed by the Ford Foundation. One hundred million villagers will be covered by 1956. (Above right) *Point Four.* Perry Jameson, one of our extension advisers, with Punjabi villagers. India is now financing 95 per cent of her Five Year Plan. (Below) *Inaugurating a village project.* At Alipore, everyone joins in the volunteer road building. Gandhi stressed that India's main capital is the free labor of her own people.

Wide World

FOA by Chapelles

(Above) *Trainees harvest rice.* Community Projects introduce better seeds, simple metal tools and fertilizer which result in spectacular increases in yields. (Below) *Land reform is essential for India's development.* Vinoba Bhave, a disciple of Gandhi, is having his feet bathed after his daily walk, collecting voluntary contributions of land. Already he has received over two million acres to be distributed to the landless. Legislation has often been slow, but Vinoba's "land-gift" pilgrimage may speed the pace. His goal is fifty million acres.

Wide World

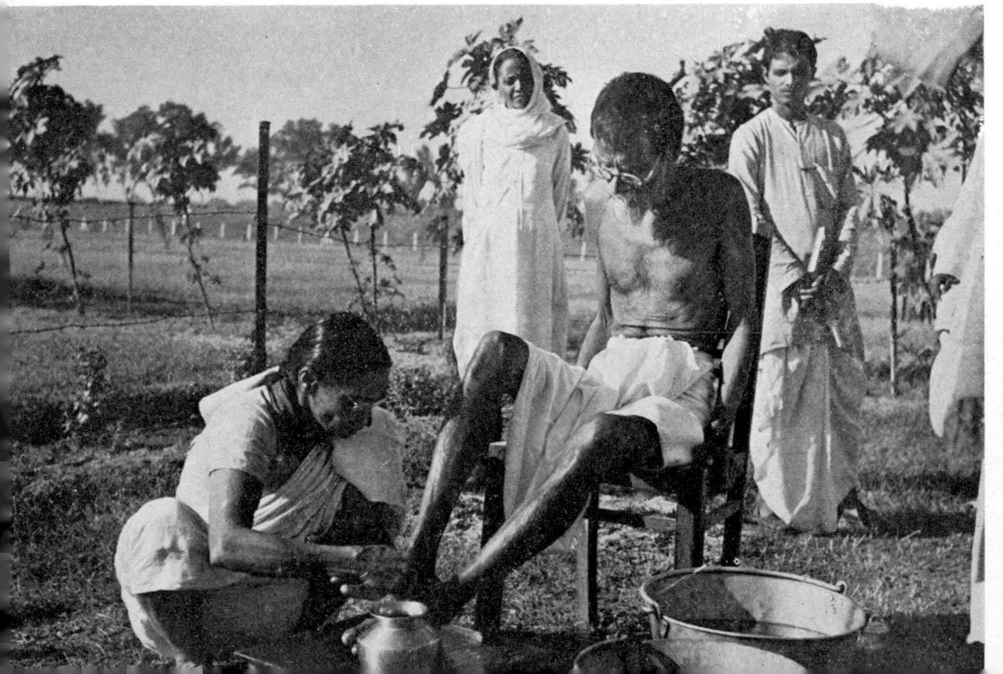

United Press

(Above) *Over the mountains to Nepal.* I was also Ambassador to this little known kingdom of ten million people which has been cut off from the world for generations between India and Tibet. In 1951 the people here overthrew the Ranas, and re-established their King as a constitutional monarch. (Right) *Immediately after my presentation to the King in Durbar Hall.* On the wall hangs a picture of Queen Victoria. At my right is M. P. Koirala, the young Prime Minister. Seated on the throne is His Majesty King Tribhuvan. (Below right) *A palace of one of the Rana family in Katmandu.* The entire furnishings and equipment for about thirty such establishments were carried over the mountains on the backs of the people. At the other extreme is the total poverty of most of the villagers. I strongly urged that land and tax reforms take place if American aid was to be used effectively.

Paul W. Rose

Paul W. Rose

(Above left) *On top of the last pass overlooking Katmandu.* Sally and Sam meet a young Nepalese. (Above right) *Tibetan horns beckon to a wedding.* In remote Pokhara valley, where people saw their first wheel—on an airplane—two years ago, we watched a wedding procession. (Below left) *Dancing on the village green.* These hill people are beginning to want modern medicine, agriculture and education in a hurry. (Below right) *A Nepalese Gurkha soldier with kukri knife.* Among the world's most famous fighters, there are still two divisions of Gurkhas in the British army and one in the Indian army.

Paul W. Rose

(Above) *Good-by to India.* Our sober looks at an Embassy farewell party are evidence that our roots in India were deeper than we realized. (Right) *On the Voice of Indonesia.* Everywhere in Asia I was asked to speak on American foreign policy. With few exceptions I found Asians receptive and understanding. On many issues I feel that they are wrong or misinformed, but they have a right to speak and we have an obligation to listen. (Below) *Talking with a Japanese farmer.* Wolf Ladejinsky, author of the far-reaching land reforms carried out under General MacArthur, a young Japanese agricultural specialist, Sam and I ask questions about the world's most efficient wheat, rice and vegetable farming.

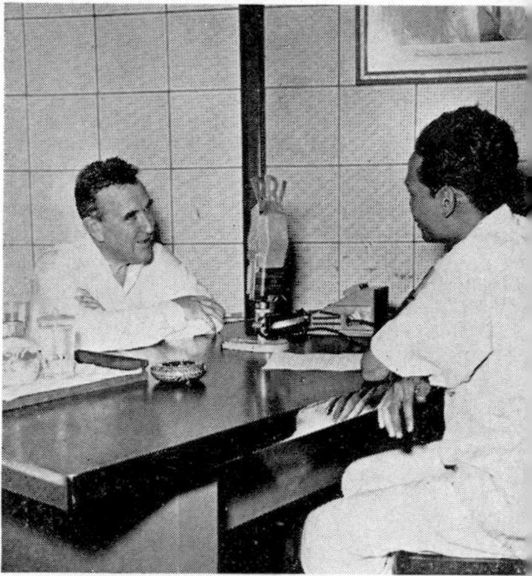

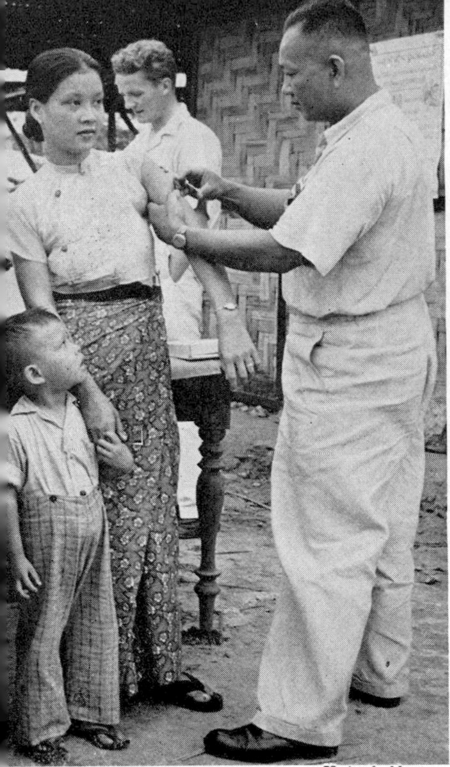

United Nations

United Nations

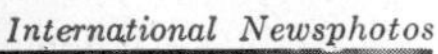

International Newsphotos

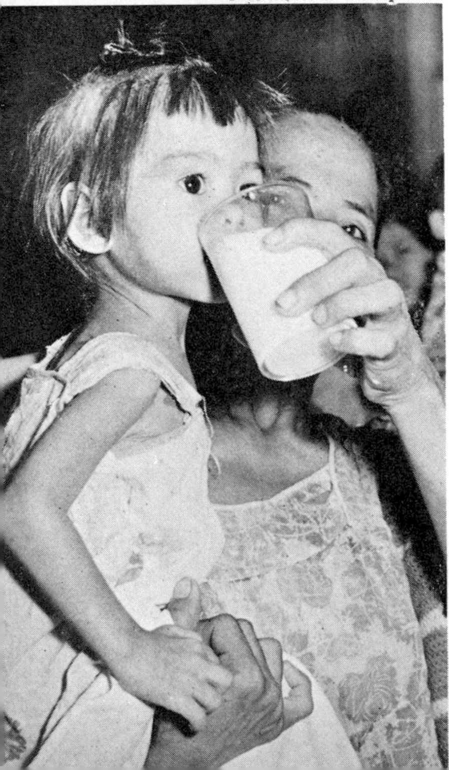

(Above left) *Public Health in Burma.* Asian people are aware of what modern science can do against disease. (Above right) *Children in Thailand.* With a life expectancy nearly twice that of India, and with two-thirds of the children in school, Thailand is an oasis in South Asia. Colonialism has never drained away its resources. (Below left) *UN Children's Fund in the Philippines.* Everywhere we were impressed with work of UN agencies. (Below right) *G.I. babies in Japan.* Our immigration policies even keep out five thousand illegitimate children of our troops in Japan. Steb visited several church orphanages. Even the effort to get them admission to Hawaii has failed.

the villagers, supported the great landlords and attempted to build their strength in the cities, while Mao steadily created the peasant following that brought him to power. Today in Formosa, after Communist prodding and with American advice, the Nationalist government is erecting the kind of rural structure which on the mainland would have made Mao's victory impossible.

In Japan the correlation between land ownership and Communist success again holds true, and in a happy way. Under General Douglas MacArthur the most extensive land reform in Asia has taken place, and Communist strength among the villagers is correspondingly slight.

Before the war the Japanese farmers were the forgotten half of the economy. Over two-thirds of them were tenants. To its everlasting credit, the MacArthur administration recognized that no sound democracy was possible on such a flimsy base.

In the first year of our occupation, as the Supreme Commander for the Allied Powers, MacArthur directed the Japanese government to "take measures to insure that those who till the soil of Japan shall have a more equal opportunity to enjoy the fruits of their labor." With the advice of our agricultural expert, Wolf Ladejinsky, a law was enacted which redistributed all land of absentee owners and all land above seven acres. About a third of the total farm acreage changed hands.

When I was in Japan in 1953, 92 per cent of the villagers owned their own land. To dozens of these farmers I put the question whether they were better off than before the war. Invariably the reply would be a grin, and an answer such as this from an old peasant: "In the former days we paid half our crop to the landlord. Now we keep it all. What do you think?"

Everyone said that the solid security which the Japanese farmers now feel is the greatest single factor for stability in modern Japan. In this atmosphere Communist propaganda has been a dismal failure, and Communist candidates won no seats in the last election.

Actually the land reform under MacArthur was more complete and with less compensation to landowners than has been carried out anywhere in free Asia. Each landlord received a modest sum in twenty-four-year bonds, which because of the sweeping inflation turned out to be worth only about 1/30 of their supposed value.

Since the tenants could also purchase the land with the inflated currency, called "Mickey Mouse" money, they got an added break. Although it was unnecessarily hard on the landowners, this reform of MacArthur may go down in history as the most decisive and beneficial step in the building of a new democratic Japan.

An examination of the land question in every Asian country demonstrates the danger of any further delay in carrying out thorough reforms. Yet this survey also suggests the difficulties involved.

Nowhere in Asia have sweeping land reforms been enacted by a free and democraticly elected legislature. In Japan, the reforms were ordered by a stroke of MacArthur's pen. Under the American occupation there could be no effective opposition. In Formosa there was no opposition permitted either, and in any event almost all of the land which the Formosa peasants have received with such excitement was formerly owned by Japanese landlords who thus paid the usual price of losing a war.

Indeed, I know of only one example in modern times of a fully democratic country carrying out a large-scale land reform: the Czechoslovakia of 1926 under Beneš and the elder Masaryk.

In India the obstacles to land reforms such as those so desperately needed in the Tanjore district are unquestionably formidable. The big landowners are educated, articulate, politically astute and often in a position to bring powerful pressure to bear on state legislatures.

Yet I believe that there are irresistible forces pressing for reforms. It is my hope that India will be the first great Asian nation to face the issue and solve it in a peaceful, decent and democratic way. Her very commitment to democracy may well compel this to be done soon. In Russia and China the peasants voted for land reform with their feet and their guns. In India they now vote for it by the ballot.

In India's first election every party, even most of the reactionary communalist parties, had to give at least lip service to land reform, and in most districts candidates were attempting to outdo each other in promising what they thought the villagers wished. Gandhi knew that the village was the key to India and to Asia. Through his genius the Congress won the allegiance of the peasants, and thus gained irresistible power.

To transform the "dung heaps of today" into "little gardens

of Eden," Gandhi knew that there was required both sweeping land reforms to shatter the old order, and patient, skilled technicians to settle in the villages and aid their development. He believed that if educated India would but throw itself into this experiment, India would be able to "evolve a new order which will astonish the whole world."

In 1942, Gandhi was arrested before he could carry out his plans, but he had written that the next phase of his liberation movement would begin by the nonpayment of taxes by peasants: "Their final step will be to seize the land."

In a free India, Gandhi told Louis Fischer in 1942, "the peasants would take the land." Fischer asked if the landowners would be compensated. "No," Gandhi replied, "that would be fiscally impossible," although he later made clear that each landowner would be allowed a family holding to till himself.

Fischer asked if this would not mean violence, but Gandhi said he was sure the landlords would co-operate, adding with his usual humor, that "they might co-operate by fleeing."

Gandhi promised the landless untouchables that with independence "the first act of the Legislature" would be to give them grants of land. "And if the landlords, zamindars, monied men," Gandhi added, "find that they are discriminated against, I shall sympathize with them, but I will not be able to help them . . . because I would seek their assistance in that process."

But unlike Mao in China, Gandhi did not want to come to power himself by means of the peasants—he wanted *them* to come to power through him.

. . .

Is the democratic government of free India taking the steps necessary to achieve what Gandhi saw was so necessary? On paper the government is committed to reform. But only in Kashmir has the "upper limit on the amount of land which an individual may hold," which the Five Year Plan recommends, been boldly set and enforced. There a man is only allowed land that he and his family can till themselves.

In one respect, an important part of the necessary program is at last well under way. Most of the states are abolishing the "zamindari" landlordism, by which the government tax collectors set up by the British Governor, Lord Cornwallis, gradually assumed ownership of the land itself. This feudal system is being rapidly liquidated with generous compensation to the landlords.

Unfortunately in some states, where in order to get legal title the tillers are required to pay ten years' rent to the landlord in installments heavier than the old rent, many tenants do not feel able to exercise their rights.

A far better system would be to give the tenant full title immediately, with compensation to the landlord, required by the Indian Constitution, to be paid by the state through twenty-year bonds. These would pay a moderate rate of interest and be non-negotiable for a period of years to guard against an increase in inflationary pressure. They could be paid off by an increase in land taxes which would still leave the peasant owner's net income far higher than it is today as a tenant farmer.

Since land values in most Indian states are incredibly high (I have seen ordinary rice paddy land in West Bengal valued at $1,500 an acre!) the fixing of compensation is most difficult. Some experts have suggested that the way to cut through the complexities and to spread land ownership more broadly is simply to limit land ownership (except for a few special crops such as jute, tea, pepper and sugar cane) to ten acres. Absentee ownership would be barred after a stated date and land rentals limited to a top of 20 per cent. This would force a wide sale of land along with a sharp drop in present prices (there would be a floor below which land prices would not be allowed to fall).

In addition to ending the zamindari system, many of the states are adopting tenancy legislation, granting occupancy rights to the present tillers and limiting the rents, which is a step in the right direction. In Tanjore district, where the village previously described was located, the Madras government finally issued an ordinance which limited the rents to 60 per cent instead of the old average of 70 to 80 per cent, prohibited evictions for five years, reinstated some of the tenants already evicted, and for the first time gave some rights to day laborers.

However, about 50 per cent of the tenants, on small plots, where fleecing by the landowners can be as serious as on the large, were not covered. Nor is the peasant's 40-per-cent share of the crop sufficient for anything but the most meager existence after he has paid the cost of production, seed, fertilizer and irrigation water. Moreover the condition of most of the landless laborers remains untouched.

In general, tenancy regulations are unworkable because the landlord is still left in a powerful position. Often he is the only literate man in the village. In the Punjab, where tenants who have tilled a certain plot for five years were finally given permanent tenure, I have been in villages where the records show that no tenant has tilled the same piece of land for more than two or three years! The village head and his associates, who owned most of the land, were able to juggle the books because he alone knew how to read them.

Furthermore, ever since tenancy legislation had been first talked about the alert landowners had been carrying out widespread evictions in order to remove many of the occupancy claims.

In 1952 I arranged to have two of America's foremost experts in land policy, Wolf Ladejinsky, the architect of the reforms in Japan, and Kenneth Parsons, Professor of Agricultural Economics at the University of Wisconsin, come to India to review the land ownership situation and to prepare recommendations for the government. After intensive studies of several states, including Madras and the Tanjore district, Ladejinsky reported that the bitter complaints of the peasants reminded him of similar complaints he heard in pre-Communist China in 1946. The land inequalities in parts of India, he said, were as bad or even worse than he had seen anywhere else in Asia.

Both Ladejinsky and Parsons concluded that progress in reforms was much too slow to meet the rising discontent of the villagers. Members of the Indian Planning Commission told me that these reports were influential in guiding the recommendations in the Five Year Plan. But when I left India the central government still had not been able to induce many of the states to take the necessary legislative action.

Why has progress been so slow? Part of the explanation undoubtedly lies in the heterogeneous make-up of the Congress party. When Gandhi was once asked about charges that Congress was supported by the vested interests, he replied frankly, "Unfortunately, they are true," adding that this "created a silent debt," but that he was sure Congress would bring about needed reforms nonetheless.

It is also true that many groups within the Congress party today are supporting the old vested interests in the villages. In many areas of South India it is difficult to find Congress workers who still champion the claims of the poorer peasants.

But since the Congress party today depends largely on Nehru for its popular strength and since he is a lifelong champion of land reform, many people in India and in other countries wonder why clear decisive action is not forthcoming. In my opinion, as I have already said, the principal reason lies in Nehru's determination that the state assemblies must be given every opportunity to carry out the responsibilities under the Constitution.

Perhaps the largest obstacle to bold action in many of the state assemblies is the frightening gap between the educated Indians and the villages, a gap which makes the political leaders hesitant and uncertain. They know that they are out of touch with village India and fear that they will make a false move that does not fit village realities. "Many of us are two generations removed from the villages," one South Indian government official told me. "The villages appall me."

In my incomplete observations of hundreds of villages, I found one distressing common denominator: the power was in the hands of old men, who were trying to hang on to the feudal past and were out of touch with the dynamic new aspirations of the younger people. Fully aware of my own lack of intimate knowledge of Indian village life, I began to realize that many of the Indian officials from Delhi on down through the state capitals to the villages themselves, brilliantly educated and competent in Western ways, were almost equally estranged, in one way or another, from village India.

I have come to believe that the key to an understanding of Asian villagers is a special reverent concept of land as the source of all wealth and goodness, which those who till the land on every continent seem to have in common. Kenneth Parsons told me the story of a Nigerian chief whose views ring true to what I saw in India. "I conceive that land belongs to a vast family," the chief said, "of which many are dead, few are living and countless numbers are still unborn."

If New India devises a land policy which meets the surging desires of its villagers and awakens the best in them, then democracy will grow from the village up. Then the heavy hand of the old village leaders, of ancient caste superstitions and prejudices will be lifted and new vital leadership will emerge with its roots deep among the people.

Land reform is not a solution, of course; it is simply a first essential step to agricultural improvement, to consolidation of fragmented holdings, and to the development of village co-operatives. Land inequality is a bottleneck, clogging the creative energy of the people; a bottleneck that must be broken.

. . .

India is a land of miracles, and strange are the shapes in which miracles come. In Hinduism's holiest book, the *Gita*, the Lord Krishna says, "Whenever there is decay of righteousness and exaltation of unrighteousness, then I myself come forth; for the protection of the good, for the destruction of evildoers; for the sake of firmly established righteousness, I am born from age to age."

When Gandhi came, despite all his denials that he was a Mahatma, the people believed that the Lord had come again to work in the world. And now just when frustration and despair were spreading among the people, a frail old disciple of Gandhi is applying the Mahatma's principles of nonviolence and truth to the solution of the problem of land.

When Vinoba Bhave left his father's home thirty years ago, he was supposed to go to college to become a chemical engineer, but the tales of the Maharashtrian saints which his mother had told him led him instead to Benares, and finally to Gandhi's ashram. There he became an obscure but dedicated disciple, practicing chastity, poverty and "bread labor."

To identify himself completely with village India, Vinoba established his own little ashram near Sevagram where he sought to prove that he and his followers could live adequately on less than one acre of land apiece. In the 1940 campaign of individual disobedience to British law, Gandhi picked the unknown Vinoba to be the "satyagrahi number one," that is, to be the first to invite a prison term.

In 1951, the Gandhian workers asked him to attend a conference in Hyderabad of the so-called movement for "Sarvodaya, the rising of all." Instead of the easy overnight train ride, Vinoba traveled the several hundred miles on foot, village by village. He was struck by the grave needs of the landless and the insufficiency of the new land legislation.

In Hyderabad he decided to tour the Telingana area where, as we have seen, in 1948 a thousand or so villages under the Communists had risen violently and been violently suppressed. On April 18, in Nalgonda district, a party of untouchables pleaded with him for land. If they were not to get land the bitter, bloody way of the Communists, how were they to get it?

He assembled the whole village, asked those who had land to give it to the landless, and incredibly they did.

Thus was born the ideas of *Bhoomi-dan Yagna,* "Worship through the Sharing of Land," in short, *Bhoodan* "land gift." From then on, to every village audience Vinoba would make this plea: "If you have four sons and a fifth is born, you would certainly give him his share. Treat me as your fifth son, and give me my share."

By the time he reached home from Hyderabad, he had collected and distributed twelve thousand acres, and soon the news came that his followers in Telingana had collected thirty-five thousand acres there. Vinoba now vowed to place this idea before the whole people of India.

Nehru asked Vinoba to come to Delhi to discuss the land problem with India's National Planning Commission, and offered to send a plane down for him. "I will come," Vinoba replied, "but in my own time, and as always." He went on foot the whole 795 miles. It was a triumphant two months' tour, with arches of palms and mango leaves erected for him to walk under in nearly every village and town. On the way he collected another eighteen thousand acres.

In Delhi he stayed in a bamboo hut near Gandhi's cremation spot, to which Nehru came several times, and the Planning Commission, and the President of India, who told him to take as much of the Prasad family lands in Bihar as he wanted.

He was in the capital for only eleven days before returning to his village mission. It was during our first weeks in India and Steb went to one of his open-air prayer meetings at the Gandhi memorial. It began with the singing of the Lord's prayer in Hindustani. She came home amazed that this frail little man of eighty-six pounds and fifty-seven years, with malaria and duodenal ulcers, could endure walking fifteen miles a day. She described his gray beard, his bifocal glasses resembling Gandhi's and his friendly quiet voice. He spoke in Hindustani, but is a master of English, as well as French, Persian, Sanskrit and a half dozen Indian languages. He eats only two cups of yogurt daily, with a little honey. When Steb left just before sundown, Nehru was arriving for consultation.

From Delhi Vinoba walked down the Ganges through the state of Uttar Pradesh to the state of Bihar. In U.P. he suggested to volunteers that they set as their first aim the settling of one landless family on five acres in every one of U.P.'s tens of thousands of villages. By the time he left, 100,000 acres were contributed, and within a year his followers had secured the necessary half million acres.

He then set as his nation-wide goal the collection of fifty million acres by the end of 1956, or about one-fifth of Indian's cultivated acreage. As a first milestone, he set the figure of 2½ million acres by April of 1954. By September, 1953, he was already the world's largest landlord, with over two million acres having been conveyed to him for redistribution. To get it he had walked 6,500 miles, the equivalent of a trip from Boston to Los Angeles and return by way of Florida.

In Bihar, he decided that he would submit his program to its strongest test. "I shall not leave this state until every landless family in Bihar has land to live on," he announced, setting his target for the state at three million acres, about one-fifth of the total cultivated land.

He established his headquarters in Gaya, where Buddha received "enlightenment." Soon he had over six hundred volunteers walking through the villages, collecting land with him. In the Hazaribagh district of Bihar alone over 700,000 acres have already been received, contributed by more than 5,000 donors.

Why are people giving their land to this extraordinary little ascetic? The Communists say that most of the gifts come from areas where the landlords have been frightened by Communist activities, or from areas where land is the most plentiful. The facts belie this. About 90 per cent of the land so far collected comes from U.P. and Bihar, on the densely populated Gangetic plains, which so far have been almost untouched by communism. Only about fifty thousand acres have come from areas of Communist strength.

A wealthy young South Indian landowner has given all his land and joined Vinoba, but he had no fear of communism. He had returned from studies in the United States with a determination to devote his life to the constructive service of the Indian people. One Maharaja has given 100,000 acres, but most of the gifts have been small.

"We have songs in the local dialects. We also cry in the villages: 'The hungry masses are waiting—share your land and wealth,'" writes a lovely young Indian girl we know who is walking with Vinoba. "The rich people hear this cry and loosen their tight bundles a little, but they do not give with the same generosity as the small landholders. We always go to the smaller people first and the rich are shamed into giving."

Of course, many motives are at work, and the force of public opinion is a crucial factor. "The God who is distributing land has come!" shout the emaciated peasants. "The Son of Gandhi," cry others, and the resulting pressures for action are very great.

"Everyone prays when Vinoba enters a district," is a current joke. The poor man prays that he will come to his village, and the rich man prays that he will go around his village. Since he can only stop for collection at two or three villages a day, at the most, and must walk by the others, the owners have a gambling chance. Some seek out Vinoba, however, and one day a small landowner walked twenty-eight miles to give one acre.

If Vinoba visits a village, the landowners face a dilemma. "How much can we afford to give? How little can we afford not to give?" One of the volunteers described how the large landowners in a village would huddle together, watching to see how much the small holders give, comparing how much the previous village had given, wondering what the next village will do. If they are too stingy they lose prestige in the district.

There is no doubt that Bhoodan has caught the imagination of the Indian villagers. All parties, except the Communist, are vying with each other in their support of Vinoba. Both the Congress and Praja Socialist parties have asked their members to heed Vinoba's call for volunteers to devote a full year to collection.

The Socialist leader, Jayaprakash Narayan, has himself vowed to spend at least the next full year on Bhoodan, and he is now collecting almost as much land as Vinoba. In one village *all* the land was contributed to him, so that a complete redistribution with consolidation of holdings was possible.

"What a misfortune it would be if we did not recognize the revolution that is taking place today all around us like the unfortunate devotee who did not recognize God when He appeared before him," Jayaprakash told the conference of Bhoodan workers. "That is why I ask all the young people of this country to give up their schools and colleges and take part in this great revolution."

Meanwhile the Communists sulk, saying that Vinoba is forestalling the *real* revolution. "The Communists may still feel unconvinced and dub me a simpleton," Vinoba replies, "but let me tell them that I know my trade." He says that he will not consider his movement successful until he has converted the Communists and received their co-operation. Members of his party are especially urged to sell Gandhian literature to the Communists, who always stand uncertainly on the outskirts of the meetings.

"Do you really believe in your ideology?" Vinoba asks such Communists. If so "why not come in the daytime instead of by night? If you want to loot the people, loot as I do, with sincerity and affection."

Vinoba does not expect his way to achieve full social revolution by itself. Legislation is also required. Communists, he says, "begin with murder and want to bring in legislation at the end, but I want to begin with pity and kindness. My aim is to bring about a three-fold revolution. Firstly, I want a change in people's hearts; secondly, I want to create a change in their lives; and thirdly, I want to change the social structure." If "looting with affection" succeeds, Vinoba has no fear of communism. "A thirsty man, if he can get good clean water will not touch dirty water," he says.

To those who began urging him to take a leading office in the government and carry out his program by law, he replied, "When two bullocks are already yoked to a cart, what use is a third bullock to the cart? The greatest help I can render is to prepare the road so that the cart can move in the right direction.

"I do not stand in the way of legislation. If I get only 50-per-cent success in the program I have adopted, it will make legislation easier. . . . I want to build up and we must build up the power of the people. . . . I shall dance with joy if it [land reform] is done entirely through the power of the people. But I shall be satisfied if it is done mainly through the power of the people."

One can hope that, as Vinoba's efforts spread, the power of the people will force the swift enactment of the long overdue land reform laws. Then all the creative energy, now of necessity going into Bhoodan, can go into the reconstruction of the country.

Thus it may be that Vinoba will accomplish far more than he imagines. He may have struck the spark which relights the Gandhian force in Indian life. With Gandhi's death, Gandhism seemed almost to go through a prism, and come out refracted in a dozen different directions. On one beam was the Prime Minister, on another were the patient dedicated Gandhian workers, on another were the Socialists. And now Vinoba, if his frail physique can stand the continuing strain, may bring all these together. He has certainly picked the paramount issue in India, on which to prove the continuing validity of the Gandhian way.

Vinoba's critics say that he lacks some of the essential "kick" of Gandhi, as well as the Mahatma's vital gaiety which prevented self-righteousness from setting in. It is argued that love was only one side of Gandhi, and that anger at, and direct resistance to, injustice was the other side.

If this is an accurate assessment, the Praja Socialists may now be adding a typically Indian ingredient of peaceful struggle to the program. In September, 1953, they launched a new kind of Gandhian satyagraha. Over one thousand peasants in Bombay province, led by Asoka Mehta, after taking a pledge of non-violence, marched onto one thousand acres of grassland which the landlords were refusing to cultivate.

Their demands were limited: "Allow us to grow food on these acres, and we will pay you whatever rent the government sets as just." They said they would call off the campaign if the landlords contributed the acres to Vinoba's Bhoodan. The landlords refused.

On the first of September, fifteen thousand villagers cheered as the "Land Army," marching three abreast, preceded by a pair of garlanded bullocks yoked to a plow, moved onto the vacant land singing gaily. Soon two hundred policemen arrested the "trespassers," including several hundred women.

Although the most active organizers were kept in custody, and the leaders were held for trial, the campaign went on as scheduled. On September 10, the *New York Times* correspondent, Bob Trumbull, reported that three thousand volunteers started to dig the tract of grassland. "As the police arrested one group it would pass its picks and shovels to another," his dispatch said. "An outgrowth of the demonstrations is that thousands of peasants in the area have taken a pledge to boycott the landlords when it comes time to cut and cart away the grass."

So far Vinoba himself has not introduced this element of jail-going against the old feudalistic land systems which one might expect in a Gandhian program. On the other hand, it is inaccurate to suggest that Vinoba seeks charity. He comes on no bended knee to the landowners. "God is standing at your door in the form of the poor and the landless," he says firmly. He demands land as a *right.*

As his program gains momentum it has some immediate practical consequences: with "land gifts" increasing, the market in land drops and the price of land falls in the area. It also becomes increasingly difficult for landlords to ask high compensation when some are giving without any compensation. Above all, Vinoba is focusing the attention of the country on the land crisis about which many others might have still procrastinated.

Whether he can accomplish his great purpose remains to be seen. But he has already inspired many Indians with new faith. An Indian girl of eighteen of whom we were very fond joined his party as a full-time volunteer.

"Mother, I think I am very lucky that I came to this world as a child of India," she wrote, in a beautiful letter which we were privileged to see. "How fortunate our country is that we have had so many great ascetics and saints, one after another, like beads in a rosary. . . .

"That is why we still have the living love of God, and the fear of his law in every village and that is why this great nonviolent revolution is taking place in our country. . . . Rivers of blood used to flow for one bit of land, and now people are giving the same land to 'God who dwells in the poor.'"

If through Vinoba, and the power of the people, and wise laws, a peaceful reconstruction of village India now takes place, then the world may at last learn the great lesson of our age: that there is no contradiction between bread and freedom. From the new-found freedom of the peasants, in land reforms, co-operatives and free elections, may come a burst of creative productive effort the like of which Asia has not yet seen.

And with this bread, translated in terms of health and energy and a chance to get an education, India may in the coming years have a new birth of freedom.

14. Community Development—A Key to Village Asia

ON THE anniversary of Gandhi's birthday, October 2, 1952, a nation-wide village program of Community Development was launched in twenty-eight Indian states. At Alipore, near Delhi, Steb, Sally, Sam and I attended the jamboree opening of one of the first fifty-five development projects, covering sixteen thousand villages and more than eleven million people, in which work commenced that day. Under a scorching sun, Nehru addressed a great crowd of peasants.

"The work which has started here today spells the revolution about which some people have been shouting for so long. This is not a revolution based on chaos and the breaking of heads, but on a sustained effort to eradicate poverty. This is no time for speeches. We must make India great by our toil."

Then he and all the officials present took shovels and started the "voluntary road building" which was to be the first joint activity in the project area covering some three hundred villages. Indian newsreel men asked me to pose with Nehru for pictures which they said would be shown throughout India, but I declined on the ground that this was India's day. Asian nations are already convinced that most Americans are brash boasters and publicity seekers.

"You are building a new India," I had already said that morning in a statement to the press. "If you succeed in this great experiment in democracy, as I am convinced you will, all the free world will be in your debt."

Actually, no Indian could have been any happier that day than I was. Although most of the money for the project was provided by the Indians, America's aid had been significant, and in the best sense, this was the Point Four idea coming to life.

When I accepted the ambassadorship to India I thought that one of the most important things I could do would be to help hammer out a practical joint program by which American aid would contribute to India's economic progress. Thus I hoped that the best in America could join hands with the best in India.

Long before coming to India I had welcomed Point Four as an exciting opportunity for America to associate her ideals and her resources with the efforts of more than a billion people to secure a better life. I had talked at length with doctors and agricultural experts, American and foreign, who had come face to face with the problems of village Asia.

Of particular interest had been the work of James Y. C. Yen in pre-Communist China. Dr. Yen, a graduate of Yale University, had returned to China after the First World War fired with determination to help set his people free from the bonds of ignorance, poverty and disease. As Minister of Education in Chiang Kai-shek's Nationalist government he had thrown his energies into an imaginative and effective program of village development which might have changed the face of China.

One of his first discoveries was the relative ineffectiveness of a haphazard, piecemeal approach. When an agricultural worker went to a village alone to induce the peasants to sow or cultivate in a more efficient way he usually made some progress. And so did a literacy expert assigned to the task of setting up schools, or a public health doctor bent on curbing malaria.

But Dr. Yen discovered that far more could be accomplished in each of these fields if these three workers went as a team, entering the villages together and developing a broad, co-ordinated development program. Later as it became clear that permanent progress was only possible when the villagers themselves controlled their local governments, a fourth worker was added whose specialty was the encouragement of democratic self-government.

Under Dr. Yen's driving energy, more than twenty million people were covered by this program before the war brought it to what he hoped was only a temporary stop. In 1945 Dr. Yen asked Chiang Kai-shek for the resources to spread this tested village development effort into all of rural China. The Generalissimo was impressed but insisted that a military victory over the Communist forces was the first order of business.

"When we have crushed Mao Tse-tung's armies we will give full support to your plan," he is supposed to have said. "But you cannot defeat communism on the battlefield," Yen is said to have replied, "until you have first conquered it in the villages and rice fields; it is the poverty and hopelessness of the peasants which is giving Mao his chance."

No one knows whether the tragic debacle that followed might have been averted if Dr. Yen had had his way, but we do know that Mao's strength in the villages continued to grow and that his peasant soldiers, fired with the hope of land and plenty, defeated the dispirited Nationalists in battle after battle. American army officers testified before Congress that the Nationalist army "could have defended the Yellow River line with broomsticks if the soldiers had had the will to fight."

When I knew that I was going to India, all that I had learned from Dr. Yen came to my mind. In theory at least his techniques seemed superior to the more diffused development programs which were being started in most of the underdeveloped countries through the United Nations Specialized Agencies and America's Point Four.

The usual procedure was to select a going agricultural center which had already accumulated some experience in village work, a clinic or hospital which had special skill in malaria or yaws control, an educational institution which had made progress in literacy work among the villages, and around these centers create individual programs. This meant that the health workers, the agricultural specialists and the literacy experts might be working hundreds of miles apart in the same country with only casual and infrequent contacts.

Although each of the scattered campaigns was often successful by itself, it seemed to me that Dr. Yen was wise to combine them into an integrated plan of broader impact which could be spread village by village. When Steb, Cynthia, Sally, Sam and I visited the Etawah development project in Uttar Pradesh two or three weeks after our arrival in India I became convinced that this was right.

Etawah was started in 1948 by the U.P. state government as a pilot study project. The original proposal came from an American architect, Albert Mayer, who, as a soldier in India during the war, had been stirred by the poverty of the Indian villagers, on the one hand, and their enormous potential strength and creativeness on the other. It was an effort to combine the Gandhian program of village development with the extension service techniques of the U.S. Department of Agriculture. It was entirely financed by the Indians themselves. Later they employed Horace Holmes, a brilliant and personable agricultural specialist from Tennessee, to assist in the training work.

When we first visited Etawah the work was being carried out in ninety-seven villages with some sixty thousand inhabitants. Village workers had been carefully trained, first to win the confidence of the villagers and then to introduce in each village new methods of fertilizing, better seeds, public health measures, primary education and literacy courses.

We were deeply impressed by the nearly 50-per-cent increase which had been achieved in food production, by the clean, healthier villages and by the earnest groups of villagers learning to read and write. But most exciting of all here I saw in action the very principles of multipurpose development which Dr. Yen had developed in China.

There was an important difference. At Etawah it had been demonstrated that a single worker could be trained as a "generalist" to cover all three fields. Although six months' training could not, of course, make him into an expert in all phases of agriculture, public health and education, he was able to learn enough about each to do effective work. When he ran up against a difficult specialized problem he was taught to call in at once one of the specialists in agriculture, public health and education who were members of the project staff. Each village worker was responsible for getting the work started in three or four villages, while the specialists covered from ten to twenty villages.

As I listened to the hard-working, dedicated instructors in the village worker school and watched workers in the fields and villages, it seemed that this was the key to the future of India and Asia. Here was an administrative framework through which modern scientific knowledge could be put to work for the benefit of the hundreds of millions of people who have so long lived in poverty.

. . .

That night I went to work with pencil and paper. How many village workers would it take to cover every village in India? How many public health specialists would be needed? How many agricultural engineers, soil conservation experts, irrigation specialists? What about literacy teachers? How long would it take to train all these people?

As soon as I had word that the Indian share of the new technical assistance program provided by Congress in 1951 would be $54 million, I was ready with a proposal for the Indian government. I called the Prime Minister's office and requested an appointment as soon as possible. It was set for 4 P.M. the next day.

Since this happened to be Thanksgiving Day, 1951, our Embassy was closed. So all morning I sat at home thinking through the conversation that lay ahead. I tried to marshal all my facts in the most persuasive possible way.

Experience had taught me that important men are often poor listeners, so I decided to put my ideas into a single, brief direct memorandum. As it was my secretary's holiday, Sally was pressed into service as a typist. At quarter of four I tucked the resulting memorandum, which had a somewhat homemade look, into my pocket, and left for Mr. Nehru's office.

On the way over an uncomfortable thought occurred to me. I had heard that the Indians were very proud and sensitive, and unwilling to ask for foreign aid. What if they refused even to accept our offer of assistance? How embarrassing it would be to hear some rabid anti-administration critic say, "Your Ambassador to India couldn't even give away $50 million!"

I opened the conversation by suggesting to Mr. Nehru that one of the most crucial questions was whether Asian democracy could compete with Asian communism unless it, too, organized its village efforts on a massive scale, substituting persuasion and cooperation for violence and concentration camps. I emphasized my lack of first-hand experience and tried to check my enthusiasm because of the humility I felt in the face of the problems about which every Asian leader is so deeply conscious. Finally, and with apologies for its inadequacies, I asked the Prime Minister to read my memorandum outlining proposals for a nation-wide plan of village development.

When he finished reading it, I told him that I had been authorized by my government to offer India $54 million in economic assistance to assist on some such village campaign and on other programs. There would be no strings, economic, political or otherwise. Our only desire was to help Indian democracy to succeed.

Nehru said that history had selected India as one of democracy's chief testing grounds. This was a contest which he and India welcomed, a challenge which must be met head on. Can a poverty-stricken country recently emerged from colonialism maintain and expand freedom while it organizes and develops its economic resources? The Communists say this cannot be done and should not be tried, but India disagrees.

For nearly two hours we talked about the exciting possibilities. When I left he thanked me earnestly for the help that the American people had offered. I said that we wanted no thanks and indeed that if India succeeded in raising her living standards by democratic means and demonstrated to Asia and to the world that men can have bread and freedom too, the whole free world would be in India's debt.

The next weeks were spent in feverish planning. First there was an agreement to be drawn up between the United States and India, a ticklish problem. Although Nehru had made it clear that he accepted at face value my assertion that our aid was not a bribe designed to buy India's allegiance, I knew that many educated Indians, perhaps even the majority, had been convinced by sad experience that the Western white man rarely offered a favor in Asia without expecting to receive a return far greater than his investment. They had not forgotten that the English came first to India as traders and stayed to conquer.

My problem as Ambassador was further complicated by the fact that some Americans are short-sighted enough to expect foreign nations to grovel for our favors like beggars in the street. And this, I knew, India and other free Asian nations will never do.

The agreement that we signed three weeks later before the Indian and American newsreel cameras was simple, direct and free of any language into which any nefarious implication could be read. I suggested that it be given to the newspapers and publicized throughout India, and the Prime Minister agreed. The editorial comment was extravagantly generous. Because America had not asked for applause or for gratitude from a proud people we received both in hearty measure.

"I have looked for hooks in this agreement," a skeptical Indian economist, who had been sharply critical of America, told me. "But I have found no fuzzy language of any kind. I am forced to respect the United States for a statesmanlike act."

The Prime Minister soon appointed as director of the Community Development program an able young Indian engineer named S. K. Dey. Mr. Dey had been educated at the University of Michigan, done graduate work at Purdue, and worked for General Electric both in America and in India. In the last few years he had made a name for himself in directing the successful efforts of eight thousand refugees from Pakistan to build the new town of Nilokheri. From the United States we brought a capable team. Clifford Willson of the Colorado River Development Authority and Bernard Loshbough, one of America's ablest development and housing administrators, headed the group which arrived during the winter months of 1951-52.

From the beginning the Indian government was faced with some difficult decisions. One school, with perfectionist leanings, felt that each development area should be almost a model utopia in itself, complete with impressive schools, hospitals, roads and industries, as well as improved agricultural and health services. The cost of such projects would be so high that it would be impossible to spread them all over India.

A second group argued that some quality must be sacrificed for a realistic program that would be carried out in every village in India. "If we concentrate on building a few show places, journalists and visitors from abroad may be impressed, but village India will remain largely untouched," they insisted. They wanted a mass program to touch as many people as possible as quickly as possible, a program that would shake villagers out of their lethargy and arouse their people to an understanding of what they themselves could accomplish for themselves.

Mr. Nehru supported this latter viewpoint and I wholeheartedly agreed. There is not enough outside capital in all the world by itself to make more than a dent on village Asia. Gandhi had always said that India's primary capital must be the labor of Indian people, and he was wholly right.

The tens of millions of dollars which the United States was ready to put in the program, and the several hundred million dollars in rupees which the Indian government could afford, could only scratch the surface. But if these funds served as a catalytic agent for the release of popular energy and enthusiasm, then the people could generate their own capital and reconstruct their villages with their own labor just as the refugee towns of Faridabad and Nilokheri had been constructed. The greatest potential capital asset of the Indian economy is the underemployment of its people. For several months a year an Indian farmer has almost nothing to do. If this vast manpower could be harnessed for village development, the achievements could be great.

Having agreed on the main line of the program we finally decided on a first phase of fifty-five community projects, each one of which was to include roughly three hundred villages and to cover about five hundred square miles. This gave each project a population of around 200,000. An Indian staff of about 125 would be assigned to each project. There would be a village worker for each three or four villages, plus specialists in agriculture, public health and education, and a few clerks and administrative people.

The cost of each project was budgeted at about one million dollars to be spent over a three-year period, after which they were supposed to be self-supporting. The Indian government provided five-sixths of the funds in rupees, while we agreed to put up the remaining one-sixth in dollars to be spent largely for equipment purchased in the United States.

By April 1, 1956, present plans call for the equivalent of four hundred community projects covering more than 100 million people or nearly 35 per cent of all village India, and considerably more than the total populations of France, Italy, Belgium and Holland. This calls for the training of some thirty thousand village workers and hundreds of specialists in soil conservation, irrigation, agricultural engineering, malaria control, public health and literacy work. Without doubt it is the greatest development effort of its kind ever launched in a democratic nation.

So far experience indicates that long before the end of the three years of subsidized work, profound improvements can be achieved in each village. Agricultural production can be increased from between 30 to 200 per cent depending on the irrigation available; malaria and some of the worst diseases can be eliminated; all of the children and many of the adults can be taught to read and write; and a good start can be made on road building and a new school. Nor will progress be confined to villages directly covered by the program. Each village which improves itself is like a stone thrown in a pond, its impact spreads out and starts others to progress.

. . .

When our first fifty-five projects were launched on October 2, 1952, I knew that the relatively small proportion of American aid would be the focal point for the inevitable Communist attack. Although the Point Four agreement with the Indian government had been widely approved throughout India, the pro-Communist Delhi *Times* devoted most of an issue to the theme that "U.S. Big Business is trying to enter India through the back door of community projects." A bold headline accused me of "condemning" the marvelous work at Nilokheri.

Late in the fall appeared a Communist-inspired 336-page handbook, *American Shadow over India*, which asserted that "the U.S.A. contributed only about one-eighth of the budget and yet rules the roost." Our fifty hard-working agricultural specialists then in India were described as "a vast network of imperialist spies."

Communist opposition was to be expected to any program of democratic reform for it is out of India's poverty that the Communists hope to forge a revolution. The question was whether their tactics of insinuation and smear would seriously dampen the enthusiasm of the people in the project areas.

One of our technicians reported that his cook had been told we were really all American agents seeking to locate good atom bomb targets in the Indian countryside! "Does the American sahib for whom you work write things on paper at night?" the servant was asked by a local Communist leader. The American was almost tempted to send his weekly "Dear Folks" letter to the Indian Communists instead of to his home town in Texas.

"What are *you* doing here?" a pro-Communist woman member of the Indian Parliament angrily accosted two of our specialists, in a rural road-building project in the South Indian state of Travancore-Cochin. Fortunately an Indian supervisor was present and promptly spoke up for the Americans, explaining the project.

But the pro-Communist agitators went up and down the whole length of the road, talking to all the villagers, urging them to oppose the work. "This road will be an American invasion route to Russia," they argued. "Don't volunteer your labor! Don't give your land unless you are paid! Don't let the Americans exploit you!"

On the day appointed for voluntary road construction to begin, several hundred villagers appeared and started to dig, along with Indian and American development workers. At this point the woman member of Parliament arrived on the scene with about one hundred supporters and tried to start an anti-American demonstration. Our people were worried that the villagers would desert their work. Although they had been petitioning the government to build them this road for eight years, the idea of doing it by themselves was new.

Fortunately, a villager who was working closely with the project spoke up loudly in the crowd: "It is true that white sahibs in the past have tried to rule us. But these Community Development projects are Indian and run by Indians. They are part of our Five Year Plan to build up the country. And this road was our own idea. Our village councils approved it and planned it. The American engineer comes only to help us to do what we ourselves want to do."

With only three or four exceptions the villagers nodded in agreement. "We are going to help ourselves by building the road," someone shouted, and it soon became a chant. About two hundred villagers took up the picks and shovels and worked hard the rest of the day. "I like people who work, not talk," said one old farmer.

To train these crucial village level workers thirty centers of instruction and on-the-job training were established by the Indian government, in co-operation with the Ford Foundation. Now thousands of young Indians are undergoing the rugged six months' course which is designed to teach those able and willing to serve and to discourage those who are lighthearted or not able to take it.

All over India I have seen these eager young men, from daybreak until after dark, being taught how to build a better seed bed, to plow more effectively, to dig compost heaps, to teach the blacksmith to make simple steel tools, to bring about a shift from an ineffective wooden plow to an iron plow which goes down twice as deep, to take care of cattle diseases, to encourage small vegetable gardens which provide a better diet.

Besides agricultural improvements, they are taught basic public health: how to get rid of rubbish, clean the well, build latrines, spray for malaria. And they are taught how to get a school started in each village.

At the centers, the trainee must break caste rules and do all his own work, such as washing his clothes and dishes. This is preparation for his significant function of dignifying manual labor by doing dirty work himself. He must also know and respect the religious background of his particular village, and be able to sing the villagers' favorite hymns. "The villager is our master," said Mr. Gupta the head of the center, at Bakshi-ka-Talab. "We must revere him almost as though he were a god. For it is only those whom we think above us whom we can serve."

The spirit of this training comes straight from Gandhi, who long ago outlined the requirements of a village worker: "Any lover of true democracy and village life can take up a village, treat it as his world and sole work, and he will find good results," Gandhi had said.

The work is hard and frustrating. When trainees first go out on bicycles to their assigned villages they often find that nobody comes near them and they are surprised and disappointed. "To say that our first trainees were not well received in the villages is putting it too mildly," an American technician, Jack Gray, reported from West Bengal. "Many of them were actively abused by the villagers and all of them were treated very coldly. They were accused of being spies for the government grain procurement department, or sent to gather information about property in order that more taxes might be collected."

One student worker was told by a villager: "We have had only two kinds of visitors before, those who collect taxes and those who come to beat us up. Which are you?" He was ordered to leave the village and not come back. In many areas the sound of an approaching automobile had long been the signal for all the poor people to disappear.

But gradually with persistence and imagination they find their way into the confidence of the villagers. Once two trainees observed that a villager was engaged in clearing the jungle from near his house in order to make a drainage ditch. They offered to help him complete the job. He treated this as a great joke, and when they actually started working at the job he quit work and called his neighbors to observe the efforts of his two city "coolies."

The villagers joined in the fun of ridiculing the two educated "Babus" who were doing coolie labor. When the trainees returned to the center that day they were about ready to abandon the idea of village service. In the group discussion, however, they were urged to take the abuse in good humor and continue the work. "Go back tomorrow and the day after tomorrow and the day after that," the instructors advised. "Keep at it until you have found the right approach." With a smile someone quoted Gandhi's old advice to remember that "it is the reformer who is anxious for the reform, and not society."

After the trainees had returned and labored industriously on the ditch for two days, first the owner and then the villagers relented and became friendly. Some of the other peasants even volunteered to help finish the work. Later, with new confidence in themselves, the trainees got the whole village to clear away a much larger section of the jungle.

Yet even when the villagers accept the sincerity of the trainees and the project workers their troubles are only beginning, for then the people often go to the other extreme and expect the government to provide everything. "Build us a school," the villagers begin to ask, or they petition for a clinic or a road. Then the worker must explain that the government's help is limited and that it will give what assistance it can to the village only if the people are prepared to work hard for their betterment.

"You and your neighbors can make over your village within three or four years," I once heard an earnest young village level worker tell a group of peasants in the Punjab. Squatting on the ground under a banyan tree, he looked directly at the three village elders, although his words were obviously addressed to the fifty or more villagers assembled.

"We will send an engineer who will show you how to plan and build a school, and lay out a road to the market. We will help you build a brick kiln which you can run as a co-operative. We will offer you better seed and fertilizer which can be paid for when your crops are harvested. But you must provide the labor."

"How will we be paid?" asked the village moneylender, who clearly looked on the worker as an intruder. "Your pay will come not in rupees," the young man answered quietly, "but in the satisfaction of seeing your children in school, of knowing that they will grow up healthier and stronger, in being able to move your extra grain to market over roads passable even during the monsoon rains, in knowing that your community is a better place in which to live and that the poverty of the past can be left behind forever. Why does any man need greater pay than that?"

When I left an hour later the group was talking excitedly, there were many volunteers, and the village worker was warning them that progress would take hard work, patience and time.

Usually the first phase of the program is agricultural improvements which rapidly increase village production and raise the eating standard of the area as well as the income. With this success the worker is then able to rally the village behind a voluntary construction program.

In a project in Assam, north of the great Brahmaputra River, near the borders of Burma and Tibet, I visited a village where, after the village worker had shown them how to double their crops, the people went on to invite a teacher to start classes under a tree. Next they built a small schoolhouse. When I visited them in December, 1952, the village volunteers were building a small irrigation dam.

The government had helped with the planning, had provided some steel to the local blacksmith for the new tools, had made available some credit to set up the brick kilns, had donated the teacher's salary for two years after which the village itself would be responsible. But all this would have been meaningless if the people had not donated many thousands of man hours of hard and grueling work.

It is not difficult to foresee the day when the agricultural phase of Community Development will everywhere lead into this second phase of building, when teams of millions of people, young and old, will give a few hours a day to their village and country, after their own work is finished. Once enough brick kilns are built, and the fuel problem is solved, I can visualize a wave of construction which can sweep through 500,000 villages and change the face of the whole subcontinent.

Already a plan has been worked out for "aided self-help housing." With easy credit for materials costing about $100 the villager himself can build a new and decent cottage. Instead of waiting for cement and steel, or for the distant day when he could hire skilled carpenters, the villager under this plan would proceed to build with materials available locally—timber, grass, bamboo, mud and stone. By providing technical advice in designing places of greater utility and more artistry, and by providing a long-term repayment, the government hopes to encourage a major face-lifting of all village India. If the investment of labor amounts to 80 per cent of village construction, it is easy to see how far a little capital can go.

Out of this construction phase must rise a network of village industries to provide work for the unemployed and those displaced from agriculture. Textiles, clothes, shoes, small-unit agricultural and household equipment, paper, processed foods, agricultural by-products and many other goods can now be manufactured efficiently in small village shops.

Gandhi's concept of a balanced village, "a little village republic," is incorporated as the goal of every Community Development project. Through these projects his dream may come to life in our lifetime. As Nehru said, "All over India there are now centers of human activity that are like lamps spreading their light more and more into the surrounding darkness. This light must grow and grow until it covers the land."

• • •

"To believe in this program," said a British visitor who came as a confirmed skeptic, "you have only to visit the villages where it is actually working." He had seen areas where within a year food production had almost doubled, schools were going up, where there was a new sense of purpose in the air.

Senator William Knowland, an outspoken critic of many Indian policies, saw this on his trip through India in September, 1953. After traveling miles through the Sikh area of Patiala, over winding dusty roads, among villages where Community Development was under way, after walking over demonstration farms and talking with villagers, he told a gathering of farm extension workers that in their work was to be found "the real basis of democracy."

I myself will never forget the contrast between villages in which work was under way and those still untouched. In nearly every part of India I had the satisfaction of seeing villages where the peasants proudly show you their community accomplishments and the children take your hand to show you to their school. And I will always be haunted by those countless other villages sunk in indifference or hopelessness, the litter and dirt everywhere, the children scurrying away and peeping out uncertainly from behind mud walls, the women nowhere to be seen, the awful hangdog look of many of the men.

Even in the first few months the progress everywhere was impressive. I have seen the scraggly smaller leafed old desi cotton growing next to a field of the new improved cotton with broad leaves. I have seen fields where last year 1,200 pounds of rice were grown on each acre and which are now producing 4,600 pounds per acre per crop.

In some projects I have joined in digging irrigation canals. In others I have walked over gravel roads built in a few days' time by villagers with only baskets and hoes.

"Last year fifty of us were sick with malaria at this time of the year," an old man in a dhoti told me. "Thanks to the DDT there are now only two cases in our village."

One of our Point Four workers told me soberly, "If the village worker is really interested in helping the people, if he treats them like men who are his equals, if he respects their opinion and ideas and does not even secretly look down upon them, then he can accomplish wonderful things."

One of the most inspiring sights is to see the villagers' efforts to become literate. Cynthia will never forget the young couple she met while doing some work in a village: every night the wife was teaching her husband to read.

"Few Americans can imagine the sacrifice and privations that Indians will endure for an education," one of our Point Four technicians, Roland Kaver, remarked. "After a hard day in the fields, they will gather for an evening of instruction." He described the classes, in which fathers sit side by side with their sons. The barnyard is their classroom. A half dozen kerosene lanterns provide the only light. For writing, each student smooths a two-square-foot area of dust in front of him on the ground, and copies the letters with a pointed stick.

One happy result of the first training work was the rapidly growing appreciation of trainees by the villagers. In the very villages where trainees were at first ordered not to return, the people themselves gave a three-day farewell festival at the end of the six months' course. Nine villages came together to prepare the party, although it was said that no more than three had ever joined in a common project. More than two thousand peasants participated in games, songs, dances, religious worship and feasts. All the villages asked the trainees to stay on and, failing that, invited new trainees. One offered a trainee land on which to build a house if he would stay.

Certainly one fruit of the program is that it is bringing America and India closer together. At least it is bringing some Americans and some Indians very close indeed. When Perry Jameson, one of our finest extension advisors, was to return to America, the villagers with whom he had worked, put on a party and sang songs, one of which contained these lines, as translated: "Sahib Jameson said plant American cotton, plant it in lines, compare it with desi cotton, decide which is best; his smiles never fade, he shakes hands with everybody, he plays with our children, he drinks our tea, and we all know he is a God-sent man to us." A village leader said that "we people who know him well know that half of his body is made of heart."

Another Point Four worker, Marshall Fox, wrote me after some months in Hyderabad, "Now I can hardly get through many of these villages, so many of the children and even the villagers themselves crowd around me, smiling and wanting to show me what they have done since my last visit to their village. Truly it is a real inspiration to see the change in expression on the faces of people who before never showed any signs of hope."

I have yet to meet any American whose heart was not won by the Indians. "We have encountered many superstitious beliefs and age-old customs in working with our villagers, but once the barrier is broken and the results are convincing I do not believe there is a more co-operative and eager people in the world than the Indian villagers themselves." So wrote Martin Howell, an able Point Four technician from Bhopal. The prevailing spirit of all our Point Four workers was perhaps summed up in the statement one American couple made to me, "We gained far more than we were able to contribute."

Perhaps the best fruit of all is that the projects are bringing together educated India and village India. Once when an American county agent was demonstrating a new way to plow, an older farmer said, "I did not know before that a man with pants on could plow." His remark was equally directed to the Western-dressed Indians who were almost as alien to him as the Americans. A Brahman cultivator explained what to him was most remarkable about the program: "The young men who come to our village are educated, some are college men, yet they work with their hands at cultivation. This is good because it will set the example for our people who believe it is beneath them to work."

Of course there is opposition. In one village where the project worker had persuaded the people to build a school by themselves, three Communist agitators arrived on the scene late in the day of the formal school opening to warn the villagers against co-operating with people who were co-operating with the Americans. The villagers, whose pride in their accomplishment was wonderful to see, scornfully told the Communists to get out.

Many flaws remain to be worked out and not all of the American Point Four workers are able to adapt themselves meaningfully. The Evaluation Program, which in the very beginning the government of India wisely established as a branch of the Planning Commission, is a needed adjunct. The Ford Foundation has contributed about half a million dollars to make the evaluation as complete and professional as possiblc.

It is important to know what the effects are on the villagers, and what is needed next. It may be true, as one of the Point Four advisors insists, that "we have found a formula that will work," but continuing independent objective study may help to improve that formula.

For one thing, I hope that Indians and other Asians will study the progress of village Japan, for there is a model of what can be accomplished in every underdeveloped nation in the world. It is also important to listen carefully to criticism of the projects among Indians outside the government.

The Gandhians wisely caution, for instance, against too much emphasis of labor-saving machinery in a country where labor is the worst problem. It is necessary for India to invent its own technology, which fits Indian conditions.

Many Gandhians also oppose any foreign aid on principle. "I can understand why America, with all her wealth, feels she should help the poverty-stricken countries," a worker at Sevagram said. "Can't you understand why I believe India should refuse outside aid? We must be self-reliant, we must do this ourselves."

Gandhi, himself, however, seemed less doctrinaire. He once said: "I should have no objection to the use of foreign capital, or to the employment of foreign talent, when such are not available in India, or when we need them—but only on condition that such capital and such talents are exclusively under the control, direction and management of Indians and are used in the interests of India." This is precisely the condition on which our aid has come.

About American aid in particular Gandhi said that if our intentions are humanitarian, "America should say, 'Well we know how to make bridges, we won't keep it a secret, but we say to the whole world, we will teach you how to make bridges. . . .'" I like to think that this is just what we are saying through Point Four.

In practice Gandhi made no fetish of self-sufficiency. He was a very hardheaded realist. Most of his constructive institutions were established and financed by large grants of money and land from Gandhi's wealthier friends. I think if more of the so-called orthodox Gandhians would visit the community projects, they would discover that they had a great deal in common. Certainly, for all their emphasis on vegetarianism, prohibition and spinning, which seems strange to most Americans, the Gandhians are the most reliable and dedicated group in India, and will always have a great deal more to offer than just criticism.

My own worries about India's ability to fulfill the promise of this program are several. At least 100,000 young men must be enlisted for village service for the program to reach full fruition. To do that it will be necessary to show that the plan is an integral part of a broad nation-building effort. In the Indo-American agreement itself it is stated that the purpose of Community Development is "to lay the proper foundation for the industrial and general economic development of the country." This must be made clear to the educated young people, who above all believe in rapid industrialization.

Similarly, popular enthusiasm in large part depends upon the fulfillment of land reforms, and this must be stressed again and again. If the benefits of increased production flow to the few instead of to the many we will have only created new and more explosive conflicts.

My main concern, however, is that the attitudes left over from colonialism will seriously hinder progress. If anything kills the vitality of the program, it may be the bureaucratic, top-down attitudes which existed under imperialism and which occasionally reappear among Indian government workers.

At first some of the village level workers asked that their title be "officer." Sometimes the old colonial approach of shouting commands from a jeep is attempted. Then failure in inevitable. Equally unsuccessful is the benevolent despot who tries to do good *to* the people and not *with* them.

A year ago in South India I visited a manufacturer who was very proud of his modern plant which employed nearly one thousand workers, but who was puzzled because he could not win the good will of his employees. A goodhearted man, he had built a school for their children and established health clinics.

Instead of the friendship he expected in return, most of his workers were restless and suspicious. At least a fourth of them had joined the local Communist party. "If you are rich enough to do these things," his employees told him, "you should have been paying us better wages."

This well-meaning employer had failed for one simple reason. The benefits which he gave his employees had been introduced as acts of charity without their knowledge, advice, participation or contribution. People need not just a higher standard of living, but a sense of purpose to fill their lives, a sense of community cooperation, above all a sense of human dignity. Properly carried out that is what I believe a Community Development project can provide.

In Madhya Pradesh, the people call the community projects *Vikash Yojna*, which means a program for self-expression. If that is the spirit everywhere adopted, the program will, I am sure, succeed.

Lao-tse, the old Chinese philosopher, wrote several hundred years before Christ that "of the best leaders the people only know that they exist; the next best they love and praise; the next they fear; and the next they revile." At this stage most of the Community Development workers are loved and praised. Occasionally a village does what the project worker says simply out of old habits of fear and obedience.

But then I have visited villages where the people feel that they have done the work themselves, where everyone is giving the credit to everyone else. In such villages the project workers have met Lao-tse's highest test of leadership: "of the best, when their task is accomplished, their work done, the people will remark, 'we have done it ourselves.'"

That is the test of leadership which the Community Development Projects, and the United States of America, must ultimately pass. The reward comes in rediscovery of the meaning of an ancient concept, the common good, an exciting new pursuit of which is now under way in the villages of India.

V. THE WORLD OUTLOOK OF INDIA

15. Russia, China and the U. S. A.

ONE DAY, in some exasperation, I asked an Indian official, "Why are you so often supercritical of American shortcomings while you seem to ignore the terrible faults of the Soviet Union?"

"We have always had great expectations about your country, while we have expected little from Soviet Russia," he replied. "You Americans set very high ideals for yourselves in your Bill of Rights and Declaration of Independence. You led us to believe in those standards. So when we think that you failed to live up to them we are disappointed and say so.

"But Russia never had liberty under the Czars. And the Communists make no bones about the fact that their government is an iron dictatorship. So whenever they do something that makes sense we are surprised, and we cannot help but show our pleasure."

This explanation has more substance to it than the casual observer might think, and yet the attitude of educated Indians toward the Soviet Union goes deeper and is far more complex.

Coming at the very time when modern India was first attempting its own rebellion, the Russian Revolution had a tremendous impact on Indian public opinion. When one famous trade union leader, now strongly anti-Communist, heard of the "ten days that shook the world" in November, 1917, he walked and rode by camel all the way across Central Asia to Moscow to sit at the feet of Lenin. Of his early thinking about Russia, Nehru himself writes that despite the dictatorship and "wholesale regimentation" which he disliked, and the "distortions of the original passion for human betterment," which he foresaw, he believed "that the Soviet revolution had advanced human society by a great leap and had lit a bright flame which could not be smothered."

As I see it there are three fundamental reasons for the initial luster of the Soviet Union in India and other Asian and Middle Eastern nations.

First, the Bolshevik Revolution destroyed one of the world's greatest autocracies, one which had been particularly hated and feared in India and the Middle East since the days of Peter the Great. The fact that the revolution also swept aside Kerensky's attempt to build a democratic state and that it brought a wave of ruthlessness in its train was little understood. What facts did come through were frequently brushed aside as "reactionary" propaganda.

Second, the Soviet Union was successful in creating a picture of its economic development as a "people's" movement of simple, rugged peasants and workers building a nation from scratch, not with foreign investments and managers, but with their own sweat and toil. Russia's problems of the 1920's were at least superficially similar to the problems faced by the underdeveloped nations of Asia.

Third, Lenin and other Russian leaders succeeded in identifying their revolution with the struggle of colonial peoples to become free, and with particular skill took up the fight of the colored peoples of Asia and Africa for equality. Asians generally became convinced that the Soviet Union was the only major nation in which there was no discrimination of race or color.

This latter point emerges in many ways as the most enduring influence of all. Very few Indians go to Russia and many Indians come to America where all too often they experience some kind of racial discrimination. Even in New York, the traditional gateway to America, two ladies in Asian dress from the Pakistan diplomatic mission, were arrested in a department store, on suspicion of being Gypsies. "What's wrong with Gypsies?" asked the Indian press.

"I have been to both America and Russia," a non-Communist Indian student told me, in an effort to describe what he believed to be an essential difference. "In your country I simply drifted around by myself. I was very lonely, and everywhere I saw the humiliating way people with my colored skin are treated. In Moscow I was met at the airport by a friendly guide who did not leave my side until I started back to India. He took me to parties and meetings and into many homes. I had a wonderful time."

So great was his preoccupation with racial discrimination that he completely overlooked the fact that in America he had been free to come and go and judge as he chose, while in Russia he had been given a rigidly guided tour with a policeman at his elbow.

Today many non-Communist Indians also find a lingering appeal in the Soviet propaganda description of Russia's modern industries, dams and farms, which have been built under forced draft in a backward land primarily through the hard labor of the people. "Because of the Soviet Five Year Plans and the vastly increased industrial production made possible by a Communist government the Russians were strong enough to withstand the whole might of the German industrial machine," say the Communist leaders and their fellow travelers throughout Asia.

Constant reiteration is neatly tailored to the desire of newly independent peoples to become strong and economically developed. It goes without saying that America's $12 billion contribution in tanks, planes and guns to the success of the Russian army is not mentioned.

In a discussion of Communist techniques on a B.B.C. program from London in 1951, Arnold Toynbee paraphrased what Russia has been saying so effectively to Asia in the following words: "Yesterday I [Russia] was an old-fashioned peasant much as you are today. Like you today, I yesterday lived depressed, ignorant, hopeless and tame. I was lying then as you are still, under the heel of a privileged native minority which was itself the creature of the Western masters of the world.

"But look at me now! See how I have pulled myself up by my bootstraps. And what I did for myself and by myself yesterday, you can do yourselves tomorrow if only you will take my advice and follow my example."

Despite the earlier success of this appeal its luster has now faded considerably. While many non-Communist Indians still have respect for the Soviet Union, the most significant development in the thinking of educated Indians during the last few years is the growing disillusionment with Russian political aims, Russian methods and even Russian claims to racial tolerance.

When after Stalin's death, Malenkov liquidated Beria, a prominent Indian politician shrugged his shoulders and said: "Whenever a great Mogul ascended to the throne in ancient India, he killed all his brothers and cousins because of fear that they might challenge his position. Russia's rulers are following this bloody custom." Such an observation would have been less likely some years ago.

With Indians who seemed to underestimate the nationalistic, expansionist nature of Kremlin policy, I often had a little fun quoting this old warning about the imperial Russia of the Czars: "Having come thus far on the way to universal empire, is it probable that this gigantic and swollen power will pause in its career?

"As sure as a conquest follows conquest and annexation, so sure would the conquest of Turkey by Russia be only the prelude, for the annexation of Hungary, Prussia, Galicia, and the ultimate realization of the Slavonic Empire. . . .

"Let but Russia get possession of Turkey and her strength is increased nearly half. She becomes superior to all the rest of Europe put together. Such an event would be an unspeakable calamity to the revolutionary cause."

This eloquent anticipation of the Truman Doctrine of 1947 was written by Karl Marx in 1853, when Czarist Russia was embarking on one of her frequent moves toward the Dardanelles and into the Balkans. In a series of long-forgotten articles in the New York *Tribune* and in the English press, Marx sought to stir up the West to resist Russia, which he said was seeking to extend its western frontier until it ran "from Stettin to Trieste."

Actually, there was little need of such reminders of traditional Russian expansion, for the memory and the fear of Russian attacks through the Khyber Pass into northwestern India was fresh in many well-informed minds. India has a number of keen observers in its diplomatic corps in Eastern Europe and Russia who report regularly and accurately to New Delhi on the imperialist aspect of modern Communist Russia.

In 1952, a delegation of Yugoslavian leaders visited India. Over and over again they told in vivid, passionate and persuasive words the story of Soviet efforts to undermine and subvert their government. The officials and leaders of Indian opinion to whom they spoke listened carefully and were deeply impressed.

Again, when a United Nations committee, headed by India's

own respected Sir Ramaswami Mudaliar, returned a carefully documented report on widespread forced labor in the Soviet Union, most educated Indians revised their earlier views that tales of forced labor were largely Western propaganda.

These, and similar incidents, piled on top of the trials and purges of the thirties, the Russian invasion of Finland, the Nazi-Soviet pact, Stalin's tirade against Tito for daring to assert his independence and the aggressive Soviet role in Korea, have led to an increasingly realistic view of Russia among most educated Indians.

Even the vaunted Soviet "peace offensive," launched during the full tide of Communist rearmament and Korean aggression, met with surprisingly little response in India. During my eighteen months in India, I watched these Cominform-organized peace rallies gradually wearing out the patience of Indian leaders. "The Communists shout loudly of peace," wrote Nehru in a public letter, "but there is little of peace in their shouting."

"Why didn't Russia disarm after the war as America did, if all she wanted was peace? Why doesn't she, even now, agree to some plan for disarmament and atomic control if she really believes that the result would be economic collapse in the West?" These were the questions I asked over and over again in India during those days. Many times I found Indian leaders asking the same questions.

"If there were a real relaxation of world tension, it would lead to a loosening of dictatorial control inside Russia and Eastern Europe. Then the Kremlin would really be in trouble," a prominent leader of the Indian government told me early in 1953. A few months later, the East German riots and the growing unrest in Hungary, Poland and Czechoslovakia seemed to prove him to be right.

I believe that one reason why Soviet propaganda lost much of its earlier effectiveness is the increase of violent language and obvious exaggeration in postwar years. Here, for instance, are three typical excerpts from the regular daily Tass press release, "News and Views from the Soviet Union," which was widely distributed throughout India:

"June 4, 1952:

It will soon be two years since the American imperialists have attacked the peace-loving Korean people. . . . These hangmen who boast of the nonexistent superiority of their race, of the notorious

American way of life have outdone the most horrible crimes of their predecessors, the Hitlerite murderers."

"June 5, 1952:

". . . The prisoners are tortured with red-hot iron, they are hung up head down and water is poured into their nostrils. In secret American laboratories prisoners of war are testing the action of new frightful poisons and deadly germs."

This official agency of the Soviet Government then went on to list some of our "crimes" as follows: "The American beasts . . . beat the children before their mother's eyes . . . bound the mothers and dragged them over to the two wells. There, right in front of their eyes, they put their bayonets through the children and threw them down into the wells . . .

"They tore the infant . . . off her back, crushed his head with a stone, gouged out both eyes, and told the mother to eat him."

This is, of course, simply an adaptation of the Nazi "big lie" technique, and most Indians are familiar enough with it to reject these extreme and repetitive stories.

In some cases, Russian propaganda moves have been more successful, at least on a short-run basis. For instance, while our Congress in the spring of 1951 was delaying on the wheat-to-India bill, the Kremlin announced that it was sending fifty thousand tons of wheat to India at once. It was announced that the grain would be loaded onto ships at Black Sea ports and that Russia would not stop to haggle about money while the Indian people were starving. Everywhere in India people cheered and for a while there was increased good feeling for the Soviet Union. Even the later arrival from America of forty times the amount of wheat sent by Russia did not erase the public memory of this quick, dramatic act of the Kremlin.

But the deal left a distinctly bad taste in Indian government circles. The price which the Russians later demanded was outrageous, and far above that which we had charged and which we had covered by a loan on generous terms. But this fact received far less publicity than the original Soviet offer. Democratic India did not take into consideration that a democracy must go through the process of debate and publicity before it can reach a decision which a dictatorship can make overnight.

During the 1952 food shortage in South India the Russians offered a large relief donation but stipulated that it must be administered and distributed through a local Indian Communist front. The Indian government bluntly refused to accept such conditions, and in embarrassment the Russians finally sent the money to be administered as India wished. Whatever illusions Indian government officials may have had about the ease of dealing with the Soviet Union have been swept away, at least for the time being, by these and other experiences.

Before I left India I could even see some signs that disillusionment was setting in about Russia's claims to racial tolerance. One night, in December, 1952, I addressed a meeting of some five thousand people in Bangalore, organized to stimulate support for the United Nations. Although I carefully avoided any political comments in my speech a member of the committee commented in his closing remarks that America was the land of lynchings and race hatred, and that on this subject at least Russia was as clean as the driven snow.

I felt that I could not allow the meeting to close on this note and requested the right to speak in reply. At that time the Slansky trials were in progress in Czechoslovakia. It was easy to expose the hypocrisy of Russian claims in the light of this blatant example of anti-Semitism. All through my vigorous rebuttal, which covered the whole range of race problems, I was interrupted by applause, and when I took my seat the audience gave me an ovation. I am sure that this response could not possibly have occurred two or three years ago when Soviet prestige, particularly on this subject, was at a much higher level.

It would be a mistake, however, to underestimate Russia's ability to develop a more effective approach in the future, including, as I shall suggest in a later chapter, the probability of a Moscow adaptation of our Point Four.

. . .

Unfortunately for the cause of world democracy, as Moscow's star declined, the People's Republic of China appeared on the distant horizon, giving Communists everywhere a new untarnished idol with which to work, a "young stronger brother" in the words of a South American Communist poet. In India the emergence of Red China was particularly opportune for the Communists, because it stirred a kind of Asian racial pride, and it revived old dreams of Asian greatness.

"The Pacific is likely to take the place of the Atlantic in the future as a nerve center of the world," Nehru had written many years ago and his vision had been of a partnership of China and India. In 1940, while urging a world-wide federation he proposed "an Eastern federation of China and India and other Eastern countries."

In 1939 Nehru had flown to Chungking to visit Chiang Kai-shek and to speak of the "imperishable links which bound India and China together." "I imagined myself as one of a long line," he said, "yet another link joining together these two ancients in history and civilization, who had found rebirth and youthful vitality again. . . ."

Although Nehru, like most Asians, considers the Nationalist Chinese hope that they may someday rule again in China completely unrealistic he still speaks with warm appreciation of Chiang Kai-shek as "the first leader of a major nation to speak out vigorously for Indian independence."

In pre-Communist days Nehru had written about China's traditional "freedom from dogma," and "her reliance on reason and common sense." There is no doubt that he and most of his associates still hope that the old "flexibility of the mind," which he found among Chinese more than any other people, will ultimately break through the rigid Communist doctrines now prevailing.

For a time these hopes were fed by the Indian Ambassador to Peking, Sardar K. M. Panikkar, a strange, unstable, brilliant man, who went all-out in his support of Mao's government, and whose daughter became a Communist. Panikkar seems to be attracted by whoever has power at the moment or whoever he believes may win power in the future. At one time he was legal advisor to the Indian princes.

When the Communists came into power in the fall of 1949, the adaptable Mr. Panikkar, then Ambassador to Nationalist China, promptly shifted gears and emerged as India's Ambassador to the new government. Although he was often critical of Moscow, perhaps in deference to the prevailing sentiments of the Indian government, he sees an Indian-Chinese entente as the world's new balance of power. In June, 1952, he was replaced by Mr. Raghavan, a tough-minded career diplomat who had served the Indian government well in Hungary, and who had no illusions about the meaning and objectives of communism.

India's stubborn hope for a more moderate and less doctrinaire China is mingled with fear of her future development. When asked to send an official cultural delegation to China, Nehru picked a group of sophisticated observers, headed by his sister Vijaya Lakshmi Pandit, present President of the United Nations General Assembly. None of them were pro-Communist, and, although they did not publicly attack China on their return, their private reports were anything but enthusiastic. They recognized the strength of the Communist government and the vast energy which it has harnessed for the development of China, but they also saw clearly the ever-present dictatorship and the complete suppression of thought.

Out of this visit came two anti-Communist books. Nehru's brother-in-law, Raja Hutheesing, who went along as press secretary, has published his account in both India and America, in *The Great Peace: An Asian's Candid Report on Red China.* "I found a government waging a ruthless class war," he says in this book. He also found that the Chinese were being reduced "to mere passionless bodies in the service of a dictatorship."

Another member of this mission, Frank Moraes, editor of the influential newspaper *Times of India*, has also published a book on his impressions, *Report on Mao's China.* "Aggression is implicit in the communism of Stalin and Mao," Moraes concludes, "as they understand it can fulfill itself only by spreading its gospel far and wide. This is the new imperialism."

China's invasion of Tibet in 1950 was an eye opener for most non-Communist Indians, especially since it occurred when India thought she was succeeding in starting negotiations between Tibet and China. Constant Communist intrigue along the northern boundary of Nepal and the steady infiltration of Chinese agents from Tibet add to the uneasiness of those Indians who know the facts.

The Indian government itself has few illusions about events in Communist China, and understands fully the cruelty that has transpired there. Once when I remarked to an official in the Ministry of External Affairs that according to our information two million people had been executed or otherwise killed by the

Chinese Communist government since 1949 the official replied, "I think that is a gross underestimate." According to his information the number ran closer to five million.

Offsetting these events to some extent is the skill with which Chinese propagandists are going about their task. Avoiding many of the mistakes of the Russians, the Chinese Communists have used more restrained and understated language and have paid close attention to persuasive and realistic detail.

A good example is their handling of the germ warfare charges. To scientists and intellectuals all over India, a book as thick as the New York City telephone directory was sent "with the compliments of the Embassy of the People's Republic of China in India," purporting to "prove beyond question" that the American government was guilty of bacteriological warfare in North Korea.

It contained page after page of fearsome, magnified photographs of insects of all kinds allegedly dropped by American planes and fairly dripping with death-dealing germs. Following this were alleged "confessions" written in convincing longhand by young American aviators captured by the Chinese who told in detail of how the "germ raids" were supposed to have been planned. Later, of course, when the Korean prisoners were returned, these confessions were repudiated and we learned of the brutal way in which they were extracted.

Along with many other Americans, I could not understand how anyone with any knowledge of the U.S. could believe these charges no matter how skillfully presented. Once again, I had failed to take account of the depth of racial sensitiveness among Indians. "If only you had not dropped the atomic bomb on Asians!" one Indian professor told me. "After that millions of Asians are willing to believe that, at least where Asian lives are concerned, you would not hesitate at even this new technique of mass killing of noncombatants."

Out of this conflicting welter of history, fact, impression, propaganda and prejudice has emerged an estimate of China and the future of the Mao government that is widely held among India's political leaders and educated people in private life. While it is at variance with the ideas of most Americans on the subject, it faithfully reflects the views of countless Asians, outside of Formosa and South Korea, who speak for almost a billion people on our side of the Iron Curtain.

If our own foreign policy is to be successful, we cannot afford to ignore a position held by so many people whose good will we seek to win. We do not have to agree with it but it is of the utmost importance that we understand it.

The first premise of this outlook toward China is the hard fact, patently clear to most Asians, that Mao has established his authority over China. Any thought that Chiang Kai-shek could return to the mainland and make a comeback, even if given substantial American air, naval and land support, they believe is the purest kind of wishful thinking. Thus, they say, whether the non-Communist world likes it or not, it is dealing and will be dealing in the future with Mao.

Secondly, they argue that China, with her 470 million people, an age-old philosophy and a history and civilization stretching back for thousands of years cannot be compared to a cowering Eastern European satellite which must jump at Moscow's bidding. The chief political fact of Eastern Europe, as they see it, is the Red army, which means, an Indian diplomat recently returned from a three-year asssignment behind the Iron Curtain told me, "that Moscow exerts direct control not only over the governments and leaders of Poland, Hungary, Czechoslovakia, Rumania, Bulgaria and Albania, but over the life and liberty of every individual."

In China, on the other hand, they see no occupying Red army or Moscow-controlled local troops. Instead, they see the world's largest country, with vast open spaces, and a large, well-trained army of its own, fanatically loyal to its own nation. "If the Russians ever tried to control China by force, it would be a military blunder which would dwarf even Hitler's invasion of Russia," I once heard a British-trained Indian general say.

From this conviction of Chinese independence the Asians do not jump quickly to the conclusion that Mao is a Tito in the making. Quite the reverse. "Mao Tse-tung will never be a Tito, because he will never have to be. He is already stronger and more independent than Tito ever dreamed of being," said an experienced Indian official who has served recently in China. "At great peril, Tito changed sides, not because he liked the West, but because it was the only way he could avoid liquidation. Russia will never be able to threaten Mao effectively, much less liquidate him."

Thus, Asians see in the Communist victory in China the emergence of a new situation in the Communist world, in sharp contrast to the abject submission of the satellites on the one hand, and the defiant independence of Yugoslavia on the other. Precisely because the relationship is unprecedented, they believe that it is a serious mistake for the free nations to react to it in terms of the patterns which have governed our attitudes toward the Eastern European Communist governments, or even toward Russia itself.

As Asians see it, the dominant note in China's future is uncertainty, but an uncertainty which is filled with possibilities for weakening the bonds that now seem to link China and Russia. To exploit these possibilities, they believe, will require flexibility combined with a cool, unemotional appraisal of the facts as they emerge.

I know of no prominent Asian leader who denies that the present rulers of China are ardent Communists with powerful ideological grounds to strengthen present Chinese-Soviet solidarity. They believe, however, that it is possible to overestimate the strength of these ideological ties and to underestimate important sources of friction and discontent. That is exactly what they think we in America are doing.

What are these points of tension that Indians and the vast majority of other Asians stress so strongly? The first is the nationalist character of the Chinese Communist movement itself, against a long background of Chinese hatred and distrust of foreigners, particularly Russians. They always point out that Mao and the men who went with him on the eight-thousand-mile "Long March" are hard, self-reliant, proud Asians who will find it increasingly hard to stay in harness with any foreign politburo.

Stalin's death, they believe, has given new importance to this factor, for Stalin was a revolutionary hero, on whom the Chinese could look with respect. Today, they see an unromantic Russian bureaucrat sitting in the Kremlin, while in Peiping, as their own leader, is the world's number-one Communist revolutionary.

Indians who have been to Peiping report that even before Stalin's death they heard Chinese Communists joke about Russian efforts to explain away Stalin's postwar assumption that Chiang Kai-shek would succeed in defeating the Red Army of Mao Tse-tung. The Russians now assigned to service in China put the blame for this error, not on the infallible Stalin, but the usual "imperialistic Wall Street agents" who had somehow crept into the Politburo, and who were now, of course, liquidated.

Another potential source of friction between Russia and China, so most Asians believe, is the needs of the Chinese economy in its drive for development. "The Chinese know their Soviet history intimately, and know that Stalin turned to Germany and the West for technical and economic help in his industrial program," an Indonesian ecnomist said to me one night at dinner. "They know that Stalin required a generation of peace to carry out his Five Year Plans. They also know that the industrialization of China is an even greater task, and there is far less to start with."

Therefore thoughtful people throughout Asia believe that at some point Communist China will be sorely tempted to seek friendly economic relations with non-Communist nations, if for no other reason than to improve her bargaining position in seeking more and more Russian assistance. Nowhere did I find this view more firmly held than in Japan, where businessmen and political leaders remember with longing the profitable economic relation with Manchuria and China in prewar years.

Asian students of world affairs often go further and interpret Russian policy and actions toward China over the last few years in the light of these factors of nationalism and economics which they believe are tending to force China and Russia apart. As they see it, the Korean War, Russia's new economic assistance program to China and what some of them even regard as Vyshinsky's successful effort to keep Red China out of the UN, are all designed to counteract the forces which might otherwise encourage a more independent China.

Non-Communist Indian leaders of all shades of political opinion are convinced that Russia launched the Korean aggression in the belief that the West would put up little or no resistance. But once the United Nations accepted the challenge they believe that the Soviet leaders saw new advantages in keeping the fighting going, even after the Chinese wanted to quit. Several Asian diplomats and private citizens who had been in Peking during the last stormy years told me that they felt that the Russians saw at least three advantages in blocking a truce.

First, the war served to tie China more closely to Russia as the only source of military supply. Second, as the bitter fighting went on, it was easier for Cominform propagandists to wipe out what remained of the legacy of good will of many Chinese for America. Third, the war delayed China's own development, kept her for the time being at least from challenging Moscow's leadership.

I shall never forget a conversation with a Yugoslav diplomat in New Delhi who had worked closely with Soviet officialdom before Tito made his break. "There are only two countries in the world which want to keep China out of the United Nations," he said. "Your own country and Russia." When I looked surprised, he went on, "Today Russia is the only spokesman for 800 million people from Warsaw to Canton. Why should she want to share that position with China? Why should Russia take the risk of exposing Chinese officials to daily contacts with the West and Western people? You will never get me to believe that Russia wants that. She wants to keep China isolated and dependent on Soviet judgments of the world situation and Soviet economic assistance."

When I pointed out that it was impossible for the United States to recognize the Communists as the legal government of China, as long as they were fighting a full-fledged war against the United Nations he nodded his head in understanding and said, "But sooner or later the war will be over and you will have to make your decision."

Most thoughtful Indians are careful to warn that Chinese communism, even if it should break loose from Russian domination, will not be easy to live with and may become increasingly dangerous to the stability of Asia. They suggest that Chinese leaders, in their first flush of revolutionary enthusiasm, are now in a sense even more militant and fanatic than the leaders in the Kremlin, and someday may become an even greater threat to world peace.

On this I agree. It is my opinion that Chinese control of the Asian Communist parties, if it comes, may prove far more effective than Russian control. As I have pointed out, the Chinese seem to have a better understanding of the psychology and techniques of village revolution, and I believe would be inclined to give much freer rein to indigenous leaders who understood local problems. And in the background is the power and prestige of the Chinese army of some 175 divisions.

. . .

This then, as accurately as I can report it, is the Asian view toward China, forcefully held in India and almost every nation from Egypt to Japan. My own conclusions differ sharply at several points. For one thing I believe that the present bonds between China and Russia are far closer than this analysis would indicate. For another, it seems clear to me that while the Soviet Union might find considerable solace, as the Yugoslav diplomat pointed out, in seeing China kept out of the UN, there would be many advantages to Soviet policy in adding China's voice to its own in the halls of the General Assembly: it gains both ways.

But of one thing I am sure: the Asians close to the scene are right in discussing the future of China in terms of deep uncertainties. And surely, as we examine this complex question of Chinese-Russian relationship we find enough valid questions about what will happen to make any reasonable person pause. Perhaps the most important conclusion of all is that Americans and other Westerners, no matter how skilled or well intentioned, cannot master mind the future development of Asia.

It is not America and Russia who are wrestling for the political soul of Asia, it is primarily India and China. Secretary of State Dulles is certainly accurate when he reports that these are the two poles in Asia. After his trip to Asia in the spring of 1953 he said of India and China, "There is occurring between these two countries a competition as to whether ways of freedom or police state methods can achieve better social progress. This competition affects directly 800 million people in these two countries. In the long run, the outcome will affect all of humanity, including ourselves."

Nehru himself is beginning to accept this competition frankly. In the parliamentary debate on the government's economic program for 1953 a Communist member of Parliament interrupted Nehru's account of the progress made in the previous three years with the suggestion that China under communism had made far more progress.

Nehru replied bluntly that he would like to see free India be compared with Communist China in every way, now and in the future. He insisted that the great works of irrigation and hydroelectric power now being undertaken in India were far greater than anything undertaken in China.

India, he said, was trying to function in a democratic way. The test would be which government "pays higher dividends for the country or the world. When I say higher dividends, I do not mean merely material dividends, although they are important, but other dividends, cultural or spiritual, call it what you will . . . an atmosphere of intellectual freedom."

If anything the attitude of most Indians toward the United States is even more complex than their thinking about Communist Russia and Communist China. They have on the one hand an extremely high ideal of what America's action should be, and on the other hand the conviction that we are not living up to that ideal in today's complex world. As a result Indian attitudes toward America have seen many ups and downs.

In April, 1940, Nehru wrote, "India is far from America, but more and more our thoughts go out to this great democratic country which seems, almost alone, to keep the torch of democratic freedom alight in a world given over to imperialism and fascism, violence and aggression and opportunism of the worst kind."

This gave way in 1942 to resentment at America's failure to support India's plea for independence. But during and immediately after the war there was a new wave of admiration and friendship for America throughout India, much of which was due to the thousands of American soldiers who had served in India. Against the background of the stiffness and aloofness of the English the natural friendliness of the Americans came as a breath of fresh air.

In addition there was the courageous position of such American diplomats as William Phillips, our first American representative in New Delhi. At the cost of his job, Phillips insisted that Britain and America could not expect India to serve as our ally against the Japanese and the Germans unless she felt that she was fighting for her independent future.

And then again in 1947 and 1948, still slow to appreciate the aggressive nature of expanding Soviet power in Eastern Europe and its dangerous surge toward Greece and Turkey, the Indians were inclined to feel that we were too belligerent and unreasonably suspicious of Communist intentions. The criticism intensified when, in 1951, India faced a desperate food shortage and reluctantly asked us for assistance.

The request came at a time when America was thoroughly fed up with the course of the Korean War and sharply critical of Indian efforts at mediation. So instead of the generous, wholehearted reaction which the Indians expected from America they found themselves the target of attacks and criticisms, demands that if they wanted help from us they must first throw their support behind us in the Cold War. To the sensitive Indians this sounded suspiciously like the use of our huge food surpluses as a political weapon against a hungry people. Even though the situation was finally ironed out and the money provided without strings, a good deal of resentment remained.

Soon, however, the pendulum of understanding swung back again, and when I left India in the spring of 1953 there was remarkably little criticism of American attitudes and policies and an enormous amount of good will. In December of 1952 I completed an eight-thousand-mile trip which took me into every major state in India. In the course of this trip I held more than twenty press conferences and spoke to a total of more than thirty thousand people. During these press conferences I did not receive a single unfriendly or loaded question.

I was not even asked the usual standby, "Is it true that in America you lynch dozens of Negroes every month?" I ran into the predictable quota of hostile questions from Communist leaders and students, but even here the questioners seemed to lack their old familiar punch. In each case it was clear that my hecklers had almost no support from the audience.

When Secretary of State John Foster Dulles visited India in 1953 he was greeted with the utmost cordiality, and Indo-American relations still seemed on a solid footing. By the fall of 1953, however, the pendulum was swinging back again, influenced by our opposition to India's presence at the Korean Truce Conference and by widely circulated stories of American intrigue in support of an independent Kashmir.

I have often said to Indians that the only people more sensitive than the Americans are the Indians themselves and I believe that this is true. Their "chip on the shoulder" attitude has developed not unnaturally during the nearly two hundred years in which they were looked upon by their colonial rulers as "natives" and as second-class citizens. Today they cannot avoid feeling that they are economically underprivileged and no matter how goodhearted our efforts may be, our very richness is resented.

And yet there is definitely a positive side to this picture. Indians instinctively respect American willingness to work, American friendliness and naturalness and even what often seems to them to be American naïveté on complex questions. Moreover, the Indians are in no sense a small-minded people.

In spite of our reluctance in 1951 to lend them $190 million at 3 per cent interest with which to buy 2 million tons of surplus American grain, there seemed to be no resentment whatever in 1953 when we, within a matter of weeks, and by unanimous vote of Congress, gave the Pakistanis a million tons as an outright gift.

Very few non-Communist Indians, in spite of what they may actually say, believe that America wants war. In the face of the maze of propaganda claims from Moscow and Peking, and despite some extremely clumsy statements from Washington, most Indians still believe that when the war was over the American people desperately wanted and planned for peace.

Often when they think we are wrong, they excuse us on one ground or another. A good example of this is that extraordinary fiasco, the Nationalist Chinese intrusion into northern Burma. Chinese Nationalist troops, driven by the Chinese Communists into northern Burma in 1949, formed an enclave, from which they sought to disrupt the Burman government, and became the base of one of the largest opium operations in Asia.

Contacts were established with the Nationalist forces on Formosa, an air strip was built at Mong Sat and, according to the Burma authorities, planes began to fly in on a regular basis. By late 1952 it is said that American arms and Chinese technicians and reinforcements began to flow in steadily.

In the troubled waters of Burma it was easy for the Chinese Nationalists to fish, and soon they began to make open contacts with the Karen rebel forces and, so it has been charged, even with Communist groups, who were eager to get support from any source in their efforts to destroy the free Burman government. Not only the Burmans but the Indians, Indonesians and most other Asians naturally assumed that if we really wanted to stop the flow of American military equipment from Formosa to this illegal army of Chinese Nationalists that we could do so.

In the winter of 1953 the Burman government, exasperated beyond measure, placed their case before the United Nations.

Belatedly we made the best of a bad situation by supporting an effort to remove the Chinese Nationalists to Formosa.

To most Indians and Asians the whole episode seemed downright stupid. "What could be more ridiculous," an Indonesian Cabinet Minister said to me in April, 1953, "than to allow American arms to be used to build up the power of a renegade group totally incapable of inflicting any damage on the Communist Chinese, but fully capable of thwarting the democratic Burman government's effort to crush her own Communist rebellion and to bring order to a harried nation?"

And yet even on this explosive subject I found a surprising amount of understanding of our political situation at home and the fact that any American administration in the election year of 1952 that dared to stop the flow of arms to the Nationalist Chinese would have been promptly charged with "following the Communist line." What a dangerously high price we often pay for our bitter partisanship in foreign affairs!

It may be fair to say that most non-Communist Indians prefer to think the best of us rather than the worst of us, although I can think of several specific instances which are dramatic and unpleasant exceptions to this generality.

One thing in my mind is clear. We cannot expect to see really friendly Indo-American relations until we are prepared to accept India's right to have a viewpoint of her own. The insistence of many Americans that anyone who "is not for us must necessarily be against us" loses us many potential friends, not only in India but throughout the world.

"What would you Americans have said," a vigorously anti-Communist college professor once asked me, "if Britain had demanded in 1939 that you must either support her in her struggle against Hitler or be classed as a nation of Nazi sympathizers?" "More than any nation on earth," a Bombay newspaper publisher once said to me, "you Americans have insisted on the right to your own opinions and the right to follow your own policies. Why cannot you grant the same rights to others?"

Mutual respect and understanding are even more important than agreement, but I believe there is one thing that is more important than either.

If I were given only a single wish for the future of our relationship with India and Asia, I would wish to see India and the other new nations of Asia *succeed* in achieving economic and political stability within the framework of freedom, regardless of what they may think of America.

A strong and democratic India is a greater guarantee of American security, even in sheer strategic terms, than any amount of verbal agreements or solemn treaties. "If democracy succeeds in India," concluded a State Department report, published after Secretary Dulles's trip in Asia in 1953, "all of South Asia is buttressed; if it fails, the outlook in Asia will be very bleak indeed."

If India wins this great victory on her own behalf we can be sure that her vast human material and spiritual resources will never be swallowed by the Communist wave. If India succeeds the Communist wave will be stopped in Asia. Then as the years move along America, India and Free Asia will surely pull closer and closer together as our stake in the same kind of future becomes clearer to us all.

16. An "Independent" Foreign Policy

AMERICANS SHOULD understand India's new foreign policy better than any other people because with its oratorical wrappings removed it is practically indistinguishable from the foreign policy of the United States from 1787 to 1937.

For 150 years we more or less faithfully tried to follow George Washington's farewell advice to avoid "entangling alliances" and to remain aloof from the "age-old struggle for power in Europe." Like India we were very busy with our own affairs and inclined to place our faith in moral judgments rather than in positive international action. Walter Lippmann says that the present Indian foreign policy, like the historic program of neutrality and isolation laid down by America's founding fathers, is "the natural expression of the vital interests of a new state."

India is sheltered by the Bay of Bengal, the Indian Ocean and the Arabian Sea on the east, south and west, and by the towering Himalayan Mountains in the north. It is faced with the most difficult kind of economic and political problems at home. Under such circumstances noninvolvement in international conflicts seems as logical now to most Indians as it did to most Americans, sheltered behind our own great oceans, before we suffered the bitter lesson of two world wars.

But it is on more positive grounds that Nehru defends what he calls his "independent foreign policy" of no military alliances and of judgment of each issue solely on its own merits. "The very process of marshalling the world into two hostile camps precipitates the conflict which it is sought to avoid," he told Columbia University in 1949, in the presence of its then president, Dwight D. Eisenhower.

"If all the world takes sides and talks of war, war becomes almost certain then," he said. "I do believe, in accordance with my master's teaching, that there is another way to meet this situation and solve the problem that faces us."

When Nehru refuses to answer Russian insults with equally

violent replies, when he insists that negotiations should always be attempted even when the outlook is forbidding, when he suggests that mutual fear feeds the Cold War conflict, he and all India believe that he is following in the footsteps of Mahatma Gandhi. And like Gandhi, he becomes angry when anyone implies that such a course means passive neutrality, or a refusal to resist evil.

To the Congress of the United States in 1949 he said, "Where freedom is menaced, or justice is threatened, or where aggression takes place, we cannot be and shall not be neutral. . . . We have to meet aggression and to resist it, and the force employed must be adequate to the purpose. But even when preparing to resist aggression, the ultimate objective, the objective of peace and reconciliation, must never be lost sight of, and heart and mind must be attuned to this supreme aim, and not swayed or clouded by hatred or fear.

"Our policy is not neutralist but one of active endeavour to preserve and, if possible, establish peace on firm foundations," he wrote to a group of American liberals who asked him why he did not "get off the fence." "On fundamental issues, such as the liberty of the individual and the rule of law, there is no difference between India and other like-minded countries. It is only as regards methods to be employed . . . that differences exist."

In my discussions with Nehru the differences in method often became strikingly apparent and important. Since the rest of the non-Communist world has been listening to India carefully, and since on most issues India's position is almost identical with that of practically all of Asia and the Middle East with the exception of Formosa and South Korea, I believe it will be worth while to review the various issues which have divided us.

Nehru has often said that we have put too much emphasis on the military side of the present world problem. During his visit to America he suggested that "a more enduring basis for peace" would be found if we channeled a larger share of "the colossal expenditure of energy and resources on armaments" into a war on "the misery and want of millions of persons." Many Americans would agree.

But most Americans would not agree with Nehru's assessment of the military situation, especially in Europe. I found that he totally misunderstood our motives in proposing the North Atlantic Treaty Organization. He often indicated his belief that the allied build-up for the military defense of Europe might frighten Russia into launching a war which she might not otherwise contemplate.

To present our perspective on NATO and to dramatize the difficult strategic problems of European defense I once asked the Prime Minister to make a series of assumptions about his own country: first, that the high Himalayas are rolled down to a flat plain; second, that four-lane highways, on which armored divisions can travel at high speed, stretch straight back across Tibet to Peking and Moscow; third, that an Iron Curtain across India's northern border completely cuts off contact with the Russians and the Chinese, and blocks any certain knowledge of what they are actually doing; fourth, that it is nevertheless known that a mechanized army of some four million men and an air force with twenty thousand modern planes including jet bombers with atom bombs are waiting across that boundary in a position to attack; and fifth, that the leaders of the Communist nations had repeatedly expressed their belief that armed conflict was someday inevitable and that their mission would not be fulfilled until the Indian Republic was destroyed.

"Then," I went on, pressing my analogy, "you call in your Army Chief of Staff and ask 'What can these people do to us?' His answer is blunt: 'If they attack we have nothing with which to stop them. Their armored divisions will reach Madras, Trivandrum and our other southernmost cities within three weeks. Their planes can utterly destroy our cities and wipe out our communications.'"

I emphasized that this was the situation that we faced in Europe in mid-1950 as we looked east across the plains of Germany and Poland toward the scowling Russians. The Korean onslaught awakened us to the realization that Europe was much more enticing and hardly less of a military vacuum than South Korea, and that a Russian Army could reach the channel ports and the Mediterranean Sea within two or three weeks.

The very existence of such a military vacuum in the world's second greatest industrial area, I argued, was an open invitation for the Soviet to seek to secure through force what they had thus far failed to win by free elections or by subversion. The history of World War II and the bloody fighting then in progress on Korean battlefields measured the cost of our failure in the past to erase such engraved invitations to expansion-minded dictators.

I do not know how convincing my case was, but the Prime Minister never again brought up the subject. He always listened attentively to my outline of American policy objectives, and particularly to my statements, repeated over and over again, that we would welcome a genuine, foolproof disarmament plan which would enable us to cut taxes and spend a higher proportion of our tax income on schools, hospitals and housing at home, and aid to such underdeveloped nations as India.

He did now and then suggest that we try to be more positive, even while firm, in our approach to Russia, and that we always come back with imaginative new proposals for every one Russia refused. Once he told me that he recognized the necessity for Western armaments, but wished that we would stop trying to match the Russians in vituperation and rancor.

NATO and European issues, however, are remote from India, while Korea is an Asian country. India, in common with most Asian and Middle Eastern peoples, has watched anxiously the course of this conflict, and it is here that some of the sharpest disagreements have arisen between ourselves and most of non-Communist Asia.

Since India's viewpoint on these questions is so broadly representative of that of these Arab-Asian countries, it might be well to review, objectively and factually, the role that India has played in the conflict from the beginning.

When the United States first asked the United Nations to take a collective stand against the aggression of North Korea, the Indian cabinet voted to support the American proposal. Since at that time the Communists held no seats, the Indian Parliament gave Nehru one of its few unanimous votes of approval. The nations of the Middle East and Southeast Asia took similar action.

The Indian representative in the Security Council, Sir B. N. Rau, voted in favor of the initial resolution which condemned the aggression and demanded a cease fire at the thirty-eighth parallel. The second resolution, which called on UN members for collective assistance was voted on before instructions from New Delhi had reached Rau. Nevertheless, the next day India announced that since "the halting of aggression and the quick restoration of peaceful conditions are essential preludes to a satisfactory settlement" she would also accept the second resolution. As a token of India's support and in the Gandhian tradition, Nehru sent an ambulance corps which served bravely throughout the fighting under the United Nations.

He did not send troops. Neither did Pakistan or any other Asian or Middle Eastern nation except Turkey, Thailand and the Philippines.

At this critical point India forthrightly supported the United States on another important issue. The United Nations Commission on Korea which was in Seoul when the invasion took place and which included an Indian member, promptly, fully and unanimously reported the facts about the Communist aggression. The government of India, three days after the thirty-eighth parallel was crossed, unequivocally adopted the conclusions of the Commission.

For Americans who take these facts for granted, the immense significance of a firm stand by the Indian government at that time is hard to appreciate. Throughout India and Asia the Communists have moved heaven and earth to prove that South Korean troops attacked first. Although they have managed to create considerable confusion, they have failed in their major objective. In my opinion, this is largely attributable to the eyewitness report of the Indian representative and the clear-cut position of the Indian government on the question of who was the aggressor in June, 1950. Without these statements, which were accepted by the majority of Asians as authoritative and impartial, the unpopularity of Syngman Rhee's regime in Asia and the repugnant prospect of white Western soldiers again fighting Asians on Asian soil might have led millions of Asians to believe the preposterous Communist claim that South Korea had started the war.

In the judgment of the veteran *New York Times* reporter in India, Robert Trumbull, these acts represented "a courageous decision in the context of the delicate state of Indian public opinion." He reported that Nehru had "risked offending a large section of the Indian public that is ultra-sensitive on the East-West question."

It was only when the United Nations forces, after MacArthur's brilliant landing at Inchon, were approaching the thirty-eighth parallel on their drive back up the Korean peninsula, that the first serious dispute began. Nehru urged that we call a halt at the parallel, which had divided North from South Korea since the end of World War II, and offer an armistice on that line. He took the view that the purpose of the UN action was to repel aggression and to defend the non-Communist world from invasion, and that this had been accomplished. Granted that the division of Korea like the division of Germany and Austria was tragic, he argued, the whole point of the UN defense of South Korea was to establish the fact that such problems could not be solved by force.

Then, on the eve of our crossing the parallel, the Indian Ambassador in Peking was awakened in the middle of the night by the Chinese government. He was given a formal warning that if United Nations troops marched north of the thirty-eighth parallel, China would take "defensive" action. The Indians relayed this information immediately to the State Department.

Although the Joint Chiefs of Staff and the State Department gave serious consideration to this information, the reports of General MacArthur's intelligence section flatly contradicted it, and the decision was left largely to his discretion as the commander on the scene. The UN troops plunged across the parallel and headed confidently toward the Yalu frontier.

Nehru announced that he had nothing further to say. "The military mind has taken over." In the United States, a full-page advertisement of a weekly news magazine appeared with the headline "Why Nehru's Face Is Red." The issue ridiculed Nehru's predictions and pointed out that although we had crossed the parallel the Chinese had not acted. It barely reached the newsstands when the thirty divisions of "Chinese People's Volunteers" suddenly struck.

In the perspective of hindsight, of course, it is easy for India to feel, perhaps a little smugly, that she was right all along. Nevertheless, despite the considerable political risks involved for him and regardless of whether other Asian nations followed suit, I believe that Nehru made a mistake in not backing up the resolution which his government approved by contributing Indian troops to the UN effort. Certainly such action would have turned the Korean fighting into an even more effective example of collective security in the face of aggression.

In the 1930's the Fascists and Nazis, following the same ugly course that the Communists took in Korea, had marched unchecked from conquest to conquest until the world was finally plunged into a war that killed thirty million people. The first victim of this aggression was Ethiopia, and here as in many other nations the costly lesson had been taken to heart. In his eloquent speech to the Ethiopian contingent leaving to join the United Nations command in Korea, Emperor Haile Selassie said, "Soldiers, you are leaving your homeland, not only to fight for the right of each people to its freedom. You are defending in a far corner of the earth the most sacred principle of collective security with which the name of Ethiopia is imperishably associated."

A prompt united defense of Ethiopia in 1935 might have prevented World War II, and who knows but that the Communists in 1950, seeing the "uncommitted world" as well as the West arrayed against them on the Korean battlefield, might have ended their bloody venture sooner with the saving of countless lives.

Nehru, however, had chosen another role, that of mediator between the two forces in the field, and there is no doubt that in that role both India and the majority of the nations of Asia and the Middle East felt considerably more comfortable. In the UN debates thereafter, India shied resolutely clear of the positions advanced both by the United States and the Soviet Union.

In December, when the Chinese troops were sweeping southward over the peninsula and many U.S. and UN units faced near encirclement, the Arab-Asian nations proposed an immediate cease fire. The Soviet delegate, Malik, angrily called this an attempt to "save the American troops" from disaster. Later India aroused equal resentment in the United States by opposing our resolution to brush aside the fiction of Chinese "volunteers" and to brand Communist China as an aggressor, because she felt that this would make a settlement more difficult.

• • •

When I reached India in October, 1951, the armistice talks, begun the previous June, were bogged down on one issue, the repatriation of the prisoners of war, and I knew of the natural and growing frustration among the American people. I did my best to give the Indian government a thorough understanding of our deep desire for an end of the fighting and our conviction that the Communists in general and the Soviet Union in particular wanted to prolong the war indefinitely.

Finally in the early fall of 1952 I expressed the blunt and perhaps undiplomatic opinion that the extension of the war was inevitable unless a satisfactory settlement was soon reached. The steady casualty lists, with no end in sight, were intolerable, and the grim logic of the situation would finally compel the United Nations to seek to win by new offensives. If the Russian or Chinese air force intervened, we would be forced to attack their bases, whether on the Chinese mainland or the Russian. In other words, if the Communists continued to defeat all efforts to secure an armistice we would not deliberately launch World War III, but we would continue to expand the Korean War until we had won it.

I argued that the time had come for further efforts to reach an armistice, and I suggested unofficially that India again take the initiative. I think this encouragement, and the realization of how earnestly America wanted peace, was an important factor in producing the Indian proposal on the prisoner-of-war issue in the fall of 1952.

The Indian proposal adopted our basic requirement that there must be no forcible repatriation of any prisoners, and a Neutral Nations Repatriations Commission was to be in full charge. It was common knowledge in New Delhi that the Chinese were shown a draft of the plan. I was told that although he did not formally approve it, the Chinese Foreign Minister, Chou En-lai gave every indication that a truce could be arranged on these or similar terms. The Indians felt completely confident that at last peace was at hand.

The Soviet, however, had other ideas. Suddenly Vyshinsky, on the floor of the UN, violently attacked the Indian resolution as totally unacceptable—"pathetic," "ludicrous," "camouflage for horrible American policy." Later the Chinese followed suit with a somewhat milder statement over the Voice of Peking. Despite this Communist denunciation the Indians nevertheless pressed their resolution and it passed the Assembly by the largest favorable vote ever achieved on any controversial issue, fifty-four to five.

It seemed clearly evident to observers in New Delhi that the Communist decision to reject the Indian resolution at that time had been made in Moscow. If China had really opposed it, they argued, she would have turned it down herself when the first informal overtures were made by India's Ambassador in Peking.

The very violence of the Vyshinsky speech suggested that its purpose may have been to force China to follow suit. The Indians, of course, believe that China had wanted to get out of the war for a long time, but that Russia had insisted on its continuation for various reasons, not the least of which is the economic and political solidarity with the Soviet Union which it imposed on China.

It may be years before we know what actually transpired, but it is interesting to note that the Indian truce resolution which Vyshinsky rejected so brusquely in November, 1952, was almost identical with the agreement which the Chinese and North Koreans finally accepted seven months later.

What is the explanation? Stalin's death occurred in the meantime. Did this mean a lessening of Moscow's influence on Peking?

In any event, to President Eisenhower Nehru cabled his congratulations on the "wise and generous part" played by the United States in the Korean truce negotiations, and the President responded with a tribute to India's "significant contribution" to making the armistice effective. That contribution was to include chairmanship of the Neutral Nations Repatriations Commission and supervision of the prisoners' exchange by five thousand Indian troops.

In retrospect India's position on the twisted course of debate on Korea in the UN was not pro-Communist. On the crucial votes, India found herself voting with the American delegates far more frequently than against them. If, as I have suggested, India must share some of the blame for the failure of the United Nations command to pay attention to her views, the fact still remains that after two additional years of fighting and dying, the war ended at just about the thirty-eighth parallel where India had urged a settlement in 1950. More than that, following the armistice in 1953, we took the same view of the purpose of the original UN resolution that India had taken earlier. We stated that the purpose of the UN action, which was not the unification of Korea by force but the ending of aggression, had been achieved.

• • •

As this book is written, another issue dividing India from the United States has assumed prominence in the United Nations. Immediately after the signing of the armistice, India reasserted her position that Communist China should be admitted to the UN.

"We think that the United Nations is incomplete without China,"

Nehru declared in July, 1953. "If China is not there, then from the point of view of population, from the point of view of world importance, nearly a quarter of the world is not there. It is not a question of anybody liking it or not. . . . You have to suffer the consequences of ignoring something which is there and which you don't recognize."

As usual most of the other Arab and Asian nations followed suit, and in this case they had the good wishes, if not always the votes, of Britain, France and many other non-Communist countries.

I believe that the lesson we drew from our analysis of India's Korean position can be applied equally to this difference of opinion. We can assume at the outset that India is not actuated by pro-Communist motives. We can assume that, even though most Americans may not agree with it, her position is an honest one, and that if we take the trouble to understand it we may save ourselves much friction and misunderstanding in the days to come.

There are, in diplomatic tradition, two views on the effect of recognition of one country by another and the exchange of ambassadors between them. The traditional British interpretation, which India has accepted since her independence, is that such recognition in no sense implies either approval or disapproval of that government's policies or philosophy. It is simply an acknowledgment that such a government's authority clearly exists as a matter of fact within its own boundaries.

From 1775 until 1913 this was also the policy of the United States. In that year General Huerta in Mexico suddenly overthrew the government of President Madero, and Woodrow Wilson, instead of recognizing the new government on the ground that it was clearly in control, proposed a period of "watchful waiting."

This introduced for the first time in American history the concept that recognition should be withheld from any new government which took power by illegal means or whose policies ran sharply in opposition to our own. On this basis we denied recognition in the following years to several governments which had assumed power through direct revolutionary action. Indian officials often point out that under this policy our own existence as a nation undoubtedly would have been ignored by most other nations following the Revolution of 1775.

In 1933 we returned temporarily to our historic policy of recognizing any government which in fact was in control of its country. Under this shift of policy the Soviet Union was recognized after much soul searching and several South American governments which had taken power by force were recognized in the following years.

After the war our policies were again modified to include the concept of nonrecognition, and this principle has carried over into the decisions on admission to membership in the United Nations.

Curiously enough in this forum the Russians adopted our approach of voting against the admission of countries whose governments they do not approve. Thus the Soviet Union turned down Japan, Ceylon, Nepal, Italy, Ireland and other nations while the United States has voted against not only Communist China, but also Bulgaria, Rumania and Albania, on the grounds that their policies are dictated by the Soviet Union.

In Britain, India, Pakistan and other nations the decision to recognize Mao's government in January, 1950, was based solely on the fact that the Communists had won and in no way involved a moral judgment. When we refused to recognize the new Chinese government and insisted that the Chinese Nationalists should continue to represent China in the UN, they disagreed with us. But following the Chinese Communist intervention in the Korean War in September, 1950, they accepted the solid sense of our argument that "we can not vote to allow China to shoot her way into the United Nations."

When the shooting ceased in July, 1953, the question again was thrown wide open. "We don't like the Communist Chinese any better than you do but the United Nations was never intended as an organization of like-minded governments," a high official in the Burma government said to me with some heat.

Perhaps the passion behind these and similar statements conceals a resentment that the only permanent Asian representative on the Security Council is Nationalist China, which Nehru says "does not represent any other part of Asia except the island of Formosa." It may well be that we could take some of the tension out of the present situation by proposing, when the UN Charter comes up for revision in 1955, that India herself be granted a permanent seat on the Security Council. This would destroy much of the effectiveness of the Soviet propaganda claim that we are not opposed to Communist China entering the United Nations because it is Communist, since Russia itself is Communist, but solely because China is Asian and her people are colored. Even when the Chinese Nationalist government controlled China four-fifths of the seats on the Council were held by the white one-third of mankind.

. . .

What about India's policy closer to home, in the areas of her immediate, vital security interests? India is flanked on the east and west by two of the most vulnerable and defenseless regions in the world today. The South Asian complex of Burma, Thailand, the Indo-Chinese states of Cambodia, Laos and Vietnam, the remaining British colony of Malaya and the scattered island chain of Indonesia lies across the eastern approaches to India. On the western flank is West Pakistan, and beyond it, Afghanistan, Iran, the troubled Arab lands of the Middle East, and Israel.

The strategic importance of these areas to the U.S. was witnessed by the men, arms and money that we devoted to their protection in World War II. Indeed, even in World War I, the Middle East, as the land bridge between Europe and Asia, claimed the attention and many lives of the Allies in its defense. Today, both these areas have indisputable military significance, for in them are to be found some of the most important raw materials—tin, rubber and, above all, oil.

These two areas are vital to the security of India, no less than our own, and perhaps it is worth a short review of their history to demonstrate their importance to the integrity of the Indian subcontinent itself and to the future of the Indian Republic.

After Britain had finally triumphed in the late eighteenth century in the race for the riches of India, she found herself faced with a new threat from Russia. Russia's objective was not only the wealth of India itself but the establishment of a firm strategic position on the Mediterranean and Arabian Seas. Thus for more than 150 years, one of the primary aims of British imperial policy was the protection of the Middle East and the sea and land routes to India, first against the Czars and later against the government of the Soviet Union.

As early as Peter the Great, Russian pressure on Iran and other Middle Eastern nations had moved in and out like a tide, and in

1813 and in 1828 Iran was forced to give up substantial amounts of territory to the Russians.

In the Crimean War of 1854-56, and later in the Turkish-Russian War of 1877 the Russians failed in their effort to force their way into the Mediterranean area, but they returned again and again to the pursuit of their objective, the domination of the Middle East, the key to India itself.

In the last half of the nineteenth century the British and the Russians were constantly at odds, not only in Persia but also in Afghanistan and along India's northwest frontier. Several British military excursions into Afghanistan were designed to keep the "bear that walks like a man" away from this historic invasion route over which Persians, Greeks, Mongols and Pathans had surged in centuries past.

In recent years, the historic Russian determination to control the Middle East, which originated under the Czars, has been given new impetus by the doctrines of world communism, and by the fact that the Soviet Union's lack of adequate oil resources represents her greatest weakness as an industrial nation. In November, 1940, in their secret negotiations with the Nazis, the documents of which were uncovered after the war, the Soviet leaders stated that their "territorial aspirations center in the direction of the Indian Ocean and the Persian Gulf."

The history of Chinese aggression into Southeast Asia is considerably less recent than Russia's interest in the Middle East. Nevertheless, in past centuries Chinese power has extended through much of Burma and Indo-China, and Chinese Communist maps today include these strategically important areas in "Greater China." Nearly twelve million Chinese settlers live in these South Asian countries to this day.

If the Communists should win the struggle of Indo-China, either with Ho Chi Minh's local troops or by the direct intervention of Chinese divisions, the consequences for India would be ominous. The Communists would then be in a position to bring overwhelming pressure on both Thailand and Burma, whether politically or by physical occupation of those countries.

Once in possession of Southeast Asia, Communist China would control some six million tons of surplus rice annually. It could then blackmail those Asian countries which are now dependent upon rice from those areas to feed their people—Indonesia, Japan, Ceylon, and to a certain extent India herself. Even more important, India would be outflanked on the east, her communications to the Pacific would be cut, and hostile armies would be poised on a common land border without significant natural obstacles, and across the comparatively narrow waters of the Bay of Bengal.

This short review of the Middle East and Southeast Asia reveal clearly that in either area the presence of an unfriendly power would be a serious threat to India's very existence as an independent nation. More than that, two associated powers, Russia and China, have historic, economic and political reasons for seeking to extend their sway into both those areas. Indeed, in Indo-China, armed fighting for that very purpose has been in progress for several years.

During the decades of British rule, the importance of these two regions to the defense of India was clearly recognized by British leaders and strategists. To defend them, Britain relied on a combination of strong words backed up by the Indian army and the British fleet, directed by a series of politically skilled British administrators with headquarters in Delhi.

Thus, in 1892, Marquis Curzon of Kedleston, who, more than any other individual, was responsible for British Middle Eastern policy, announced: "I should regard the concession by any power of a port upon the Persian Gulf to Russia as a deliberate insult to Britain, as a wanton rupture of the status quo and as an intentional provocation to war." What is more the Czar knew that the British had the ships and the soldiers to make his words stick.

The soldiers, it should be stressed, who gave Curzon's words meaning, and who had traditionally guarded British interests in the Middle East against the Russians and later against the Germans, belonged to the Indian army. In World War I they were the backbone of Allenby's army in the Mesopotamian campaign. In World War II, with the Gurkhas, they played a major role in Montgomery's defense of Suez and his defeat of Rommel's Afrika Korps. In 1941 they blocked a Nazi effort to take over Iraq by a coup d'état. In 1942 Indian troops also played a major role in the campaign against the Japanese in Burma and Assam.

Thus while British diplomats master-minded this early "containment" strategy, the military power on which their success depended rested largely in the Indian army.

Today the British are gone from India and with them has gone the combination of strong talk and strong forces which for the benefit of the British Empire had long provided stability in these two historic danger areas. In an effort to fill the resulting vacuum of the Middle East, the United States took up where Britain left off in clearly asserting our intention to resist any incursion by the Russian army.

In 1946 we took the lead in forcing Russia's withdrawal from Iran. In 1947 through the Truman Doctrine we threw our military and economic support behind Greece and Turkey, which were faced with Soviet pressures toward the Mediterranean in the classic pattern of the Czars.

In New Delhi, as Ambassador to India, I took the position that we should be equally precise in stating the lines that we were prepared to defend in Asia. It seemed to me that the wisest, and in the long run the safest, course was to announce firmly that a Chinese Communist invasion of any Asian country, including Indo-China, Thailand and Burma would be met by full military force.

But the administration was under heavy political fire over the long, dragged-out war in Korea. An election was in the offing and no statement was forthcoming.

As a result I took the liberty of speaking on my own initiative as a private citizen to Prime Minister Nehru. Several times I expressed to him in strong terms my personal conviction that if the Chinese Communists attacked Indo-China we would promptly go into full military action against China, with or without the United Nations. Although I emphasized that I was speaking unofficially I said that I thought my assessment of the temper of the American people and its government was accurate. I know that this expression of opinion was passed on to the Chinese Communist government in the spring of 1952 for whatever good it might do.

Although I was worried about whether or not I had done the right thing, I immediately reported the conversation to Washington and received no contradiction.

Two or three months later the situation was confused by a newspaper report that Mr. Eisenhower, who was then seeking the

Republican nomination for president, had stated at a press conference that he would not commit American troops in the jungles and rice paddies of Vietnam. I pointed out, however, that this limited answer to a limited question did not mean that he would not favor all-out military action against China at a place of our own choosing, and my explanation was generally accepted.

On September 3, 1953, in his speech before the American Legion, John Foster Dulles made the first clear-cut official statement of what we would do if an attack occurred. "There is the risk," he said wisely, "that as in Korea Red China might send its army into Indo-China. The Chinese Communist regime must realize that such an action could not occur without grave consequences which might not be confined to Indo-China. I say this soberly in the interest of peace, in the hope of preventing another aggressive miscalculation."

Thus America's categorical guarantees of the integrity of these two areas have replaced those of Britain. But the crack Indian army which had put the teeth into the earlier British guarantees no longer stands behind those which we have made. If Russia and China should decide to risk defeat in a third world war their armies could fill these two vacuums in a matter of weeks.

"Why should this be?" many thoughtful Americans have asked me. "At least in these two vital areas where India's interests coincide so closely with our own, why cannot India put aside her 'independent' policy and co-operate with us to assure stability? And if India cannot join a formal defense alliance with us why doesn't she act independently with other Asian and Arab nations to protect her own interests and theirs?"

There are, it seems to me, three principal reasons why India has seemed slow to act decisively about these strategic flanks.

First there is the same obsession of India and all Asians with colonialism, which recurs as an excuse for the commission or omission of so many things which disturb us of the West. When we look at the Middle East we see lack of adequate military defense stretching from Turkey to Pakistan. We see Communist intrigue in Iran and other nations. We see the great military base at Suez under heavy pressure from Egyptian nationalism.

When we look toward Southeast Asia we see Communist-led troops supplied from China fighting to take over Vietnam, Cambodia and Laos. We see Chinese Communist divisions on the northern borders of Burma and Thailand in a position to attack. We see Malaya and Indonesia as logical objectives for Chinese ambitions.

Over and over again I said to Indians, "Of course Asians hate and oppose colonialism. But can't you see that communism is the new imperialism, and that it's an infinitely greater threat to the new India you are trying to build?"

India sees the danger and she is worried by it. Nehru has stated clearly, "World Communism in its expansionist aspect, just as any expansionist movement, is a danger to peace and freedom." But for India the picture is clouded because she also sees her old colonial masters, the British at Suez and at Singapore, with oil interests in Iran, and the French in Indo-China. The habits of thinking built up over two hundred years under colonial rule, and sharpened for many Indian leaders by long terms in British imperial prisons, cannot easily be forgotten.

The second reason why India has largely ignored her own strategic problem is her conviction that her first order of business must be to create internal stability and build a solid base for industrial expansion. To reach this objective she has been pushing her resources to the limit, and this has made her particularly hesitant to stretch her commitments beyond her power to fulfill them. "If the Communists moved into Burma or the Middle East," an Indian political leader said to me, "our future would be threatened, but if we fail to build a modern nation here in India, the Communists will take over and that will be the end."

The third reason for India's reluctance to take the lead in creating a practical defense organization is her conflict with Pakistan. As long as these two nations feel obliged to station the bulk of their troops on guard against each other, neither feels in a position to contribute what it might to the broader problems of Middle Eastern and Southeast Asian security.

Whatever one may think of the necessity for the partition of British India into two separate nations, it is now a fact, and both those nations must now grapple with the consequences, some of which are tragic. The subcontinent with Burma and Ceylon had been a traditionally self-supporting area and partition resulted in fantastic economic distortions of both the Indian and Pakistan economies.

Not only was Mountbatten well aware of the economic consequences of partition, he was equally aware of the military and political weakness which was bound to follow. Even after partition had been decided upon he urged the establishment of a mutual defense organization under a single command. The passion of partition, however, had gone too far for that. Thus the troops which were once the military mainstay of South Asia and the Middle East and which together still comprise the strongest non-Communist Asian military force between Suez and Tokyo were split tragically into two rival armies.

The riots in the fall of 1947, the vast exchange of refugees, totaling close to fifteen million on both sides, the confiscation of property by both governments and the abrupt shutting off of rail communications and even essential trade have embittered the relationship between the two new nations of South Asia which above all should stand together.

As Ambassador to India I was naturally better acquainted with the Indian case. But I tried to keep an open mind, and to understand the perspective of the dynamic developing country which is Pakistan. Certainly there is much to be said on both sides. Many Indians are not reconciled to partition, and many Pakistanis know and fear this fact. Pakistan's avowed aim to build an "Islamic" state inevitably comes in conflict with the Indian goal of a subcontinent pledged to complete religious freedom and equality.

The greatest single conflict arose over Kashmir, a subject on which, unhappily, there has been much misinformation, and, in my opinion, ill-advised action. Very briefly, the Maharaja of Kashmir in October, 1947, after a large-scale invasion by Muslim tribesmen from across the border, announced his decision to throw in his lot with India and called upon the Indian government for protection. Lord Mountbatten, Governor General, accepted this accession to India as legal, and the Indian government flew troops into Kashmir to defend its capital against the invading tribesmen.

At the same time Nehru stated that he would hold a plebiscite to determine the true wishes of the people as soon as the invaders had been driven from "Indian soil." As the fighting continued the Indian government brought the dispute before the Security Council on January 1, 1948, charging that the situation which existed endangered the maintenance of international peace.

The government of Pakistan vigorously denied the Indian charges and promptly filed countercharges. It stated that the inhabitants of the area were principally Muslim and that they would vote in favor of Pakistan if they had the opportunity.

Twenty days later the Security Council established the United Nations Commission for India and Pakistan. Eventually a cease fire was brought about, and efforts were launched to secure an agreement. For the most part the negotiations centered around the question of the number of troops which each nation would be allowed to maintain within the boundaries of Kashmir during the proposed plebiscite. This approach was foredoomed to failure, since India had always said that she would not agree to any plebiscite until all foreign troops had been withdrawn from the Kashmir territory, which she argued, had legally acceded to India.

I have always felt that with a little more flexibility on the part of the Security Council, and particularly on the part of the United States and the United Kingdom, an agreement might have been reached in the winter of 1952. At that time there was considerable indication that if the Azad-Kashmir area, then occupied by Pakistan troops, were given outright to Pakistan, and the Jammu and Ladakh areas, which are comprised almost wholly of Hindus and Buddhists, given outright to India, it might have been possible to agree on a plebiscite confined to the valley of Kashmir itself. Various legal advisors, however, rigidly held that the negotiators could not stray from the narrow "terms of reference," for a plebiscite of the whole state, laid down by the Security Council, and this eliminated any hope that a new approach to an agreement might be explored.

As the stalemate dragged on, sentiment in Kashmir for independence from both Pakistan and India seemed to develop, although it is hard to tell how strong this actually was. After an involved series of political maneuvers, this came to a head in the summer of 1953, after I had left India. Sheikh Abdullah, the Kashmir leader who had earlier taken the lead in the defense of the state against the tribal raiders, and who since the 1930's had been the popular hero of the long Kashmir struggle for freedom, was deposed as Prime Minister on the ground that he was "plotting" for an independent Kashmir.

Whatever the facts, this crisis brought further meetings between Mohammed Ali, Prime Minister of Pakistan, and Nehru in New

Delhi. High officials of both governments have argued from the beginning that the conflict can only be solved by direct negotiations.

It is likely, however, that Kashmir may be plagued with increasing internal conflicts. At least one member of the new government is openly a Soviet fellow traveler and Communist intrigue in this critical area where India and the U.S.S.R. have their one common frontier is now at a feverish peak. If the situation becomes dangerous I have no doubt that the Indian government will react vigorously. Under such circumstances it is even possible that Sheik Abdullah, who thoroughly understands the present Communist danger, may someday be re-established as Chief Minister.

Out of this tangled history of the events in Kashmir, some lessons, both for us and the Indians, emerge very clearly. When I was in Kashmir in the fall of 1952, some two-thirds of the officers on the cease-fire line were Americans, and not all of them handled themselves with discretion. The last negotiator appointed by the United Nations was a distinguished American, Frank Graham, and the administrator who was selected by the United Nations to take charge of the plebiscite, if and when it was conducted, was still another American, Admiral Chester Nimitz.

Despite the high caliber of these men, and all the good will in the world, the UN effort to achieve a Kashmir settlement inevitably took on the character of an American operation. In a situation where passions run high, we have not only failed to achieve a settlement, but have inevitably come in for sharp criticism.

Our failure to recognize fully the explosive nature of this issue as well as the whole India-Pakistan dissension, is one of the reasons for the collapse of our proposal for a Middle East Defense Organization in the fall of 1952. At the time, discussions were held with the British and others on the possibility of developing a Middle East alliance including Pakistan, but not India. When rumors of this development reached India, her opposition was so prompt and vigorous that the project was dropped.

As long as the present dispute continues, and in view of the many threats that have been made, Indians will look on any expansion of the Pakistan army as a direct threat to themselves. Since Pakistan did not send troops to Korea and has been one of the key members of the Arab-Asian bloc in the UN, many Indians honestly believe that the only reason for Pakistan's readiness for

American military aid is an attempt to get ahead of India in their own tragic little arms race.

Americans may ask angrily why India and Pakistan should criticize us for our failure to find a way to end the Cold War and to establish a basis for coexistence with the expansionist-minded Soviet Union, while their own costly Cold War continues. But such irritation with these new, proud nations, even though justified, accomplishes nothing.

Certainly to do anything to heighten Indian-Pakistan tension only delays the reconciliation which I believe to be the main hope for stability in the whole Middle East and Southeast Asia areas. It is a deeply emotional situation which we must seek to understand sympathetically and objectively. Since our aim is to see peace and friendly co-operative action between India and Pakistan, it will be a grave mistake for us to become partisans of either. The best hope is that they will find their own way to agreement.

. . .

In the meantime we need not despair of progress.

I believe that the number of Indians who understand the danger of allowing the present vacuums to continue will grow steadily once France makes clear beyond all question her intention to give unconditional freedom to Vietnam, Cambodia, and Laos; once Britain and Egypt come to an agreement on Suez; and the dust settles in Iran.

The unpredictable Mr. K. M. Panikkar, who has never been known as a supporter of Western "containment," but is an astute geopolitician, has already gone further than most Indian leaders in discussing the danger which India would face with an unfriendly power in the area of the Indian Ocean and the Persian Gulf.

Mr. Panikkar pointed out that "while to other nations the Indian Ocean is one of several important oceanic areas, to India it is the vital sea. Her life lines are concentrated in that area. . . . No industrial development, no commercial growth, no stable political structure, is possible for her unless the Indian Ocean is free and her shores protected."

Mr. Panikkar proposed long-term and short-term policies to cope with this situation which borrow freely from the theories of our own great naval geopolitician, Admiral Mahan. The long-term policy, as he sees it, calls for the gradual development of a navy strong enough to defend India's interests in this vital area. The short-term policy must be based on co-operation "with the high seas fleets of friendly nations in the strategy of global naval warfare."

These quotations are from Panikkar's book, *India and the Indian Ocean*, which was originally published in 1945 and later revised and republished in 1950. It would be interesting to know if as Indian Ambassador to Egypt he still thinks in these terms.

Indian leaders know, of course, that military guarantees and agreements will never in themselves bring peace and security to the Middle East or any other part of the world as long as the great majority of the people remain impoverished, frustrated and with nothing to defend. Thus Indians have kept in close touch with turbulent events in Tunisia, Morocco, Iran, Egypt and Indo-China. They know that their own military power may someday become the principal factor in the regional defense, but they believe that there can be no real stability until the rising Arab and South Asian popular demands for freedom, reform and development are met. In the UN the Arab-Asian bloc has championed those demands.

Fortunately the economic opportunities throughout the Middle East are almost without limit. Through irrigation projects on the Tigris, Euphrates, Jordan and other rivers much of this barren land could be brought dramatically to life again to provide a good standard of living for tens of millions of additional people. The great oil resources of the region offer a major source of development funds with both private and governmental contributions.

Today much of the Middle East seems faced with the bitter choice between archaic landlord feudalism on the one hand and a Communist dictatorship on the other. Let us hope that before it is too late a third choice is made available: democratic development, perhaps under a regional program which will turn the present negative, mob-ridden, anti-Western nationalism into a positive force for progress and stability. If India and Pakistan can play an effective role in helping to create this new kind of future, backed by a sound mutual defense system, the free world would be everlastingly in their debt.

Even today, while India's own internal problems are so staggering, and she is hesitant to spread her resources too thin in outside commitments, she has, after the Chinese invasion of Tibet, taken action to guarantee the security of the tiny northern states of Bhutan and Sikhim as well as the larger kingdom of Nepal, and she is in close consultation with Burma. In a later chapter I describe the large-scale participation by India in the defense and strengthening of Nepal. And on at least one occasion, Indian parachute troops stood by when rumors reached New Delhi of the possibility of a Communist-oriented political upheaval in that mountain country.

I think it is entirely possible that we shall see a similar Indian move in the future in these more important areas of vulnerability to Communist encroachment that we have been discussing, at least in Burma. Certainly such a move would not be in conflict with India's independent foreign policy. Indeed it would be a logical extension of it.

Many Indians with whom I talked, including various officials of the Indian government, were keenly interested in my outline of the development of our own Monroe Doctrine in 1823. The parallels are striking indeed.

This Doctrine grew out of the fear, following the end of the Napoleonic Wars, that the Holy Alliance of Continental power under the leadership of the Austrian Metternich would re-establish Portuguese and Spanish control over their former colonies in South America which had broken away in a series of revolutionary wars. Our policy of noninvolvement in European disputes was at least as well established as India's is today. But George Canning, the British Foreign Minister and deadly opponent of Metternich, proposed to our ambassador in London that we make a joint statement guaranteeing the integrity of the new South American republics.

In some secrecy, because of the important implications of this proposal, President Monroe and Secretary of State John Quincy Adams consulted with the cabinet and with Thomas Jefferson, then in his eightieth year and a traditional critic of Britain. Jefferson not only agreed that a statement should be made, but stressed that only through such a policy could our policy of noninvolvement be maintained. The warning against imperialist intrusions on the American continents which resulted, was a unilateral American declaration, addressed to all nations of the world, the British equally with the members of the Holy Alliance.

In presenting his new Doctrine President Monroe emphasized

that "we must consider any effort on the part of outsiders to extend their system to any part of our hemisphere as dangerous to our peace and safety." Secretary of State Adams in deference to our own established policy of noninvolvement added reassuringly that "the principle of neutrality in foreign wars remains fundamental to our liberties and our union."

Will India, together with Pakistan, Egypt, Burma and Indonesia, move in the direction of some kind of multilateral Monroe Doctrine for the whole region? If so, will we of the West be as wise as the nineteenth-century British, and welcome it quietly as a reduction in our own burden of defense?

But whatever lessons India may draw from her experiences in foreign policy, and from her study of history, and whatever course that policy may take as a result, we may be certain of two things at least: her foreign policy will remain "independent," and it will not be pro-Communist, so long as the present government or any of its democratic opposition parties are in power. India will not sell her soul for a bowl of rice. She is no more willing to accept Chinese or Soviet domination of herself or of her neighbors than she is willing to accept the return of Western colonial rulers. On the scale of history this fierce independence may turn out to be decisive in stopping the Communist expansion in Asia.

When Harold Stassen returned from a visit to India in 1950, he reported that not only had he found Nehru to be "thoroughly alert to the evils of Soviet Communist imperialism," but that he saw Indian policy in a new light. It was "neither an echo of America or a voice of Moscow." "I strongly believe," he said, "that if we in America develop a policy toward them [Nehru and his country] that accords full recognition of their third position, tremendous goodwill will result for the people of both countries."

At his press conference on his visit to India in the spring of 1953, Secretary of State John Foster Dulles said that he was "thoroughly convinced that India is acting according to its best judgment to promote democracy in the world and prevent the spread of totalitarianism."

Other Americans may not agree, but in any case, there is no doubt that much of Nehru's present popularity in India and the strength of his democratic government stems from the almost universal Indian approval of his foreign policy. Its very independence puts Indian Communists on the defensive. If Nehru became a formal ally of the West in the Cold War, he would be going against the whole grain of Asian anticolonial sentiment. He would be under constant and effective attack as a "stooge of Western imperialism." By his independence of either bloc, he is able to draw on all the pride of Indian nationalism, and to charge convincingly that it is the Asian Communists who are the foreign stooges.

In any event we are going to have to live with an "independent" foreign policy on the part not only of India but of most other newly free nations, like it or not, and for many years to come. If this disturbs us we can console ourselves with the thought that it may turn out to be of great benefit to the free world in many places where we least expect it.

One such place is Africa, where India and other Asian nations, based on their own experience in gaining freedom, have taken the lead in offering to tens of millions of frustrated people a third path that is neither Communist nor colonial. For example, in July of 1953, Nehru announced that India would oppose racial oppression in Africa "with every measure short of war." Declaring the supreme importance of Africa, he warned that unless more liberal policies are followed "the world may well have to face major explosions and eruptions in Africa of the worst type."

When Nehru says these things he is speaking a language that Africa as well as Asia understands. Indeed he is only saying publicly and eloquently what millions of people are saying every day in the bazaars, coffee shops, villages and universities of two continents.

India has also made a constructive effort to help. To British Central and East Africa Nehru sent a splendid Commissioner, A. B. Pant, who is persuading the important Indian trading community there to lend increasing support to the Africans, including the building of schools and donations of scholarships to Indian universities. The Indians hope to see a new kind of white, black and brown partnership emerge, based on complete equality, under which all groups may benefit.

If our need for the support of France and Britain in Europe, as we see it, leads us to soft-pedal our own support of freedom and independence for all men, should we not be glad that independent democratic voices are being raised to champion the nationalist movements in Africa and elsewhere? If this support did not exist, where would the subject peoples turn except, in desperation, to the Soviet Union, which is always ready to exploit the difficulties of the democratic world for her own ends?

If India sometimes seems intransigent and difficult to deal with, let us remember our own years of antiforeign attitudes, high tariffs and isolation, while we built a continent and a great democracy. And just as the world listened to us in the vigor of our democratic youth, we should listen to India, tell her frankly when we think she is wrong, but listen.

VI. NEPAL AWAKENS

17. A Revolution Comes Over the Mountains

SITTING HERE in Essex and looking out over the peaceful Connecticut River and the green gentle hills on either side, nothing seems more remote and unbelievable than the picture of the New Delhi branch of the Bowles family, astride long-haired mountain ponies, breaking over the crest of Chandragiri Pass on the narrow trail into Nepal.

There, a few months after our arrival on the Indian subcontinent, we saw close at hand for the first time the mighty sweep of the Himalayas, traced against the horizon to the north. Mt. Everest lifts its serenely majestic head over a host of other peaks of twenty-five thousand feet or more, some of which no one has even bothered to name.

Just below us was the beautiful central valley of Nepal and its capital city of Katmandu. I was bound there to present my credentials as the first United States Ambassador to Nepal, in addition to my duties in India. Probably in all the non-Communist world there is no country more effectively cut off from contacts with foreigners and none in which democratic forces face a greater challenge.

Nestled high on the southern slopes of the Himalayas, Nepal extends for some five hundred miles, roughly east and west, between Communist Tibet and free India. Its breadth from north to south averages one hundred miles and its size is approximately that of Florida, larger than Belgium and Holland combined. No one knows its exact population, but an educated guess might be ten million.

We had heard much of this country ringed about by almost

impassable mountains and for centuries systematically cut off by its rulers. We knew that, although Nepal is celebrated throughout Asia as the birthplace of Buddha, human slavery had existed there less than thirty years ago.

Our first trip into Nepal and the many that followed were to teach us more, however, for we discovered the same determination of the people and their leaders to achieve freedom and dignity which is so powerfully at work over the rest of the continent. And here too we found, in perhaps the greatest degree in any underdeveloped country, the same bitter obstacles—disease, ignorance and grinding poverty for the great majority of the people.

Curiously enough Nepal had never been under colonial rule. Its modern history begins in the last half of the eighteenth century, just about the time the American colonies were winning their independence. The Gurkhas, who originally were Hindus driven from India by the Muslim conquest, moved gradually northward through the mountains, and in 1768, under a strong king, Prithwi Narayana, conquered the native Mongol rulers of Nepal.

For the next sixty years the monarchy deteriorated rapidly as a succession of weak and ineffectual rulers followed each other. In an effort to take advantage of the confusion and add to their empire, the Chinese Manchu Emperor invaded Nepal through the Himalayan passes to the north in 1792. The Gurkhas, however, were stout warriors, and aided by the natural barriers which surrounded their country, they were able to maintain their independence. In 1814 the British from India made their first of several attempts to conquer Nepal and also failed.

Finally, in 1846, a Nepalese nobleman named Jung Bahadur succeeded, by ability and intrigue, and with the support of the British, in establishing himself firmly as Prime Minister. He swept the ineffectual king into the background and set up the autocratic political system under which Nepal was governed until 1951.

Under Jung, the office of Prime Minister became hereditary, passing from one to another of the Rana family to which he belonged. The Prime Minister was in fact a supreme dictator, exercising all the power of the government, while the king remained a figurehead.

The first Rana ruler initiated a policy of friendship with England under which Nepalese soldiers were recruited for service in the British army in India. When the Indian "Mutiny" of 1857 broke out, he sent his own Nepalese army of Gurkhas to the aid of the British. And later, in both World War I and World War II, tens of thousands of Gurkhas, either in British army units or in the uniform of Nepal, fought valiantly beside the British and other allies on all the major battle fronts of the world.

A Nepalese once said to me, with a sad smile, "The chief export of my country has always been soldiers." Even today, the Gurkhas in the British army amount to about two divisions, and I saw several units in Malaya fighting the Communist guerrillas. There is another division of Gurkhas in the Indian army.

The policy of friendship with the British did nothing to overcome Nepal's isolation and hostility to foreigners. Except for a British Resident at Katmandu, the old ways prevailed and probably no more than a dozen Westerners have entered the country in a single year. Even fewer crossed the mountains into the isolated central valleys where most of the people live and where the few towns are located.

No roads were built through the mountains, no schools were established, no motion pictures were allowed. As far as it was humanly possible, the Ranas saw to it that Nepal was hermetically sealed from the outside world and the possibility of democratic contamination.

But there were inevitable gaps in this iron curtain. Gurkha soldiers who went abroad during the first World War brought with them tales of the outer world and of the great democratic ferment stirring everywhere under the impact of Woodrow Wilson's idealism. Buddhist priests wandering into faraway countries returned to tell of new progress being made in other lands to combat poverty and disease.

Then, too, some of the younger noblemen were going to India to be educated, for there were no adequate schools in Nepal. There they learned of mankind's long fight for liberty and justice and they saw all around them the national struggle of Indians against imperial rule.

As history has proved time and again, these ideas are dynamic and explosive. They take firm root in the minds and hearts where they are planted. The man or government who tries to ignore or suppress them sets his face against the future and will fail in the end.

Nepal was no different. In the early 1920's a small movement directed at ending the autocratic rule of the Ranas arose. The Ranas responded with ruthless suppression. Here, it seemed, their long support of the British paid off, for the Viceroys in New Delhi refused to permit agitation and organization against the Ranas by the Nepalese political exiles who took refuge in India.

But despite everything the Ranas could do, the revolutionary movement remained alive, and slowly grew. With Indian independence in 1947, and with the old British suppression ended, the movement for a democratic Nepal among the Nepalese in India grew rapidly. In response to growing pressure from across their mountain border the Ranas finally promised new reforms and in 1948 even proposed a Constitution. But these concessions had been too long postponed. In 1950 the Nepalese National Congress was openly formed in India, pledged to full democratic reform and bringing together all the groups who were opposed to Rana rule.

Even King Tribhubana himself, a man with deep respect for democratic principles whom the Ranas had kept in the background, became involved in the fight to establish a modern state. Late in 1950, he escaped from Nepal to India. By then the young Nepalese revolutionaries felt strong enough to invade their homeland, in the name of their King, where they were greeted with enthusiasm.

The short revolution, which was largely free of bloodshed, began on November 11, 1950, six days after the King left Nepal, and ended in January, 1951, in the overthrow of the century-old autocracy of the Ranas. The idealistic young liberators, led by M. P. Koirala and his half brother, B. P. Koirala of the Nepalese Congress movement, announced their determination to set up under King Tribhubana a constitutional monarchy much like that in Britain. M. P. Koirala, a brilliant young man for whom I developed real respect and affection, became the first democratic Prime Minister of Nepal.

Since then the new government has faced grave difficulties. There were almost no trained people to take over the operation of the public services. The only people who had any experience at all were some of the Ranas themselves and the few who had worked under them. Nepal did not even have a budget. The heavy taxes, collected from the poorest people at the point of a bayonet, had been paid directly into the Rana's private account to be used as the rulers had seen fit.

The only communication between the various valleys was by ponies which were able to cover no more than fifteen miles a day over the incredibly rugged terrain. I doubt that any new government ever faced a more bewildering series of obstacles than did that of M. P. Koirala and his associates in 1951.

Diplomatic relations between the United States and Nepal had been established with the Rana government in 1947, and in 1951, after the revolution, our first Point Four technician, a mining engineer, entered the country.

It did not seem to us either practical or economical to establish a separate and permanent embassy in Katmandu. With the help of a carefully chosen group of specialists from our New Delhi staff and frequent trips to the Nepalese capital I felt that I would be able to keep in close touch with developments there, work out a program which would convince the government and people of Nepal of America's friendship, and assist them in their efforts to become a modern democracy.

I knew that Nepal would understand this part-time ambassadorship because she herself has often practiced it. For several generations Nepal sent its ambassador to China only once every five years, and even that has for some years been abandoned. Today Nepal maintains diplomatic relations with only four countries: India, Britain, France and the United States.

Although a rough air strip had just been laid down in Katmandu we decided to make our first trip in by pony over the historic, rugged trail through the mountains. Steb and I felt that in this way we could get a far clearer idea of the people and the country. In January, 1952, when Cynnie, Sally and Sam heard that I would soon be presenting my credentials at the colorful court of King Tribhubana they said firmly that we could not leave them out.

So the five of us and six staff members, including Loyd Steere, Fraser Wilkins, Clifford Taylor and our army attaché, Colonel King Henderson, flew first to Lucknow, where, after visiting the new American information library and lunching with Governor

Modi of Uttar Pradesh, we took an overnight train to Rauxal on the Nepalese frontier.

As we walked across the border we were met by a group of Nepalese officials who spoke English, and I was asked to review an honor guard of Gurkha soldiers who were drawn up at attention. Their Teddy Roosevelt hats were cocked jauntily on the side of their heads, their khaki uniforms immaculate, and their famous long Gurkha kukri knives dangling at their belts.

Then a special train of three cars carried us over a narrow-gauge railroad up the gently sloping land called the Terai which stretches from the Indian border to the first range of mountains of some twelve thousand feet elevation. This strip is perhaps thirty to forty miles wide and contains rich agricultural and forest land. But the Terai is blighted by some of the worst malaria in the world. In some places, as many as 95 per cent of the villagers have the disease each year.

After leaving the tiny train with its engine and almost miniature coaches, we drove in antiquated automobiles another ten miles through rolling foothills to Bhimphedi. There the road ends and travel is only possible on foot or by pony. We reached the lodge there at sunset on the second day out from New Delhi.

At villages along the way we had been greeted warmly with garlands of flowers, and here at Bhimphedi, in the growing dusk, Nepalese women and children stood with flickering oil lamps, waiting for us by the roadside with more flowers in lovely brass pots.

As do mountain people everywhere, the Nepalese struck us at once as friendly, open and self-reliant. We were all impressed by the rather marked difference in appearance of these northern neighbors of the Indians. They were generally shorter and fairer-skinned than Indians, and their high cheekbones and slightly slanted eyes recalled their mixed Mongol and Hindu descent.

The dress of the people also was different from that of India and the familiar Indian dhoti was replaced by warmer clothing more suited to the mountain temperatures. Many of the men wore three-quarter-length wool coats over knee breeches and wrap-around leggings of the kind worn by American soldiers in World War I. And on their heads was invariably the small Nepalese cap, resembling an overseas cap, with one side higher than the other so that it looks perpetually cocked at a jaunty angle.

There can be few places in the world with a climate more perfect than that of the Nepalese valleys. In the spring the thermometer climbs to ninety or more but the air is dry and clear. The monsoon rains come in July for a few weeks and then follows month upon month of beautiful weather. Even in Katmandu in the shadow of the Himalayas the winter temperature usually manages to climb above 70 degrees at noon with nights rarely below 45 degrees.

Next morning, after an early breakfast, we started our long-awaited trek over the final twenty-mile stretch of rugged mountain trails to the capital. An electrically operated ropeway picked up our bags, which went over the mountains in a little steel cage swinging from high point to high point. They would be in Katmandu long before we would.

This ropeway, which has been in operation for some years, provides the only mechanical transportation into the capital, other than airplane. Its capacity is small, however, and by far the greatest bulk of equipment and goods going into the interior is carried on the backs of men over the precarious trail we were soon to climb ourselves. We found later that all of the three hundred odd automobiles to be found in Katmandu had been carried intact over this mountain trail by one-hundred-man crews.

We selected our ponies, each of which was accompanied by a Nepalese guide or *syce*. His job was to stay at the pony's head, guiding it along the trail, and taking the bridle now and then to help the pony pick his way over some of the slipperiest and steepest sections.

Sally had done a little riding but Cynthia and Sam had scarcely been on a horse. Almost immediately they both looked extremely grateful for their *syces*, for the trail rose at once at angles of thirty and even forty degrees. The path was narrow, and needless to say there was no railing or barricade. In almost no time, we were looking out over gorges with sheer drops of thousands of feet and the ponies sure-footedly (we hoped) were stepping only a few inches from the edge. At several particularly rugged points we dismounted and walked.

With us was a Nepalese army colonel who had served in the

British army and who spoke excellent English, and an honor guard of some thirty Gurkha soldiers.

Many who are competent to judge consider the Gurkhas the finest infantry soldiers in the world. Their toughness is legendary. Although they are small, they are wiry and strong and can carry heavy burdens over the most difficult terrain. The colonel, seeing my obvious admiration at their lithe, sure movements, told me the story of the famous Khud Race, which took place in 1907.

"A Scottish infantry unit attached to the Indian army," he said, "had grown weary of hearing about the Gurkhas' great ability to cover ground rapidly on foot. This regiment, the 60th Scottish Rifles, challenged a Gurkha regiment to a cross-country race. The story got out and the British army headquarters at first issued orders to cancel the race since it was against their policy to permit competition between troops of different nationalities. By this time, however, there was so much excitement and interest in the race that a special exception to the rule was made.

"One hundred picked men were chosen from each of the regiments," he continued. "They were loaded with full field equipment, and started out over twenty miles of the roughest kind of country imaginable, including two steep ranges of hills. It is said that the Scots were holding their own on the way up those ridges, but coming down the Rifles were simply not in it. The first ninety-nine men to cross the finish line were Gurkhas."

I found myself wondering what was said by his fellows to the hundredth Gurkha, who had somehow permitted himself to be nosed out by a Scotsman!

Gurkha troops, wherever they go, carry, in addition to modern weapons, their ancient kukri knife, with its fifteen-inch curved blade, razor-sharp. I was told that with a single stroke of the kukri, which is swung like an axe, a Gurkha can cut off the head of a buffalo. And, after talking to American veterans of World War II, who fought alongside the Gurkhas, I am inclined to believe it. I bought one later in Katmandu as a souvenir for eighty cents.

There are today about forty-five thousand of these well-trained soldiers in the Nepalese army, and they are backed up by a large trained reserve, many of whom have combat experience.

Along the trail we met many Tibetans, some of them traders

and others apparently on pilgrimage to the Buddhist holy places of North India, and even in Ceylon. On their backs in baskets many of them were carrying old men who wanted to pay homage to Buddha before they died. They eyed us with friendly curiosity, and we did the same with them. They are big, jolly-looking people, with high cheek bones and red cheeks which reminded Steb of some of our own American Indians. All were dressed in loose belted robes, and many of them carried prayer symbols and long knives.

This was not the only time during our visit that we were reminded of Nepal's larger northern neighbor, now occupied by the Chinese Communists. There has always been some trade between Tibet and Nepal, mostly in salt and grain. And to this day, Tibet pays ten thousand rupees yearly in tribute to Nepal under a treaty signed in 1856 after a war between the two countries. For some reason the Communist Chinese masters of Tibet have not yet cut off the payments.

Later in Katmandu, we ran across a youthful and bewildered Chinese soldier who had deserted from the Chinese army in Tibet. No one in the city spoke Chinese, and since a member of our party did so fluently, he was asked by the Nepalese army to interview this man.

He said that he had been a member of a Communist youth brigade. This was his second attempt to escape and he knew that he would be shot summarily if he ever returned. He had been working on Tibetan roads, and had slipped away over the Himalayan passes into what he thought was India. He was amazed to find himself in a place called Nepal, of which he had never heard.

He told us that there were then some twenty thousand Chinese troops in Tibet. Immediately after the invasion in 1950 there had been considerable friction with the Tibetans, but this was quieter recently, and the Chinese had relaxed a number of restrictions which they had imposed on the local people. The Dalai Lama, believed by the Tibetan people to be a reincarnation of Buddha, still maintained a strong hold on the affections of his people, who admired him for his decision to stay behind in the capital city of Lhasa rather than to take refuge in India.

All this simply confirmed what I had learned from many talks with Indian travelers and others who had recently visited Tibet, some of whom had covered thousands of miles on foot. Through these frequent talks in Delhi and on later visits to Nepal, we were able to keep pretty well informed on happenings in this highest country in the world. We knew, for example, that there had been frequent riots in Lhasa, the capital city, principally over food shortages.

We also knew that the Tibetans strongly resented the invasion of their country by the Chinese. Most of their history has been the record of a slow, patient struggle to rid themselves of Chinese rule. At the time of the Communist invasion they were wholly unprepared to repel the attack, and many Tibetan soldiers were frightened into surrendering simply by a Chinese display of strange rockets and fireworks.

The continued presence of Chinese Communists on its northern border makes what happens in Nepal all the more important to India, and to the whole non-Communist world. If Nepal should fall before an invasion from Tibet, or from an internal Communist revolution, the Communists would be poised right on the Indian border, above the great heartland of the country, and less than four hundred miles from Delhi.

. . .

Besides the Tibetans, there were other claims to our attention along the trail. Occasionally we would catch a breathtaking glimpse of the snow-topped Himalayas. And as we went further the country began to take on a new look. The houses that occasionally clustered along the trail were of homemade brick and frequently two stories high. Although their owners were obviously very poor, they impressed us as sturdier than Indian village houses, and with their up-slanted eaves, some of them recalled the architecture of Chinese pagodas.

Here, too, we saw for the first time the complicated and perfectly engineered Nepali terraces on which much of the food of the country is grown. On what seem to be sheer cliffs, these little shelves of land, sometimes only four or five feet wide, have been cut out and tilled for hundreds of years.

Torrential mountain streams are carried off among the terraces by a series of canals along the face of the mountainside, often at several different levels, so carefully graded that the water barely moves in them. These canals are sometimes several miles in length, with the water being drawn off every few yards to nourish one of the terraces below.

By dint of this loving use of the precious soil, the most intricate that I saw in any country in Asia including even Japan, the Nepalese are able to grow enough rice for their own subsistence even without the full use of the fertile but malaria-infested Terai through which we had passed the previous day. With better agricultural methods, disease control and improved communications, they will be able not only to raise their own dietary level but even to export some rice to grain-hungry India.

After a lunchtime rest at which some of our guides treated us to Nepalese songs and dancing, we made the final climb to Chandragiri Pass with its sudden panorama of a vast Himalayan skyline, and the valley of Katmandu green and dim in the haze below.

From there, the descent was easy. Paul Rose, who had just reached Katmandu to head our budding Point Four program, had come up to meet us at the pass and accompanied us to Thankot on the outskirts of Katmandu.

We climbed gingerly down from our ponies. It was already past six o'clock, growing dark, and we had been riding and walking since early morning.

More than anything else I wanted to lie down but there were two full companies of the King's bodyguard in spectacular crimson uniforms drawn up for review. Since there was no level space anywhere, much less a parade ground, the men were lined up along a hillside at an angle that looked to me about forty-five degrees. On legs that suddenly felt unable or unwilling to bend at the knees I had to climb up hill and down between each of the eight ranks. But then I thought of the one hundred Gurkhas who had run and scrambled twenty miles under full pack in the Khud Race and what they would think of an American Ambassador who succumbed to a twenty-mile ride on a horse, and I managed to hold out.

When it was over, I remembered what the Nepalese Ambassador to India had told us when we suggested the overland trip into his country. "If I were you I would take the plane," he had said with emphasis. "Anyone who has not been doing a lot of riding will be stiff for a week." But in forty-eight hours we were all back to normal, and thankful that we had stuck to our plan.

Three cars drove us through the town to the Government Guest House where we were to stay. By diplomatic custom, this automatically became the American Embassy while we were living there and the Nepalese had decorated it with the flags of the United States and Nepal. The American flags had all been made by hand for the occasion.

Another honor guard of Gurkhas was drawn up in front of the house, and after reviewing them we went inside, where we found a cordial staff of servants, and best of all the news that since no function was planned we could go to bed immediately after dinner. Sam and Cynthia soon reported that their bathtubs were fully seven feet long.

It was not until the next day that we were able to see something of the city by daylight and to observe, as in so many other places, the terrible contrast between the luxury of our Guest House, the government buildings and a few palaces and the desperate pervasive poverty that surrounded them. Life for most of the 150,000 people of Katmandu was, like that of millions all over Asia, short and hard.

In slum-ridden Katmandu, however, there are some thirty palaces belonging to members of the Rana family. Most of them were built between 1800 and 1850 from materials carried to Nepal on human backs over the rough mountain trails from India. They have great marble bathtubs, carved staircases, and crystal chandeliers. In one palace I even saw a series of Coney Island distortion mirrors, some of which made us appear to be four feet high and at least four feet across, while others pulled us out like elongated stringbeans.

The government protocol officer arrived soon after breakfast and with him we worked out our schedule of official calls and conferences, and other activities. It was not until the second day after our arrival in Katmandu that the ceremony of presenting credentials as United States Ambassador took place. Cynthia must have been getting inured to this kind of thing by now, for she remarked with relief that there was "surprisingly little pomp and foolishness."

There was certainly enough of it for me. For one thing it meant putting on for the second time the ridiculous diplomatic garb of striped trousers, long-tail cutaway and silk hat. I found that my own aged version did not fit me as well as the "lend-lease" edition that I had borrowed from the Italian Ambassador for the similar occasion in New Delhi a few weeks before.

The presentation was to take place in the old Durbar Hall, a huge royal throne room in the center of the city. Thousands of men and children, although only a few women, had gathered on the steps of the Hindu temples near the Hall.

I was driven to the Hall in a resplendent coach with an honor guard of cavalry with lances and brilliant crimson uniforms, to the tune of "The Star-Spangled Banner" played by two Nepalese military bands. Like many of the Rana palaces, the old Durbar Hall might have been transported from Versailles. It glittered with chandeliers, and these reflected in the deep polished floor.

A long carpet led from the doorway to the red and gold velvet throne. Steb and the children sat in a high balcony above the King in his ornate military uniform. The walls were lined with life-sized paintings of the kings of Nepal, and behind the throne itself was a portrait of the present King and one of Queen Victoria.

The ceremony was over in a few minutes. Following the careful coaching I had received from Nepalese officials, I bowed once as I entered the room, once in the center of the hall and once when I reached the throne. I handed His Majesty my credentials and a letter of friendship from President Truman. The King stood while I introduced the others in the party. Then he offered us *pan*, an Asian chewing concoction of leaves and seeds, and rose water in the traditional gesture of hospitality of Nepal and India.

That night the Prime Minister gave a buffet dinner for us at which we had a chance to meet and talk to the King and his two Queens. And the following night it was our turn to give a dinner for His Majesty the King.

I was seated between the two Queens, who are sisters and whom the King married when they were ten and eleven years old and he only thirteen. They are known respectively as the Junior and Senior Queens. Since they spoke only Nepali it was rather slow going until Prime Minister Koirala volunteered as an interpreter. Steb found that she could talk to them quite easily through her knowledge of Hindi which is similar in many ways to Nepali.

We had brought gifts for His Majesty which we gave him after dinner. They included an encyclopedia, a tape recorder, and a walkie-talkie sending and receiving apparatus which was by all odds the greatest success with the King.

Sam went out into the garden a few hundred yards away with his end of the outfit and soon his voice came through, with youthful ignorance of the proper way to address His Majesty: "Can you hear me, King?" But the King was as pleased as Sam. "I can hear you, Sam." (Like our Indian friends he pronounced it "Som.") "Can you hear me?"

At all of the parties given for us by Nepalese officials and by the British and Indian Ambassadors, there were many ladies, for many of whom it was their first appearance in public. In Nepal the tradition of seclusion for women is still powerful but democracy is breaking it down.

. . .

I was very glad indeed when the formal festivities were over for there was much work to be done in getting to know the Nepalese ministers and their problems, and I was eager to start.

I was immediately impressed with the Prime Minister, M. P. Koirala, a man of great sensitivity, integrity, and intelligence. At the age of thirty-nine he became the new Nepal's first Prime Minister, at the head of an earnest team of associates, most of whom had had even less experience in government than he. We had many long talks and I found him well informed on the world situation, keenly aware of the nature of the Communist movement, friendly toward America and determined to build a democratic nation.

However, he failed to keep his grip on the political machinery which had put him into power, and came into sharp conflict with his younger half-brother, B. P. Koirala, who had won control of the Nepalese Congress party. From this position B. P. Koirala sought to control the actions of his brother and his ministers.

M. P. Koirala had the King behind him, but he was not sufficiently sure of the temper of the people to risk an outright break with his own political organization which had cracked the power of the Ranas two years before. So in the summer of 1952 he resigned, and set out on a tour of Nepal on foot and by pony.

He visited the most remote villages explaining the meaning of

Nepal's new democracy to attentive groups of villagers. Everywhere he denounced communism as a new imperialist tyranny as evil as the government of the Ranas. He appealed for mass support, and when he returned from his tour, he had strengthened his position considerably. A few months later he was again heading the government.

In the meantime the Communists were by no means quiet. Within four months after the end of the revolution there was an uprising, supported by the Communist party, which for twenty-four hours held control of most of the capital city of Katmandu. The government, with the help of the loyal Gurkha army, broke the rebellion, restored its authority and outlawed the Communist party.

K. I. Singh, the Communist leader, is now a fugitive with the Chinese in Tibet, while the Nepalese party is racked by a bitter internal struggle over whether it should continue to take orders from Moscow through the Indian Communist Party or shift its allegiance to the Chinese Communists across the Himalayas. I will be surprised if we do not hear further from K. I. Singh. Recently B. P. Koirala has rejoined his older brother as a member of the cabinet, so that "a strong united front can be organized against communism."

Among the many dedicated young members of the new government whom I met on my first visit was also a man named Singh, with the same initial K. But no two men could be more different than Khadgaman Singh, then Foreign Minister, and the Communist Singh.

I came to know Khadgaman Singh very well in the next year or so, and I know of no man whose story more needs telling to the world. Already in Nepal it is a story the children learn, for he was one of the early heroes of the revolutionary struggle.

Khadgaman Singh is now only forty-three years old. A son of one of the lesser Rana families, he was sent to India for his education. He went to the University of Patna, in Bihar province in the northeast of India and scene of Gandhi's first struggle in India. "There," he said, "I met a young anarchist who tried to convince me that all government was evil and that until government was completely destroyed everywhere the people would never be free.

"But my anarchist friend was not content merely to talk or to indulge in philosophy. He knew how to make bombs, and he wanted to teach me how, so that together we could put his ideas into action. At the time, I was completely uninterested. After all, I was getting my education to prepare me for a good post in the government when I returned to Nepal. Why should I want to destroy it?"

But Khadgaman Singh had not seen the last of his explosive-minded fellow student. When he returned to Nepal, riding his pony over the high mountains just as we did, he became deeply depressed by the miserable lot of his people, the rigid autocracy under which they lived, the disease and dirt and ignorance, above all the terrible contrast between the riches of the Ranas and the cruel burden of poverty borne by the great majority of the people.

He found among his educated friends, many of whom had also been in India, a number of young men equally horrified by the condition of their country, and equally determined that only by democratic processes could a new nation be built and the ancient ills erased. But the Rana government stood squarely in the way and it seemed clear that until it had been destroyed the people of Nepal could never hope to live as free men.

So Khadgaman Singh, then only twenty-one, returned to Patna in 1930 and looked up his anarchist friend. "This time," he said, "I was an apt and determined pupil. I learned how to make bombs well. I made a good supply of them, loaded them on my pony and carried them back over the mountains to Katmandu."

With the bombs at hand, Khadgaman Singh and his young friends laid their plans to end the Rana rule. Each year all the members of the Rana family who were in the line of succession to the office of Prime Minister rode out together in a large ceremonial carriage to pledge their allegiance at a shrine near Katmandu. If this carriage could be bombed, all eight Ranas who had any present or future claim to the top office of the land could be wiped out by a single blow. With no one to succeed to the hereditary office, Khadgaman Singh hoped the way would be clear for the establishment of a democratic government.

Everything was in readiness. Then, a few days before the date set for the assassination Khadgaman Singh began to worry. "My anarchist friend had taught me to make bombs," he told me, "but he had not convinced me of his theories about government. I knew that we would need a responsible force after the elimination of the principal Ranas, to exercise the powers of the state and to act as a symbol of authority during the time we were organizing our new democratic government.

"My friends agreed with me, and we decided, after some discussion, that the King, who had been in the background all these years, was the man we needed. Unfortunately none of us knew him, so we decided to take the risk of revealing our plot to one of our acquaintances who did have access to His Majesty."

The new recruit listened intently and then lost no time in taking the entire story to the Ranas. Khadgaman Singh and his four companions were promptly arrested and faced what they thought was certain death.

But luck was with them. The Ranas had been under considerable criticism for their medieval judicial system. Under strong British pressure they had recently enacted a new judicial code, cutting down the severity of criminal penalties and abolishing capital punishment.

This placed the Ranas in a dilemma. They wanted very much to be rid of Khadgaman Singh and his revolutionary friends once and for all. Still they did not dare to make a complete mockery of the recent reform of which they had boasted so proudly to the British and to their own subjects. Reluctantly, they decided to stick to the newly passed law.

Khadgaman Singh and his friends were, of course, imprisoned, and in a manner deliberately calculated to shorten their life expectancy by many years. "All five of us were put in one cell," he told me. "It was only five feet high, so that we could not stand erect. It was no more than ten feet long and six feet wide. It was my home for twelve years." One by one, his friends died. Only one of them survived the long ordeal with him.

In prison he was completely cut off from the outside world. He wrote poems, a little book of which he gave me. And he induced a guard to take a picture of him, which was smuggled out of the prison. I have a copy of that picture in my library now. It shows a handsome man behind bars in a kind of cage, dressed in rags, with an eighty-pound iron ball and chain around one ankle, and heavy manacles at his wrists and throat. But on his face was a look of complete peace and dignity.

He explained that the inspiration of Gandhi had reached even into this remote Nepalese prison. The Mahatma's cheerful courting of jail in India, news of which was smuggled in, made a deep impression on him. "Through Gandhi I came to realize how wrong our bombing plot had been. I gave up all thought of violence. I decided that if our country were to be free it should be by Gandhi's way."

Khadgaman Singh proved willing to follow his newfound ideals though it meant hardship and suffering. In 1934 an earthquake destroyed much of Katmandu and with it the prison in which Khadgaman Singh was held. "I could have walked out without anyone trying to stop me," he said. Because of his Gandhian beliefs, however, he remained where he was while order was being restored to the devastated city.

In 1943 he was taken out of his cage and put into a more conventional prison. "Here," he said, "I could stand up straight and get some exercise. But I still could not see the sun."

It was not until the revolution of 1951 that Singh at last gained his freedom. He was, of course, a hero from one end of the country to the other. And he immediately assumed an important post in the new free government of Nepal.

I asked him if he felt any bitterness or hatred toward the Ranas who had taken twenty-one years of his life from him. He looked almost surprised at my question. "No," he replied, "why should I hate them? They did only what seemed to them to be right. It was their duty to do that, just as it was my duty to oppose them."

Now it was his duty to help build a free Nepal. In his hands, and in the hands of the other young men who carried out the revolution, lies the hopes for creating a democracy out of a country without roads or communications, with only an infinitesimally small portion of the people able to read, and with many of the population living on the remote and windswept slopes of the highest mountains in the world.

One of the first orders of business has been the preparation for a nationwide election to establish a permanent government in the place of the provisional one now ruling the country. The problems involved in this undertaking are hard for us even to imagine. There is, of course, no census, and there is not even an accurate estimate of the population of Nepal. Nor are there maps accurate enough for establishing proper election districts.

Nevertheless, the work has been pushed ahead. Sukumar Sen, the Chief Election Commissioner for India, to whom much of the credit for the success of India's great election of 1951 is due, has been sent by India at the request of the Nepalese government to assist in the preparations. Sen's report makes interesting reading to us who are used to polling places just around the corner from our homes, especially where he discusses the difficulties of assuring the vote to the 10 per cent of Nepal's people who live in the snowy highlands. Yet he and the government are confident that these obstacles can be overcome.

When I left the Indian subcontinent, registration of voters was under way. In many of the more populous districts it was already complete, and for the country as a whole about one-third to one-half of the job was done. The government has announced its plans to hold a general election in early 1954, and the first elective assembly of Nepal is scheduled to meet in June of that year.

I had become convinced after the Indian election that the strength a new nation gains from such universal suffrage, the education of the public inevitable in the campaigning, and the knowledge of how much public support lies behind each political faction, outweigh the obvious risks.

The work of political reform has been going forward. Before the revolution, the Rana's word was law in the literal sense. He sat personally as the highest court in the land, hearing appeals from district and village judges and dispensing "personal justice." This has all been changed by the Supreme Court Act of 1951, which sets up an independent judicial system, much like our own, and which assures, among other things, the writ of habeas corpus. A Press Act has also been passed, which guarantees full freedom to all publishers except those who incite violence against the government. The new government is making an earnest effort to develop a democratic Nepal in the form of a constitutional monarchy, much like Great Britain's.

Much will depend on Nepal's relationship with India and here there are many uncertainties. Although the Indian government of Nehru has stood solidly behind the revolution in Nepal which brought an end to the Rana autocracy, there is a certain irony in the fact that India now faces in Nepal some of the same difficulties which America itself faces in other parts of the world.

Indians are aware of the danger to their own security from a Communist Nepal, and they know that this danger could come about not only by an armed attack from Tibet but also by infiltration, subversion and a sudden coup d'état. A Communist Nepal is something that the Indian government is determined to prevent.

So India has done on a small scale in Nepal what we have done on a far broader scale on two continents. Her first step has been to put her own troops side by side with the Nepalese Gurkhas in the Himalayan passes on the Tibetan frontier. Then she has gone to work to help Nepal to strengthen her army so that she can defend herself.

An Indian military mission has helped to reorganize the army, including the weeding out of officers who earned titles running as high as general by inheritance rather than by ability. New equipment has arrived from India and today the Nepalese army, in addition to its traditional individual fighting qualities, is far better trained and with high morale.

Indian army engineers have also built, in the short space of one year, a remarkable road over the mountains which not only opens Nepal to easier contacts with the outside world, but makes possible quick military support in time of emergency.

Knowing, as we do, that an impoverished people led by frustrated young intellectuals can be an easy target for Communist subversion, India has offered its assistance in Nepal's effort to build a modern state. India's civil servants and technicians are now working effectively in Nepal, setting up a tax system and organizing new government departments. And again, just as in the case of America, the result has often been abuse and criticism!

For all over Nepal, wherever people gather, India is being charged with "interference," with "attempting to turn Nepal into a colony," with plotting and scheming against the best interests of the Nepalese people. These accusations are as false, in my opinion, as the very similar accusations leveled at the United States in India and other Asian countries. And, of course, those loudest with such accusations in these countries are the Communists.

There is no doubt that Indians have sometimes been tactless in dealing with the sensitive Nepalese, just as we have too often been tactless in dealing with Asians. Fortunately the present Indian Ambassador and his excellent staff have done much to relieve the tense anti-Indian sentiment that existed in 1952.

Despite the helpful assistance of India, the new interest of the United States, and the vigorous efforts of the Nepalese people, everyone is aware of an undercurrent of restlessness. It is apparent that the people are willing to give their new government a fair chance, but the situation can deteriorate very rapidly if their hopes for democratic progress are dashed again.

As elsewhere in Asia, the people of Nepal will not long be satisfied with the trappings of political democracy, unless they find they can use their freedom to attack the ancient plagues of hunger, ignorance and disease which still oppress them.

18. Point Four in the Himalayas

IT WAS not until I first sat down with the Nepalese government officials to take a systematic look at the obstacles facing them that I really began to grasp the magnitude of the problem.

At the head of the list was lack of people with any kind of technical training, either for the operation of the government itself or for the guidance of the people in the improvement of their living conditions. This could hardly be otherwise in a country where education was almost unknown.

It was difficult even to begin training government personnel or health, agricultural and other workers because fully 98 per cent of the people could not read or write. At Godivari, outside Katmandu, is one of the few new schools, which was founded just before our arrival by a Jesuit priest, Father Marshall D. Moran, of Erie, Pennsylvania, who had given outstanding service in India. When we last saw the school there were some one hundred students, all boys, between the ages of eight and twelve, and plans were being made for its expansion.

Most travel in Nepal is over narrow foot or pony tracks. Even bullock power is little used either for plowing or for transportation. Practically everything is carried on the people's backs. In the entire country of some 50,000 square miles there were only 170 miles of road over which an automobile could be driven.

Total electric power capacity amounts to only 2,825 kilowatts, scarcely enough to light an American town, and this is despite the fact that the snow-fed rivers plunging down from the Himalayas offer an abundant source of cheap power.

Health problems are staggering. Nepal has one of the highest concentrations of tropical diseases in the world. Forty per cent of the people have malaria. Tuberculosis, typhoid and typhus, dysentery, hookworm, elephantiasis, trachoma and venereal disease are also rampant.

In the face of this, there are only 650 hospital beds in the entire country, only three doctors with the equivalent of a medical school education, fifty more with some medical training, and ten nurses.

Modern equipment, drugs and other medical supplies are almost unavailable.

A small hospital for the treatment of eye diseases was established in 1951 at Katmandu by a dedicated Nepalese, Dr. G. C. Sood. "We are still performing eye surgery under kerosene lanterns," he told me. "Bandages are so scarce that we must carefully wash each one and reuse it many times."

In 1953 more than half the land was still owned by large landowners charging rents averaging 50 per cent of the yearly crop—with many rents running far higher. The villagers lived under a staggering burden of debt, which was passed on inexorably from generation to generation. Seventy per cent of the peasants were making payments to village moneylenders at interest rates ranging from 20 to 100 per cent annually.

There was no accurate record of government revenues and expenditures, and other statistics were almost nil. There were not even accurate maps of most of the country. Because of the lack of communications, the central government could only operate to full effectiveness in two or three principal valleys, including Katmandu.

Distances between these valleys, and indeed between all points within Nepal, are usually expressed in days of travel by pony, instead of in miles. Beautiful Pokhara Valley, for instance, is "fourteen days" from Katmandu. We flew there once in forty minutes and learned that the actual distance is only 135 miles in a straight line. It was a magnificently clear day and the towering snow-clad Himalayas, only a few miles to the north, stood out dramatically against a cold blue sky.

I sat beside the pilot and we checked off the great mountains as we passed. We saw three or four that according to the map were over twenty-five thousand feet. We flew through the valleys with their swift-flowing rivers at an altitude of ten thousand feet. Every tiny patch of land which was level, or which hard patient work could make level, was cultivated, much of it irrigated even at heights of eight thousand feet.

When we had flown over Pokhara Valley before, we had been unable to find the level pasture where it was supposed to be possible to land a plane. This time we had better luck. The valley itself was easy to pick out, ten or fifteen miles in length with a river flowing through it, a large lake at each end. Mt. Dhaulagiri,

26,810 feet high, was thirty miles to the west, and an unnamed peak of 26,405 feet twenty miles to the north.

After circling the "field" several times we strapped our seat belts tightly and took a long deep breath as the pilot came in for a landing. We bounced high off the ground, but soon settled safely to a stop.

Our plane was almost immediately surrounded by an excited, good-natured, jostling crowd of two thousand or more men, women and children, most of whom seemed to be Tibetans. To our amazement we saw three middle-aged Western women standing at the edge of the crowd.

They told us that they were British women doctors who had heard of the extraordinary concentration of disease in this remote valley and had come over the mountains from India to do what they could to help. A smallpox epidemic had broken out "two days" away, and they had hoped that we were bringing the serum which they had requested by radio. The Tibetans, they said, had come down through the passes to the north, the lowest of which is some fourteen thousand feet, to find relief from what they described as the worst winter in any man's memory.

Pokhara, like other valleys of Nepal, is today probably much the way it was a thousand years ago. The tools, the clothes and the customs are the same. Once we followed the bass notes of the five-foot-long Tibetan horn to a village where a marriage was taking place in the same ceremony followed for countless centuries.

Perhaps I could say three thousand years as accurately as one thousand, for today there is said to be not a single wheel of any kind in the entire valley. Indeed the people say that the first wheel they ever saw in the valley of Pokhara was on an airplane that had landed there two years ago. Thus they had simply skipped the stage of animal-drawn and automotive transportation, and had jumped straight into the air age.

When, after a day of exploring the countryside, we took off just before sunset we had a better understanding of the challenge which faces the new government of Nepal as it tries to leap in one bound into the twentieth century.

. . .

To assist the government the United States, at my request, had agreed to send a group of nine Point Four technicians, agricultural and public health experts, who with their families totaled some thirty people. I shall never forget the trouble we had finding places for them to live. Except for a few of the old Rana palaces, there were no houses with even the crudest comforts or sanitary facilities.

Although several of the palaces were available, we were determined to find some other solution. Point Four people are supposed to, and generally are anxious to, live close to the people among whom they work. Only in this way can they establish the confidence and mutual respect needed for their success.

We looked and looked and finally gave up, settling reluctantly for one of the smaller palaces, which we purchased from the Nepalese government. Let me add that it was the farthest thing from luxury. There was no heat, no refrigeration, inadequate cooking facilities and toilets. Until they were able to break the palace up into separate apartments, all the families had to live together with little privacy.

But it had a nice garden, a wonderful view of the Himalayas, and everyone turned to in good spirits to make the quarters livable and comfortable. Mary Rose, the wife of the head of the mission, did a good job breaking in new families, helping the wives and children to get settled, and starting a school with the help of the Calvert system of "education by mail."

In many ways this Point Four group typifies the many Americans now spread all over Asia, Africa and Latin America, meeting the exciting challenge of a new frontier. It is a wonderful experience to see these eager men and women, in strange and unfamiliar surroundings far from friends and families, turning willingly to the mammoth job of helping to build a nation. They have had to endure considerable discomfort, and some of them, who are working in the malarial districts, have faced the dangers of a virulent disease.

They have had to buck the red tape of our own government as well as the delays and inefficiencies of the new government of Nepal, unequipped as yet to deal decisively with its end of the program. They have to learn a new language, and make friends among people who for centuries have deliberately kept foreigners out of their country.

Of course, in one sense our Nepalese Point Four mission is

lucky; their opportunity is without limit. "It's so easy to show quick progress here," said Paul Rose, then the head of the mission, an experienced agricultural extension worker. "Practically all the plowing in Nepal is done by simply breaking the earth up with a wooden pick. Very few of the villagers have ever heard of a plow with a steel plowshare. If we can just show these people how to make and use simple tools, how to sow in rows, and get them to use natural manures, the increase in food production will be tremendous."

Paul Rose and his co-workers also saw immediately that the wheat and rice grown in Nepal were pure strains and were subject to continual blight and disease. They brought in over three hundred types of seeds from wheats grown in mountain areas in Mexico, South America, Morocco and other places, where conditions were roughly comparable to Nepal; they planted these carefully in test areas in the various regions in the country to see which were best suited for use there.

On my last visit to Nepal in late February, 1953, the Nepalese agricultural trainees were already proudly showing me several varieties in the test plantings which had produced an increase of 30 to 40 per cent above the average yield. Early in 1954 the most successful varieties of seeds will begin to be distributed to the villagers. Even if they continue to plant in the old medieval way, they can look forward to at least a 15 to 20 per cent increase in the crops which they harvest.

As we knew from our experience in India another job which could show quick results was malaria control, backed up by a broader public health program. Dr. George Moore, our Point Four public health specialist, gave me a grim report on his preliminary malaria survey. "In the middle Terai, where I've just come from," he said, "I have seen whole villages deserted and fertile land unused. Four out of every five babies born die before their first year is out."

Dr. Moore had counted up the amount of money a family has to pay for cures where malaria strikes. He did not include the loss of crop production because of weakness or because the family had to move away from its land during the worst of the season. And yet these payments came to more than the average family income in Nepal.

When he told me this, it was easy to understand how so many of the villagers get into debt and stay there, year in, year out. "Malaria cripples the whole country," Dr. Moore concluded, and he was right.

With the help of Dr. Robert Watson, Director of the Rockefeller Foundation mission in Southeast Asia, and one of the world's top malaria experts, whom I brought with me on one trip into Nepal, we worked out a program for the control of malaria which should wipe out the disease all over Nepal within a five-year period. The cost of this program in American dollars over the entire five years would be less than $450,000. Already a start has been made in the valley around Katmandu, and Nepalese students are being sent to the Indian Malaria Institute to be trained to take the lead in the control work upon their return.

A third major task for the economic development of the country was to open up roads between the various sections of Nepal and between Nepal and India. Here, as I have said, the Indian government, through its army engineers, shouldered most of the burden. When I heard that a motor road was being built along a steep pony track similar to the one by which we had come into Nepal, I knew that some extraordinary engineering skill would be required.

Yet by March, 1953, when I left India, the road was already "jeepable." It will be followed up by a similar north-south road from Pokhara to the Indian border, and within two or three years the valley that so recently saw its first pair of wheels on an airplane will be opened to motor traffic.

The next step in the plan is to cut an east-west road across the Terai between these first two roads. Katmandu and Pokhara will then be connected by a motor road for the first time in history. Unless you have been in a country without roads at all, it is almost impossible to realize how much this road construction will mean.

But the heart of Asia is in the villages, and Nepal is no exception. Here too, as in India, it seemed clear to all of us that the best way to begin a frontal attack on the related problems of food production, health, roads and literacy was by a co-ordinated village development program. By adapting the Community Development program from India and by training Nepalese young men and women for agricultural, public health and literacy work in the villages, we could reach the largest number of people quickly with some of the basic knowledge they needed to attack their own problems.

Equally important, we knew that this was the only way that we could gain the participation of the people themselves in the work, and their support and understanding, without which even the best development scheme is bound to fail. Nepalese government officials from Prime Minister Koirala on down agreed with me that this was the most practical approach.

The first thing to do was to set up a training center for village workers, for there was nobody in Nepal with the experience to take on that job. We arranged with the Nepalese government to assign a building for the school, which in the beginning our Point Four staff would run, and by the end of July, 1952, the first class of fifty village workers was enrolled.

The handicaps were great. Unlike India, where pilot projects such as Etawah had long since shown what village extension work can do, there was at first little recognition of its importance in Nepal. Many of the students in the beginning seemed more interested in the cultural opportunities that they thought the school would offer, and did not see the necessity of getting their hands dirty.

But as soon as they understood the possibilities of the work for which they were being trained they became enthusiastic and eager to help their country. I shall never forget my several visits with them, and the excitement we felt as we saw their progress from month to month.

In part to provide practical experience for the students, and in part to demonstrate concretely the value of the village development work, we suggested that the government immediately select several villages near Katmandu to be turned into model demonstration villages. Here, under the direct supervision of three American technicians, students put into operation the lessons in malaria control, fertilizing, irrigation and other improved agricultural techniques, local road building and literacy instruction, that they had learned in their classroom hours.

It was remarkable what a few months' effort was able to do in the five or six villages in which work was started before I left. People from neighboring villages came to these model villages to see and compare. The most dramatic results were still in the future, but even after a few months you could feel the hearts of the people in the model villages begin to lift, and the interest of their neighbors quicken.

In the village workers' training school, practically all training and instruction materials, from many of the tools to the charts, had to be improvised by the American teachers and the Nepalese trainees as they went along. Dr. Laubach, our Point Four literacy expert who was helping to open up such new horizons in India, prepared materials in the Nepali language for teaching villagers how to read and write. These will be distributed by the village development workers in evening classes.

The first class of fifty trainees graduated after only three months and were serving in the villages soon afterward. The second class received somewhat more thorough training, lasting for six months, and was made up of one hundred students. A third class of one hundred had already been started by the time I left.

As in India, the villagers are being grouped into Community Development areas. The first plans called for six of these areas, each of which contains about sixty thousand people. Each development area is to be headed by a trained director, and American technicians will be available at the area headquarters to help village workers on the more difficult problems that arise. We had already sent nine Nepalese students to America for special technical training. When they return, I hope that some of them will be ready to take their places as area directors.

Over a period of six years, with continuing American help, I believe they will be able to train enough village workers to cover all of Nepal and to bring improved seeds, complete malaria control, improved village sanitation, some roads, better agricultural methods and the beginnings of a school system to all but the most inaccessible mountain areas.

The total cost to the United States of this country-wide effort would be less than $800,000 a year. I don't believe that there is any place in the world where democracy can achieve such spectacular results for such a relatively small sum, or where the people are more ready to respond.

If the Nepal government does its part and if we give it the modest support through Point Four which I strongly recommended, there is every reason to hope for steady progress. But there is a long way to go and much to be done. Communist propaganda is persistent and because of the lack of book stores and libraries there often is nothing else for the few thousand literate leaders to read.

To help fill this need and to stimulate greater understanding of America we felt that it would be wise to establish a small library in Katamandu. Three months later it was in operation under the direction of a single American and four Nepalese assistants.

An old three-story building in the center of Katmandu was leased for the library site. On the ground floor were some doors which were usually left open and which permitted easy entrance from the street. Here we kept magazines, picture displays, posters and hundreds of books. On the upper floors were a reading room, more books and a projection room for our Information Service movies.

The movies were probably the most popular feature of the library for ours were among the first motion pictures ever shown in Nepal. We had three showings daily covering everything from the operation of our American public school system and the building of TVA to films showing how germs spread disease.

There was an average of five hundred visitors each day, and in spite of the fact that many of them could not read their own language, much less English, their desire to learn something of the world outside their country was so great that they would often stay for hours looking at picture books and magazines.

The library also was the only real source in the country of technical books on many of the problems that were confronting the new government. As a result, journalists, government officials and students made constant use of it.

Once the library was under way, there was time to work on other methods of explaining our views to the people of Nepal. Specially prepared English-language textbooks were supplied to schools as well as an inexpensive collection of several books which we worked out in India.

News in Nepal is hard to come by, and the library when I left was preparing to translate for local papers news stories that came in. Equipment was ordered to enable the government radio to broadcast some of our Voice of America recordings. Just before I left we were working out a program of taking magic lantern slides and film strips out among the villages to people who had hardly heard of the city of Katmandu.

At best we were working under difficulties and with inadequate equipment. Our librarian, Nancy Dammann, told me, "We could get a lot more people reading if we had the right kind of books. Here, where most of our readers are just learning to read, they need simple books that tell about their daily problems, mostly food and health. Descriptions of life in American cities and farms are too far beyond their experience." Our best-read pamphlet was a description of the Indian Development project at PEPSU.

. . .

There is, however, at least one thing that Point Four assistance cannot do, and that the government of Nepal, despite its lack of technical proficiency, can do. In Nepal too, the land, which is the only basis of wealth, is not in the hands of the men and women who till it. Without question the control of the moneylenders and landlords is the most pressing grievance of the people. Unless some way can be found to assure that bigger crops, better roads and schools bring tangible benefits in the way of life of the families who work the land, they will not long retain their enthusiasm for village improvement, nor for the government which permits their bondage to continue.

The Communists, though officially banned in Nepal, have begun new agitation under cover of front organizations. On one of my visits, I saw a parade of three thousand young men in Katmandu, marching through the streets with clenched fists. While most of these young people were not Communists, they were certainly Communist organized and led. Whether this smoldering Communist movement grows more powerful or not will depend to a major degree on whether the new government is able and willing to move swiftly to distribute land to the villagers.

The present land system in Nepal is somewhat different from that in India. Technically all the land is owned by the state, and the cultivator pays about 5 per cent of his crop to the state as rent for the right to use it. If this really worked out in practice, there might be no complaint, but there are two major flaws.

The first is the *birtar* lands, large holdings given generations ago by the Ranas to individual supporters as reward for their loyalty, and which are still tax free. They are worked, of course, not by the owners or their families, but by impoverished tenants. Forty per cent of all the agricultural land in Nepal is *birtar* land.

Secondly, although the peasant rents his land from the state, he may sell his right to work it, and moneylenders in the villages have been avidly taking advantage of this situation for centuries. They loan the peasant the cash he needs when sickness strikes, or to perform religious obligations, or to provide a dowry for his daughter. The villager gives his land as security or gives up his right to work it for a period of years. In such cases the moneylender assumes the position of landlord and rents the land back to its rightful owner.

The interest rates on these loans were fantastic, ranging in some extreme cases as high as 300 per cent. And there is no such thing as a "statute of limitations." All over Nepal today, villagers are paying on debts incurred by their grandfathers and great grandfathers. It is easy to see that once in debt it is almost impossible to get out.

During my stay in Asia I became convinced that American aid will be so much more money down the drain unless basic reforms are put through by the individual governments.

The American people can provide bulldozers, DDT, Diesel pumps, fertilizer and technicians. They cannot, however, pass legislation putting land reforms into effect and establishing tax systems which do not fall primarily on the very poor as in Nepal, Thailand, the Philippines and many other Asian countries, as well as in much of South America. And yet without such legislation, backed by determined administration, our American aid may actually increase existing inequalities and thus speed the day of revolutionary explosion.

For this reason I have always believed that we should insist on some basic, essential reforms as a condition of American assistance. If such a requirement had been part of our policy in dealing with Europe under the Marshall Plan I believe that the injustices which go far to explain why 32 per cent of the Italian people in desperation voted for the Communist party in 1953 would long since have been wiped out.

Nepal seemed to me a textbook example of a similar situation and I felt it would be foolish indeed for America to offer its Point Four funds year after year if the government itself was unprepared to tax its own wealthy groups, and to take a courageous and effective stand in behalf of its own people.

So a few weeks before leaving India and Nepal I decided to write directly to the King and his government and to lay down what seemed to me a basic requirement for continued American assistance.

Surely the King's titles and name, which I copied carefully, were the most formidable I have ever addressed:

"His Royal Majesty, Shri Shri Shri Maharaja Tribhubana Vir,
Bikram Jang Bahadur Shah Badadur Shamsher,
Jang Devanam Sadasamarvijayinam"

I first outlined briefly the work which had already begun and congratulated His Majesty on the imagination he had shown in grasping what Nepal could someday become. I said that with help from India, America and the UN, Nepal could make "spectacular economic, social and political progress in the next few years."

I then went on to say: "In the revolutionary world in which we are living such progress is no less than essential. In Asia, Africa, and South America, hundreds of millions of people who have long existed in a state of abject ignorance, misery and ill health are awakening to the possibilities of a better life.

"Your own people of Nepal have felt the impact of this world-wide economic and political restlessness. In the last few years they have become constantly more aware that their impoverished conditions can be remedied; that modern science and technology can enable them to overcome the threat of malaria, to open up inaccessible mountain valleys, to harness the streams for electric power, increase the yield of human labor many times over, and to secure a more fair return for their labor."

I stated our willingness to help but stressed the urgent need for Nepal to put through the reforms which were basic to all economic progress. More income to the state so that Nepal could provide the local funds necessary for her own development could come from a graduated income tax, by more efficient customs collectors, and by taxing for the first time the *birtar* lands.

I then passed on to land reform: "One final problem which I believe needs the most careful consideration is the question of land reforms. I understand that most of the *birtar* land and about half of all the cultivated land in Nepal is now tilled under tenancy arrangements of a type which is being rapidly abandoned in agricultural countries throughout the world. Communist agitation for land reforms, which has already become intense in India and other underdeveloped countries, is beginning to show itself in Nepal.

"Unless broad ownership of the land is developed, the cultivator has but little personal stake in its development, the benefits from increased yields will flow largely into the hands of the few, and the majority of the people will come to consider them a fraud and a delusion."

I ended my letter with the following paragraphs: "The American people and their government feel a deep sense of friendship and respect for Your Majesty and for your people. We are sincerely anxious to help you in every practicable way, and we seek nothing in return.

"If my understanding is correct that the Nepalese government intends to move forward along the lines which I have sketched in this memorandum, I have every reason to expect that American assistance will be forthcoming and I can assure you that I shall do everything in my power to speed up this aid."

I took the letter to Nepal, presented one copy to the King, and read another slowly to the King's Council which acted as an interim government when Prime Minister Koirala resigned temporarily to carry his case to the people. Three or four of the Council members were among the largest landowners in Nepal and I was uncertain about the kind of reception which my proposals would receive.

As I watched their expressions out of the corner of my eye, it seemed to me that it was going far better than I had dared to expect. When I had finished reading I put aside the letter and quoted an old Hindi proverb: "The wise man, when faced with total disaster, gives up half and saves the rest."

There was immediate laughter and two or three of the group including one of the larger landlords spoke up promptly to say that he welcomed my firm stand, that clearly Nepal was going through a revolution and that the old days of great riches side by side with intolerable poverty were over.

The Indian Ambassador, one of the ablest men in India's able civil service, took a similar stand and a few days later we were cheered by news that the King had stated over the Nepalese radio that a land reform commission was being set up which would break up the great estates; that all peasants would be given full rights to the land they till, with their own committees to assure the success of the program; that the *birtar* lands would be taxed for the first time; and that a graduated income tax would be introduced. That was in the early spring of 1953, and I hope by now that these assurances, so earnestly and hopefully given, have taken tangible form.

I have often thought that someday Nepal could become the Switzerland of Asia, and perhaps the Swiss think so too, for, working side by side with our own Point Four people in Nepal, are two Swiss agricultural specialists, the only Swiss technical assistance mission in the world.

Someday we will revisit this beautiful land in the Himalayas, for we developed a deep affection there for its leaders and its people. As I drove to the airport through the old streets, turbulent with humanity, one early evening in February, 1953, on my last visit to Nepal, I felt saddened that my time among these friendly, dynamic people had been so short.

VII. WEST MEETS EAST

19. Voices of America

"YOUR INFORMATION Service library here in Delhi is wonderful," an Indian friend of ours said to Steb. "I was there just yesterday morning looking for some material on American cooperatives. The young lady in charge couldn't have been nicer. She went with me to the shelves, and helped me to find just what I wanted."

Encouraged by this we urged him to give us more of his impressions about our information program. He told us how he had stayed on in the library to look at some of the posters and photographs of American farmers atop harvesting combines, of workers seated at their benches in clean, well-lighted plants, of children eagerly gathered about a pretty young teacher in a glass-walled modern classroom. In the auditorium at the back of the library they were showing a movie about TVA.

I must have beamed with satisfaction, for I had put a great deal of effort into these and other U.S. Information Service activities since our arrival. But our friend seemed to have something more on his mind, and I urged him to give me his frank criticisms.

After some hesitation he said, "Of course, your government's information effort is only one of a great many factors which affect an Asian people's thinking about America. For instance, what were the headlines on the front page of the *Times of India* the other day? A member of your American Congress urged that the help you are giving to our Five Year Plan be cut off completely if we do not accept your views on Indo-China and meet a whole long list of other American demands.

"In another paper a day or two ago there was a story about two Indian women students traveling in your South who were refused hotel accommodations because their skins were dark like Negroes, and another giving a retired American general's view that America should attack Russia while you still have superior atomic strength.

"Then there are your movies. Some of them are splendid. But so many deal with nothing but divorce, night clubs, murder and other violence. And your comic books! Yesterday after I left your fine library, feeling so good about America, I went home to find my son with one of your particularly violent comic books called "The Mongol Bloodsuckers.'"

Steb and I were already embarrassed enough. Only a few days before we had been horrified to see a copy of that particular comic book which depicted a superman character struggling against half-human, colored Mongolian tribesmen who had been recruited by the Communists to raid American hospitals in Korea and drink the plasma in the blood banks.

In every picture they were portrayed with yellow skins, slanted eyes, hideous faces and dripping jaws. At the climax of the story, their leader summoned his followers to an attack on American troops. "Follow me, blood drinkers of Mongolia!" he cried. "To-night we dine well of red nectar." A few panels later he is shown leaping on an American soldier with the shout, "One rip at the throat, red blood spills over white skins. And we drink deep."

In Asia it is impossible to explain such things away by pointing out that it is pure fantasy. The Communist propagandists themselves could not possibly devise a more persuasive way to convince color-sensitive Indians that Americans believe in the superior civilization of people with white skins, and that we are indoctrinating our children with bitter racial prejudice from the time they learn to read.

At least we were thankful that our friend had not gone to a wild west movie which Sam had seen the previous week, where the American "Indians" were called "savages" and "dirty redskins" who regularly "hit the dust" to the tune of American six shooters. We were thankful too that he had not heard recent stories of tactlessness and rudeness on the part of some color-conscious American tourists which had just come to our ears.

I knew how such occasional incidents in India and other countries of Asia are picked up by Communists, fellow travelers and the Soviet propaganda machine, multiplied, garnished, and otherwise tailored to fit the requirements of the never-ceasing anti-American campaign, and broadcast by one means or another to every corner of India.

It is important, of course, to improve our information programs in every possible way, and to expand it in many areas. But in a sense every American abroad, every American activity is a "Voice of America." It seemed to me that one of the chief duties of an ambassador should be to try to co-ordinate these many "voices" into an effective, integrated program. That we, who consider ourselves the greatest nation of salesmen in history, should have neglected this task for so long is only another indication of how deep was our isolationism.

Fortunately, in 1945 a small group of Americans set about to do something about it. Perhaps the most effective of these men was William Benton, an old friend and former business associate of mine who in that year became the first Assistant Secretary of State in charge of our world-wide information program.

At the head of a devoted group of people in the State Department, Bill Benton, by dint of his own unbelievably hard work and imagination, succeeded in building, in a few short years, an information program of which this country could be proud.

Some mistakes in such a new kind of effort were inevitable. But by far the most serious resulted from the quite understandable pressure from Congressmen and public leaders that we follow tried and tested American advertising techniques.

In America, we are all conditioned to the radio commercials by which everything is sold from breakfast food to baby carriages. Many busy people in high places insisted that we could sell America and stop communism in the same way. As a result our information activities throughout the world have all too often taken on the character of those commercials. Sometimes we have sounded as though we thought communism were some kind of international halitosis which could be effectively eliminated only by our special American brand of democracy cast in the role of Listerine.

Often the picture of America we tried to present was too extravagantly perfect to be believed by even the Europeans who knew us reasonably well. To Indians and other Asians the picture of a fabulous America with the biggest skyscrapers, the richest millionaires and the happiest babies, and with everyone 100 per cent satisfied appeared smug and arrogant. Because it was so completely unrelated to anything in their own experience it was also without meaning. Even those who accepted the accuracy of the picture resented our concentration on what seemed to them pure materialism.

Unfortunately too, some people who think that Communists can best be defeated by their own methods picked up the unhappy phrase "psychological warfare." The very words, like the word "propaganda," imply deviousness and insincerity, an implication which destroys the effectiveness of any information program. In warfare everything is supposed to be fair. But in our information effort to win the confidence of other peoples we cannot succeed unless we prove ourselves to be truthful and sincere.

For instance, this mistaken application of "psychological warfare" was demonstrated by the *way* we offered to send food in the summer of 1953 to the hungry people of Eastern Germany. Almost every American news broadcast and newspaper carefully explained to their readers and to the world that this was a brilliant psychological move that put the Communists on the spot. Whether the Russians accepted the food or turned it down, in either case they would be publicly embarrassed. Only a handful of the more sophisticated observers thought to warn, "Don't look now but our technique is showing."

In Europe in spite of the well-publicized psychological warfare approach, this move was not only to our advantage, but also to the advantage of hundreds of thousands of hungry Germans who got our food packages in West Berlin. But in Asia food is a sacred emotion-packed subject, connected in people's memories with famines in which millions perished. Asia's reaction to our "clever move" was a shocked gasp that we should seem to play such cynical politics with a life-and-death matter like food.

• • •

Having from the first considered the information effort one of the three principal fields for America's diplomacy, I tried to divide my time equally among the more traditional diplomatic and reporting functions and the two new fields of economic aid and information.

It seemed to me we needed to adopt a simple, positive and

completely candid approach in all the lines of our information activity. This meant admitting our shortcomings as well as showing our achievements. It meant trying to explain both our successes and failures honestly in terms that Indians would understand.

It meant also emphasizing things which were of direct interest to the Indians and clearly related to their own problems and struggles. It is vital that Indians and indeed all Asians come to a full appreciation of the evils of communism, but the best way for us to be believed in our comments and reports on communism is to show that anti-communism is not our sole concern. Above all, it seemed to me that our keynote had to be our desire to see India succeed in its efforts to build a strong and happy democracy for its own sake and not just because the Communists opposed it.

We started at once to put this approach into effect in each of the five media through which USIS (the United States Information Service) was trying to reach the Indian public. In India as elsewhere these are *libraries, radio, movies, publications and pamphlets,* and *work with the local press.*

All over Asia, as I have pointed out in a previous chapter, fantastically inexpensive literature is provided by Russia or China to local Communist parties seeking to undermine democratic governments such as Nehru's. It gives educated Indians their only access to really cheap full-length books selling for as little as five to thirty cents a copy.

When I arrived there were USIS libraries in the four main Indian cities, Bombay, Delhi, Madras and Calcutta. During my stay we added four more in India and one in Nepal. In Trivandrum, capital of Travancore-Cochin, where the Communists did well in the election, we discovered in our survey that the only American book available in a city of numerous Communist bookstalls was *Uncle Fitzgerald's Bedtime Stories.* We set up a USIS library there, as we did in Bangalore, capital of Mysore, Lucknow in Uttar Pradesh and in the city of Hyderabad.

Even the biggest of these libraries was not very large, having only eight thousand or so volumes, and most of them had nearer three thousand. Yet the total number of visitors in all of them averaged over five thousand a day.

We have heard a great deal recently about the character of the books to be found on the shelves of American libraries abroad. Of course, I can speak only for those in India and Nepal, but I do not believe we had any books in those libraries which in any way advocated or condoned communism.

In most free public libraries in America you would expect to find books advocating every "ism" of any importance in the history of mankind, and these would undoubtedly include not only books advocating fascism, such as Adolf Hitler's *Mein Kampf*, but books advocating communism by Marx and Lenin. I assume that an American Communist might even find books by such Communists as Trotsky and Beria, which have long since been burned in Russia!

In India I could see no point in using American funds to add to the Communist literature which was already flooding the country. But we did try to get a variety of non-Communist points of view on most of the important issues which were being debated in America.

I made it a practice to attend the opening of every new library during my stay in India. "This library proves that in America we believe deeply in freedom of information and in full freedom of discussion," I would always say on these occasions. "If any of you here today are concerned about the racial discrimination which still exists in the United States, you will find books in this library, such as Gunnar Myrdal's *An American Dilemma* which objectively discuss this entire subject and which do not spare our feelings. You will find books which approve and books which criticize every phase of our democratic life. Here you can see with your own eyes what Americans are thinking about, talking about and arguing about."

In Bombay a young Indian student after walking through our library said to me, "This is a very strange place. There are books here on everything and from a dozen different viewpoints. In Communist bookstalls there are only books on Communism, and even there it is limited to books which reflect the exact party line. It hadn't occurred to me but right there may be the difference between communism and democracy."

In addition to our own libraries, the USIS accepted the recommendation of Teg Grondhal, the able head of information whom the State Department sent to India in 1952, for the development of a small, inexpensive library of pocket books. These books were suitable for presentation to schools, colleges, community centers and other organizations which maintained reading rooms or circulating facilities. Each collection contained 102 books ranging from the *Autobiography of Benjamin Franklin*, Charnwood's *Abraham Lincoln, The Education of Henry Adams*, and Dr. Benjamin Spock's famous baby book, to such tough anti-Communist literature as *Darkness at Noon, The God That Failed, 1984* and David Shub's devastating life of Lenin.

It was often possible to present these sets to village councils or to schools in remote areas which did not have access to our permanent USIS libraries. They were eagerly welcomed in book-starved India and some five thousand sets were distributed during the time I was there.

As for the Voice of America broadcasts to India, the second of our information media, it was almost impossible to hear the programs on most of India's 400,000 radio sets. Broadcast from New York, the Voice was relayed first to Tangier in North Africa, then to Ceylon, and finally to India where it arrived complete with the accumulated static of twelve thousand miles.

By contrast, the Voice of Moscow comes in strong and clear from the Soviet city of Tashkent only a few hundred miles away and so, fortunately, does the British B.B.C. This is why a leading Indian politician, when visiting this country, replied to a journalist's question about the effectiveness of the Voice of America, "What is this Voice of America? I never heard of it."

Since India is well covered by the government-owned All-India radio, in whose fairness and objectivity most citizens have confidence, they simply will not put up with static and other reception difficulties as did people in the occupied countries during the war or as people do today behind the Iron Curtain.

We made efforts to arrange to eliminate this long series of pickups and have the programs originate in Ceylon, which would have given excellent reception all over India, but the wheels of bureaucracy grind slowly and there was still no decision from Washington when I left for home. We also were making arrangements for the broadcast of some of our transcriptions over Radio Nepal, as soon as the station there could be supplied with a proper turntable and other equipment.

I had one experience in connection with Voice of America which illustrates vividly the difficulties of information work abroad and the sensitive understanding that it requires.

One day in the Madras state assembly the Chief Minister and leader of the Congress Party, Mr. Rajagopalachari, delivered his now famous remark that the Communists were his number one enemy and he theirs, and his views were given wide coverage in the press. I was particularly pleased because some months earlier I had discussed with him the misunderstandings that result from the fact that men like him, with a strong religious or Gandhian background, took it for granted that their opposition to communism was obvious, and so rarely bothered to express their real views on the subject.

Without sensing the complex Indian attitudes the Voice of America immediately picked up his speech in its news broadcasts, implying over and over again that at last Rajagopalachari had taken his stand on the side of the West.

At once his Communist opponents took up the cry that this proved that he was a "captive" of the "Wall Street imperialists" from America. The result was a threat to his already shaky coalition in the Madras assembly. To counter it, a mutual friend told me sadly that Rajagopalachari would have to "square accounts" by making a statement critical of the United States.

In discussing this development, the conservative journal of Indian businessmen, *The Eastern Economist*, noted, "The main charge made by Moscow against Pandit Nehru is that he is 'an Anglo-American Imperialist stooge,' and while he, as an Indian, is free to criticize fellow Indians who are Communists, it is obviously embarrassing to him and helpful to the Communists if his statements are emphasized by a foreign government in its propaganda. Why enable Radio Moscow to say: 'Listen in to the Voice of America for proof of our assertion that Nehru is in American pay?' "

The *Economist* suggested that a fatal mistake for Americans would be "to use arguments overseas that appeal to their own national opinions at home. Surely if you want to convince somebody that a certain course of action, such as rejecting Communism, is good for him, the first task should be to study his situation and psychology and to try to ascertain what arguments are likely to appeal to him." Although we Americans with our reputation of salesmanship may think it strange to be educated on the subject by even so friendly a critic as *The Eastern Economist*, there is no question in my mind but that their advice is entirely valid.

Some months later while visiting Washington for consultations, I told this story about Rajagopalachari to a staff meeting in the Department of State as an illustration of the need for sensitivity and caution in our treatment of Indian political leaders, so as not to drive them into criticizing *us*. Washington, in turn, passed it on to the Voice of America people in New York. A year later I was amazed to hear that this story was distorted by a government witness before Senator Joseph McCarthy's committee investigating the operations of the Voice of America, into an accusation that I had urged the Voice to tone down anti-communist statements in its broadcasts to India!

. . .

In contrast to the difficulties of getting good radio reception in India, we were very successful in reaching the Indian people with motion picture films. There was a theater in each library, where as many as four or five hundred people could witness a single showing of our movies.

In addition we sent motion picture projection crews to universities all over India, and we had twenty-six mobile truck units almost constantly on the road which showed the movies right in the villages, far from permanent movie theaters. As a result, millions and millions of Indians saw good American documentary films each year. The impact of these movies on people who have few other opportunities for entertainment, and most of whom cannot read, was tremendous.

In the beginning we found that many of the pictures simply did not fit India and others needed considerable revision. In order to meet this problem we set up juries of some twenty Indians each to view each of our five hundred pictures and to give us their frank criticism. Some of the films passed their test with flying colors. Others were entirely worthless. A third group, we found, could be used effectively with a three- or four-minute explanation at the beginning to relate them to Indian life or to clear up other difficulties.

The Indian government used many of our films in its own educational work. They especially welcomed the twelve documentary films which we made to show Indians the progress being made through their own Five Year Plan. These were effective proof of our sincerity in saying over and over again, "Our one and only objective is your success in building a free democratic India."

The night I showed some of the films to Nehru, Lady Mountbatten who is often accused of being anti-American, was present. "Why on earth did you make these films?" she asked me. I told her we wanted India to succeed. She looked skeptical but after a moment said, "I can't for the life of me think of any other reason, so I must congratulate you."

I only wish that Indian officials were as aware of the need for public information among their own people as are, for instance, the Indonesians. During its all-out literacy drive the Indonesian government equipped all village instructors with short-wave radio sending and receiving sets. At a certain hour each day, all channels on these sets were cleared for news broadcasts from the capital, principally devoted to reporting on progress in the literacy program and other economic and social achievements of the new government.

Each village worker would make notes and then relay the news to the population of his village by means of a loudspeaker system with which he was also supplied.

At another hour, the channels were cleared again, and the village workers sent progress reports and stories in to the central government for use in the next day's broadcast.

In this way the people were kept up to date on what their government was doing for them, and often had the satisfaction of hearing the accomplishments of their own village recited for people all over the country to hear.

The Indian government, unfortunately, had no such network of village workers to spread news, and in any event was, as I have said, prone to hide the very substantial light of its own progress under a bushel. I was convinced that this attitude was a mistake, and that democracy in India would be strengthened immeasurably by wider knowledge among the people of just what was being accomplished to better their lives.

. . .

Magazines, pamphlets and other printed matter from Washington, much of it excellent, were mailed out frequently to Indian leaders, educators and officials. But, as with other information media, I believe the most effective publications were those prepared on the spot by people with an intimate knowledge of local politics, interests, customs and needs.

While I was in India, the principal United States publication was *American Reporter*, a news magazine issued every two weeks in English and in the major Indian languages. When I arrived the *Reporter* had a circulation of about 300,000 request subscriptions, which we increased to about 500,000 without any difficulty. Indeed we could easily have distributed over two million if the funds had been available. As it was, each copy was seen by as many as six or seven readers, and our research showed that 60 per cent of them were under thirty years of age.

Our subscription list was the largest of any publication in India, thirty-two times the circulation of the official Communist weekly, *Crossroads*, and nearly ten times that of the weekly *Blitz*, the most violently anti-American paper in India.

The *American Reporter* was edited by Jean Joyce, one of the three people whom I took to India with me. She is an extremely capable woman, with a broad background of newspaper and magazine experience, and with the advice of Leigh Danenberg, as American publisher who came to India for three months as a consultant, did a remarkable job in making the *Reporter* an effective and respected organ.

A typical issue of the *Reporter* while I was there had as its lead article a description of a new method of planting rice, being developed by the Indian government on the basis of Japanese experience, which promised to quadruple production per acre.

Other front-page stories told of the world première of the film *Mahatma Gandhi* in Washington attended by President Eisenhower; of three new U.S. aid agreements for economic development; of the publication by the Michigan State College Press of a novel by an Indian author.

A box contained the news that Soviet-controlled Poland had withdrawn from UNESCO, a U.N. agency particularly respected in India. Still another story reported that thirteen American Communists, convicted under the Smith Act of plotting to destroy our government by force had been offered a choice between deportation to Russia and jail, and that all had chosen jail.

Inside pages had stories on the beginning of an Indian program for controlling TB; comments by an American Negro leader on the progress made in reducing discrimination against outcastes in India, and urging the outcastes to use the techniques by which American Negroes had improved their social and economic status; reports on water-power research in India; a description of our own Grand Coulee dam; articles on Indian industrial development, village school building, the American ballet, and UN aid to India's public health services.

There were a number of special features just as in any American newspaper. A page was devoted to excerpts from Herman Melville's *Moby Dick*. The women's column gave hints to homemakers, including a recipe for brownies.

A large amount of space was devoted to answering questions from readers ranging from the height of the UN Building, to annual wheat production in the United States, to the nature and purpose of 4-H clubs, and the American tax and social security system.

Our mail response to the *Reporter* was phenomenal. In the first year I was in India the *Reporter* received over a half million letters, the vast majority distinctly favorable in their reactions. We also had another interesting test of its effectiveness.

In co-operation with the State Department, Bantam Books, Inc., agreed to send free of charge a copy of *Roosevelt and Hopkins* to anyone in a number of countries who would send a certain amount in stamps to their offices in New York. This offer was published in a number of advertising media all over the world, including the *American Reporter*. Of a total of thirty thousand requests for the book, almost half came from India.

In addition to the *Reporter* we prepared in New Delhi a series of timely question-and-answer pamphlets, called *What Are the Facts?* which included explanations of the American position on disarmament, U.S. aid to India, the question of a divided Germany, the progress of American Negroes toward political and economic equality, and the Korean War. I became so interested in the possibilities that I wrote three of them myself. They were written in simple language giving the facts on specific questions which all of us knew from our public speeches and private conversations were uppermost in the minds of almost all educated Indians.

The fifth medium of the United States Information Service is direct work with newspapers and magazines. In India, Arthur Bartlett, an outstanding newspaperman from Maine, was our chief press officer.

I made it my business to keep in close personal touch with the Indian working press, and the many contacts that Arthur was able to make among them were a great help. In my thousands of miles of travel throughout India, I held press conferences in each city I visited, and answered questions until the reporters themselves were ready to call it quits.

Only once was I ever misquoted in the Indian papers, and then it turned out to be a deliberate falsification by a Communist working on one of the wire services. The newspaper which published this misquotation promptly offered its public apologies as soon as it was discovered.

Of course, there are a number of Communist or fellow-traveling newspapers, most of them printed in English, but several in the various Indian languages. The most effective of these is *Blitz*, whose editor, although claiming not to carry a communist card, follows every tortured twist and turn of the party line, and is bitterly anti-American.

His paper is widely read, partly because of its skilled sensationalist, scandal-mongering make-up, and partly because it caters shrewdly to frustration and bitterness among the students of India. I am told that each copy of this paper, which boasts a circulation of around sixty thousand, is read by an average of ten students.

For months *Blitz* reporters bombarded my office with requests that I answer a series of questions for their paper. My first inclination was to refuse on the ground that anything I said would surely be distorted, and on the ground that I had already answered identical questions over and over again in press conferences throughout India.

As I thought it over, however, it seemed to me that an interview for *Blitz*, if there were reasonable safeguards to assure that what I said was printed exactly as I said it, would enable us for the first time to present the true facts about American foreign policy to some half million or more people. Some of these, to be sure, would be doctrinaire Communists, but most of them confused students who might still maintain some degree of open-mindedness.

So, I agreed to answer their questions, provided Blitz would print my answers exactly as I gave them. The editor agreed, adding that he planned to print all letters which he received commenting on the interview. I insisted that I must also have an opportunity to comment finally in rebuttal.

A young *Blitz* reporter read me a list of some thirty skillfully loaded questions, covering the whole field of American-Indian and American-Asian relations in the Cold War. Although most of them sounded much like the questions I had heard from fellow travelers all over India, they gave me an excuse to say all that I wanted to say.

Here are a few samples:

"Do you really believe the paltry sums of money that you have made available under TCA and Point Four would substantially aid India's economic development under the Five Year Plan? Would it be wrong to describe this meager economic aid as at best an extension of the propaganda expenditure which the United States is incurring in this country?"

"What in your view is the reason for the growing unpopularity—or lack of understanding, if you prefer to call it that—of American policy in Asia?"

"There is widespread feeling in Asia, particularly in India, that the Americans have lately begun interfering more and more in our domestic affairs. . . . How do you justify this sort of interference in the domestic affairs of foreign countries?"

"On the one hand, the U.S. claims to champion freedom and democracy all over the world, but on the other hand she promotes French colonial aggression and imperialism in Indo-China. How do you explain this contradiction?"

I answered each question frankly and fully, trying to give the background of the particular issue, the true facts involved, and to explain the reasons behind our policies.

Blitz published four solid pages devoted to a verbatim transcript of the questions and answers, calling it "an exclusive interview." The only thing exclusive about it was that *Blitz* alone had never before printed my many previous answers to similar questions asked by correspondents at press conferences in all parts of India.

Then the fun began in the letters-to-the-editor department. It was open season on the American Ambassador. Everyone in public life soon learns to accept, with at least outward calm, the inevitable mud-slinging and abuse that unhappily go with it, and I had my share in the United States. But until you have been subjected to the full treatment by professional Communist hatemongers it is hard to imagine the depths to which name calling and invective can sink. I was worked over by party-line experts. Every top Communist in India was called in to tear me to pieces.

An occasional letter was allowed to appear in support of what I had said, but the editors made it clear that their readers were overwhelmingly opposed to the American viewpoint which I expressed. They even professed to be shocked that anyone, even the "capitalistic" "war mongering, Wall Street dominated" American Ambassador, had the temerity to stand up for such views in public.

But I had my own private check on the effectiveness of the interview. I received over a thousand letters from *Blitz* readers. Fully 99 per cent of these were from students thanking me for giving them the opportunity, for the first time, of hearing the American point of view on world affairs fully and fairly stated. Wherever I went in India, people commented on the interview. In the end, I think all of us were convinced, despite our earlier misgivings, that the effect was well worth the obvious risks.

When the *Blitz* editors finally decided to end the controversy, I prepared a rebuttal letter in accordance with my understanding with the editor. In it I was careful to maintain a moderate tone, in contrast to the extravagant bitterness of the pro-Communist letters. I remarked that it was surprising and disheartening to find any group in India which so thoroughly rejected the Gandhian principles of tolerance and nonviolence, and which so completely embraced the totalitarian creed of invective, slander and bitterness.

For two weeks the editor of *Blitz* refused to publish my letter. So I released it to the other newspapers, together with the agreement I had made with *Blitz* at the time of the interview. When these papers published the letter, *Blitz* belatedly followed suit.

For a time, this seemed to close the incident, except for the news that the young man who had conducted the interview had thrown up his job, repudiated *Blitz* and communism and joined the staff of the staunchly pro-democracy *Times of India.*

But the Communists do not give up easily. Several weeks later photostatic copies of what was supposed to be an exchange of letters between me and the pro-Communist editor of *Blitz* were "leaked" to another sensationalist newspaper. In them he was alleged to have invited me to meet some of his Communist friends "at a quiet party in my home." I was alleged to have replied that I was eager to meet his Communist friends so long as he "did not make too much noise about it."

Of course, these letters were bare-faced forgeries, and I lost no time in saying so. The only exchange of letters with the editor was a perfunctory three-sentence acknowledgment of a letter concerning the interview. I requested the Indian government to make a thorough investigation of the case, which it immediately did. As a result, criminal charges of forgery were brought against the editor of *Blitz* and the editor of the anti-Communist paper which printed the letters.

Both defendants freely admitted that the letters were forgeries and the judge agreed. "First and foremost," he stated, "there is no question at all that the photostats are forgeries and forgeries of a contemptible and disgraceful nature . . . it is common ground that they are downright forgeries."

The trial dragged for several weeks. Each editor accused the other of perpetrating the crime. Eventually the charges were dismissed because the evidence was not sufficiently clear as to exactly who was actually guilty.

. . .

These then are the five methods by which the USIS operates in India—libraries, radio, movies, publications and work with the Indian press. Judged by the over-all objective of gaining greater understanding of America, its attitudes and policies, I think we made considerable progress through these established media.

Blitz itself unwittingly paid our efforts the most authentic kind of compliment in the following words: "Spearheaded by the United States Information Service a 'Sixth Column' infinitely more diabolical in ingenuity than the infamous breed sired by Franco, has been operating in India for some time now with its destructive cells planted in practically every sphere of our lives."

On another occasion *Blitz* complained of the "plethora of American musical soirees, film group discussions, gramophone record afternoons and a whole gamut of tricks, the infectious reactions of which, are so keyed that no Indian attending these whoopees returns home without feeling that the Americans are their blood brothers and Washington is their spiritual home."

In the last analysis, however, our government information service with its divisions for five media, no matter how well supported or how imaginative, can accomplish very little unless it is supported by what I came to call "the sixth medium:" the real voice of America projected in the everyday statements and actions of its leaders and its ordinary citizens as they come in contact with the new free Asia.

There were altogether about four thousand Americans in India, more than half of them missionaries, but I knew that the place to start paying attention to the "sixth medium" was in the Embassy staff itself. I have already described the efforts we made to teach Hindi to American personnel, to give them some background in Indian history, culture and religion, to imbue them with a sense of the importance of their mission, and to emphasize the simple courtesies which many of us overlook in the bewildering strangeness of a foreign land.

Above all, we encouraged Embassy employees to break out of the cocktail-party set, to make friends among the Indian people in all walks of life, to make themselves a part of Indian life. With a handful of exceptions they responded with the greatest enthusiasm and understanding.

We even prepared a "check list" which all of us found useful as an occasional reminder. These are some of the questions:

"How do you drive? Does the American Embassy tag on your car give you a sense of added responsibility? Or a feeling of license to flash by bewildered, barefoot pedestrians and to scatter herds of goats and cattle?"

"The Indian people lived under a colonial government for 200 years and as a result they are deeply sensitive to any hint of foreign influence or interference. Are you doing your part to convince them that America respects their new freedom as much as they do?"

"Are you honestly interested in *why* things are as they are, and why Indians feel as they do? Do you respect the view of others even when it varies from your own?"

"Deep in your heart are you prejudiced in even the slightest degree against those of a different race, religion or color?"

"Eventually, you may someday feel the accumulative impact of difference and frustration—the dirt, the heat, the strange foods and new ways of living. To these things will be added plumbing that doesn't always work, plane connections that seem slow. Then one day you may find yourself defensive, impatient or downright nasty. Can you quickly recover your sense of values and proportion?"

Every American who visits India for business, pleasure, study or government service, hour by hour and day by day, is creating an impression by which all America is judged. I have often thought that it would be well worth while for the State Department to make available some sort of briefing for private travelers who are going as far away from home as Asian countries.

I tried to see all American visitors to India soon after their arrival in the country, and I found as I expected that the vast majority of them were very much aware of their role and eager to be the best kind of unofficial ambassadors that they could. Without exception they were grateful for all the help that we could give them on how to better understand India and to support our efforts.

Often the Indians accepted in good humor occasional tactlessness on our part. For instance, when a group of American baseball players arrived in Bombay, which is carrying out prohibition on religious grounds, the boys greeted the Indian officials singing, "How dry you are!" Everyone seemed amused—except *Blitz.*

Sometimes we can even get too concerned about the impression we are making and become tight and self-conscious. On at least one occasion I was guilty of this mistake.

In the winter of 1953 the Navy expressed a desire to have an American cruiser stop in India for a few days. I knew the sensitiveness of the Indian people on the subject of their independence, and at first thought this might seem reminiscent of "showing the flag," as we were once charged with doing in Latin American ports to bring pressure upon reluctant governments.

My forebodings could not have been more wrong. One of our new, large cruisers steamed into Madras, the crew went ashore and in no time flat completely won over the town, just by having a good time and being their natural selves. The gobs took the handles of the rickshaws, put the rickshaw drivers in the seats, and set up rickshaw races with other sailors through the main streets of the city.

First, the townspeople smiled uncertainly and then they began to join in the fun. American flags came out. The boys jitterbugged. The Indians reciprocated by showing them some Indian dances. A festival atmosphere took over whole sections of the city. Not a single instance of violence or other misbehavior was reported.

I shouldn't have been surprised. After a few months in India I was so impressed with the possibilities of promoting a fairer view of the United States through personal contact with representative Americans that I developed a plan for systematically using this medium. We decided to adopt it on one of our toughest information problems, the Indian students.

One of the first things that strikes any visitor to India is the apparent strength of anti-American sentiment and the lack of accurate information about America among the student bodies of India's eight hundred odd universities and colleges. It is from this group that the leaders and intellectuals of future India will be drawn, and it seemed desperately important to me that some plan should be developed which would enable us to reach them.

I took every opportunity I could to speak to student audiences. After visiting every major university and scores of smaller colleges, I found that most of these young men and women were fair-minded people. Their lack of a sense of purpose, the absence of job opportunities after graduation, and the poverty all around them had convinced them that they were living in a bad world which needed changing. They were desperately searching for answers, and almost the only ones that had been given them up to now had come from the Communists.

Everywhere I found these students not only eager for the information I could give them, but for the most part open-minded about considering what I said. It was as if they wanted to believe in America.

Young Indians were much more interested in hearing about our struggles than our accomplishments. They used to listen delightedly to my description of Andrew Jackson's early fight against the United States National Bank; of Lincoln's battle to free the slaves; of Teddy Roosevelt tackling the great monopolies; of F.D.R. declaring war on the depression of the early 1930's.

When I would talk of our tragic failure to join the League of Nations and our slowness in resisting Nazism, invariably one of the students would get up to suggest with a smile that in criticizing American isolationism of the twenties and thirties I was gently chiding the Indians for their present "independence."

Several times to Marxist-conscious groups of students I gave a talk entitled, "If Karl Marx Returned," in which I pointed out how surprised he would be to see the high living standards of the supposedly "exploited" American workers, and how shocked he would be at the centralized dictatorship of the Soviet Union, where he would find the very opposite of the "withering away of the state" under communism which he predicted. I asked if they thought Marx could even get a visa to Russia, and how long they thought he would be out of prison if he tried to speak his mind in Moscow.

Once, to an audience which I felt must be weary of talk about momentous international problems, I described in detail the state and town I came from in America. I told about Connecticut, its population, whose ancestors had come from Ireland, Poland, Italy, England, Holland, Greece, Rumania, Lithuania, and many other countries.

I told about our public school system. I told how every pupil took his seat in alphabetical order, regardless of how wealthy his parents were, or the color of his skin, or his religion, or his national origin.

Then I told of our town of Essex, lying near the mouth of the Connecticut River, with its thirty-five hundred people. I emphasized our Jeffersonian type of economy in Essex which made it possible for many heads of families to work in a small factory for a few months of the year, do some fishing in the spring when the river was full of shad, raise some vegetables and sell them in the summertime, and do handicraft on the side.

To an audience in which every person of even moderate means had several servants I explained that out of our seven hundred families, no more than twenty had full-time servants. I emphasized that there were no very rich people and no very poor.

Such talks by all of us on the staff no doubt did much good. But there are so many universities and colleges in India that even with the help of people in our consulate offices we could not hope to cover them all adequately.

Soon it became clear that what we needed to reach this vitally important student group was a systematic program of visits by Americans sent over from the United States specially for the purpose. This was finally inaugurated in the spring of 1952.

In all, twenty prominent Americans visited India at our request under this program. They stayed two or three months each. This group included President William Stevenson of Oberlin College, Mrs. Mildred McAfee Horton, former president of Wellesley, Dr. James Robinson, a prominent New York Negro clergyman, Ralph McGill, editor of the Atlanta *Constitution*, and other prominent editors, educators and public figures.

Wherever they went most of the visitors announced that their time was completely at the disposal of students and faculty, and the Indians took them at their word. "If they have awakened me at 5 A.M. (and they have) to ask whether 'Indian literature and history are known and respected in America,' they have also kept me up until the small hours to visit with them," reported one of our lecturers. Another said to me that the only way in which he could get any time for himself, even for sleeping or for preparing his talks, was simply to lock his door and ignore the knocking as one student after another came with a question to ask.

Three of our visiting speakers, who were Negroes, played a particularly important role in counteracting the distortions of our racial problem, simply by giving a thoroughly honest picture.

"Until I came out to India I had no idea that there was so great a dormant urge to defend my country," wrote J. Saunders Redding a Negro political scientist, "nor had I any idea that there were so many dangerous untruths to defend her against." A sample of the mixed-up truths, half-truths and untruths is seen in the questions which were asked of Dr. Redding:

"Aren't Negroes prohibited public education in America?"

"Don't all people who are not white in America have a certain place to walk in the public streets?"

"Why has no colored person held high office in America?"

"Isn't it true that the Haitian Ambassador to the U.S. must live in a ghetto in Washington?"

To stimulate such questions Blitz and other Communist publications never ceased their stream of distortions and untruths. Once *Blitz* reported that there were 530 American Negroes lynched in 1947, exactly 529 more than there were.

In all, eighteen hundred visits were made to Indian campuses between July 1, 1952, when the program really got under way, and the time I left the following March. That meant that most colleges in India had been visited on the average more than twice in the nine-month period and many even more often.

When I left India we were also planning to set up reading rooms at eight of the universities for the use of the students. Each was to be staffed by local Indian employees and supplied with about a thousand books from our regular USIS libraries, as well as current issues of a number of American magazines.

You could almost feel the anti-American agitation in some of the universities begin to diminish under the impact of these typically good American people, standing up there before the students and talking things over with them in a candid, straightforward way.

Could anyone imagine a similar group of Russian Communist visitors talking freely to young Indian students on an endless list of embarrassing questions about the Soviet Union? The difference between November, 1951, and January, 1953, when I last talked to Indian university audiences was no less than extraordinary.

I am confident that we could achieve the same results in country after country throughout Asia. Certainly my own experiences and those of others I talked to, in addressing student audiences in other Asian countries, were remarkably similar to those that had impressed me so deeply in India.

• • •

Of course, when I say "we" could carry out such an information program everywhere in Asia, I should stress the limitations on the program if the "we" only means America.

Washington is but the capital of one nation state. Moscow is the headquarters of a world party. There is, and can be, no "American party" in India or Asia, nor any mass party taking orders from us or disseminating our information. There is, and will be for a long time, a Communist party in every Asian country, which does willingly take orders from the Kremlin, and which in the towns and villages of Asia is feverishly distributing Soviet propaganda.

This points up a fundamental limitation on American information programs, and raises the question whether the democratic forces in the world do not need an international rallying point which transcends any one nation.

Meanwhile, the United States need not try to carry all the burden of the West's information work in the uncommitted world of Asia. If our aim is not so much to make Asians love us but to help more of them to see the dynamic strength of the democratic way and the pitfalls of world communism, we should encourage countries on the edge of the Iron Curtain, such as Yugoslavia, Turkey, Norway and Sweden, to tell their stories. The dramatic Yugoslav estimate of Soviet communism as a new and far more dangerous kind of imperialism, which an effective Yugoslav mission told all over India in 1952, had a tremendous impact.

I suggest these added considerations as an amplification, not a diminution, of our present information program.

Many Asian students these days are going to America, as well as Americans traveling to India. The provisions of the Smith-Mundt Act and the Fulbright scholarships have done much to direct the eyes of Indian students to the United States, where formerly they looked almost exclusively to England for advanced education. Each year almost three hundred Indians come to America for study and training, either under these laws, or on TCA grants, or with funds supplied by the Ford Foundation and other philanthropic institutions, and several hundred others come with their own resources.

Applications for these grants far exceed the number that are available. The actual selection of the students under the Fulbright and Mundt-Smith bills is made by the United States Educational Foundation in India, consisting of four Indians and four Americans who review the applications and decide who are to get the places. Most of the Indians return with a more sympathetic understanding of the United States, and this valuable program will gain much additional momentum from the interest on the Indian wheat loan, which, under the law, is to be devoted for five years to the furtherance of Indian education by the exchange of students and teachers between the two countries.

These Asian students, whether on scholarship or traveling with their own funds, are becoming increasingly more evident on American campuses and in American cities. Here all of us can contribute to better understanding of America among the people of Asia, for these students observe us constantly when we least expect it, and when they return home and speak of American life, they are accepted as "experts" by their fellow countrymen.

I remember one Indian medical student who wrote me from the University of Minnesota about a trip south that he and his Indian friends had made during the winter vacation. He told me that his party had been thrown out of hotel lobbies, refused accommodations, and discriminated against on trains and in other public facilities. I spent two years in correspondence with this one student and his friends in an effort to erase some of the early bitterness against America that that trip had created.

This year I wrote to nearly all the Indians who were in the United States on some kind of U.S. grant, asking for their full and frank impressions of America, and suggestions for the future. I wish all Americans could read the long and careful letters I received from them. I was fascinated to see the similarity of viewpoint toward America among students in widely separated parts of our country. They loved our friendly informality, good humor and social equality. They hated our racial discriminations; and they were immensely puzzled by our inconsistent attitudes, our alternating indifference and irritation toward Asia.

Whether we like it or not, what America says and thinks is news all over the world. But what our country *does* is even more important than what it *says*. When the wheat loan to hungry India was stalled in our Congress month after month, nothing we could say for ourselves could then answer what we were saying against ourselves by the delay.

A good information program can be a strong right arm to a positive policy, but is unable to be of much assistance to a negative or mistaken policy. We cannot, for instance, convince Indians that America opposes colonialism unless we have a clear-cut policy that in practice does oppose colonialism. We cannot convince Indians that we respect Asians and believe that Asia is important unless in practice we do pay attention to Asia and do listen respectfully to the views of Asians.

Sermon on The Mount

from The Herblock Book (Beacon Press)

For years the exclusion of Asians in our immigration laws made a mockery of our championship of the equality of all peoples. Even now, the McCarran Act, with its high walls to the world, causes constant embarrassment.

I started this chapter by saying that the tricks of advertising and salesmanship that we take so for granted often play us false in our information work. But in a deeper sense, the method of the American salesmen can pay rich dividends in today's world. No insurance agent ever sold a policy by telling a client that since he, the agent, was richer and stronger and knew more about actuarial equations, the client would just have to buy his policy and lump it, and if he dared even to listen to a competitor he would be read right out of the community.

On the contrary, our salesmen, whether their product is steel mills, breakfast food or ideas, spend countless hours analyzing their prospects, studying their habits, their modes of thought, their convictions and their prejudices. Above all they have the patience to wait for results and to recognize the value of easy and open friendship, of relaxed give and take with each prospect, who, according to our American selling tradition, is "always right."

It would be one of the greatest ironies of history, if America, which prides herself on these characteristics, should fail to use them in the most important task which she has ever undertaken.

Postscript—November 18, 1953

As this book goes to press I am distressed to hear that much of the United States Information Service effort described in this chapter has become a victim of the economy drive in foreign operations.

The *Reporter* circulation has been reduced nearly 50 per cent and the Telegu language edition, which went largely to the now Communist-ridden state of Andhra, eliminated entirely. The village motion picture program has been stopped, and the university program sharply reduced. The staff has been cut nearly in half.

America is understandably impatient with high taxes and with crises which never seem to end, and inevitably many members of Congress reflect this impatience. But as we cut and fire, the Soviet global propaganda machine, backed by at least ten times the resources available to our own government even before the recent slashes, grinds on relentlessly, in India, in Asia, and throughout the world.

Democratic America has an honest, exciting story that must be told and retold to our friends and potential friends everywhere. We will court no less than national disaster if we fail to tell it.

20. Role of Foreign Aid

HELP FOR a neighbor is as old in American history as the frontier communities where everyone turned out to lend a hand in rebuilding a burned-out barn. Assistance was offered not as charity or to instill a sense of gratitude or obligation. It was given because it was the decent thing to do, and because in an exposed and struggling settlement the fact of each man's dependence upon the strength and success of his neighbor was too plain to mistake.

The tradition of spontaneous aid from man to man broadened from its original setting of the pioneer community, first into America as a whole and finally into the world through churches, philanthropic institutions and the Red Cross, and after World War I through Herbert Hoover's efforts in Belgium and France.

After World War II, when it became clear that only the United States was in a position to help the devastated economies of Europe back to their feet, Secretary of State Marshall had the courage and vision to propose a plan of aid "not directed against anyone but against hunger, chaos and poverty." Perhaps because those enemies of mankind are among the main allies of communism the Soviet Union flatly refused to participate in the European Recovery Program.

About $14 billion and five years later, it is clear that the Marshall Plan worked in restoring the productivity of Western Europe, and, as a by-product, in stopping the Communist advance. Since the total final cost of World War II, including veterans' payments and interest on the national debt, is estimated to have run about $30 billion a month, the Marshall Plan, costing the equivalent of two weeks of warfare, may easily be the best investment ever made by this country. It may well have prevented the Communist sweep of Europe which would have led directly to World War III.

It has always seemed to me symbolic that the Marshall Plan was adopted and the first money appropriated by a Republican Congress on the recommendation of a Democratic President to aid European governments, many of which had socialist economies. To the hard-working administrator of the Plan, Paul Hoffman, a Willkie Republican of outstanding business experience, the free world will always owe a debt of gratitude.

Having offered such creative leadership in helping Europe back to its feet, we were shocked to realize the extent of our new responsibilities when, on the other side of the globe, the largest country in the world, China, swiftly started to collapse into Communism. We discovered that not only Europe, but even more so all of poverty-stricken Asia and the vast underdeveloped world were in the midst of a "revolution of rising expectations."

Our age, the great British historian, Arnold Toynbee, tells us, will be remembered "not for its horrifying crimes or its astonishing inventions but because it is the first age since the dawn of history in which mankind dared to believe it practical to make the benefits of civilization available to the whole human race." This belief that a better life is possible for the two-thirds of the world who go to bed hungry every night was to a large extent carried to the underdeveloped world by American missionaries, travelers, troops, machines, mass production, medicines and movies.

In any case, the news is out and spreading fast from Japan to South Asia, from the Middle East to the southern tip of Africa, from South America to Mexico. It is shattering old concepts, weakening old societies and leaving revolutionary vacuums in its wake.

In an imaginative recognition of the world's new facts of life, President Truman, in the fourth point of his inaugural address in 1949, proposed a "bold new program for making the benefits of our scientific advances available for the improvement and growth of underdeveloped areas." His words were heard and cheered on every continent:

"Our aim should be to help the free peoples of the world, through their own efforts, to produce more food, more clothing, more materials for housing, and more mechanical power to lighten their burdens . . .

"The old imperialism—exploitation for foreign profit—has no place in our plans. . . . Only by helping the least fortunate of its members to help themselves can the human family achieve the decent, satisfying life that is the right of all people."

Hope stirred throughout the world that the United States of America, which Wilson called "the colony of mankind," was now to join all free peoples in a partnership for the great new business of world development. "Point Four" became a symbol of what people everywhere wanted.

The members of the British Commonwealth organized their own version called the Colombo Plan, and the United Nations instituted its projects of Technical Assistance. Even little Norway adopted a Technical Aid Program which, among other things, supplied the Indian state of Travancore-Cochin with equipment and advice on the development of modern fisheries. Private American foundations expanded their operations into dozens of such new fields.

It was my good fortune, not only to have played some small part in developing the original concept in the early days before President Truman's inaugural, but later to have been responsible for the establishment and day-to-day operation of Point Four programs in India and in Nepal. In addition, I kept in close touch with the progress of the work in many other countries of Asia and the Middle East.

As a result, I am convinced that Point Four is potentially the most powerful constructive program against chaos and communism which the free world has devised. After seeing Point Four in action in the villages of Asia I predict that it will go down in history as the most creative idea of our generation.

Now is the time to take up this idea and apply it on an adequate scale. That this is what the non-Communist world is waiting for was shown in the universal enthusiasm following President Eisenhower's first major foreign policy speech on April 16, 1953. The President announced that his administration was ready "to ask its people to join with all nations in directing a substantial percentage of any savings achieved by real disarmament to a fund for world aid and reconstruction."

Nothing may come of the President's offer for multilateral disarmament, because the leaders of the Kremlin are committed to an ideology which by its nature seeks world dominion. But even if the present chances are poor for any lasting settlement with the Soviet Union, which in my opinion is the case, that only leaves the problem of our relationship with the "uncommitted world" all the more crucial.

If a sound aid program can help the two-thirds of mankind who are now living in poverty achieve some of their aspirations, then the opportunity for Communist subversion or outright aggression will be substantially lessened. For instance, an economically strong and developing India would have millions of loyal men ready to defend her from internal or external attack. But a hungry and depressed India would be hard to defend with a million American troops and a hundred atom bombs.

The last thing the Kremlin wants to see is a successful democratic program of world development for nothing would more thoroughly discredit the theories of Karl Marx. Therefore, if we continue to condition any increase in our economic aid to underdeveloped nations on the Soviet Union's willingness to reduce armaments, we will only give Russia another reason to postpone agreement.

If the United States should fail to pursue Point Four with added vigor and resources, it would be one of the most tragic mistakes in the history of American foreign policy. This is the time for Point Four in Asia, Africa and South America to become Point One, to rank equally with our program for military defense.

Of course, Point Four, although in the right direction, is no panacea, and still has many flaws which need to be corrected. Before I left India and Asia I asked all our Point Four people to give me their suggestions for improvements, many of which are included in the following ten points.

In these "do's" and "don't's" I have tried to sum up the lessons that many of us feel that we have learned from our experience.

1. *Neither small-scale "technical assistance," nor indiscriminate giveaway will suffice.*

In America two major viewpoints have emerged about what Point Four involves. One school of thought, impressed by the vision of a few thousand American experts in agriculture, health and literacy carrying our "know how" to the underdeveloped nations, has suggested that pure technical assistance is sufficient.

This view has considerable appeal. It is flattering to think that all the world needs is some good old Yankee ingenuity. Furthermore, the costs would be comparatively modest, a matter of importance to harried American taxpayers in these days of huge military budgets.

Then there is a second school which sees the need for large-scale economic development and the lack of capital in underdeveloped countries, and therefore concludes that the United States should provide billions of dollars to all non-Communist countries who want and need it.

In my opinion both of these extreme views are unsound. The first approach is not only inadequate but also too inflexible. It is true, of course, that a few countries with a resource for export such as oil can earn ample foreign exchange of their own for purchases of Western machinery and equipment. Here the help from engineers, public health specialists and other technicians may be enough.

But in most underdeveloped countries we have discovered that there is simply no means of earning the necessary foreign exchange to import what is needed. Without new seeds, commercial fertilizer, DDT, sprayers, bulldozers, metal for improved plows, pumps, drugs and antibiotics, most of which must come from abroad, any program of development finally grinds to a halt.

Moreover, these Asian countries need increases in capital goods, dams and power projects, roads, communications systems and large irrigation works. They cannot get these by simply rubbing two technical assistants together.

Yet an indiscriminate flood of dollars, or of U.S. surplus goods, is no solution. If dollars grew on trees in America, the development of Asia could still not be achieved by shipping them overseas in infinite quantities. Complex engineering projects such as river valley developments and industrial plants require huge amounts of technical skill, which is limited even in America.

As a nation's development progresses its capacity to make use of capital goods increases, but in the early stages there is a limit to what each underdeveloped country can absorb. The amount will vary greatly depending on its resources, its administrative abilities, the extent of its problems and the competence of its planning.

Particularly difficult for the underdeveloped nations is the question of local currency. Usually American aid covers the cost of goods bought abroad plus their overseas transportation and the salaries of American technicians. The recipient country with its own funds pays for all other wages, materials and expenses. As we have seen in India, these local costs often amount to many times the volume of the American assistance.

Once taxes have been raised to the limit and all other resources fully tapped, any further expenditure of local currency based on excessive deficit financing or money printing results in runaway inflation, thus destroying the very confidence among the people which the aid program was designed to create.

2. *Free Asia's handicaps in its competition with China should be a yardstick for Western aid.*

The development of India, like that of America, Russia and every country, is dependent primarily on "savings," the difference between what it produces and what it consumes. In order to move ahead economically any nation, democracy or dictatorship, must produce more than it consumes. These savings are then invested in industrial construction which will raise the productivity of the economy sometime in the future.

The kind of voluntary savings we know in the U.S. today is only possible in a highly productive economy, where most people are already getting enough of the necessities of life and a little bit more. If most people are hungry, or sick or ragged, they will spend everything they have on more food, medicine and clothes. A few generations ago in the earlier stages of the Industrial Revolution, both in Western Europe and America, a large part of the savings necessary for industrial growth were secured from the high profits made possible by low wage rates and sweatshop working conditions.

In America there was also the vast wealth released in the opening of the frontier, and before the First World War the large sums provided by European, and particularly British, investors. In Europe, as we have seen in an earlier chapter, the "forced savings" of industrial workers were swelled by additional savings, squeezed out of the colonial peoples of Asia and Africa by the same process: extremely low wages and miserable working conditions.

One of India's leading economists estimated that British investors extracted from India an average of $250 million a year up to the Second World War, over and above the amount of their annual investment in India.

For a nation entering the industrial race in the twentieth century there are no colonies and no frontiers, and very little time to meet the awakened needs of the people. This stark fact lends a terrible plausibility to the argument of the Communists who say that the only alternative is a ruthless dictatorship which will force sufficient savings from the people regardless of their suffering.

They point for confirmation to the Soviet Union, where the "dictatorship of the proletariat" has rigidly limited consumption by low wages, forced labor and strict limits on the amount of consumer goods that can be produced. Through such controls, Russia has squeezed from the people for industrial investment nearly 30 per cent of their total production each year. Thus in less than two generations the Soviet Union created a modern industrial state, whose steel production is now second only to our own.

Russia's development has certainly been phenomenal. But like nineteenth-century America it had a vast open frontier. And recently it has had its own "colonies" in East Germany, Poland, Czechoslovakia, Hungary, Bulgaria and Rumania which have been bled in a way which makes the western imperialism of Queen Victoria's day look inefficient by comparison.

The situation facing Asia is so different that any comparison is questionable. Communist China and democratic India, for instance, are both desperately poor and heavily populated. Both are almost completely agricultural countries, with only the barest rudiments of an industrial economy. Neither has open lands or colonial dependencies. And yet, as we have seen, there is an inevitable and fateful competition between them.

Although China has several clear-cut advantages her prospects may not be quite so rosy as the statistics and logic indicate. For instance, Communist Russia began with much more productive equipment per person than has Communist China and with the wealth of an underpopulated land. In other words the Soviet planners had something to squeeze.

In China, as in India, where the majority of people live close to the hunger line it's my guess that savings beyond a certain point spell catastrophic starvation. Even in Russia, Stalin pressed the peasants too far and in the 1920's famines devastated the economy.

In 1953, according to recent stories from Moscow, Soviet agricultural production has still not fully recovered from this "mistake."

Nor do round percentage figures tell the whole story. First of all, dictatorship is not always the smoothly running, highly efficient machine it sometimes appears. Its ruthless demands evoke protest, silent opposition and rebelliousness.

Otherwise productive resources must be drawn off into an elaborate police and administrative system to keep the people in line, and into the expanded military power which most dictators seem to feel they need to keep them safe. The Chinese Red Army plus the Chinese security police are nearly seven times larger than their Indian counterparts and the costs must be nearly in proportion, even though the equipment from Russia comes as a loan.

India, moreover, has a special advantage: she need not really win the race in terms of material construction. Perhaps she does not even have to tie. She must only make substantial improvements in her economy and in the welfare of her people. Asians have been brought up in the democratic, liberal tradition. It is only if they feel that the democratic way has failed utterly to provide the decencies of life that they will abandon it.

Thus, if both India and China were left to their own resources, there might still be doubt about the outcome of the contest, but India and free Asia would definitely be a good bet. The difficulty is that Russia has made it clear that she will support the Chinese effort with a substantial "Point Four" program from Moscow.

In September, 1953, in announcing a promised vast new Soviet program of economic aid to China's Five Year Plan, the Communist *Peiping People's Daily* stated bluntly "we need international aid." It added: "This means that we not only needed assistance in the past, but need it now and will continue to need it in the future." The editorial admitted that "obviously, but for the Soviet, it would not be possible for us to carry out our five year plan over such a big area on such a scale."

In addition to military assistance it is reliably reported that the Soviet Union has committed funds totaling $1.6 billion in long-term loans to the development of the Chinese Communist economy, in addition to the services of some forty-five hundred Russian technicians. This is at least ten times the amount of capital goods that we have been willing to make available to India, and perhaps twenty-five times more technicians.

This is not only the dilemma of India; it is the dilemma of all free Asia. On the one hand the people everywhere are demanding the kind of economic progress which the Communists claim is occurring in China and which did occur in Russia. On the other hand, they are unable to accept under democratic governments the awful sacrifices which the Communists would impose by force. And we are unwilling to make up the difference.

Thus far, the Soviet Union has confined its economic assistance programs to Communist China and North Korea. In the non-Communist nations of Asia and Africa they have relied almost exclusively on propaganda and on the organizational efforts of the Communist parties.

But already there are disturbing signs that Moscow's indifference to the possibilities of technical and financial assistance in the non-Communist underdeveloped areas may be changing and that a new period of "ruble diplomacy" may lie ahead.

As I was leaving India, Novikov, the Russian Ambassador, was also replaced. The present Ambassador is a foremost Communist expert on foreign trade, who has already offered some enticing propositions.

Then there is the trade agreement between Communist China and the free government of Ceylon which may well have been subsidized by Moscow. The Chinese agreed to purchase one-half the Ceylonese rubber crop annually for the next five years at a price 34 per cent above the world price. They agreed to pay in rice for which they would charge some 4 per cent less than the world price. The Ceylonese government, one of the most conservative in Asia, simply could not refuse such favorable terms.

The possibilities of that kind of approach on a broad scale are sobering to contemplate. Japan needs raw materials which Communist China can supply. The food deficit countries need grain wherever they can get it. Iran needs more customers for its oil. All of the underdeveloped nations need machinery and technical experts. If the Communist governments offer to fill these needs, it will take more than our warning that it is dangerous to sup with the devil to keep Asian nations from responding.

Many thoughtful observers argue that Russian resources simply cannot be stretched to cover the present level of Soviet armament,

Malenkov's promise of substantially higher living standards for the Russian people "in the next two or three years," and a major program of economic aid, not only for China but also for other underdeveloped Asian nations.

They may be right. But the record shows that for thirty years we have consistently underestimated the industrial progress of the Soviet Union in every development field including steel production and atomic energy. The gross national income of the Soviet Union is in excess of $120 billion annually and said to be growing at the rate of 7 per cent each year. A devastatingly effective Soviet version of Point Four could be financed for less than one-third of the present $8 billion annual increase in Russia's national income, which would amount to far more than we are putting into our own Point Four effort.

If we continue to ignore the challenge and put our faith in negation, we will lose our big chance. What is now required is an American aid program, on a large enough scale and soundly enough conceived, to fill the gap between the *maximum* possible savings of nations like India and the *minimum* needs for a program of economic development. The time has passed for "pilot plant." We have pilot-studied Asia almost to death. The funds required to do the job as it needs to be done will not amount to more than 5 or 10 per cent of what we must spend on armaments. And let's not forget that expanding development in Asia will encourage full production and full employment in America, for as Asia becomes prosperous she may ultimately become the greatest customer for our goods that we have yet found.

If the West musters the imagination and the means to meet this new Soviet challenge, there will be many reasons for satisfaction. Not the least of these will be the belated justice in the fact that the former colonial nations of Asia, which for many generations were forced to contribute to the prosperity of the Western powers, may now, in a more enlightened age, receive from the West the resources essential to their own growth and freedom.

3. *Private capital should not be expected to play a major part in the early stages of world development.*

Most American studies of foreign aid have emphasized that vastly increased contributions of private capital are necessary if the burden otherwise to be assumed by the government is to be significantly decreased. "Partners in Progress," the report of the Nelson Rockefeller committee on economic aid to underdeveloped areas, recommends, for example, an annual net investment in these countries of $2 billion a year. Such investment for sound projects is wholly desirable.

But actually the total new American private investment abroad for the years 1946-50 was on the order of only $1 billion a year, and all but $250 million a year went to South America. Something between 60 and 80 per cent of this has been spent by the American oil industry.

These figures show that private investment abroad is hardly approaching a scale necessary to play a significant role in the development work of Asia and Africa. The reasons for this are partly economic and partly questions of outlook and attitude.

Among the real obstacles which confront American businessmen are provisions of our own tax and antitrust laws which are said to be interpreted and enforced so as to discriminate against foreign enterprises financed by American funds.

On the other hand, the laws of many of the underdeveloped nations, reflecting long memories of colonial exploitation, place restrictions upon the direct operation of foreign business within their borders. Frequently they provide for large local participation in the ownership of the company. They may limit very stringently the amount of profits that can be withdrawn from the country. There may even be outright discrimination in taxation and other fields against the foreign businessman.

Many such factors serve to dampen the enthusiasm for this type of investment. And beyond this is the fear of general governmental instability so that the businessman does not know where he stands from day to day. In the turbulent politics of Asian countries the co-operative government officials with whom an agreement for a new plant or concession is concluded may be replaced tomorrow by others far less friendly who are in a position to change the rules.

Thus there is a vicious circle: the very revolutionary instability in Asia which leads everyone to recommend economic development as an essential cure is a major cause for the reluctance of private capital to go there.

On their part, most Asians tend to view American industrialists with a suspicion derived from their experience with exploitation, from their ardent nationalism and from their rather theoretical predisposition toward democratic socialism. Even the most anti-Communist Indian leaders accept, to some degree, the shopworn Marxist thesis that capitalism must inevitably lead to imperialism.

When independence had been won from British rule, Indians genuinely feared that Western capital would come rushing to get a new form of colonial grip upon them. They braced themselves to stop this new threat or hold it in check. To their astonishment practically none of this tainted capital made its appearance. Gradually they have become alarmed by its absence, and are now beginning to try to coax it into coming.

In a few areas, such as oil refineries, the Indian government has been so acutely anxious to get American private capital into a few specific fields that they have taken energetic steps to attract it. By giving Standard-Vacuum and Caltex a thirty-year guarantee against nationalization, and some other incentives, they have secured two valuable modern refineries. They have also made a similar deal for oil exploration in northeastern India, which may result in the discovery of an oil field rivaling those of the Middle East.

I followed the negotiation of these agreements very closely, talking to both Indian and American representatives at every stage. I found the Americans impressed with the competence, knowledge and businesslike attitude and procedures of the Indian officials, especially Finance Minister Deshmukh. The Indians were equally taken with the fair, open and straightforward dealing of the Americans.

Already in most Asian nations the standing of the American businessman is well above that of his French, Dutch and British counterparts. Of course one reason is that we have no colonial tradition. It is also due to the relatively enlightened policies followed by many American enterprises in Africa, the Middle East and South Asia.

Some steps can be taken, by both sides, to encourage investment abroad. But the attitude of mutual suspicion between most American businessmen and most Asian officials cannot be wished away or made to disappear by some magic governmental formula. It will take a history of responsible action on both sides extending over quite a few years to replace mistrust with confidence. We must face realistically the fact that for the next crucial years, most of the American money which is required for the success of development programs in Asia and Africa must come in the form of government assistance, and to whatever extent possible from the foundations and private agencies.

After all is said and done, there is one very simple reason why this is so. The type of activity required during the early stages of economic development is not very well fitted for private investment in the first place. What is needed at the outset is agricultural improvement, higher health and educational standards, mineral development, the construction of dams, power plants and other public utilities, and roads.

Of these, only one, the exploitation of mineral resources, is a job typically done by private industry. Significantly enough, that is just where most of the American private investment has been directed. Mineral development is readily profitable, but all the other basic development fields are at best profitable only in a long-term sense. Yet it is only after a groundwork in these fields has been laid that rapid industrialization can take place. India's problem is to finance that groundwork.

4. *Economic conditions should be attached to our aid.*

We have been properly hesitant to attach strings to American aid. To require a recipient country to think as we do about foreign policy or to vote as we do in the UN would amount to a bribe which any self-respecting people would refuse. As we shall see in a later point, even the implication of such a commitment will cause proud Asians to decline the aid altogether.

But, as I suggested in the chapter on Point Four in Nepal, there is a distinction between political strings that spell a new imperialism, and practical conditions which are simply necessary to assure that our funds are spent where they will produce the results intended.

Our assistance is generally a waste of money in any country which is unwilling to put its own house in order. Since success in development requires a climate of popular enthusiasm, America should, as I see it, offer its aid first of all to nations which are taking the necessary steps to create such a climate.

If a government has no over-all plan to mobilize its own resources to the utmost, if there is an inadequate and unjust tax system which bears primarily on those least able to pay, if there are no controls over luxury spending in the midst of poverty, if there are no land reforms, then American assistance will go to perpetuate bad leadership and to increase inequalities. Such a climate makes substantial development impossible and communism probable.

Asians have often asked me, "Why on earth do you Americans keep on subsidizing governments in Asia which won't lift their fingers to help themselves? They will never put through the necessary reforms as long as American aid is there to bail them out."

Of course, there may be cases where we will decide that aid, even without reforms, is more likely to strengthen the democratic forces than no aid. But even in such instances, and I hope they will be rare, we must find a way to make it clear that we are there to help the people.

If America openly required a sound national plan, an equitable fiscal system, and land reforms as a precondition to aid, there would certainly be risks of antagonizing some governments. But would the risks be as great as they are now? On one side we are subject to blackmail by governments who let black markets run uncontrolled and refuse to tax their own wealthy people, and then come to us hat in hand pleading, "Help us quick or we will go Communist." On the other side we are easy targets for the Communists because of our support of just such governments. The idea of "guilt by association" is not the exclusive property of a few Americans. The Russians use it too.

In the Philippines we took the risk of irritating a friendly government by issuing the Bell Report, and it paid solid dividends in our future relationship with the Philippine people. Headed by the president of the American Security and Trust Company, the U.S. Economic Survey Mission recommended $250 million of aid "strictly conditioned" on a new tax program bearing more heavily on high incomes and large property holders, on minimum wages and on a program of land reforms.

The report caused considerable irritation among Philippine officials, but it proved to the people of the Philippines that we are on their side and that is what counts most.

I believe that one mistake we made in the Marshall Plan was

our tendency to put our faith, more or less unconsciously, in the "trickle-down" theory of prosperity. Perhaps because time was short and the program was without precedent, we took the short cut of letting much of this money go in at the top, in the hope that enough of it would work its way down to the workers and consumers of the country.

As a result, the old European monopoly economies of scarcity and price rigging remained largely intact and the hoped-for dynamic rebirth of democratic faith failed to develop among the people. Production indices rose steadily, economic collapse was avoided, communism was stopped, but democracy itself remained on dead center. One-third of the Italian and one-fourth of the French people still voted Communist.

Monopoly capitalism is a defunct system, and the trickle-down theory will no more work in Asia than it will in Europe. To encourage the growth of healthy democracies we should see that our programs in Asia get directly to the people, that they are participated in by the people, and that they are in support of the people's organizations, such as the democratic farm groups, trade unions and co-operatives.

5. *Regional planning and participation should be increased, as far as practicable through UN.*

By far the best way to establish economic conditions on aid would be through standards agreed upon by a world or regional body, in which all the participating countries were represented. Both the conditions and the aid itself are likely to be much more acceptable this way. There is no doubt that aid from one nation to another looks to some people like charity, and to many it touches sore points of national pride.

President Truman's fourth point stressed that "this should be a co-operative enterprise in which all nations work together through the United Nations and its specialized agencies wherever practical." So far, unfortunately, the UN technical assistance has been starved for lack of funds.

In India the budgets for the projects of UNESCO, World Health Organization, Food and Agricultural Organization, International Labor Organization, the Children's Fund and Technical Assistance all put together amounted to only a little more than a million dollars a year. Nevertheless, within this limitation the UN agencies did fine work. WHO's part in the malaria control program has been mentioned. Their teams had also tested about seventeen million people for tuberculosis and vaccinated over five million when I left India. Thanks to the Planning Commission there was no overlapping between Point Four and the UN projects, and a good deal of co-operation.

For several years the Middle East-Asian-South American countries have been proposing a World Development Authority which would finance and administer a co-ordinated world aid program. Both the Soviet Union and the United States, for their separate reasons have each time opposed this proposal. One can see why the Soviet Union wishes to prevent the UN from becoming a vital world agency affecting the lives of hundreds of millions of people, but it would seem to be in the sheer security interest of the United States to try to turn the UN into the center for world economic development.

In any case, regional organization for mutual aid is within the grasp of the Middle East–Asian countries themselves. No one can veto their action if they try to pool their resources and skills for a regionally integrated assault on their common problems. Certainly in India our Point Four people not only would have welcomed closer relations with similar work in other Asian countries but we actually tried to promote it in small ways. We were all struck by how much the Asian nations had to offer each other.

The ingenious Indonesian program of fish farming in the rice paddies, which can be adapted in many parts of Asia, we have discussed. It is as old as Confucius, but is being introduced abroad for the first time, including Arkansas, where the yield is not yet up to the Indonesian average. When I was walking through some of the fifty thousand acres on which the fish are growing, an old Indonesian farmer, with a twinkle in his eye, offered to go to America to give us a little technical assistance in this field.

He would certainly be welcomed in India, and Indian experts in malaria control, who are among the world's best, could be of great service in Indonesia. Both India and Indonesia could use advice from Japan on how to develop deep-sea fisheries. Already Japanese methods of rice cultivation, the most efficient in the world, are being introduced in India, with the assistance of experts brought from Japan. India has the iron ore and manganese which Japan needs, just as India is a potential market for many of Japan's products.

Why not borrow from our experience in Europe and put this interchange on a more systematic basis? Mr. Dulles and Mr. Stassen now might take much the same kind of initiative that Secretary Marshall took in Europe, by inviting the South and East Asian nations to set up a regional development board. The present ECAFE, the United Nations Economic Commission for Asia and the Far East, would be the logical starting point. At first its functions might be modest, but the aim should be to become responsible for the co-ordination of all foreign economic aid programs in all of free Asia.

One of the problems which might be handled on a regional basis is that of achieving some kind of stability in the price of raw materials such as rubber and tin. The entire economy of many of these countries is completely dependent upon the sale of one or two of these materials in the world market.

Since synthetic products and substitutes are gaining ground, any price stabilization effort should probably be a temporary stopgap to give the one-crop or two-crop countries a little time to diversify their economies so that they are no longer in such an unhealthy and dangerous dependence.

Another long-range subject for regional planning is how to devise an industrial system and technology that really fits Asian conditions. The American approach is often too large-scale and mechanized, and some new answers must be found. Eventually Asia may succeed in developing balanced and decentralized economies which would warm the hearts of both Thomas Jefferson and Mahatma Gandhi.

6. *Economic and military aid should be kept as parallel but completely separate programs.*

There are two hurdles to get over for America's foreign aid program in underdeveloped countries to become a reality: the United States Congress, with wide public support, must pass the necessary year-to-year appropriations, and the recipient governments must agree to accept the program. Right now the second hurdle seems to me almost as high as the first.

Anyone who knows South Asia also knows that if Point Four aid seems to be in any way tied to our military and alliance system it will be rejected by most of the nations which are in greatest need of help. For their own reasons, which we have discussed in previous chapters, these countries are determined not to become formally identified with either the American or Soviet side in the Cold War, and if our offer of assistance has even the most indirect military overtones, that will be the end of it.

In India this was the first question raised about our Point Four offer in 1951 by everyone from the Prime Minister to journalists in the most remote Indian towns. It was because I was able to assure them that the program was independent and nonmilitary that we were able to draft the Indo-American agreement and undertake the Community Development projects, malaria control program and other efforts.

The Communists, anxious to bring about the failure of India's Five Year Plan, agitated violently against accepting any foreign aid from America or even the World Bank. And they are not concerned with their lack of consistency. In China the Communist government states publicly that for a country in their situation substantial outside aid is absolutely essential.

They failed to stop our program in India for only one reason: we could prove that charges that this was merely part of a military deal were false. By maintaining the integrity of Point Four as a separate program, we placed ourselves in an invincible position.

No one needs to be theoretical about what would happen if Point Four ever really became entangled with our military efforts. While we were moving ahead with the projects in India, the issue exploded on precisely this point in Indonesia. The Prime Minister there had agreed to an aid program that was primarily technical assistance. But because some weapons for the local constabulary were included as a small item, it came under the Mutual Security program, with the implied commitment to support the West.

So violent was the popular uproar that the cabinet repudiated the agreement; nor was popular clamor satisfied until the cabinet was overthrown. Thus a friendly government disappeared overnight, and it was months before negotiations for a separate Point Four agreement could make any progress again.

To most Congressmen in America it probably makes sense to

combine all overseas operations in one integrated program. Although this sounds efficient, it overlooks some of the basic facts of Asian life and attitudes. If the two programs are on separate tracks they may actually parallel each other. If they are put on the same track, in Asia at least, they may cancel each other out.

7. *Nongovernmental groups should be encouraged to undertake their own projects.*

Someday someone must give the American people a full report of the work of the Ford Foundation in India. The several million dollars in total Ford expenditures in the country do not tell one-tenth of the story. Under the leadership of Douglas Ensminger, the Ford staff in India became closely associated with the Planning Commission which administers the Five Year Plan. Wherever there was a gap, they filled it, whether it was agricultural, health education or administration. They took over, financed and administered the crucial village-level worker training schools. Their kind of straightforward service is in the finest traditions of our country. Similarly, as I have also pointed out, the Rockefeller Foundation has done excellent work in public health and education and I understand they are considering additional work in agriculture.

No less encouraging has been the trend of the churches toward accepting wider responsibility in the field of Point Four and humanitarian aid. The American Friends Service Committee has its own Point Four kind of project at Barpali in the state of Orissa under Alston Waring, where some excellent techniques of village work have been developed, and another in Madhya Pradesh.

"The more that Indian groups or communities are approached not by the U.S. government, but by their counterpart local, community, or private organizations from America, the less this curse of national humiliation stands in the way," Henry Hart, one of our Fulbright Lecturers at the University of Mysore, wrote me recently. "I wish I knew how to extend the town-to-town, union-to-union, farm coop-to-farm coop relations between India and America," he concluded.

I wish I knew too. Because the result would be a two-way street from which both towns, both unions, both co-ops and business groups on both sides of the world would come off richer.

With a new approach and vigor, the International Development

Placement Association has started to send young American volunteers to work with Gandhian institutions in India and with various African co-operatives and schools in Uganda and West Africa. IDPA seeks to place qualified Americans to work at local wages and live under local conditions in useful jobs in the whole field of economic and social development.

Obviously these groups do not solve the problem of getting adequate outside capital to the underdeveloped countries, but they provide the human links which make the work lasting. Most of these Americans are wisely coming to Asia in the conviction that they will learn more than they will contribute, but they will probably contribute more than they realize.

8. *Point Four people should be carefully selected and trained.*

I have seen our Point Four technicians and their wives in the mountains of Nepal, at the dam sites along the broad-flowing Damodar, in the rice paddies of Burma, Malaya, Indonesia and the Philippines. With few exceptions they are dedicated people, representative of the best that is in America. Unfortunately there are some who were chosen on the basis of competence in their technical specialties alone, without regard to their broader personal qualities. There are even a few who came because they had nothing else to do, or couldn't make the grade back home. Often even the best selections are so unprepared for what is awaiting them that their ability and good will cannot immediately make up for their ignorance.

A little knowledge of history and some sense of perspective about his job seem to be indispensable qualifications for a technician or volunteer arriving in a proud and ancient land. Once at Bhakra Dam I met a group of American engineers, hired by the Indian government with its own funds at going rates, up to $75,000 a year. They were a group of doers, experts in their field, and they freely expressed the exasperation they felt at the red tape around them. As a result relations with the Indian personnel were rapidly deteriorating.

I admired their spirit when they argued: "We've come to build dams." But that day I spoke bluntly. "You are not just here to build dams, but also to build *men.* Every day that you come home without giving new confidence to an Indian whom you are training, that day is a failure, regardless of how much earth you moved." We had a frank and good talk, and I believe they came to see their job with this new dimension added.

The Russians are apparently putting their own technicians through careful preliminary training. A member of the Indian cultural mission to China reported that at a Chinese airport there were a number of Russian technicians. They were wearing the same clothes as the Chinese, lived in the same kind of dwellings, and cleaned out their own latrines. They are said to be excellently trained in the Chinese language, and in skills of getting along with an Asian people.

Russia is currently turning out thirty thousand engineers a year from a five-year curriculum of six-day weeks and ten-month years. The United States output is twenty-three thousand engineers from four-year, five-day-a-week courses. Is that extra year devoted to training in more than engineering? How many of Russia's engineers are being prepared for assignments not only in China but in South Asia as well?

Wherever those engineers go, it is a safe guess that they seek to build communism as well as to build dams. We need to train people to help build Asian democracy, whatever their special assignment. No effort is too great to assure that our Point Four people, who are the only personal contact that millions of Asians have with America, represent in fact the America we would like to have Asia know.

I have often thought that we would do well to establish special schools, where people who chose this field for their careers can be given the specialized education which is needed. There, in addition to training in their technical specialties, they could take courses in the languages, history, governments and social and economic structures of the countries in the area of the world in which they planned to work.

9. *Not mere anti-communism but building strong democracies should be our main emphasis.*

In India I was often asked, "would America be concerned about our poverty if she were not afraid of our going Communist?" My answer was that I believed we would. I fervently hope I am right.

There is an apocryphal story going the rounds of Asian capitals which by indirection says something which we should take to heart. It seems that when the Prime Minister of the tiny state of Monaco heard about the Marshall Plan he flew to Washington to apply for aid. His modest request was viewed favorably until an official happened to ask, "By the way, how is your Communist problem?"

The Prime Minister replied proudly, "We have no Communists in Monaco. We are a poor but sensible people." Our official was embarrassed and explained reluctantly that if there was no Communist problem it would be nearly impossible to get Congress to vote the necessary funds, however sound the projects.

Not to be so easily daunted, the Prime Minister went home by way of Paris, where he called on the French Foreign Minister. "Please be good enough to loan me some of your surplus French Communists," he requested, after presenting his problem. "Just enough to break some windows and put on a good demonstration for the American newsreels."

The Frenchman said he would like to help Monaco get its aid, but after some hesitation he is supposed to have replied, "I'm sorry, my friend, we would like to be good neighbors, but we need every Communist we've got."

Here is a point worth remembering. How silly we must sometimes seem reducing every question to the Communist equation. Some of the questions are bigger than communism. World development, symbolized by the concept of Point Four, is potentially far bigger than communism. If all the Communists on earth disappeared overnight, the need for foreign aid to assist new struggling peoples to achieve stable democratic societies would still be there.

The challenge is to do what we ought to have done without the Communist challenge. But can we do what needs to be done out of fear or negation? We did not build our own country in order to oppose some foreign ideology but because we had a positive faith of our own. Only in that way can Asians build their new countries, and only in that spirit can our presence be of any real assistance.

It is essential that we should ask ourselves some blunt questions about our real objective in extending Point Four aid in Asia and Africa.

Is it to make America popular?

Is it to buy the people's gratitude?

Is it to win allies in the Cold War?

Is it to increase the acceptance of capitalism abroad?

Most of these objectives, like stopping communism, are desirable by themselves, but if we make them the direct essential goals of our foreign aid I am confident that we will achieve none of them.

As I see it our primary objective is to strengthen democracy in the new free nations of Asia for its own sake, without regard to occasional disagreements with them which are certain to rise. Democracy presupposes disagreements, and it is democracy to which we as a nation are above all committed.

If these new nations are successful in creating governments which are strong, democratic and solidly supported by their people, we can stop worrying about the spread of communism in Asia. Then we can surely expect to see many of the other objectives which I have listed achieved as by-products.

If we ask for thanks we will get none. But if we concentrate on the work that needs to be done we will be embarrassed by all the thanks we will get. In Assam, in northeast India, where not a cent of U.S. aid had gone at the time, I was once greeted with floral arches in half a dozen villages, and lavish thanks for several constructive projects which had been started solely from Indian funds. Because we had not stopped to ask for credit for what we did, people assumed that we had done far more than was the case.

The following letter, which reached a group of American engineers on Bhakra Dam in October 1952, illustrates this important point.

The American Specialists
on Dam, in Bhakra
Nangal Township.
Dear Sir,

We the undersigned villagers of Achalpur, Nainwan, Bhowanipur, Indowal, Sikhowal, Benewal, Holiowal, Kalewal, Kharali, Sihwan, Kanewal, Chottelal, Gondpur Dohkar, Joengpur and Majori, send our warm greetings to you, and through you, to your great country and its finest Democratic Govt. and great American people.

We the villagers of above mentioned villages welcome you in our soil. We are grateful to you for your valuable assistance in helping us in building Bhakra Dam which after completion will bring us prosperity and happiness.

We also thank you and your country for rendering us financial aid to change the face of rural areas, in carrying out the *Community Projects.*

We also very much appreciate the efforts you individuals are putting up here, in doing all odd jobs yourself. We know that you left your near and dears in U.S.A. to help us. We shall always keep this in mind, shall repay you in join our efforts to remain as free men.

(signatures of 566 villagers)

10. *We should act boldly while the initiative is still ours and not wait for a crisis.*

We Americans have a tendency to wait until a crisis comes and then go all out in its solution, at the very time when its solution is most costly.

In early 1952 it was clear that India required about $200 million for each of the remaining three years of the Five Year Plan to ensure that the Plan went over the top. I knew that India would not bring herself to ask for it.

So I presented the picture to the Department of State, the Senate Foreign Relations Committee and the House Foreign Affairs Committee. "In Asia the hour is late," I said. I did not mean that free Asia would collapse within a year or two. I meant that these were the years to bolster free Asia so that she would never collapse.

That three-year sum which I requested can be viewed in several perspectives. Historically, it happens to be less than the sum which the British extracted from colonial India, year after year, when the dollar was worth two or three times what it is worth today. In current terms, taking the three years together, it is less than the cost to the American taxpayer of one or two days of World War II. It is approximately half what we gave to Greece with its eight million people between 1947 and 1951.

It is half of one per cent of our military expenditures of the last three years. It is one third of what we did give to Chiang Kai-shek in China, which many people now say was too little and too late. It is also one-third what the Soviet Union is now giving Communist China. It is less than the military aid which we are putting into Indo-China in 1953 alone. Is this really too much for America to invest in democratic India at a time when such an investment might make the difference between democracy's success or failure?

There are some timid "realists" who oppose education in Asia, for fear the students will succumb to Marxist literature; who would stop assistance in malaria control or agricultural improvements,

"I Ain't Interested in Countries Till They're Lost"

Herblock in The Washington Post

for fear that these will only produce healthier, better-fed revolutionaries; who would refuse aid for fear any little change for the better in the villages of Asia will only whet the appetite for faster changes. If America should accept their arguments it will mean our abdication from the twentieth century.

Having seen how the people of Asia are on the move, I believe that in this century, by what means I do not know, change is coming to every village. The industrially backward continents are now moving on to the center of the world's stage. Our choice is whether we hinder and oppose them, turning them into totalitarian enemies, or whether we find a way to join hands with them in a democratic development.

If the development of these continents does become the primary field for the encounter between communism and the democracies, how much better that will be than war, and how much better fit we will be for such a contest. This challenge, which is in line with our American traditions, should call for the best from us in ingenuity, constructive skills, generosity of viewpoint and political intelligence.

VIII. FREE ASIA AND THE UNITED STATES

21. Farewell to India

EDUCATED INDIA'S attention to the U.S. presidential campaign in 1952 demonstrated once again the significance of our country to men everywhere. In August Steb and I took a 15,000-mile trip through Southeast Asia. We found the same pre-election excitement and the same concern about the development of American foreign policy, whether we were talking with the leaders of Burma, Indo-China, Thailand or the Philippines.

For twenty years they had been accustomed to a Democratic administration. Although they all felt that the United States had made mistakes during those years, they had come to have confidence in our desire for peace and in our refusal to escape into isolationism. There was a general nervousness about what a change of administration might mean for Asia and the world.

It seemed to me that my role should be to assure these people that the world would not come to an end regardless of who won. Since Stevenson's eloquence, which is somewhat similar to Nehru's, had particularly attracted Indian sympathy, I often found it necessary to remind Indians of Eisenhower's remarkable wartime record of international teamwork.

I pointed out that, although some of our political talk might sound as if we were about to embark on another civil war, we had developed over recent years a broad unity on foreign affairs, and I thought there would be few, if any, fundamental changes in our world policies.

Some of my friends in America had suggested that I should give up my work, return home, and plunge into the campaign in an effort to help elect a President of the United States. I did not agree, and I am confident that Adlai Stevenson would not have agreed. He was an old friend, and a schoolmate, whom I admire a great deal. But when I went to India as Ambassador I did not go as a Democrat or as a Republican, but as an American citizen anxious to represent his country regardless of party.

During my stay in India I did not discuss politics with the members of the staff, and I literally had no idea how most of them voted, nor did I care. They were working in the completely nonpartisan way that befits career civil servants. It seemed to me that my primary responsibility was in India, especially during a period when Indians sought reassurance.

Immediately after the election, several steps were taken which led Indians to believe that a drastic change in our policy had occurred, although the new administration had not even come into office and was in no way responsible. There was the British-American resolution on Kashmir, introduced largely out of impatience, and the ill-timed bid to Pakistan to join a Middle East Defense Organization, both of which moves were seriously misunderstood in India.

When the new administration withdrew the Seventh Fleet from Formosa and seemed to imply that we were preparing to back Chiang Kai-shek in an invasion of the Chinese mainland, most Asians concluded that a decision had been made in favor of aggressive action which could only result in a third world war.

I was confident that this was not the case, and did my best to explain the inevitable difficulties and initial uncertainties of a completely new crew, but the worries increased. "If these new American moves are just psychological warfare against the Communists, I can only hope your enemies are as worried by them as are your friends," one Indian official told me.

In late January I made a speech before a large dinner meeting in New Delhi in which I sought to clear the atmosphere by pointing out the widespread agreement on foreign affairs between the responsible leaders of both parties in spite of all the political charges and countercharges. I stressed the fact that above all the American people wanted peace and that all through the campaign the two parties had attempted to outdo each other in establishing their determination to achieve peace. I expressed the conviction that President Eisenhower's deepest wish was to bring the world a little closer together.

This speech was reported throughout India and everyone felt that its effect was reassuring.

During the period of transition after the election, communications with Washington broke down and it was hard to get answers on anything. From the beginning I was in the dark about my future position. After twenty years out of office the Republicans were naturally jittery about their new associates, whom they found already carrying out government assignments. It would be hard for them to know whom they could trust to follow new policies. In any case, President Eisenhower clearly was entitled to his own choice of ambassadors, and I would formally resign, as was the custom, to give the President a free hand.

The timing of my resignation seemed to me quite important. If it was clear that I would be relieved of my responsibilities, I wanted to resign as of January 19. Then Mr. Truman would accept my resignation and Mr. Eisenhower would not be forced to make a public decision which might in any way be embarrassing to him.

If, on the other hand, it seemed likely that the new administration intended to keep me, I would normally resign on January 20, and then if I were asked to stay, I would expect to come home and talk the situation over with the President and the new Secretary of State before making my decision.

After the election several wholly unofficial letters came, saying that while nothing was certain, it looked as though no change would be made in New Delhi. So my resignation went in to Mr. Eisenhower to be effective on January 20, his first day as President.

It was increasingly difficult to get anything done as the whole State Department machinery had ground to a stop, waiting for the new administration, and, weary after many months of intensive work, Steb, Sally, Sam and I (Cynthia was in college at Santiniketan in Bengal) decided to go to Ceylon for Christmas and a vacation on the beach.

The swimming was wonderful, and the chance for some quiet reading in this gorgeous country was appreciated. We had Christmas dinner with Ambassador Joseph Satterthwaite and his family, who somehow managed to make the day seem "Christmasy" in spite of the palm trees and flowers in full bloom.

Everywhere we found constant reminders of India in the ever-present Hindu and Buddhist art, and in the Tamil-speaking plantation laborers from South India, who comprise about 10 per cent of the population. Because Ceylon refused to grant full citizenship to these Indian immigrants, who still have many ties to Madras and Travancore, relations with the big northern neighbor are uneasy. But like India, Ceylon, also a newly free member of the British Commonwealth, is in a hurry to achieve economic development.

While we were there the Chinese Communist government completed the previously discussed trade deal with the relatively conservative government of Ceylon. We were all pleased when we heard later that the government of India refused Ceylon's request for ships to transport the rubber to China. So far, India does practically no trading with either China or Russia—probably far less of such trading than any other major nation.

On our return from Ceylon, instead of the ambassadorship situation having clarified, we found a climate of rumors and uncertainty which made dealing with the Indian government, to say the least, difficult. Hardly a day passed that some new successor was not indicated in the newspapers. By the second week in February, although there had been no word from either the White House or the State Department it became clear that the administration intended to make a change in India as elsewhere. I wrote the President suggesting that the change I assumed he was planning should be made as soon as possible so that someone could take over with full responsibility.

Within a few hours after my letter was mailed, a cable arrived announcing that the new Ambassador to India would be George Allen, who was then our Ambassador to Yugoslavia. When I heard that Allen was coming, I suddenly realized how much I had worried about the nature of my successor.

Steb and I both felt a deep sense of relief that evening. We had put everything into our work in New Delhi and Katmandu, and it would have broken our hearts to have felt that some deserving politician, without real qualifications, no matter how well-meaning, was taking over. Although I had not met Allen, I had heard high praise of his abilities and had corresponded with him considerably on the subject of Yugoslavia's interest in Asia.

Steb had to tell the servants, with whom we had enjoyed many good times together. We had grown very close to them and their families, and were touched by their fears that we might leave. Several of them were in tears over the first rumors. Steb said she would talk everything over with them as soon as anything was definite.

When the day came that she had to tell her story, she called all of them together and spoke in Hindi. There was a silence. Then she was enormously pleased to see that the first person to speak was Madan, the outcaste sweeper. Now he felt equal to anyone, and all the other servants nodded to show that Madan spoke for them, and, of course, they each added their words, too.

As soon as we knew we were leaving, we wrote Cynthia at Santiniketan. She said she would come to Delhi in early March, several weeks before we were planning to depart. When she arrived she told us she wanted to stay on in India until midsummer. She said that there was a great deal she had not seen, and that she would feel her experience was only half completed if she left then. She particularly wanted to go into more villages and live there as normally as she could. She also wanted to visit some of the big dams she had not seen, where fathers of her friends at Santiniketan were employed as engineers.

We were sorry to leave her behind, but she had become very grown up in her eighteen months in Asia, and had fallen in love with what she called "the real India." We were pleased when Dr. Sushila Nayar, a good friend of ours who was the Health Minister of Delhi State, offered to take Cynnie into her home and to keep an eye on her. Sushila was an active Gandhian worker, who had been Gandhi's personal physician.

We gave a farewell party for all the Embassy staff, Indian and American. Whatever had been accomplished was done through the teamwork of those men and women and their families, more than five hundred of whom attended and joined in our usual square dancing. We hoped to keep it as unsentimental as possible, but we did not succeed. The staff had chipped in to give us a lovely silver tray, inscribed to Steb and me "with affectionate good wishes."

The following Sunday we gave a party for all the chauffeurs, bearers and night watchmen, their wives and children. Several hundred came and it was a gala event. Steb had found a portable merry-go-round and a Ferris wheel which we rented all set up and complete with attendants for ten dollars. There was a pony to ride, a trained bear, popcorn and endless quantities of soda pop. There was a photographer, too, who took separate pictures of each family, more than eighty in all.

Later the Indian employees gave us a party of their own, at which I thanked them for accepting all of us Americans as we came, from year to year, and helping us to carry out our assignments. Without the highly trained Indian members of the staff, we American newcomers would soon be adrift.

On the eve of our departure I prepared answers to a series of questions from Indian journalists. I said that the most outstanding impression of India I would carry home was her "determination to master, by democratic means, the vast problems which she faces in building a better future for her people." But I added bluntly that "Americans are often puzzled by the failure of some Indians of strong democratic convictions to recognize the danger to their country presented by a new imperial power which has already subjugated the once free nations of Eastern Europe and which has openly vowed to turn all Asia into a Communist appendage of the Soviet Union."

I said that in an effort to make a small contribution to better understanding between our peoples I would devote the next twelve months in the United States to writing and speaking on the subject of American foreign policy with special emphasis on the problems of India and Asia. The fifteen-page transcript of my answers was printed in full by many newspapers throughout India.

We had long since decided that we would return through the Pacific. Our previous extended trip through Southeast Asia, which had helped us with many problems in India, had only whetted our appetites to see and learn more of this vital section of the world.

Also we wanted the children, who had not been able to go along on our previous trip, to have a chance to see other parts of Asia. We arranged to go on a small Dutch freighter which would wind its way from Calcutta to Rangoon, and down the Malayan coast to Singapore and then Djakarta.

With seven or eight weeks of slow, casual travel we hoped to renew our acquaintances through Indonesia and in other Asian countries, and above all to filter and digest all we had learned since we first arrived in this vast and vital continent.

I had been anxious to talk with my successor before he arrived in India, just as Loy Henderson had made it a point to see me. We hoped to meet at some midway point such as Lebanon. Mr. Allen cordially invited me to spend a few days with him in Yugoslavia, but in the end our schedules just did not fit and we had to give it up.

As the day of departure arrived, Sam and Sally became sadder and sadder in their last visits with friends, just as they had before they left their friends in Essex in 1951. When it came time to pull up the roots we had grown in India, we all realized that those roots went down deeper than we knew.

Nothing could have been more anticlimactic than the series of false departures and long farewells which awaited us. The freighter, which was in Ceylon picking up a cargo, could not make up its mind when it was going to go. After it had postponed its sailing a number of times we finally decided to take a plane to Thailand and then to Indonesia, and to use the time saved on the island of Bali.

We said good-by to all our friends, packed our bags, and took care of last-minute problems at the office. I had a last long earnest talk with Nehru.

Tichat, now a grown-up and dignified cat, departed by air by the more direct Atlantic route. On her crate the children had tacked a note introducing her to their older brother and sister-in-law in Essex. "This is Tichat," it said. "She speaks Hindustani fluently, a little French, and English if it is spoken very slowly."

But our own travel plans continued to go wrong. Our plane was supposed to leave at eight o'clock Sunday night and many of our friends went out to the airport to say good-by. At the last moment we were notified that the plane was still down in Karachi with motor trouble and would not leave till six the next morning.

After one false alarm and in view of the early hour we did not expect to see many people on that last day but when we reached the airport at 5:30 A.M. we were touched to see that almost the whole embassy staff, as well as a great many friends from other embassies, from the press and from government offices had come out to say good-by. They gave us a wonderful send-off.

As the plane left the soil of India it was barely light. We settled back in our seats, a little stunned, almost shell-shocked, after those frantic last weeks and emotional farewells. For all of us there was a kind of sinking feeling as India disappeared in the mists below.

But we would not be leaving the Indian subcontinent for several hours yet. Far below us were the great central states of India, as we followed the Ganges River east toward Calcutta. The sky became clear as we flew over Bihar, and I looked down on the hundreds of dots in the countryside which I knew were the villages. These were the fields through which Vinoba was now walking, collecting land and resurrecting the Gandhian ideals. And here and there we would see the new irrigation canals of the Five Year Plan.

What was in store for India? Who could say? I had seen great projects under way, but I had also seen the delay in reforms. In her history I had studied India's bright periods when she produced great and creative men, and I also knew of her dimmer days of inertia and disunion.

Surely the vitality and idealism generated by the independence movement could not be lost, yet no one could doubt the awful obstacles in the way of Indian progress.

What was in store for America in Asia? We had so much to offer Asia, and yet so much to learn. In America there was so much criticism of India which the Indians could not understand, and in India so much criticism of America which we cannot understand. We had made a start in breaking down that wall of misunderstanding. But would the harsh logic of events give us time for wisdom and generosity to come fully into play on both sides?

In my last long talk with Nehru we had discussed all these questions, but the answers belonged to no man. They were hidden in the history of our time which will be written when all of us have passed away. Will history say that Nehru and India lived up to their best potentiality? Will it say that we in America, in this era, lived up to our best?

When I came to India I asked myself many questions. Some of these had been answered, but I was returning with more questions than I had brought with me.

Our thoughts were interrupted by a short stopover in Calcutta, which we had almost forgotten. Friends from Bengal and Calcutta were on hand at the airport for a second farewell. After we completed the painful task of saying good-by to India all over again, the plane quickly carried us up over the Hooghly River, out over the Bay of Bengal. India dropped rapidly behind us.

22. Homeward Through Asia

WE WERE sorry to miss Burma on our homeward flight, but we were headed for Indonesia, the only South Asian country which we had not visited on previous trips. As our plane skirted the Burman coast we thought of the friendly people and the earnest democratic young government which had so impressed us the previous summer.

Prime Minister U Nu at forty-six is the oldest member of the Burman cabinet. The popular Defense Minister, U Ba Swe, is thirty-three. These men, who are vigorously anti-Communist, took over from the British in 1948 when their new nation was literally falling to pieces, have carried out many basic reforms, including the broadening of land ownership, which have won them the support of their people. With this support, they have been able to put down a half-dozen rebellions, including two by the Communists, without any outside aid, and today Burma is moving steadily toward stability.

Nu, who is a devout Buddhist in a Buddhist country, has an extra hold on the hearts of his countrymen. Once he told me his secret: "Heads of state everywhere have often threatened that if their governments or associates do not do as they wish, they will resign and sulk in their tents or even go into the opposition. But I doubt if anyone has quite such a heartfelt alternative as I. Often I tell my associates that unless they co-operate with me to build a new democratic Burma I will enter a monastery."

Nehru and U Nu are good friends and their foreign policies are almost identical, as I discovered in many talks with Burman officials in New Delhi and in Rangoon, which we visited in the summer of 1952.

"Perhaps it is just as well we are missing Burma this time," I told Steb. I knew that the whole mess about the Chinese Nationalist soldiers in Burma was about to blow up again. Burma's Ambassador to India, in one of my last talks in Delhi, had told me that his country had been as patient as it could, that it wanted to believe the best about us, but that Burma could no longer tolerate the disruption to its economy and its efforts to establish internal security from these Chinese who were being armed by Formosa. I knew that I would have been bombarded by many hard-to-answer questions!

We spent the night in Bangkok, the capital of Thailand, formerly known as Siam. We had a good visit with Ambassador Ed Stanton, an exceptionally able Foreign Service veteran who had been there for more than five years, with several years in China before that. We had seen a great deal of him on our previous visit. We discovered that he, too, would be leaving shortly.

Like Burma, Thailand is a country of some twenty million people with a rich rice surplus and unused land. But Thailand in most ways is a striking contrast to Burma, Indo-China, India and the rest of Asia. With China and Japan it is one of the three Asian countries of any size which has never been taken over by a Western colonial power.

Because of this lack of direct colonial experience, Thailand has seemed more friendly to the West than most of the rest of Asia. But the very Thai success in avoiding Western colonialism by shrewd maneuvering and outright bargaining has hardly encouraged a high sense of political morality. It has also thrown doubt on how deep Thailand's commitment to the West really goes. The Thai troops which we are arming are good soldiers, but many foreign observers say there is one thing wrong with them: if past experience is any guide, they will never be ordered really to hold out against an invading force.

"Of course we declared war on the United States and England in 1941. But we did it only to protect your American and British investments," a Thai official once told me with a straight face.

Partly because of its lack of colonial exploitation and partly because of its natural wealth, the difficulties which Thailand faces today are substantially less than those of most Asian countries. It is particularly interesting to compare traditionally independent Thailand with Burma and Indo-China which spent so many generations under the British and French.

Although all three are about equally blessed with resources, the latter two countries, after colonial rule, were no more than

15 per cent literate; while in Thailand the figure is over 50 per cent. Almost equally sharp differences existed in public health and life expectancy. Of course, the Thais have exploited each other scandalously, but at least the nation's wealth has not gone outside its borders to Paris, London or The Hague, and the good results seemed apparent everywhere we went.

Unlike most of the newly free nations of Asia, the Thai government, a relatively benevolent military dictatorship, has no strong roots among the people. Lacking the tradition of national struggle which supports Nehru and U Nu of Burma, the leaders of Thailand are constantly in danger of being supplanted by a military coup. A popular former leader, who is said to have strong Communist leanings, is now in the underground, and possibly in China. The Communist party is outlawed and not yet strong, but the young people of the country who are studying abroad are increasingly dissatisfied with a system of strong men.

"How fortunate we are," an attractive Thai girl, who had attended an American university, told me ironically. "We are just as united as the Soviet Union. We have no political parties whatsoever because we are so wonderfully united."

Yet with all this, I found that the Prime Minister, Pibul Songgram had much the same attitude toward colonialism as those who had fought it all their lives. He carried his anticolonialism so far that in spite of the fact that the war against communism in Vietnam was only next door, he did not appear alarmed at the possibility that the French might suddenly leave the Vietnamese to handle the Communists by themselves. He thought that the very fact of independence alone would give Vietnam the spirit necessary to defeat the Communists.

I agreed with him that real independence of Vietnam, Cambodia and Laos was long overdue and that it was essential for victory, but I pointed out that until the Communists actually laid down their arms, it would be extremely dangerous for the French to pull out. Like so many other Asians, he simply shrugged his shoulders and said that he would take his chances.

• • •

From Bangkok we flew to Djakarta, capital of the Indonesian Republic, a government which rules eighty-five million people who live on islands that stretch for thirty-five hundred miles, further than from New York to San Francisco. Pakistan and Indonesia, with about the same population, are by far the two biggest Muslim nations in the world.

Members of the government met us at the airport, and we were pleased to hear that what we had been trying to do in India had been carefully followed and understood. For our part, we had long had a special interest in Indonesia. Our good friends the Soedarsonos, the Indonesian Ambassador to India and his wife, had told us much about their country's struggle. Their daughter, Sofi, and Sally were almost inseparable.

We were anxious to meet the Indonesian leaders and have a chance to look at their problems, but we were dead tired and first wanted our long-promised week or so of quiet. So we flew east to the island of Bali. Our plane passed over a live volcano from which bellowed huge clouds of red flame, and then we landed on the famed island which looked just as the artists picture it.

We arrived during the full moon, and the tiny hotel on the beach was in the midst of a setting right out of a tropical picture postcard. I have seen lovely places but none of them have ever quite equaled Bali.

While Steb, Sally and Sam were looking forward to a vacation, I had privately planned to start writing this book during my week's retreat. For that purpose I had with me a dictaphone, especially adjusted for all kinds of electric currents. When I heard that we were the only people then staying at the little hotel, I thought how much work I would be able to get done. Then suddenly I noticed the kerosene lamps all around us. They had scarcely dreamed of electricity!

One evening we heard music that sounded familiarly like India, and walked up the village road in the moonlight to find it. The friendly people invited us to watch their dancing and singing, and among their beautiful performances we recognized the Indian monkey dance. Bali is the last stronghold of Hinduism in Indonesia, the last remnant of the early Indian colonization.

Looking at the peacefulness and natural plenty of Bali, where the villages are democratically organized and almost all of the children go to school, I wondered whether modern technology, even my dictaphone machine with all its speed and efficiency, was so necessary after all. Gandhi once said that "modern civilization is not an incurable disease."

However, when we returned to Djakarta on the main island of Java for two crowded weeks of traveling and talking, we discovered that in most of Indonesia the process of introducing modern civilization was in full swing.

As in other countries which we visited Steb and I followed quite different schedules. While I talked to government officials and our own embassy experts, visited Point Four projects and tried to get as close as possible to the problems of the villages, Steb concentrated on education and public health. Everywhere she visited primary schools, secondary schools and universities in the cities and in the rural areas, and also clinics and hospitals. But her main interest was the new younger generation and I have often wondered if this didn't bring her closer to the heart of each country than my talks with the heads of state.

Fortunately our visit to Djakarta coincided with that of Adlai Stevenson, whom we met at the airport and took for a ride through the bustling capital city. He was dead tired, but determined to see the leaders, meet the people, catch the spirit of the country, and understand some of its problems. Optimistically he had expected to see Asia quietly, poking around in the back streets, talking with whomever he wanted. But to his surprise he found that the governments everywhere had prepared great receptions and were eager to talk with him.

Many Asian leaders had read and been deeply impressed by Stevenson's speeches, but the cause of his widespread popularity in Asia is simpler than that. Asians sensed that he was interested in people as people, and that is their first test of a man's *bona fides*. Anyone who looks on the world as a mass of statistics, treaties, and power relations is distrusted and disregarded by the sensitive Asians.

Indonesia and India contrasted in many ways. Like the Indians the Indonesians struggled to oust their European rulers, but they fought with guns instead of with Gandhi. And unlike the British, the Dutch tried to hang on to the last minute and thus lost everything. We Americans worried the Indonesians when at first we condoned the Dutch attempt to reconquer Java. But then under the prodding of Frank Graham, who had been appointed a special American Commissioner, and Merle Cochran, our First Ambassador to Indonesia, we realized our early mistakes and effectively used our influence in the UN to help make the Dutch yield.

But the memory of that period of hard-fought warfare still galls young Indonesians. I was told the story of the return of Dutch troops to Djakarta, then called Batavia, after the surrender of the Japanese, which Edmond Taylor also recounts in his book *Richer By Asia.* They are said to have come in American army trucks, armed with American weapons, supplied with American ammunition, and supported by American-built war planes. When American newsmen entered the city with these Dutch troops they found two slogans written in bitter mockery waiting for them on the walls of the buildings of Batavia: "Give me liberty or give me death," and "All men are created free and equal."

"If only America would really understand us," President Soekarno told me. "We are not primarily interested in your money although we need help. What we want most is your understanding. We want you to believe in what we are trying to do. Our only aim is to become a successful democracy. We are not going to become Communist, but we naturally cannot take direction from you or anyone else. We must have a forthright independence. It means everything to us."

Throughout Indonesia what constantly surprised me was the extraordinary similarity of attitudes of this predominantly Muslim people to those of the Indians. When I spoke to a large audience at the University of Indonesia, giving almost the same kind of talk I had given in India, I was asked politely but persistently exactly the same questions about American attitudes toward colonialism and toward world problems in general that I had come to expect in India.

That night at dinner an Indonesian professor talked to me about his students. "Many of them talk like Communists, but I can assure you they are not Communists," he said. "They don't want to live under Russian or Chinese domination any more than they wanted the rule of the Dutch or Japanese. But they do want change. They are ready to like America, if America will give them reason to like her, by supporting the new kind of world they want to see."

As in India, it was the little things one does unconsciously which seemed to assure Asians that you respect their dignity. A leading Indonesian newspaper carried a much too generous article about us, pegged on the simple fact that on a warm afternoon Sally and Sam went alone to swim in the Manggrai public pool. A perfectly natural thing for most American children to do, but apparently new in Indonesia.

Although a Muslim and no follower of India, Soekarno reminded me of Nehru. He is good-looking, earnest and very articulate in excellent English. Now fifty-two years old, he led the nonco-operation movement against the Dutch from 1927, serving many years in jail, only to be released by the Japanese in 1942. He holds himself above party politics as the universally respected symbol of the national struggle.

Vice President Hatta, a Socialist of firm anti-Communist convictions who served fourteen years in Dutch prisons, and Finance Minister Sumitro Djojohadikusumo, a brilliant and flexible economist who wants to find the most practical way to national development, were both impressive. Having had much the same experience with Dutch businessmen that the Indians had with the British, all of these people are skeptical of capitalism, although they are very anxious to get capital on fair terms.

The respected Socialist leader, Dr. Sjahrir, who was also a leader of the independence struggle, is in the democratic opposition. No one could be more firmly anti-Communist. It is interesting that the two groups in Asia which are most firmly and militantly aware of the world Communist danger are such otherwise diverse groups as the Socialists of India, Burma and Indonesia on the one hand, and the Chinese and Korean supporters of Chiang Kai-shek and Syngman Rhee on the other. Actually many of these Socialists are more like Jeffersonians or Gandhians than Marxists.

While we were in Djakarta we stayed at the residence of the American Ambassador. For seven months after Merle Cochran resigned in February, 1953, we had no ambassador in Indonesia, although this new nation has a larger population than France and Italy combined. For several months there was no head of Point Four. The staff of the American Embassy were anxious to do a good job, but they felt lost and forgotten, not knowing what to do about the lack of attention from home. When we were there the only American newspaperman in the entire country was working as a free lance.

• • •

America had paid more attention to our next homeward stop, Singapore. Once the crossroads of empire, Singapore is still the crossroads of Asia as well as the center of the long-drawn-out battle for Malaya between British troops, including many Gurkhas from Nepal, and Communist guerrillas.

Sam was fascinated by the huge harbor, with hundreds of ships of all kinds from many nations coming and going. I do not think he quite approved of my concentration on the political, economic and military situations when we could have been watching such a waterfront spectacle.

When I had last been in Singapore, in August, 1952, I came down with a bad case of dysentery which kept me in bed at the home of the American Consul General, Charles Baldwin. He was good enough to provide me with a steady stream of Malayan and Chinese visitors, who impressed me with the difficulties of a rational political solution in Malaya. About 40 per cent of the people are Malayan, 40 per cent Chinese and 20 per cent Indian.

As everywhere, the Chinese settlers are remarkably hard-working, and the Malayans fear that the Chinese will eventually take over the country. Thus the Malayans hesitate to grant political equality to the Chinese, a precondition for any real independence, which all sides say they want.

"Usually in such a situation you can be pretty sure that the colonial power is behind the scenes stimulating the racial and religious divisions," said a Malayan Indian who had seen the divide-and-rule policy of the British in India. "In this case it is probably not true. I think the British genuinely want to work something out."

Many Malayans and Chinese told me that they wanted independence but that they did not want it any harder than Malcolm MacDonald, the popular British High Commissioner—more popular with the Asians than with some of his own countrymen. It is said that the local British aristocracy have never forgiven him for the night when he broke one of their conventions by taking off his coat at a concert when it was very hot. Even in April, 1953, the European clubs in Singapore still did not admit Malayans, Chinese or Indians to eat or to swim.

An interesting contrast to MacDonald is Sir Gerald Templer, the hard-bitten British commander in the war against the Communist guerrillas. Somewhat in the style of the eighteenth-century Clive in India, Templer is said to go into villages and announce,

"I will chop off your heads if you co-operate with the Communists," but then he adds a modern touch: "Now that you understand that, tell me your problems and I will do my best to help you."

Sir Gerald's predecessor had been killed in an ambush, and when he arrived in mid-1952 there were about five hundred such ambushes and similar incidents a month. Since then there has been steady improvement and the roads are now safe in the daytime.

I found him very temperamental, very opinionated and very intelligent. We stayed with him at his home, "King's House" in Kuala Lumpur, capital of the Malay states. After a large dinner, he leaned over to me and said, "Although it's only ten o'clock, let's call the evening off. However, you and I must talk. We'll all say goodnight, then you come back down and we'll have a conversation." So the party broke up and up we went to bed and down again the back way.

"You Americans know nothing of the East," he began argumentatively. "You have only been interested in it for a few years. We have been here for 250 years." I agreed that we, of course, did not know much about Asia and should certainly approach it with humility. And then I added, "You came to Asia 250 years ago but you, too, should feel humility for now you are only hanging on by your teeth."

He seemed to like a straight discussion, and we continued until after 3:00 A.M. I asked him to analyze the nature of his insurgent enemies. He estimated that they were about 10 per cent tough, disciplined Communists, who organized and led the guerrillas; 10 per cent idealistic, frustrated schoolboys, about 40 per cent people who had broken with the law and were living in the jungles to avoid the penalty for some minor crime, and about 40 per cent habitual bandits. He believed that 95 per cent of all the people in Malaya were now anti-Communist. But finally to defeat the Communists, he said, "we must win these people. We must get them land."

Sir Gerald was building new villages in which to settle people from the jungle areas, one of which we visited. With new hospitals and schools which are now educating nearly two-thirds of the children, the people are getting a far better break than before.

From an entirely different perspective, Sir Gerald, a tough-minded military strategist and a political conservative, agreed with MacDonald that above all the people count. That was the same point which nearly everyone stressed about the war in Indo-China, our next homeward stop.

• • •

During my previous summer's visit to Saigon, I had spoken to President of the Council, Van Tam, of the anti-Communist Vietnam government, who had then been just appointed by Bao Dai, the French-backed Emperor. He told me then that the country would never be free of Communist trouble until the people became convinced that they were fighting for genuine freedom. He told me that at least two-thirds of the rebel Vietminh forces in his judgment were ardent nationalists, not Communists: they thought they were fighting to get rid of French colonialism. Tam was entirely clear in his own mind that a Vietminh victory would only replace French colonial rule with Chinese Communist rule, which he knew would be worse. But he emphasized that the people did not understand this, and the French did not help them to understand it.

Now on my second visit in the spring of 1953 the French still clung to all the appearances of power, their High Commissioner still lived in the principal palace where he has always lived, and their agents still tightly controlled the customs, taxes, foreign affairs and army. This was hardly the way to convince the Vietnamese people that they were a free people.

Without the determined backing of the people of Indo-China the full weight of the French army seemed to be unable to uproot the Vietminh. Despite 150,000 French Union troops and more than that number of Vietnam soldiers under French command, despite 275 shiploads of American war materials (over two million tons) in the last year and a half, despite an expenditure of money greater than all the aid France received under the Marshall plan, despite the loss of the cream of the French officer corps, the Communist-led rebels still controlled a large part of the countryside and many of the cities were still oases in an unfriendly desert.

"War upon rebellion was messy and slow, like eating soup with a knife," wrote Lawrence of Arabia after the First World War. But Lawrence was helping the nationalist Arab rebels backed by Britain in their struggle against Turkish rule.

Like the Vietminh in Indo-China, Lawrence's Arabs did not

advance with banners. They were "an influence, an idea, a thing intangible, invulnerable, without front or back, drifting about like a gas." Lawrence said that success came because "our kingdoms lay in each man's mind."

The French troubles came because their dominion was not at all over the minds of the Indo-Chinese. "When the people of a village are with us, we can hold that village with one sentry," said an anti-Communist Vietnam commander. "When the people are against us we need a whole battalion to hold the same village."

The tragedy of Indo-China is that while the French have been fighting with magnificent courage, they failed in the beginning to take the necessary steps to win the people, which alone can bring the fighting to a triumphant conclusion.

Yet many Frenchmen understand the problem thoroughly. General Chassin, who was commander of the French air force in Indo-China when we were there, has written a searching analysis of the military situation he faced. The Communists' system, he said, "places its reliance on men rather than on machines and gives first priority to winning the support of the people. Opposing it is the Western system, which seeks to save the maximum possible number of lives and therefore relies largely on the machine."

For the Communists, General Chassin notes, "political action always precedes military action, the establishment of political 'bases' being the first and most important step." For the French to win, he says, they too must recognize that "this is largely a political problem." He urges the French to "promote essential reforms" and "build as rapidly as possible a Vietnamese army. . . . If we are to fight a Far Eastern jungle war, we must rid ourselves of heavy equipment and rely on mobility rather than shovels."

Donald Heath, our Ambassador to the Indo-Chinese states of Vietnam, Cambodia and Laos, is patiently behind the scenes doing his best to help bring about a good solution of the political problem. An old and good friend of mine, Heath has had a series of the toughests posts the Foreign Service can offer: West Berlin, Bulgaria and now Indo-China. He has great faith in the French, and feels sure that they are going to come out of this situation successfully. He admits that they have been slow to change, but he points out that the change is already great and that patience is necessary.

Before I left Indo-China, a Vietnam leader said to me in the privacy of his home, "Before we can be a free people, we must win three wars: first, against the Communists; second, against the French; third, against the landlords and economic exploiters of our people." He then asked me to drink to the Vietnamese success in these three "wars."

I replied that I could not drink with him to victory "against the French" who had so often and gallantly helped my country, but I would join him if he modified his toast to say "freedom from foreign rule." He agreed, and so at eleven o'clock in the morning we drank this triple toast in French champagne.

In June and July, 1953, two months after we left Saigon, French policy in Vietnam, Cambodia and Laos started to undergo some encouraging changes. Let us hope that these are solid steps on the road to full freedom for these three new nations, and full defeat for the Communist forces.

From Saigon we took a small French steamer down the river and up the coast to Hong Kong, an easy three-day trip.

Sam and Sally were especially sorry that we had to bypass the Philippines, which they had never seen. We would have liked them to see this new nation where most Americans are not only liked as individuals, as they are everywhere, but where America itself is popular.

During our visit the previous August, Steb and I had been greatly impressed by Admiral Spruance, our Ambassador to the Philippines, and his wonderful wife, and his persistent effort to induce the Philippine government to put through the reforms which had long been promised.

The Philippines and India are widely separated by geography and history, and have few contacts. We had been amused and a little amazed to discover that one member of the Philippine cabinet had no clear idea of who Nehru was.

"Is India's Prime Minister going to get well?" he asked me. When I said that he was not sick, the cabinet member told me that he had read all about him governing from a sickbed in pajamas, and weeping in public when it helped his purposes. He had Nehru and Mossadegh of Iran mixed up.

Yet even in the Philippines I found much the same attitudes toward the world that I had once thought to be only Indian attitudes. Here, too, was a proud people, fiercely anticolonial, determined to be respected as the equals of any Westerners, above all concerned with how to develop into a modern economy.

• • •

When our ship steamed into Hong Kong, Sally and Sam commented at first glance that they could see why the British wanted to keep such a magnificent place. The city slopes up a high hill, with lovely British homes in rows all the way to the top. The sweep up from the harbor is equaled only by San Francisco. At night when the whole hillside is dotted with lights and other lights shine from the steamers, freighters and Chinese junks which bob up and down in the harbor, the beauty is breathtaking.

For the Communists, sitting on all sides only a few miles away, Hong Kong must be a tempting morsel. Although thirty thousand British troops are stationed there, everyone knows that the powerful Chinese force across the border could drive them out if they were really determined to do so. Yet British settlers in Hong Kong, with their typical national optimism, are undertaking an amazing building program in the very shadow of Chinese communism. Everywhere we noticed banks and apartments going up. Everyone brushes aside the fear of war, whistles cheerfully and moves ahead.

Hong Kong is the free world's principal listening post in China. Hundreds of thousands of Chinese refugees from communism have come to the island, and there is terror among these people at the thought of the Communists taking over.

Also coming and going are thousands of Chinese from South Asia. A crucial factor in non-Communist Asia is the vast number of Chinese settlers throughout the region. The Communists are said to be stepping up their campaign to turn these ten to twelve million outside Chinese into a fifth column. When it is remembered that Malaya is 40 per cent Chinese, that Thailand and Indonesia have about two and a half million Chinese each, and that there are many Chinese Communists in most South Asian cities, the potential danger becomes clear. By Chinese law, overseas Chinese can never lose their nationality.

Young Chinese from this entire area were constantly receiving scholarships to study in China and some of these were returning as trained Communist agitators.

So far, I gather that about 90 per cent of these overseas Chinese have no interest in politics. Although they have pride in China, they have no special love for either Mao Tse-tung or Chiang Kai-shek. However, if Communist China really started to thrive and to expand, it is possible that their pride in the homeland might sweep a majority of them into full support of the Communists.

All those who come out of China through Hong Kong are closely questioned by the large corps of newsmen, diplomats and intelligence agents of all countries. From my talks with many people, including Chinese refugees, I put together a kind of rough consensus of what is happening in China.

Everyone says that the Communists have achieved an unprecedented national unity. To avoid future war lords, such as those who helped wreck Chiang, the Communists practice a steady rotation of their administrators, on both regional and provincial levels. About five million Communist party members, most of them young, provide the backbone for the brutally tight state controls along with the Red Army, which is now growing to 175 divisions, much of it modern equipped, with an additional one million security police.

So far the Communist leaders seem to have shown more flexibility than their European and Russian counterparts. They have demonstrated greater readiness to admit mistakes and to back away from programs which do not work. The top leadership has remained intact and there has been no purge among Mao Tse-tung's immediate associates since 1938.

Everyone reports that the war in Korea was skillfully used to unite the Chinese people. White Western soldiers on the soil of the Asian mainland, their mission completely distorted by Communist propaganda, provided a public enemy that aroused Chinese nationalism to fever pitch. However, the war was also very costly to the Chinese and undoubtedly set back their development considerably. Taxes are high and the peasants are being squeezed hard to secure the rice needed to feed people in the cities and provide a surplus for export.

Most of the people with contacts in China said that the Russians were dealing skillfully with the Chinese. The thousands of Soviet experts and advisers were staying behind the scenes and living according to Chinese standards. But I met no one who expected this Chinese-Soviet honeymoon to last indefinitely.

As I listened to reports of what is going on behind the "bamboo curtain," I came back again and again to the competition between free India and Communist China which I believe is one of the most important facts of our time.

Of the 219,000 students officially enrolled in Chinese universities, somewhat less than in India, over 50 per cent were "assigned" to engineering courses. While most Indian schools remain British-modeled liberal arts centers, the Chinese universities are factories to turn out technicians for their Five Year Plan.

A key to China's future is Manchuria, the former industrial center of the mainland which the Russians wrecked and dismantled after the war, in the apparent expectation that Chiang Kai-shek would win. With the surprise collapse of Chiang, the Russians reversed gears and began restoring some of the equipment. Although this may give China a substantial lift on her industrial development program, the road ahead will be hard and long and only time can decide the result.

We flew on to the beautiful island of Formosa, to visit the headquarters of the man who had done more than any other except Sun Yat-sen to awaken modern China. Over and over again as I traveled around the island I thought to myself: If only Chiang Kai-shek's government had done as well on the mainland as it is now doing on Formosa it would still be there, and the world would be closer to peace.

At first, the influx of two million Chinese from the mainland into an area already holding seven million Formosans, plus their first notoriously bad Provincial Governor General, caused deep resentment on the part of the Formosans. But Chiang insisted upon a housecleaning, appointed the honest and able Dr. K. C. Wu, former Mayor of Shanghai and a graduate of Princeton, as governor, and saw to it that good relations were established between the Chinese and the Formosans. Somehow in defeat the Nationalists seem to have found the regeneration they had so desperately lacked on the mainland.

With American assistance, the Nationalists are determined to turn Formosa into a model of economic development for Asia. They say that they are moving toward local elections and real democracy and I hope and believe that they are sincere. In any event I know that they have already carried out more sweeping land reforms than yet enacted in any Asian nation except Japan.

These nine million people use almost as much fertilizer as is used in all of India, and the rice yield per acre is double India's. In spite of its increased population Formosa still exports rice.

Their sense of political realities seemed to me less well developed. Most of the leaders still talk and think about the day when they will rule on the mainland, but no one explains how this may come about, short of a third world war.

In Korea 400,000 American and other United Nations troops, plus 600,000 tough South Koreans and unchallenged air power, fighting on a narrow front with both flanks guarded by the United States Navy, finally settled for a stalemate truce. This truce came, not because we could not win, but because, rightly or wrongly, both Democratic and Republican administrations felt that the cost of victory would be too high. How could a far less formidable Chinese Nationalist force hope to succeed from Formosa without the all-out American commitment which we decided against in South Korea?

In a sense the course of events has given the Chinese Nationalists a kind of vested interest in World War III, which would bring the United States into an all-out struggle with China and Russia, and which they hope would destroy Communist domination of the mainland. In the meantime Chiang's 400,000 troops, although well-trained, are not getting any younger.

One night I asked a world-wise old Chinese diplomat what he thought would happen on the mainland. "Have you ever been in China?" he asked me. When I said I had not, he said that all over China I would find villages, much as in India, and that in every village there would be a tea house. Every day at the tea hour the people, especially the wiser people of the village, gather to talk. At that same time people all over China are talking in nearly a million villages.

"Chiang lost because this great 'village jury' decided that he had failed," the old man explained. "The villagers came to the point where they felt that the Communists could not be any worse." He said that there were military battles after that, but once the jury decided that Chiang was through, it was just a question of time.

"As long as the 'tea house jury' of China supports Mao Tse-tung his government will remain strong and there is little that Chiang or the United States can do," the elder statesman continued. "But, if that jury ever brings in a verdict against Mao, then his regime will fall or be ready for a change."

Like several other Chinese Nationalists, he scoffed at the thought of Russia ever really dominating China. "Only the United States or someone who does not know China believes in this theory of a Soviet satellite," he insisted. This did not mean that he had any illusions about Chinese communism being less dangerous than the Russian variety. On the contrary, he thought, as do many throughout free Asia, that Red China might someday become more of a threat to the world than Russia.

"Who knows," he said with a faraway smile, "someday Russia may be allied with the democracies fighting Communist China." This struck me as fantastic, but it is a fantastic world in which the democracies find themselves again close friends with Germany and Japan.

Unfortunately we did not get a chance to talk with Generalissimo and Madame Chiang, who were then out of the city. I remembered that although Nehru now disagreed with Chiang on many questions, he always spoke about their old friendship with warm feelings. During the war Madame Chiang took care of Mrs. Pandit's daughter at Wellesley College. It should never be forgotten that the Generalissimo and his wife were the first, and for many years the only, spokesmen for Asian anticolonialism among the world leaders.

. . .

Our plane for Japan stopped over briefly on the tremendous American base at Okinawa, stretching as far as the eye can see, a reminder of our vital new interests in the Pacific, and of the precious loss of lives which our pre-Pearl Harbor blindness to Asia had cost us. Sam and Sally were reminded of home when for the first time in many long months they saw 100 per cent American milk bars and soda fountains.

In Tokyo Mr. Robert Murphy, one of our most experienced ambassadors, was about to leave for a new assignment in the United States. However, he and his wife took us in and were very kind in showing us around Japan for more than a week.

Seeing Japan was like seeing the other pole of free Asia. In many ways it is India's opposite. Smaller than California, Japan is highly industrialized with the most efficient agriculture in the world. Eighty-three million people live on the one-fifth of the land which is not rugged mountain terrain. When you look at the terraced plots winding up the hillsides, it seems as if every cultivable inch of soil is tilled. Nearly everyone is literate, and public health standards are high.

Also, as I have pointed out in an earlier chapter, sweeping land reform has taken place, thanks to General MacArthur. I spent several days with Wolf Ladejinsky, the architect of those reforms, seeing the effects in the villages myself. It was exciting to talk with villager after villager who felt pride in the ownership of a bit of land and confidence that his future held so much more in store than had the past.

Even some of the former landlords feel satisfied with the change. One woman who was working on her reduced acreage said she now felt self-respecting and productive, and was glad that her neighbors no longer looked down on her as an idler. She said that the new system was best for Japan.

It is true that Japan's former plan of an East Asia Co-Prosperity Sphere adopted all the worst forms of Western imperialism. Even so the very slogans of "Asia for the Asians" had a powerful effect, and the Japanese were at first welcomed as liberators in country after country of South Asia. If they had gone on to grant genuine independence, the leaders of such new nations as Burma and Indonesia might never have turned against them.

India would be a good place for Japan to begin to offer Asian co-operation on new terms of equality and peace. India is one of the few Asian nations which does not have the scars of a Japanese occupation, and has great need for many Japanese skills, goods and capital.

I was surprised to see the extent to which the Japanese and Indians seem to think alike on many major world questions. I had expected to find Japanese attitudes quite different from those of the rest of Asia. Unlike the others Japan has never been overrun by any conquerors, except for its unique occupation by the United States. Yet, particularly among the young people, there seemed to be the same inclination toward an independent position in the Cold War, side by side with the same underlying anticommunism, so common throughout Asia. We will delude ourselves if we think that Japan is our docile ally; she is a great nation with powerful aspirations of her own.

I will not forget my talk with a nineteen-year-old Japanese boy who lost his mother at Hiroshima. He does not want anything to do with the present world struggle. He opposes Russia and communism, but insists that there must be no further war. Essentially he is now a pacifist. He, like most of his generation, is voting Socialist.

He believed MacArthur when our Supreme Commander instructed Japan to lead the way in renouncing war for all time, and in adopting Article Nine of the new Japanese Constitution, which prohibits military armament, even for defense. That millions of Japanese wish the American troops to leave, do not wish to rearm themselves, and yet have no desire to become a military vacuum tempting Soviet aggression from nearby bases seems completely contradictory, but it is just such conflict in the minds of Asians which we must strive to understand.

The afternoon I spent talking with a group of Japanese bankers about the possibility of trade with China reminded me of talks I had had in many other Asian capitals. But here there was an added factor. The Japanese businessmen idealize the old days when they got coal and manganese and iron ore cheaply from nearby Manchuria, ignoring the fact that those were days when Manchuria was a colonial area, whose prices could be determined in Japan to Japan's favor.

Today they are forced to buy coal and iron ore from the United States and South America with huge transportation charges. I remember my own attempt to buy steel from Japan for the Indian Point Four program. It had to be abandoned because the high prices Japan had to charge made the costs prohibitive.

I think that the Japanese are naïvely optimistic about the terms they can get from China, and about the possibility of dealing with China without Communist inroads occurring in Japan. On the other hand, there is not much we can do about it once Asia settles down. If, as I suspect, the Chinese terms are unscrupulous, the Japanese will soon discover it.

If Japan does not reopen her Chinese markets, then she must either work out a new self-supporting relationship with non-

Communist Asia, or the United States will have to keep her from economic collapse by the contribution of at least $700 million a year, which directly or indirectly is what we are now putting into her economy.

The billions of dollars we have spent to help our former enemy is a kind of ironic joke to many Asians. When Norman Cousins, editor of the *Saturday Review*, visited India on a lecture tour in 1951, he frequently cited our huge aid to the reconstruction of Japan as our greatest achievement in Asia. "The Japanese are now eating better than they ever did before," he said.

At one of his meetings, held while the wheat loan to India was being delayed in the Senate, a professor asked this question: "Would you then say, sir, that India's mistake is in not ever having declared war on the United States of America?"

Yet no one can be flippant about war who has seen Korea. On April 25, General Mark Clark arranged for me to be flown to Seoul in General MacArthur's old plane, the *Bataan*. I had been reluctant to go over to Korea, only because it seemed to me that there had probably been enough junkets there by visiting Americans. But General Clark and others said they wanted me to go, and of course I was glad to have the chance. The children and Steb wanted to go too, but we all agreed that it was not the place for them just then.

The cruel devastation overcomes you even on landing. Seoul was itself 50 per cent uninhabitable. Of the twenty-two million people of South Korea, a fourth were homeless.

Contrary to some predictions, I had a long, relaxed talk with President Syngman Rhee, who was in a remarkably friendly mood. He is a tired, hard, crafty old man. It was a beautiful spring day, much like April in Connecticut, and he talked about his dogs and his cherry blossoms.

Other than that he only wanted to talk about the war and the unification of Korea. He had waited a long time to get a chance to unite his country and did not want to let what looked like an opportunity slip out of his aging hands. Since the turn of the century he had been in the forefront of the Korean struggle for independence, which cost him seven years in prison and thirty-three years in exile. "He is too old to be patient," his wife says.

I had heard a great deal about Dr. Rhee from Everett Drumright, then our Consul General in Bombay, who had been second in charge of American operations in Korea, and was one of the last Americans to leave Seoul when the North Koreans moved in. Everett and I had started from somewhat different viewpoints, but we ended fast friends, and, I think, in close agreement about India and most of Asia. Since Dr. Rhee had fought his own lifelong fight against colonialism, Everett even hoped that some better understanding could be reached between him and Nehru.

But Dr. Rhee did not want to talk about India. "It is perfectly clear to me that communism can be defeated only by war," he said, and it was only war on which he could concentrate.

In Korea I can see why it would be hard to concentrate on anything else but war. I saw the first wounded American prisoners to be brought in by helicopter from the front. And all through the streets were signs, "Unification or Death," "Yalu or Death," testifying to Rhee's belief that only by war could Korea be united.

Written in English, the signs were clearly intended for American eyes, as pressure against the pending armistice. The Americans with whom I talked said that without question the anti-armistice riots were carefully engineered. Police were said to have gone from house to house, ordering each family to provide one demonstrator at a certain place at a certain time to oppose American "appeasement."

Talk about American or United Nations "appeasement" in Korea strikes me as no less than absurd. For two years the Communists refused to agree to a truce unless all prisoners were repatriated, regardless of their wishes. Then in July, 1953, they suddenly reversed themselves and agreed to the very terms which they had rejected so many times before. Exactly who is appeasing whom?

When I visited the international cemetery in Korea, I realized again what a brave and history-making act was this amazing collective defense of South Korea. It is an awesome experience to walk by the graves of men of many nations, buried side by side as they fought side by side, Turks, Englishmen, Greeks, Frenchmen, Ethiopians, Filipinos, Americans. Here, you feel, was the beginning of a United Nations army. Here in Asia the first successful collective resistance to aggression had taken place. Perhaps here the third world war was stopped before it started.

From the Korean struggle there is reason to hope that the Communists have learned not to attempt any further open military aggression. Almost half of North Korea's civilian population was killed or driven from the country. Nearly half of all habitations were demolished by bombs and napalm strafing. The Chinese and North Korean armies lost more than a million of their best-trained young men. It was a costly lesson.

America under two administrations has acted boldly and responsibly in Korea at the moment of crisis, but this only marks the beginning of our responsibilities in Asia. Elsewhere our task is to act ahead of time to so help strengthen democratic countries that no enemy will be tempted to attack them from within or from without.

Even in the deep spring mud and the blasted ruins of Seoul and Pusan and the Korean countryside, I saw much to give me confidence that America would understand her role and grasp the future with both hands: the navy, army and air force units that had raised thousands of dollars each to build schools for Korean children; the earnest good will of the American M.P.'s as they guided homeless Koreans to soup kitchens and clinics; the twenty-five hundred young American soldiers who were seeking visas so that they might adopt Korean orphans whom they had picked up in the streets.

After a crowded two days in Korea, I rejoined the family in Japan, where we said good-by to our hosts, the Murphys, and other friends new and old, and took off for Hawaii and home.

As we flew eastward across the Pacific our thoughts raced back through our many months in Asia. For all the variety of this great continent, I realized again the deep currents running throughout the whole area. The attitudes we had found were not merely Indian, or Burman or Japanese. They were unmistakably Asian.

In my imagination I began to gather these leaders of the new free Asia together in one room, Nehru, U Nu, Soekarno, Naguib, Van Tam, Mohammed Ali, Magsaysay and the others. Was their firm determination to be free so different from that of the men who created our own America? Many of them had the kind of prestige among their people that George Washington had among Americans in the 1790's.

Their suspicions of foreign entanglements, their feeling of being

Asian, their blunt rejection of colonialism and communism alike, above all, their belief in people—would this not be recognizable ground for our own Jefferson, Adams, Paine, Jackson, Lincoln and Wilson?

In any event, for better or for worse, they represent together one-third of the human race, and if we do not want to isolate ourselves from a good one-third of mankind, we had better listen to them.

All night we flew across the Pacific, which American boys had "island-hopped" with such tenacious bravery. At dawn we paused for breakfast at Wake Island, an isolated spot which has its page in our history, and just after dark we landed on American soil at Honolulu.

The next morning Sally took a travel-wrinkled dress to the hotel desk, asking how she could get it pressed. "Dearie, you can press it yourself," the cheery clerk responded, "I'll get you an electric iron."

Sally smiled and said, "Now I know I am home."

23. Policy for Americans

AS WE sat on the deck of the S.S. *President Cleveland* plowing steadily through the peaceful waters from Hawaii to San Francisco, Steb and I wondered what we would find in America. From far away, America had seemed so strong and so vital. Just as the thoughts and actions of the people of Asia will affect America, so we know that the policies of the American people will profoundly affect the future of Asia.

The first thing that struck me is that the United States has never really had an Asian policy. We have never developed a set of concrete and positive goals to govern our relations with the Asian nations, backed up by realistic measures for reaching those goals and supported by agreement along a broad spectrum of American opinion.

This is very surprising in one sense, because we certainly have been involved in Asia, in some ways more directly than we have in Europe. For half a century before 1946, an American possession, the Philippines, was in the heart of South Asia. Even today a string of island territories stretching from Hawaii to Okinawa flies the American flag. At Pearl Harbor we were treacherously attacked by an Asian power and defeated it only after an arduous and bloody war. With all this, however, we have not, before the war or after, evolved a coherent and articulate policy toward that part of the world.

Since the turn of the century we have pretended to have a policy, summed up principally in the doctrine of the Open Door in China. But the Open Door was like many of the statements of moral principle which we too frequently like to identify with foreign policy. It amounted to no more than a pious wish that the great powers should refrain from carving up China.

We proved that we were unwilling to take real responsibility for this position within a few years after we announced it, when we refused to join Japan in opposing Russian advances in Manchuria. And later, when Japan herself began a decade of conquest on the Chinese mainland, we confined ourselves to caustic letters of disapproval.

We ourselves did not even relinquish the colonial-like rights we had wrung out of the Manchu emperors several generations before until 1942, when they had, in any event, been canceled by the fact of Japanese conquest.

During World War II, we joined with the British in the stirring declaration of the Atlantic Charter which brought the conquered peoples of Europe rallying to our side. But, although we watched the Philippines, Indo-China, the whole Malay peninsula and rich Indonesia fall before the Japanese armies crying anti-imperialist and anticolonial slogans, we silently acquiesced in Churchill's assertion that the principles of the Atlantic Charter did not apply to the Asian countries.

After the war we took one great and important step. In 1945 we stuck resolutely to our commitment to grant independence to the Philippines.

That promising move was never followed up by other actions. Instead we limited ourselves to the essentially negative policy of opposing Communist expansion almost entirely with military force, whether in the form of arms, staff advice or combat troops. In Korea at great cost, but to our everlasting credit, we succeeded in stopping Communist aggression. In Indo-China, as this book is written, the issue is still in doubt. In China, the attempt was a dismal failure which led to bitter and costly partisan wrangling at home.

Above this checkered record one fact stands out. We have done very little since 1945 to capture the imagination of the Asian peoples, or even to reaffirm concretely our historic position as champion of expanding political and economic freedom for all men.

During the long decades of colonial rule in Asia, we thought of our relations with Asian peoples, when we thought of them at all, as a kind of appendage to our relations with their Western rulers. The result is a vast ignorance of Asia among Americans, an ignorance which we ourselves confirm in our use of such phrases as "the mysterious East" and "the inscrutable Oriental."

American attitudes and relations toward Europe after World War II were markedly different. Here we had a clearly defined objective upon which we all agreed: to prevent our Atlantic frontier in Western Europe from coming under the domination of an aggressive and expansionist power. Fifty years of bitter experience, climaxed by two world wars from which we had vainly tried to stand apart, had etched in blood and treasure the lesson that the security of Western Europe is vital to our own national security and to the peace of the world. And with an understanding of Europe and its people based on common ties of history, religion, culture and even ancestry, we were successful in developing imaginative, large-minded and yet practical measures for securing this objective.

Our Asian policy must reflect the same characteristics as our postwar European policies. There must be a clear-cut set of objectives with a program which realistically takes into account the political, economic and social forces at work in Asia and the national interests of the Asian nations. Above all there must be the maximum possible nonpartisan agreement here at home on what needs to be done and how best to do it.

Even if there were not a Communist in Asia, even if Karl Marx had never been born, our need for a positive and effective Asian policy would still be with us. The tidal forces which have been released on that continent, and which are even now being released in Africa, must find an outlet along channels of peaceful and orderly development. If not, Communists or no Communists, a Pandora's box of discontent, tension and violence will open which cannot fail to menace the peace of the world for generations to come.

All this is *not* to say that Asia should have priority. No debate could be more futile than that of *Asia First* versus *Europe First*. The fact is that the problem we have is global, and we cannot risk denuding our defenses in one quarter by concentrating our attention and effort upon another.

Certainly we cannot afford to relax in Europe. Western Europe remains the biggest potential prize for Moscow outside the United States itself. NATO has, for the moment, eased the threat of the Soviet legions poised in East Germany, the Russian zone of Austria and the satellite states. But it would be imprudent to the point of foolishness not to assume the possibility of Russia launching World War III to achieve world domination. Although we should grasp every reasonable opportunity to thrash out our differences at the

Council table we should read any whisperings of peace and coexistence that come from Moscow with caution and reserve.

In my view there remain three conditions under which the men in the Kremlin might risk all-out war. The first is their possession of some weapon which they believed would assure a quick knock-out victory.

The second is a preventive war psychology on their part. They might react in panic to the spectacle of mounting Western military strength or to the signs of rising dissatisfaction inside their own borders, recognize that, contrary to Marx, time is not on their side and strike while some chance remains for maintaining their rule.

The third is the reverse of the second. If the Russians see allied military and economic co-operation grind to a halt and begin to crumble, they might be tempted to undertake a policy of expansion by force.

To the first of these possibilities, the answer is renewed effort through the UN for atomic disarmament, with inspection, coupled with high priority attention to our own striking power and to civilian defenses.

To the other two, the answer is the continued full support of NATO, which, as Secretary Dulles pointed out in the UN, by its very make-up as a council of still sovereign nations, combines maximum defensive potential with the smallest aggressive threat—together with continued efforts to bring about the economic strength and political union of Western Europe, and indeed, of the whole North Atlantic community.

The true meaning of a third world war has been brought home to all of us by the news that the Soviet Union has developed a hydrogen bomb. Many Americans, who have always felt remote from the consequences of conflict in Europe, now realize for the first time the terrible impact of war on our own country with its vulnerable, crowded cities.

In the last few years when Europeans, who have been forced to recognize their inevitable situation in the front line of a new world conflict, cautioned us against rash moves or rigid policies, many Americans charged them with appeasement and a desire to embark on a "new Munich." Our own new awareness of the awful disaster of war may help to bring us closer together on a firm and yet flexible course of action.

The unity of the free nations of Europe from Norway to Turkey is a foundation block of our world policy, hewn at the price of bitter debate, hard work and billions of dollars. Much needs to be done to perfect this unity and to enhance its military, political and economic strength, but the job is well under way. Now the same imagination and resourcefulness, the same national effort at understanding that have served us so well in Europe in recent years must be directed to the new Asia that is taking shape.

I do not see any easy solution to the problem of Russian imperialism, which I fear will be around to plague us and the world for many more years. But such tempered pessimism about our relations with Russia only adds urgency to the problem of finding a successful relationship with the new nations of Asia. If they can become strong democracies, if we can establish friendly ties with them, the prospects for peace will be much better, and the prospects for further Communist expansion will be diminished.

. . .

As more and more Americans begin to turn their attention to Asia, their first reaction is frequently, "Well, if NATO has worked so well in Europe, why can't we do the same thing in Asia? Why not a military alliance of the free nations of Asia, under the leadership of the United States?"

The answer to this lies in the wholly different strategic situation. Europe is essentially a single peninsula which can be defended along clearly established defense lines. Most of the nations of Europe are industrialized and capable of producing the weapons of modern war. Their populations have had long experience as soldiers in modern warfare. Most important of all, the principal European threat is Russia, itself an industrialized country, vulnerable to atomic attack from the American air force.

In Asia, none of these conditions is present. Free Asia is a series of peninsulas, subcontinents and island chains scattered along the vast fringes of the central mass of the Soviet Union and China. It is not a geographic unity. It is far from the United States over hazardous and exposed supply routes. The principal threat, China, is not an industrialized nation, capable of being laid low by concentrated atomic attack.

We must remember that the conditions that prevailed in the Pacific during the war against Japan are unlikely to be repeated if a major war again breaks out in Asia. Then our enemy was a tight, integrated industrial nation, centered upon islands with extremely vulnerable communications. Through the maneuver of highly mobile sea power to cut those lines of communication, and the use of heavy air strikes against the industrial concentrations, we were able to bypass large Japanese armies, cutting off their supplies and reinforcements, and leaving them to wither in remote outposts. By these tactics we were able to conduct the war in the Pacific with only a few hundred thousand ground troops, and to achieve victory without invading the Japanese home islands.

The enthusiasm of some of our military leaders for this victorious strategy was evident in the way they urged a blockade of the China coast during the fighting in Korea. Such a blockade would undoubtedly have hurt China. But it is difficult to see how, even in combination with air attack, it could bring China to her knees.

The Chinese mainland, unlike Japan, does not present a concentrated target. Although the industrial structure and system of communications are, by our standards, primitive, they are not nearly so vulnerable to air attack or sea strangulation as is a more highly developed and interdependent industrial economy.

Chinese armies, schooled in long years of guerrilla warfare, have learned to live off the land with a minimum of reliance on complicated and exposed supply and communication networks. A high Indian army officer once emphasized this point when he said to me, "In considering the possibility of war in Asia your Joint Chiefs of Staff have more to learn from the campaigns of Genghis Khan than from those of Douglas MacArthur."

As I have suggested in the previous chapter the limits on our military power in Asia were demonstrated in the Korean War. The fighting was confined to a long, narrow peninsula, both flanks of which were open to the striking power of our navy. All supplies and communications had to funnel down this peninsula through a narrow neck less than one hundred miles across. We had absolute and unchallenged control of the sea and air.

We shall not find another battleground on all the Asian mainland so well adapted to the air-power–sea-power strategy which developed naturally out of our success in the Second World War and which now dominates much of our military thinking. Yet our inability to crush an Asian army that was determined, well-trained and competently led without the commitment of additional and overwhelming ground strength was apparent to the world, including the new independent nations of Asia. What was also apparent is the fact that the United States will not be able to commit large armies in any future Asian conflict without stripping the free world's defenses elsewhere.

This lesson of our Korean experience was learned at great cost by the Japanese before and during the Second World War. Beginning in 1931, they put an army which eventually numbered three million tough soldiers on the Chinese mainland. It was well equipped with tanks, planes and ammunition. The Japanese navy dominated Chinese waters and her air force was almost unopposed. Yet at no time was Japan able to control more than the large cities and the major arteries of communication. She was unable to subdue a China that was weak and divided and that lacked equipment, trained manpower and fighting allies.

Nor can our own deficiencies in the ground strength needed for Asian warfare be supplied by any presently achievable alliance with Asian nations. The most populous countries of free Asia and the Middle East, Egypt, Indonesia, India, Burma, and probably Japan and Pakistan are unlikely to join such an alliance at the present time.

In the case of obvious aggression from Russia or China which clearly threatened their immediate security, I am confident that they would range themselves without hesitation on the side of freedom. But they are as unwilling to bind themselves in advance to a military alliance, as we were to offer advance assurances to the European democracies before World War I and World War II.

That leaves South Korea, Formosa, Thailand, the Philippines, Australia and New Zealand as the only likely participants in any such pact, and they make up less than 15 per cent of the population of free Asia. To rely on an alliance of these nations would be like trying to hold Europe with a NATO consisting of Spain, Portugal and Greece, with the rest of Europe sitting on the sidelines. It would be welcome assistance, but it could hardly be decisive.

Nothing I have said implies that we can afford to neglect our military position in Asia or anywhere else. But since manpower is the immediate key to military power in Asia, it does suggest that the great strategic goal for the democracies in Asia should be to create new economic and political stability in South Asia, especially the Indian subcontinent, the only large source of non-Communist manpower outside of Japan. Only if such democratic strength is firmly established in both India and Pakistan can we overbalance the Communist strategic position in North Asia. But this is a long-term proposition.

Thus we must squarely face the fact that atomic weapons, control of the air and sea and any presently feasible military alliance with Asian nations cannot in themselves keep more of the Asian mainland from slipping behind the Iron Curtain; nor can such sources of power assure a cheap victory if war should come.

In Asia our military power, although important to the preservation of peace, is a backstop and not a policy. To mistake it for a policy is to accept the disastrous mentality of the Maginot Line.

If we are to develop a dynamic and positive approach toward free Asia, we must understand and keep constantly in mind some additional hard facts about that continent. Some of these facts are displeasing to us, but that will not make them go away. Policy, to be effective, must operate within the framework of these intractable facts, whether we like them or not.

The *first* of these, and perhaps the most important as I have stressed in previous chapters, is the existence of an Asian viewpoint, held by half of all the people in the world, from Japan to the Mediterranean, and beyond to Tunis and Morocco and much of Africa.

The fezzed Lebanese, the Pakistani jute farmer, the student leader in India, the Burman cabinet minister, the Vietnam jungle scout, the head man in the Indonesian village, the formal and correct Japanese businessman will all answer in almost the same words questions about America, Russia, China. They will reveal the same preconceptions about Western materialism and Eastern spirituality, the same attitudes toward the Cold War and the atom bomb. They will condemn with equal vigor American racial discrimination wherever it comes to light. They will react with equal quickness to every evidence of foreign domination from any source.

Some of their views are clearly, even dangerously wrong. Almost all seem to me oversimplified. But that is beside the point. They are there, and no successful Asian policy can run against their grain.

Those few Asian leaders who reject these predominant views may be more satisfying associates at the moment, but they speak only for a small minority and to follow their leadership is to cut ourselves off from nine-tenths of Asia.

The convictions which make up the majority Asian viewpoint are deeply held and, if we have the vision to understand them, they cannot help but work in our favor. The rallying cries of freedom from foreign rule, economic opportunity for everyone, and the dignity and worth of each human being are essential democratic ideas, indeed they are the very bloodstream of the Western liberal tradition. All three are irrevocably at war with the iron despotism of the Kremlin. All three have profound and practical implications for American policy.

The *second* of the hard facts to which our Asian policy must bend is that we have only a very limited control over the course of events in Asia. This is a fact that we have ignored to our damage in the past. When things have not worked out to our liking, we have immediately jumped to the conclusion that some American group or individual must be at fault.

This constant search for culprits in America to explain away unfavorable events in Asia leads us to assume rigid and dogmatic positions, frequently dictated by partisan considerations. The result is an exaggerated picture of American naïveté and disunity abroad and an ugly political squabble at home.

The days when a Western nation could call the tune and the Asian subject peoples would dance to it have ended in the smoke and fire of revolution across a whole continent. The new free nations of South and East Asia have demonstrated conclusively that they have the power to make and enforce their own decisions about their future.

When Vyshinsky taunted us that America would "lose" Asia, he himself was going against the grain of Asia. Asians know that America never had Asia to "lose," and will be wary of any democratic or totalitarian power that wants to "win" it.

If we cannot impose our decisions by force, neither can we buy adherence with our dollars and our technical aid. The fight has been too costly and the satisfactions of independence too deep for these nations ever again to accept foreign, and especially Western, direction of their policies. Americans cannot change this. Indeed, if we are to be successful in our larger purpose we must respect and nourish this new, and for them highly meaningful, captaincy of their fate.

The *third* hard fact is the existence of several crucial questions to which no one at present has an answer. We must recognize that we are not as a nation, any more than as individuals, omniscient. If each of us looks back honestly and objectively over the record of great international events in his own lifetime, the First World War, the League of Nations, the rise of Hitler and Stalin, Munich, the Second World War, the fall of Nationalist China, I am sure hindsight will convince him that his contemporary judgments of their meaning and of the best American policy toward them were something less than 100 per cent correct.

There is no reason to suppose that today's judgments and predictions on the future of Asia will be any more correct, and there is every reason to avoid dogmatic conclusions, to keep our objectives clear but our methods flexible, and to be ready to respond to the pattern of events as it emerges.

The future of the three key countries in Asia, China, Japan and India, bristles with particularly important questions marks. With our first-hand experience in Eastern Europe it has been natural for most Americans to think of China as another satellite of Soviet Russia. But China is much more of a partner with Russia, a junior partner to be sure, and one which up to now has seemed to defer to the senior on almost every issue of broad, basic policy, but a partner nonetheless.

Recognition of this fact simply opens questions for the future, it does not answer them. The partnership, as most Americans assume, may continue with increasingly close co-ordination and association between Peking and Moscow. Or China may, under the pressure of her own national interests, develop a policy independent of Russia's in many respects and even divergent in some. This need not go so far as an open break with the Kremlin. There are many whistle stops and stations along the way.

Even China's future role in Asia in uncertain. She may turn inward, call on the Soviet Union for continued all out help and concentrate her energies in perfecting Communist control and in economic development and industrialization. Again, if she can mobilize her resources quickly, she may contest with Moscow the direction of the Asian Communist movements.

Or, either because of growing internal resistance and unrest or because of her own explosive ambitions she may embark on further military adventures. These uncertainties will not be resolved by our own preconceived notions, but by facts and events carefully observed and expertly interpreted.

Another Asian question mark is the development of Japan with her eighty million energetic people, cooped up on her islands, importing 20 per cent of her food and dependent upon foreign resources for virtually all the raw materials needed for her highly industrialized economy. Every American has a good reason to remember that the explosive potential of this situation once before turned all Asia upside down.

The Japanese have recovered remarkably from their crushing defeat, but it is still too soon to say what their relations will be with Russia, with China, with non-Communist Asia and with the West. It is possible that Russia or China or both will seek to dominate Japan by force. I have always believed that the invasion of South Korea, directed of course by the Soviet, was in essence an attempt of this sort. Now that we have blocked this thrust, we may see an intensification of internal Communist activity in Japan.

It may be more probable than we like to think that Japan and China will move closer together over a period of time. It is conceivable that a Chinese attempt to limit Russia's Far Eastern strength, to reduce her own dependence on Moscow or to extend her own influence, would take the form of a persuasive effort to cultivate Japan.

China could exchange iron ore, coal and manganese, which Japan needs to feed her industries, for some of the machine tools, motors, steel and heavy equipment which China now gets from Russia. Most Japanese are convinced that they will have no choice but to enter into such trade if it is offered.

Finally, what of India? Will her great democratic effort succeed? India started on this democratic experiment at almost the same time that China started down the road of regimentation, "brain washing" and terror. While India struggles to achieve her Five Year Plan in the welter of pressures and politics and red tape that inevitably accompanies government by the people, China throws ruthless discipline and iron control into her struggle to mobilize her far-flung human and material resources.

If India succeeds, no matter what happens to China, if free India can bring land and bread and hope to her people, it will expose the Communist myth more than anything we can possibly do. It will strengthen immeasurably the hands of democratic leaders all over Asia. There will be an almost audible sigh of relief as people begin to believe again that they need not go through a pitiless and bloody wringer to achieve the economic progress they are so desperately seeking.

But if India fails, it will have a profound effect upon the future of every American and indeed of the world. The people of Asia will say: "With all the advantages of friendship with the West, of trained technicians and a good civil service, democracy in India failed to produce for its people. What can it offer us?"

And so they will turn to solutions of despair. If that happens, the balance of world power will shift fatally toward Moscow without a shot being fired.

. . .

Against this background our policy, as I see it, is confronted with two principal problems. The first is how to deal with the immediate points of conflict where fighting is now going on, or is likely to break out. These are the danger points for the outbreak of World War III in Asia.

The second problem is the development of a long-range program which will assist in the triumph of democracy in the developing lands of Asia, Africa and South America.

The immediate danger spots are easily identified. They are Korea, Indo-China and Formosa. There are also other issues which, although not involving such high-voltage threats to peace, are none the less important, such as the continued Cominform campaign throughout Asia of virulent hate against America, and the question of Red China's participation in the UN.

All of these questions directly involve our relations with China, which in addition to their own inherent complexity, have unhappily become so involved in domestic politics that it has become difficult for us to think objectively.

There are, as I see it, three possible ways of dealing with Communist China. We can make up our minds to destroy her government by force if we can, and to substitute a government more friendly to the United States. We can go to the other extreme and attempt to woo China through such concessions as the abandonment of Formosa and the withdrawal of our support of anti-Communist forces in Indo-China. Or we can adopt a policy of tough-minded but patient firmness coupled with a willingness to meet any genuine Chinese concessions to the peace of Asia halfway.

I have already suggested why a war with China could not be won by bombings and blockades, and why we cannot count on free Asia to supply the vast additional manpower that would be needed for ground warfare in China. For these reasons alone, war with China would be a political disaster, and if it is brought about by our own blindness and folly, it will represent the bankruptcy of American diplomacy.

Although the Soviet Union has a military alliance with China, I am inclined to believe that she would not enter such a war directly if she could avoid doing so. The Russians would, of course, provide the necessary equipment and act as China's skilled propaganda advocate in the court of world opinion.

Otherwise they would be content to watch us bomb crowded Chinese cities, thereby turning hundreds of millions of people against us throughout the world, and to hope fervently that we would finally commit our own infantry in the expectation that our troops could succeed where the Japanese failed. Under no circumstances, of course, could the Soviet Union allow China to go under, and if this became a possibility the Kremlin would undoubtedly throw its armies into the balance.

If Russia decided to take this fatal step her attack would probably be through the front door of Europe, which we would have left open by our commitment on the Asian mainland. Indeed the very circumstance which might make Russia think that she could defeat the democracies in a third world war might be such an American involvement in a major war with China.

What then should our policy be? To give up in Asia? To turn our backs on Chiang in Formosa, Syngman Rhee in Korea and on the courageous anti-Communists of Vietnam, Cambodia and Laos? To settle for peace at any price?

Such a course would be equally disastrous. The result would probably be all Asia in Communist hands within a decade. We would find ourselves faced with an overpowering military force with internal lines of communications stretching six thousand miles from Budapest to Canton and from the Indian Ocean to the Arctic Circle, backed by more than half the world's people united by an ideology pledged to our complete annihilation.

The most hardheaded and the most hopeful policy is one based on restraint, firmness, patience and flexibility. It promises no magic results or clear and immediate decision. But it offers us a real hope of avoiding a war that could only be won at prohibitive cost, gradually improving the prospects for peace and associating ourselves firmly with the forces of democratic Asian strength that are steadily emerging from Cairo to Tokyo.

I have already suggested that we should continue calmly, firmly but without arrogance to make it clear that we will resist with force any Chinese army or organized "Chinese volunteers" which move across any Asian boundary, be it Korea, Burma, Vietnam, Cambodia or Laos.

In addition we must enter the period of prolonged negotiation and conference that probably lies before us in Asia with a set of concrete, reasonable proposals, which, if accepted would assure immediate relief of tension without sacrificing any of our vital interests, and which, if rejected, would make it clear before the whole world which side was the intransigent one. The exact content and detailed scope of such a set of proposals would have to be hammered out first by our own government and its allies and later at the conference table.

These proposals might cover not only the unification of Korea but the Communist threat in Indo-China, the independence of Vietnam, Cambodia and Laos, the subversive activities of the Cominform in Asia, the hate propaganda emanating from Peking and the future status and relationship to the UN of Nationalist and Communist China.

Would the Chinese Communist government accept a broad all-Asia settlement backed by effective guarantees? Although no one can be sure I am not optimistic. I do know, however, that if Mao refused to accept it, Communist China's position before Asia and the world would be seriously weakened, and ours would be correspondingly enhanced for having made an honest effort toward peace.

On the other hand, if Communist China did agree, many developments over a period of years would become possible. Such a settlement, for instance, would certainly encourage Chinese independence from Russia, and for this very reason we can assume that the Soviet Union would do everything in its power to prevent it. But even if the uniting influence of a common Marxist ideology and the drive for world revolution sets the pattern of Sino-Russian relationships for the indefinite future, no one would then be able to charge us with arrogance or stumbling blindly into chaos.

Whether such a settlement of immediate tensions is possible or not, and I am inclined to be doubtful, our major objective for the long haul must be to help in the strengthening of struggling democratic governments in Asia. Our preoccupation with the problem of putting out fires, however urgent, cannot be permitted to obscure the larger task of fireproofing the buildings.

. . .

What are the positive elements of a long-run Asian policy which gives hope of bringing peace and order to this vital area?

To begin with, the almost pathologic dominance of nationalism in Asian thinking, as well as our historic convictions, demands that we take a clear stand against colonialism. Our action in the Philippines was in line with our finest traditions. But during the last few years in Indo-China and in parts of Africa we have permitted ourselves to be maneuvered into the position of seeming to support French colonial controls which were galling and demeaning to the people of those places, and which brought our good faith into question by the rest of Asia.

Many argue that we have had no choice, and that our underwriting French colonialism is the price of French support in Europe, and continued French resistance in Indo-China. This is exactly the kind of unreal dilemma into which we can be led by an Asian policy which consists of unrelated reactions to individual crisis situations.

The real question for the French is not whether they will relinquish their hold, but how? Meanly and grudgingly, leaving a legacy of ineradicable hate and bitterness, or with the kind of bold and generous statesmanship of which they are capable?

It was in the French Revolution, after all, that the ideals now animating those colonies received one of their earliest and most glorious expressions. What is needed in France is the leadership to mobilize this opinion and to restate the principles. The French government's promise of July 3, 1953, to negotiate a settlement with Vietnam, Cambodia and Laos for their free and independent status is a promising omen.

Indo-China is only the most immediate of the current crises of colonialism. It does not take clairvoyance to see that Africa will be equally aflame within a few years, unless practical and meaningful steps are taken while there is still time. By proposing such steps we can go a long way toward dispelling the notion among the old colonial peoples, Asian and African, that there is something half-hearted or hypocritical about our belief in political freedom.

We must also examine with a cold and objective eye the argument of the professional "realists" that willynilly we must take our allies where and as we find them. If in taking such allies we alienate and repel much greater sources of potential strength, we are being dangerously unrealistic.

Except in the most desperate circumstances we must avoid spending money, effort and time propping up leaders who have exhausted their claim on the loyalties and enthusiasm of their people, and who stand as symbols of the feudalism and corruption from which Asia is trying to escape. If we are to help establish a more stable and more democratic Asia we must for the long run associate ourselves with something deeper and more powerful than mere breast-beating anticommunism even when it is backed up by troops. Wherever such alternatives exist we must support the new representatives of the Asia of peaceful change.

Another aspect of the Asian revolution, the demand for economic opportunity, the determination to make an end of squalor, poverty, disease, has direct relevance to our aid program in Asian nations which we discussed at length in the chapter on foreign aid. As I have suggested, this is the time to take the initiative in Asia, much as we did through the Marshall Plan in Europe in 1947.

Still another element of the Asian revolution, the demand for human dignity among the Asian peoples, has repercussions for one of the most difficult problems of American domestic policy: racial discrimination. Our world responsibilities and the requirements of our national security no longer permit us the luxury of temporizing and evasion on civil rights here in America.

Over and over again in this book I have emphasized the painful sensitivity of all Asian peoples on this subject, and the fantastic success which Communist propaganda has had in creating anti-American feeling through distorted pictures of our racial conflicts. Unfortunately, enough factual examples of racial discrimination here reach Asia to make these distortions plausible.

Despite the emphasis I have given this point, I am not yet sure that I have succeeded in making it as important as it really is in the Asian mind. Of one thing I am certain. I have not exaggerated. It is impossible to exaggerate.

Finally, we must come to terms with the insistence of the new independent Asian countries that their foreign policies must be independent in fact as well as deed. We can gain nothing, and will lose much, if we insist on trying to badger or buy Asian governments into line.

And yet this is not an easy proposition for many Americans to accept. One of the most exasperating symptoms of our inability to control the situation in Asia is the unwillingness of most Asian nations to commit themselves firmly to our side, to stand up and be counted on what we believe to be the clear-cut issues of the Cold War. Our bewilderment and irritation at their position have grown to the point where many of us, including some in places of responsibility, have turned upon Asian countries with a snarling "if you're not for us, you're against us."

Again, it makes little difference whether we are right or wrong, for no American argument or threat can change matters. The idea of noninvolvement in the present world struggle is deeply held throughout most of Asia except Formosa and South Korea, and we will not make it go away by striking out blindly. We will gain far more by trying earnestly and patiently to understand it and the fears and realities on which it is based.

Part of its basis is psychological. These nations are proud of their new independence, and one of the hallmarks of independence is an independent foreign policy. It should not be hard for us to understand it or to assure the right of these nations to decide upon their own commitments in line with their own resources and interests.

A second factor is less easy for us to understand. The danger of the world Communist movement directed from Moscow and

Peking is still remote and unreal to most Asians. It does not have for them the awful immediacy it does for us.

On the positive side there is a steadily increasing awareness of the threat among more thoughtful leaders, and as memories of colonialism recede, and if democratic institutions are able to provide an improved life for the great bulk of Asia's people, this awareness should grow and intensify. But again we cannot hasten the process by getting hysterical about it.

Over a period of time I believe the Asian Middle East nations will take increasing responsibility for the defense of their own vital interests. This I have suggested might ultimately take the form of a kind of Asian Monroe Doctrine perhaps issued jointly by India and Pakistan and other South Asian and Middle Eastern countries. Such a pronouncement might guarantee the security of independent nations in the area against all comers, including ourselves.

The effect of any commitment of this sort would be to relieve our already overextended resources in such areas where we are less effective than a combination of free Asian nations might be.

We achieve nothing by calling upon the free Asian nations for resounding moral statements which they cannot back up by real power, and which, rightly or wrongly, they believe will involve them in issues which are no concern of theirs. We have much more to gain by patient effort to define the areas where our interests and theirs coalesce and by concentrating our diplomacy and persuasion on obtaining their co-operation and indeed their leadership in safeguarding these interests.

These then, as I see it, are the ingredients of an American policy which may help non-Communist Asia achieve long-range stability and freedom. But it can only succeed if it is based on a deep faith in the very principles which made this country great.

In Asia less than any place in the world can we afford to appear frightened or confused, to speak with the whine of frustration or the snarl of the bully. We cannot light the faith of Asians in our ideals if we ourselves act meanly from fear rather than boldly from faith. And yet it is natural that many of us are frustrated and weary of responsibility.

The war ended on a note of high hope for the American people. With great expectations we embraced the United Nations in our determination not to repeat the mistake of 1920 when the League of Nations was put to death in the United States Senate.

These early exultant hopes were snuffed out as the chill, creeping dusk of Cold War spread across the world. Instead of stability and peace we faced implacable hostility, high taxes, a thousand and one turbulent and tortuous new problems and, finally, even another war in Korea.

Can we throw off our weariness and rally now to the challenge of free Asia? It will require statesmanship, patience, understanding, imagination, respect for the people of all races, religions and nations, all the qualities that are so traditionally rare in the field of international relations.

The greatest idea the world has yet developed is the dream of independence and individualism, the opportunity for every man to build a full and meaningful life. For 150 years it has been the rock on which we have built our nation.

Today in Asia this dream has more meaning and more importance than ever before in history. As the Asian peoples reach out to us for reassurance and understanding will we be true to our tradition? Or will we rebuff them with the monotonous chant, "The Russians will get you if you don't watch out"?

Empires such as Rome and Britain have had their hours of greatness and courage. But has any nation ever faced as great a test as ours?

To remain strong militarily without becoming militarists.

To develop an expanding peace-time economy which continues full employment and full production.

To find a sound way for our enormous productivity to be fully useful in a world so full of want.

To banish discrimination against any man because of his race, creed or color.

To strengthen the United Nations so it can more fully win the allegiance of all free peoples, and point the way to a lessening of all tensions.

To form a great international team of free nations, on which we co-operate and listen to our teammates, as well as lead.

To enter the work of world development with the boldness and vision which the revolutionary continents require.

To come to terms with the Asian half of the human race.

It may be that no nation, no matter how wise or how good, can meet such a challenge. Toynbee writes that twenty civilizations before ours of the West have faced lesser questions and failed.

History only asks that we try our best. Above all, that we act in faith, not fear.

Postscript

November, 1953

AS I WRITE the final words of this report, the Bowles family is scattered temporarily to the four winds. Steb, Sam and I are home in Essex where Sam is in his first year in high school. Sally is at school near Boston. Cynthia has gone off to college. Our older married children are living in New Haven and in Cambridge.

As I look out on the Connecticut hills where the leaves are changing color, and over the blue water of Essex harbor, I realize how easy it would be to cut ourselves off from distant seething continents, and relax amid the blessings of the richest standard of living the world has ever seen.

As I followed the newspaper reports from India and Asia in the months after our return I confess that I had a few moments when I thought many of us Americans were yielding to this temptation.

I read of our quarrel over the Korean Peace Conference with nations which should be among our staunchest friends. And I read of Mr. Nehru's angry remarks in Parliament that "The countries of Asia, however weak they might be, do not propose to be ignored, do not propose to be by-passed, and certainly do not propose to be sat upon."

I also read about the "book burning" that was supposed to have taken place in some of our information libraries abroad, and I wondered how many Indians remembered my opening-day speeches at several of those reading rooms in which I discussed with such assurance the sacred freedom of the mind.

I read that our United States Information Service in India has been drastically reduced, with the *American Reporter* eliminated in four of the major Indian languages.

I read that the outlook for the expansion of our Point Four

program is becoming steadily more gloomy, and that many of its most experienced administrators have resigned.

I read that many members of Congress are expressing increasing impatience with non-Communist nations which fail to see the complex problems of the world exactly as we see them.

There is much that divides us from the people of Asia, and while we grope toward more effective policies, time is steadily running out. Those who make American policy in Asia as elsewhere carry heavy responsibilities.

If in five or ten or fifteen years free Asia has failed, for lack of our sufficient moral and material support or for any other reason, it takes no fortuneteller with a crystal ball to imagine the angry Congressional committees sitting on the fateful questions, "Why did our public officials fail to learn from the failure in China? Who is responsible for the collapse of free India and free Asia?"

In that grim session I would have no interest.

Yet today I have deep faith that the American people will overcome the natural temptation to isolation and indifference, just as I have faith that Asians will overcome the temptation to totalitarianism.

In India, Burma, Pakistan and Indonesia, and half a dozen other new nations, I have seen free Asians pulling themselves up by their own bootstraps, fiercely determined to resist any encroachment on their new freedom. Whatever disagreements we may have with them, how fortunate we are that governments so committed to democracy exist in this vast area!

In America during the months since our return I have spoken to groups large and small in many parts of our country. Instead of isolationism and indifference I found an eager desire for greater understanding of Asia and Asians, and for bold and constructive policies with which to meet the challenge of our time.

As I listened to the people talk I thought that now, as in so many other critical periods in our history, it is government that lags behind its citizens, fearful to give the positive, nonpartisan leadership which the majority is so clearly seeking.

We Americans are a pioneer people, still respectful of the old Puritan concepts of common decency and hard work, still guided by moral principles, still stirred by the call of the frontier. Now a new frontier awaits us, working with peoples of all races and religions in the economic, social and political development of every underdeveloped continent and country, which is this century's main adventure.

If that becomes the great positive mission of America, then I deeply believe that we will rediscover the creative, courageous spirit of our frontier days, and relearn the truths which once we held self-evident.

Suggested Reading

A BIBLIOGRAPHY would be impractical since it would include most of my personal files. For those who wish to read further, I suggest the following books, which in various ways have been particularly helpful to me:

India

By Jawaharlal Nehru, *Toward Freedom* (his autobiography), *The Discovery of India, Glimpses of World History, Nehru on Gandhi, Visit to America, Independence and After,* and others, all published by John Day.

By Mohandas K. Gandhi, *My Experiments with Truth* (his autobiography), published in the United States by the Public Affairs Press; *Satyagraha in South Africa, The Gita According to Gandhi, Non-Violence in War and Peace* (compilation in two volumes), *Delhi Diary,* and others, all available in cheap editions from the Navajivan Publishing House, Ahmedabad, India. Navajivan will send a list of its Gandhian books in English upon request.

By Vinoba Bhave, *Bhoodan Yajna,* Navajivan Publishing House, Ahmedabad, India.

The First Five Year Plan—A Summary, Planning Commission, Government of India. An interesting discussion of the problems of an underdeveloped country is in C. N. Vakil and P. R. Brahmananda, *Planning for a Shortage Economy.*

Excellent views of Gandhi and of modern India are found in these books by Americans: Margaret Bourke-White, *Halfway to Freedom* (with magnificent photographs), Simon and Schuster; Louis Fischer, *The Life of Mahatma Gandhi* (the best basic biography), Harper; John Frederick Muehl, *Interview with India,* John Day; Gardner Murphy, *In the Minds of Men* (a study of tensions in India), Basic Books; Vincent Sheean, *Lead Kindly Light,* Random House; Clare and Harris Wofford, *India Afire,* John Day.

Indian history is presented in Gertrude Emerson Sen, *The Pageant of Indian History,* Longmans, Green; Sir George Dunbar, *History of*

India, 2 Vols., Nicholson and Watson, London, and *An Advanced History of India* by Majumdar and others published by Macmillan. The story of the British departure is well told in Alan Campbell-Johnson, *Mission with Mountbatten*, Robert Hale, London. A sidelight on British rule is in R. G. Casey (former British Governor of Bengal and at present Foreign Minster of Australia), *An Australian in India*, Hollis and Carter, London.

Hinduism and Indian culture is discussed in S. Radhakrishnan, *Indian Philosophy*, 2 Vols., Allen and Unwin, London; Robert Ernest Hume, *The Thirteen Principal Upanishads*, Oxford University Press; B. G. Tilak, *Gita Rahasya*, Tilak Brothers, Poona, India; C. Rajagopalachari, *Mahabharata*, H. V. Divatia, *The Art of Life in the Bhagavad Gita*, B. V. Bhusan, *Things of Beauty*, all published by the Bharatirya Vidya Bhavan, Bombay, India. In the United States there is Kenneth W. Morgan's recent book, *The Religion of the Hindus*, Ronald Press. An excellent book on Indian art, dancing and music is Kay Ambrose's *Classical Dances and Costumes of India*, published by Adam and Charles Black in London.

Indian views of Gandhi are presented in Chandrashanker Shukla, *Gandhi's View of Life*, and K. M. Munshi's *Sparks from the Anvil*, Bharatirya Vidya Bhavan, Bombay. A compilation of his writings is found in *The Mind of Mahatma Gandhi*, edited by R. K. Pradhu and U. R. Rao, Oxford University Press.

China

Two interesting recent accounts of Communist China by non-Communist Indian observers have been published in America: Raja Hutheesing, *The Great Peace: An Asian's Candid Report on Red China*, Harper; and Frank Moraes, *Report On Mao's China*, Macmillan.

The following books also help in understanding China's role in Asia: John King Fairbank, *The U. S. and China*, Harvard University Press; Herbert Feis, *The China Tangle*, Princeton University Press, an account of the successes and failures of American Policy in China. Renè Grousset, *Rise and Splendour of the Chinese Empire*, University of California Press, an excellent recent Chinese history; Rhoads Murphy, *Shanghai—Key to Modern China*, Harvard University Press; Edward Hunter, *Brain-Washing in Red China*, Vanguard; Nathaniel Peffer, *China: Collapse of a Civilization*, John Day; John W. Riley, Jr., and Wilbur Schramm, *The Reds Take a City*, Rutgers University Press; Sun Yat-sen, *The International Development of China*, Putnam; Leonard S. Hsu, *Sun Yat Sen, His Political and Social Ideas*, University of Southern California Press.

Communism's role in Asia is discussed in Harriet Moore, *Soviet Far Eastern Policy 1931-1945*, Princeton University Press; in Charles S. Braden, *War, Communism and World Religions*, Harper, in Benjamin I. Schwartz's *Chinese Communism and the Rise of Mao*, Harvard University Press, and *Moscow and the Chinese Communists* by Robert C. North, Stanford University Press. Also relevant is *The God That Failed: Six Studies in Communism*, by Koestler, Silone, Gide, Wright, Fischer, and Spender, published by Harper.

Elsewhere in Asia and Africa

Nepal by Perceval Landon, Constable, London, describes that amazing mountain kingdom. Modern Indonesia's story is told in George McTurnan Kahin, *Nationalism and Revolution in Indonesia*, Cornell University Press. One of Indonesia's great modern leaders, Soetan Sjahrir, tells his exciting story of the drive for independence in *Out of Exile*, John Day. *The New World of Southeast Asia*, by Lennox Mills and Associates, University of Minnesota Press, is good source material. *The Island of Bali* by the Mexican artist Miguel Covarrubias, Knopf, is well worth reading for its sensitive account of Bali's rich culture. The thinking of this whole region is evidenced in *Asian Nationalism and the West*, edited by William Holland, Macmillan.

Justice William O. Douglas has written three fascinating reports about faraway corners of Asia: *Strange Lands and Friendly People*, Harper; *Beyond the High Himalayas* and *North from Malaya*, Doubleday.

The Arab revolt in World War I is pictured in a great piece of literature, T. E. Lawrence, *Seven Pillars of Wisdom*, Garden City.

For the feelings of people in the Asian-African half of the world, I suggest Alan Paton, *Cry the Beloved Country*, Scribner's; Santha Rama Rau, *East of Home*, Harper; and Eleanor Roosevelt, *India and the Awakening East*, Harper.

Policy Discussions

For background on the power-politics and policies of this region, there are many books: W. Norman Brown, *The United States and India and Pakistan*, Harvard University Press, is particularly good; Olaf Caroe, *Wells of Power*, Macmillan; Richard Frye, ed., *The Near East and the Great Powers*, Harvard University Press; A. Whitney Griswold, *The Far Eastern Policy of the United States*, Harcourt; *Japan and America Today* by Edwin O. Reischaurer and others, Stanford University Press; Werner Levi, *Free India and Asia*, University of Minnesota Press; John J. McCloy, *The Challenge of American Foreign Policy*, Harvard University

Press; K. M. Panikkar, *India and the Indian Ocean,* Allen and Unwin, London, and George Kennan's *Fifty Years of American Foreign Policy.*

The problems of the present world revolution coming out of Asia are considered in Edmond Taylor, *Richer by Asia,* Houghton Mifflin; Arnold Toynbee, *The World and the West,* Oxford University Press; Stringfellow Barr, *Citizens of the World,* Doubleday. Nor should anyone forget to reread the first great report on this subject by Wendell Willkie, *One World,* Simon & Schuster.

INDEX

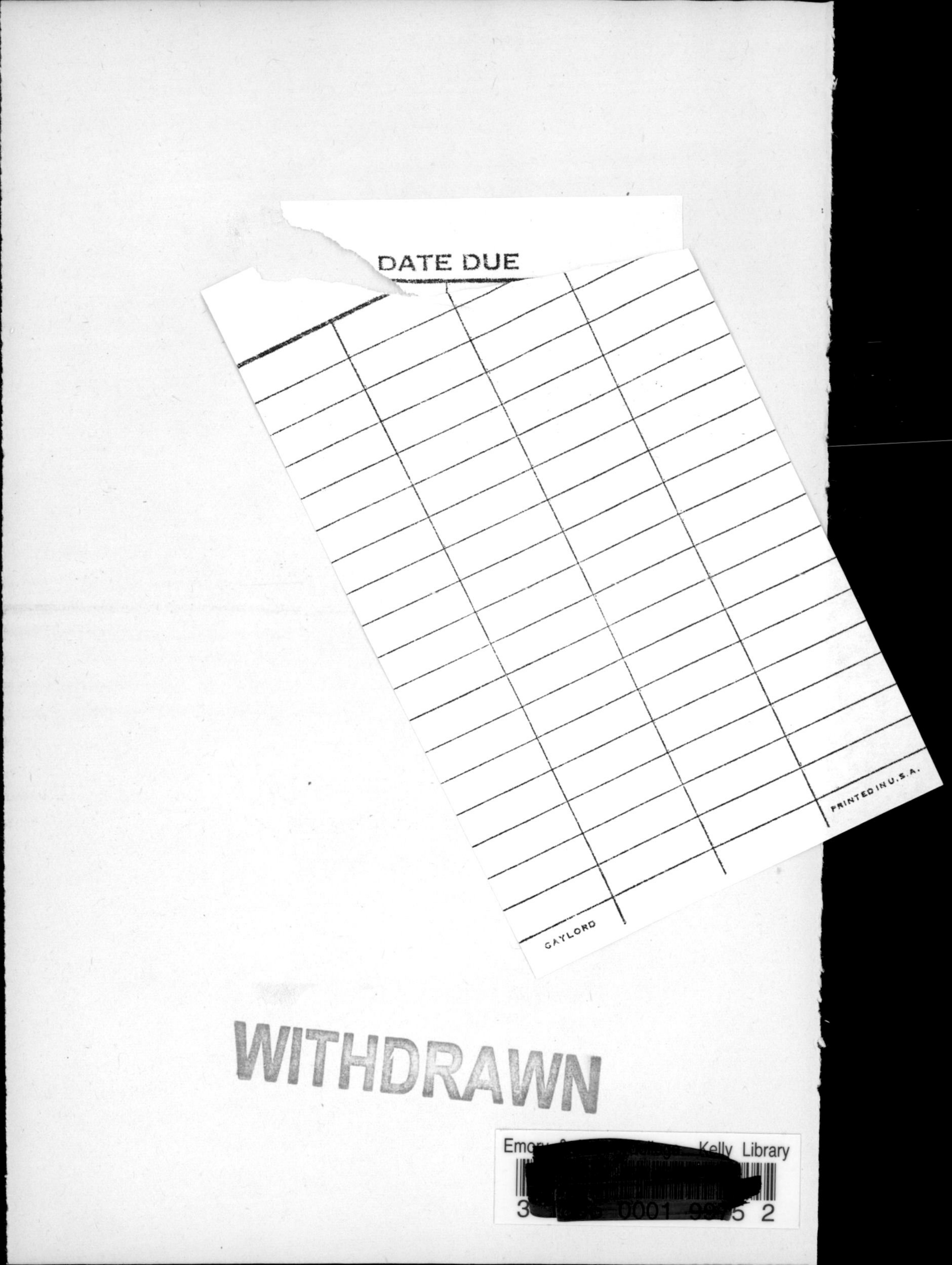
DATE DUE
GAYLORD
PRINTED IN U.S.A.

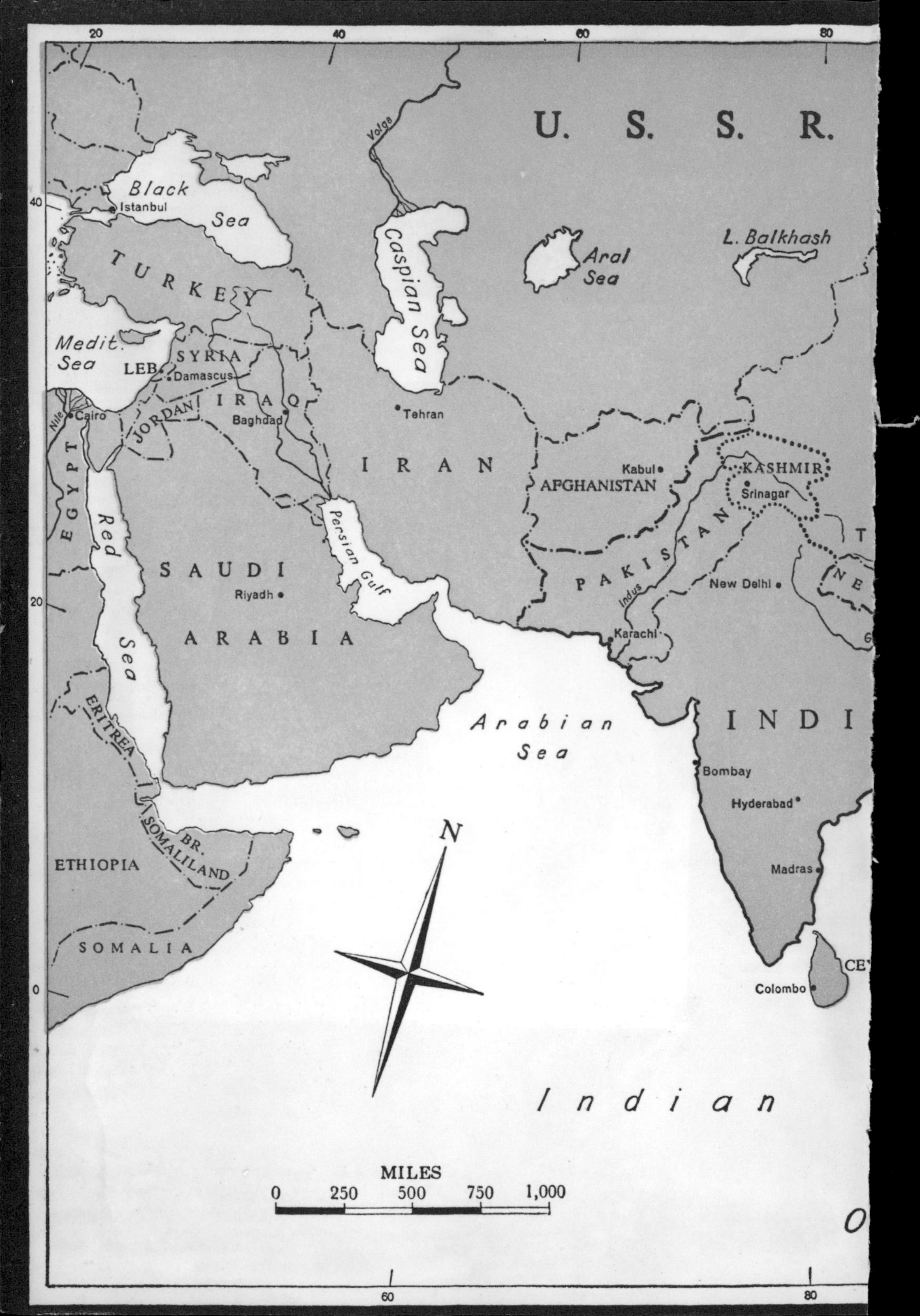
20
40
60
80
U. S. S. R.
Volga
Black Sea
Istanbul
Caspian Sea
Aral Sea
L. Balkhash
TURKEY
Medit. Sea
LEB
SYRIA
Damascus
IRAQ
Baghdad
Tehran
JORDAN
Nile
Cairo
EGYPT
IRAN
Kabul
AFGHANISTAN
KASHMIR
Srinagar
Red Sea
Persian Gulf
SAUDI ARABIA
Riyadh
PAKISTAN
Indus
New Delhi
Karachi
ERITREA
Arabian Sea
INDI
Bombay
Hyderabad
N
BR. SOMALILAND
ETHIOPIA
Madras
SOMALIA
Colombo
Indian
MILES
0 250 500 750 1,000